History of the Philippine Islands

From their discovery by Magellan in 1521 to the beginning of the XVII Century; with descriptions of Japan, China and adjacent countries

by

Dr. Antonio de Morga

Translated by E H. Blair and J. A. Robertson

Printed on acid free ANSI archival quality paper.
ISBN: 978-1-78139-016-0

Contents

Volume I   1
  Preface   2
  Introduction   12
  Chapter 1   17
  Chapter 2   24
  Chapter 3   26
  Chapter 4   30
  Chapter 5   33
  Chapter 6   48
  Chapter 7   138
  Appendix A: Expedition of Thomas Candish   159
  Appendix B: Early Years of the Dutch in the East Indies 165
Volume II   187
  Preface   188
  Chapter 7 (cont.)   192
  Chapter 8   214
  Notes   275

Volume I

Preface

In this volume is presented the first installment of Dr. Antonio de Morga's Sucesos de las Islas Filipinas. Events here described cover the years 1493-1603, and the history proper of the islands from 1565. Morga's work is important, as being written by a royal official and a keen observer and participator in affairs. Consequently he touches more on the practical everyday affairs of the islands, and in his narrative shows forth the policies of the government, its ideals, and its strengths and weaknesses. His book is written in the true historic spirit, and the various threads of the history of the islands are followed systematically. As being one of the first of published books regarding the Philippines, it has especial value. Political, social, and economic phases of life, both among the natives and their conquerors, are treated. The futility of the Spanish policy in making external expeditions, and its consequent neglect of internal affairs; the great Chinese question; the growth of trade; communication with Japan; missionary movements from the islands to surrounding countries; the jealous and envious opposition of the Portuguese; the dangers of sea-voyages: all these are portrayed vividly, yet soberly. Morga's position in the state allowed him access to many documents, and he seems to have been on general good terms with all classes, so that he readily gained a knowledge of facts. The character of Morga's work and his comprehensive treatment of the history, institutions, and products of the Philippines, render possible and desirable the copious annotations of this and the succeeding volume. These annotations are contributed in part by those of Lord Stanley's translation of Morga, and those of Rizal's reprint, while the Recopilacion de leyes de Indias furnishes a considerable number of laws.

The book is preceded by the usual licenses and authorizations, followed by the author's dedication and introduction. In the latter he declares his purpose in writing his book to be that "the deeds achieved by our Spaniards in the discovery, conquest, and conversion of the Filipinas Islands—as well as various fortunes that they have had from time to time in the great kingdoms and among the pagan peoples surrounding the islands" may be known. The first seven chapters of the book treat of "discoveries, conquests, and other events ... until the death of Don Pedro de Acuna." The eighth chapter treats of the natives, government, conversion, and other details.

In rapid survey the author passes the line of demarcation of Alexander VI, and the voyages of Magalhaes and Elcano, Loaisa, Villalobos, and others, down to the expedition of Legazpi. The salient points of this expedition are briefly outlined, his peaceful reception by Tupas and the natives, but their later hostility, because the Spaniards "seized their provisions," their defeat, the Spaniards' first settlement in Sebu, and the despatching of the advice-boat to Nueva Espana to discover the return passage, and inform the viceroy of the success of the expedition. From Sebu the conquest and settlement is extended to other islands, and the Spanish capital is finally moved to Manila. Events come rapidly. The conquest proceeds "by force of arms or by the efforts of the religious who have sown the good seeds of the gospel." Land is allotted to the conquerors, and towns are gradually founded, and the amount of the natives' tribute is fixed.

At Legazpi's death Guido de Lavezaris assumes his responsibilities by virtue of a royal despatch among Legazpi's papers, and continues the latter's plans. The pirate Limahon is defeated after having slain Martin de Goiti. Trade with China is established "and as a consequence has been growing ever since." The two towns of Betis and Lubao allotted by Lavezaris to himself are taken from him later by order of his successor, Dr. Francisco de Sande, but are restored to him by express order of the king, together with the office of master-of-camp.

Succeeding Lavezaris in 1575, Dr. Francisco de Sande continues "the pacification of the islands .... especially that of the province of Camarines." The town of Nueva Caceres is founded, and Sande's partially effective campaign to Borneo, and its offshoot—that of Estevan Rodriguez de Figueroa to Mindanao—undertaken. The "San Juanillo" is despatched to Nueva Espana, "but it was lost at sea and never heard of again." Sande is relieved of his governorship by Gonzalo Ronquillo de Peñalosa, and after his residencia returns "to Nueva Espana as auditor of Mexico."

Chapter III details the events of Gonzalo Ronquillo de Peñalosa's administration and the interim of government of Diego Ronquillo. Events, with the greater stability constantly given the islands, follow more quickly. Gonzalo de Peñalosa, by an agreement with the king, is to take six hundred colonists—married and single—to the islands, in return for which he is to be governor for life. He establishes the town of Arevalo in Panay, builds the Chinese Parian, endeavors, although unsuccessfully, to discover a return passage to Nueva Espana, by the South Sea, and despatches "a ship to Peru with merchandise to trade for certain goods which he said that the Filipinas needed." He imposes the two per cent export duty on goods to Nueva Espana, and the three per cent duty on Chinese merchandise, and "although he was censured for having done this without his Majesty's orders" they "remained in force, and continued to be imposed thenceforward." The first expedition in aid of Tidore is sent for the conquest of the island of Ternate, but proves a failure. Cagayan is first pacified, and the town of Nueva Caceres founded. Gabriel de Rivera, after an expedition to Borneo, is sent to Spain to consult the best interests of the islands. Domingo de Salazar receives his appointment as bishop, and is accompanied to the islands by Antonio Sedeno and Alonso Sanchez, the first Jesuits in the islands. In 1583 Gonzalo de Penalosa dies, and is succeeded by his kinsman Diego Ronquillo. Shortly after occurs Manila's first disastrous fire, but the city is rebuilt, although with difficulty. In consequence of Rivera's trip to Spain, the royal Audiencia of Manila is established with Santiago de Vera as its president and governor of the islands.

In the fourth chapter are related the events of Santiago de Vera's administration, and the suppression of the Audiencia. Vera reaches the islands in 1584, whence shortly afterwards he despatches another expedition to the Malucos which also fails. The pacification continues, and the islands are freed from a rebellion and insurrection conspired between Manila and Pampanga chiefs. Fortifications are built and an artillery foundry established under the charge of natives. During this term Candish makes his memorable voyage, passing through some of the islands. Finally the Audiencia is suppressed, through the representations made by Alonso Sanchez, who is sent to Spain and Rome with authority to act for all classes of society. On his return he brings from Rome "many relics, bulls, and letters for the Filipinas." Through the influence of the Jesuit, Gomez Perez Dasmarinas receives appointment as governor of the islands; and with his salary increased to "ten thousand Castilian ducados" and with despatches for the suppression of the Audiencia, and the establishment of regular soldiers, he arrives at Manila in May, 1590.

Chapter V deals with the term of Gomez Perez Dasmarinas and the interims of Pedro de Rojas and Luis Perez Dasmarinas. The term of the new governor is characterized by his great energy and enthusiasm. The Manila wall and other fortifications, the building of galleys, the regulation of trade, various pacifications, the rebuilding of Manila, and the opening of negotiations with Japan, are all a part of his administration, and he is the inspirer of them all. The first note to the future expeditions to, and troubles with, Camboja and Siam is struck by an embassy from the first

4

country in charge of Diego Belloso with offers of trade and friendship and requests for aid against Siam, the latter being at the time deferred. In accordance with his great desire to conquer Ternate, the governor fits out a great fleet in 1593, sending the advance vessels to the Pintados in care of his son. Shortly after, leaving the city in charge of Diego Ronquillo, although with too few troops for defense, Gomez Perez sets out to join his son, but is assassinated by his Chinese rowers, who mutiny and make off with the galley. After his death, the contests for his office begin, for the dead governor had assured various people that they would be appointed in case of his death. Especially had he done this with Estevan Rodriguez de Figueroa, a wealthy man of the Pintados, to whom he "had shown an appointment drawn in his favor." In Manila, Pedro de Rojas, lieutenant-assessor, is chosen governor ad interim, but after forty days Luis Perez Dasmarinas takes the office by virtue of an appointment regularly drawn in his favor. The return of the troops to Manila proves an efficacious relief from fears of a Chinese invasion. The vessels sent to Nueva Espana in 1593 fail to make the voyage because of stormy weather, but the governor's death is learned in Spain by way of India. The troubles between the bishop and governor culminate somewhat before the latter's death, in the departure of the former for Spain, as a result of which an archbishopric with suffragan bishops is established in the islands, and the Audiencia is reestablished. The office of lieutenant-assessor is given more weight and Morga is sent out to fill it in 1595 under its changed title of lieutenant-governor. In the administration of Luis Perez Dasmarinas affairs begin actively with Camboja through the expedition despatched under Juan Xuarez Gallinato, and Blas Ruiz de Hernan Gonzalez and Diego Belloso. The governor, completely under the influence of the Dominicans, although against the advice of the "majority of people in the city" sends a fleet to Camboja. Gallinato fails to reach that country until after Blas Ruiz and Belloso have quarreled with the Chinese there, killed the usurping Cambodian king, Anacaparan, and thrown the country into confusion. Much to their displeasure Gallinato refuses to continue the conquest, chides the others harshly, and departs for Manila by way of Cochinchina. At Cochinchina Blas Ruiz and Belloso go to the kingdom of Lao to find the legitimate king of Camboja, Prauncar. On their arrival they find that he has died, but partly through their efforts and those of two Malays, the king's younger son, who still survives, is placed on the throne. Gallinato experiences difficulty in Cochinchina, where he endeavors to regain the standard and various other articles from the galley of Gomez Perez that had been stolen by the Chinese, but finally returns safely to Manila. Meanwhile Estevan Rodriguez de Figueroa agrees to subdue Mindanao at his own expense, in return for which he is to have its governorship for two generations. In pursuance of this he fits out a large expedition, but shortly after reaching the island is killed in a fight and ambush, whereupon his first commanding officer Juan de la Xara schemes to continue the expedition, and establishes his men in a settlement near Tampacan, called Murcia.

The administration of Governor Francisco Tello forms the subject-matter of chapter VI. At his arrival in 1596, news is received in the island of the appointment of Fray Ignacio de Santibanez as archbishop, and of two appointments for bishops. News of the death of Estevan Rodriguez is brought to Manila, and the machinations of Juan de la Xara to carry on the expedition independently of Manila learned. His death shortly after arrest, while on his way to Oton to push his suit with Rodriguez's widow, frustrates his plans. Juan Ronquillo is sent to Mindanao and takes over the command there, but being discouraged by the outlook advises an evacuation of the river of Mindanao and the fortifying of La Caldera, on the Mindanao coast. However he gains a complete victory over the combined forces of Mindanaos and Ternatans, which causes him to send another despatch to Tello. But the latter's reply to the first despatch having been received, in accordance with its orders he burns his fort, and after establishing a garrison at La Caldera, returns to Manila with the rest of his command. There he is arrested for not awaiting Tello's second despatch, but is liberated on producing a letter ordering him in any event to return to Manila. Gallinato, on his return from Cochinchina is accused by his own men of not following up the victory at Camboja, for had he done so, "all that had been hoped in that kingdom would have been attained." An incipient rebellion in Cagayan is checked by the murder of its leader by his own countrymen "who had offered to do it for a reward." In the year 1596, the remnants of Alvaro de Mendana de Neira's expedition that had set out from Peru to rediscover the Solomon Islands reaches the Philippines after great sufferings from famine and disease, and after the death of many men, among them the commander himself. The voyage is related in detail in a letter from the chief pilot, Pedro Fernandez de Quiros to Morga; it is full of stirring adventure, and of keen and appreciative observation. One of the vessels, the "San Geronymo" despatched to Nueva Espana in 1596, is forced to put in at a Japanese port because of storms. There they receive ill-treatment, and the efforts of the Franciscan missionaries in Japan in their behalf lead to the edict sentencing them to death, in accordance with which six Franciscans, three Jesuits, and seventeen native helpers are crucified in 1597. Taicosama's wrath, intensified by the accusation that the Spaniards conquered kingdoms "by first sending their religious to the kingdom" and by entering afterward "with their arms," is satisfied by the crucifixion of the religious and their assistants, and the men of the "San Geronymo" are allowed to return to Manila. The religious write a letter of farewell to Dr. Morga, in which they inform him that Japan intends to attack the Philippines. Luis Navarrete Fajardo is sent to Japan to demand satisfaction, but accomplishes little. Faranda Quiemon, one of Taicosama's vassals, a man of obscure birth, obtaining permission to make an expedition of conquest, sets about his preparations, but owing to lack of resources and initiative fails to complete them. Meanwhile great caution is exercised in Manila, and the Japanese residing there are sent back to Japan, while those coming on trading vessels are well treated but gotten rid of as soon as possible. Cambodian affairs are again set on foot, although against the advice of some, through the instrumentality of Father Alonso Ximenez, a Dominican who had accompanied Gallinato on the former expedition, but who had been left behind at Cochinchina through his own disobedience of orders. Affairs in Mindanao and Jolo assume a threatening aspect. One Juan Pacho, commander of La Caldera, is killed in an incursion into Jolo with twenty of his men, and a new commander of La Caldera is appointed until a punitive expedition can be undertaken. In 1598 the archbishop arrives, and the Manila Audiencia is reestablished by royal order, and the seal received with great pomp and ceremony. A letter received that same year by Morga from Blas Ruiz details events in Camboja since he and Belloso went there with Gallinato's expedition. Blas Ruiz seeks to excuse their actions in Camboja and holds out the hope of Spanish conquest and influence on the mainland, and asks help from the islands. As a consequence of this letter, Luis Perez Dasmarinas secures permission to attempt an expedition to the mainland at his own expense to aid the king of Camboja and then to seize the kingdom of Champan, whose king was a constant menace to all navigators throughout that region. Negotiations with China and the granting of an open port to Spaniards called El Pinal, are opened and secured through the efforts of Juan de Zamudio who is sent to China for saltpeter and metals, although with great and vindictive opposition from the Portuguese, who fear the loss of their own trade at Macao. At El Pinal the survivors of two of Luis Perez's three ships meet with Juan de Zamudio, after suffering great storms, hardships, and wrecks. The same favor is extended him by the Chinese as to Zamudio, but the Portuguese show their hostility to him also, imprisoning the men sent by him to Macao to ask for help, and even attempting force against him. Both Zamudio and a messenger from Luis Perez carry news of the latter's disaster to Manila, whereupon a ship and supplies are sent him with orders to return to Manila. Hernando de los Rios Coronel, sent to Canton by Luis Perez to negotiate with the Chinese, writes from that city to Dr. Morga concerning China and the possibility, desirability, and advantages of the Chinese trade in China instead of Manila, and the opposition of the Portuguese. China he describes as a country "full of rivers and towns, and without a palmo of ground left lying idle." Meanwhile the third vessel of Luis Perez's fleet, commanded by Luis Ortiz, reaches Camboja, where he and his companions join the Spanish, Portuguese, and Japanese already there. This small force, which is eyed askance by the Malay leaders and others envious of, and hostile to them on account of their prowess and their influence with the weak king, is further increased by Captain Juan de Mendoza Gamboa and Fray Juan Maldonado, a learned Dominican, and their men. The former, having obtained permission to go on a trading expedition to Siam, for which he is given letters of embassy, is also entrusted to convey certain supplies to Don Luis at Camboja, where he fails to find him. Maldonado is sent by his order as a companion to Don Luis. This addition to their forces is welcomed by the Spaniards in Camboja, and they refuse to let them depart until hearing definite news of Luis Perez. The arrival of a contingent of Japanese, mestizos, and one Spaniard, who had left Japan on a piratical expedition, still further increases the force in Camboja. The leaders Blas Ruiz, Belloso, and Maldonado treat with the king on their own account, but not so satisfactorily as they wish. Conflicts and quarrels arising between their forces and the Malays, the latter finally overpower and kill the Spaniards, Portuguese, and Japanese, except several who remain in the country and Mendoza, Maldonado and a few men who escape in the former's vessel. In Camboja confusion and anarchy again reign and the king is bullied and finally killed by the Malays. The Joloans and Mindanaos are emboldened by the final abandonment and dismantling of the fort at La Caldera—which is decided upon by the governor against the opinion of the Audiencia—and, joined in self-defense by the peaceful natives of Mindanao, make an incursion against Spaniards and natives in the Pintados in 1599, in which they take immense booty and many captives. The next year they return with a larger force, but are defeated by the alcalde-mayor of Arevalo, whereupon they resolve to be revenged. In Japan the death of Taicosama encourages Geronimo de Jesus, a Franciscan who has escaped crucifixion, to open negotiations with his successor Daifusama. The latter, desiring trade for his own northern province of Quanto, requests the governor of Manila, through the religious, for commerce, and men to build ships for the Nueva Espana trade which he wishes to open. He does not negotiate concerning religion, for "the profit and benefit to be derived from friendship and commerce with the Spaniards was more to the taste of Daifusama than what he had heard concerning their religion." However, the religious writes that freedom is given to evangelize throughout Japan, although the only concession given is that the religious could establish a house at their trading station. In October of 1600 news reaches Manila of the coming and depredations of Oliver van Noordt's two vessels. The description of the preparations, made by Morga, the instructions given him by the governor, his instructions to Juan de Alcega, and the fight and its consequences follow. In the same year of 1600 the vessels "Santa Margarita" and "San Geronymo" are both unable to reach Nueva Espana, and are wrecked—the latter near Catanduanes, and the former in the Ladrones, where it is rifled by the natives and the men surviving distributed through the different villages. In 1600 the "Santo Tomas" on its way to the islands puts in at the Ladrones, but the commander, fearing storms, refuses to wait for the Spanish prisoners of the "Santa Margarita," although petitioned to do so by the religious and others. Accordingly a Franciscan, Juan Pobre, full of pity for the unfortunate men, casts in his lot with them and voluntarily remains behind. The "San Felipe" is wrecked eighty leguas from Manila, and its cargo taken overland to that city. Mindanao and Jolo affairs are meanwhile given into command of Gallinato, and although he is partially successful, the rains, hunger, and disease work for the natives, and finally in May of 1602, Gallinato sends to Manila for instructions. Juan de Mendoza and Fray Juan Maldonado, after leaving Camboja proceed on their journey to Siam, but are received there coldly by the king, and their trading is unsatisfactory. Fearing violence they depart one night without notifying the Siamese, taking with them certain Portuguese held in Siam as partial prisoners, but are pursued by the Siamese who molest them until in the open sea. From wounds received during the week's continual conflict both Mendoza and Maldonado die, the latter first writing to his Order and advising them "on their consciences not to again become instruments of a return to Camboja." Troubles in Maluco between the Dutch and natives on the one side and the Portuguese and Spanish on the other, render it necessary to send aid several times from Manila. In March of 1601, a letter is written by the king of Tidore to Morga requesting aid against Ternate and the Dutch, in response to which supplies and reenforcements are sent in 1602.

The seventh chapter deals with events during the period of Pedro de Acuna's administration. With his arrival in May of 1602, new life and energy are infused in public affairs. The new governor first concerns himself with home affairs. He constructs galleys but has to postpone an intended visit to Pintados, in order to attend to Japan and Jolo, and despatch the vessels to Nueva Espana. It is determined to open commerce with Quanto, but to defer the matter of sending workmen to Japan to show the Japanese how to construct ships, as that will be detrimental.

Religious of the various orders go to Japan, but are received less warmly than Geronymo de Jesus's letter leads them to expect. The latter pressed by Daifusama for the performance of his promises finally asks permission to go to Manila to advocate them in person, whence he brings back assurance of trade with Quanto. The vessel despatched there is forced to put in at another port, but is allowed to trade there and to return. Two vessels despatched to Nueva Espana in 1602 are forced to return, putting in on the way—the first at the Ladrones and the other at Japan. The first brings back most of the men wrecked at the Ladrones. The second after rough treatment in Japan finally escapes. As a result of an embassy sent to Daifusama from this vessel chapas or writs of safety are provided to the Spaniards so that any vessel putting into Japanese ports will be well treated in the future. The reenforcements sent to Gallinato at Jolo serve only to enable him to break camp and return to Manila. While Acuna is on his way to Pintados to inspect those islands, a raiding expedition of Moros goes as far as Luzon and Mindoro, committing many depredations, thus compelling the governor to return, who narrowly escapes capture. A punitive expedition of Spaniards and Indians sent in pursuit of the Moros inflicts but slight damage. Shortly before this a fleet prepared at Goa for the chastisement of the Malucos sets out under Andrea Furtado de Mendoza, but is separated by storms. Some of the vessels with the commander reach Amboina, but in so crippled and destitute a condition that they are forced to ask help from Manila. Acuna, although arranging independently for an expedition to Maluco, sends a force there under Gallinato in 1603 to aid the Portuguese. Early in that year the prelude to the Chinese troubles of that same year is given by the coming of the Chinese mandarins to see the island of gold, which causes many, among them the archbishop and some religious, to counsel watchfulness. In 1603 occurs the second disastrous fire in Manila, with a loss of over one million pesos.

The victorious Malays in Camboja are finally driven out by a combination of patriotic mandarins, and make the brother of their old king sovereign, whereupon relations between Camboja and the Philippines are again established by sending there a number of religious. In May of 1603 two ships with reenforcements arrive at Manila, bringing certain ecclesiastical news. The aid rendered Furtado de Mendoza by Gallinato does not prove sufficient to subdue the Ternatans, and Gallinato returns to Manila. The present installment of Morga ends with the courteous letter written to Acuna by Furtado de Mendoza, in which he renders praise to Gallinato and his men. The remainder of the book will appear in the succeeding volume.

The present volume ends with two appendices: the first an abstract of Thomas Candish's circumnavigation; the second an abstract of Dutch expeditions to the East Indies.

THE EDITORS
May, 1904. ¶

Introduction

EVENTS IN THE FILIPINAS ISLANDS

By order of the most excellent Don Luis de Velasco, viceroy of this Nueva Espana, and of the most illustrious and reverend Don Fray Garcia Guerra, archbishop of Mexico, and member of his Majesty's council, I have examined this book of the Events in the Philipinas Islands, written by Doctor Antonio de Morga, alcalde of the court in the royal Audiencia of Mexico. In my judgment it is entertaining, profitable, and worthy of publication. The author has strictly obeyed the laws of history therein, in the excellent arrangement of his work, in which he shows his soundness of intellect and a concise style to which few attain, together with a true exposition of the subject matter, as it was written by one who was so fully conversant with it, during the years that he governed those islands. I have accordingly affixed my signature to this instrument here at the professed house of the Society of Jesus in Mexico, on the first of April, 1609.

JUAN SANCHEZ

Don Luys de Velasco, knight of the Order of Sanctiago, viceroy-lieutenant of the king our sovereign, governor and captain-general of Nueva Espana, and president of the royal Audiencia and Chancilleria established therein, etc. Whereas Doctor Antonio de Morga, alcalde of criminal causes in this royal Audiencia, informed me that he had written a book and treatise on the Events in the Filipinas Islands, from their earliest discoveries and conquest until the end of the past year six hundred and seven, and requested me to grant him permission and privilege to have it printed, to the exclusion of all others doing the same for a certain period; and whereas I entrusted Father Juan Sanchez, of the Society of Jesus, with the inspection of the said book, as my proxy: therefore, I hereby grant permission to the said Doctor Antonio de Morga, so that, for the period of the next ten years, he, or his appointee, may freely have the said book printed by whatever printer he pleases; and I forbid any other person to do the same within the said time and without the said permission, under penalty of losing—and he shall lose—the type and accessories with which the said impression shall be made, and the same shall be applied in equal shares to his Majesty's exchequer and to the said Doctor Antonio de Morga. Given in Mexico, on the seventh of the month of April, one thousand six hundred and nine.

DON LUYS DE VELASCO

By order of the viceroy:
MARTIN LOPEZ GAUNA

Don Fray Garcia Guerra, by the divine grace and that of the holy apostolic see, archbishop of Mexico, member of his Majesty's Council, etc. Having seen the opinion expressed by Father Juan Sanchez, of the Society of Jesus, after he had examined the book presented to us by Doctor Antonio de Morga, alcalde in this court and Chancilleria, entitled Events in the Filipinas Islands, their Conquest and Conversion, for which we granted him authority; and since it is evident, by the above-mentioned opinion, that it contains nothing against our holy Catholic faith, or good morals, but that, on the contrary, it is useful and profitable to all persons who may read it: therefore we do hereby grant permission to the said Doctor Antonio de Morga, to have the said book of the said conquest and conversion of the Filipinas Islands printed in any of the printing establishments of the city. Given in Mexico, on the seventh of April, one thousand six hundred and nine.

FRAY GARCIA, archbishop of Mexico.

By order of his most illustrious Lordship, the archbishop of Mexico: DON JUAN DE PORTILLA, secretary.

¶To Don Cristoval Gomez de Sandoval y Rojas, duke of Cea [1]

I offer your Excellency this small work, worthy of a kind reception as much for its faithful relation as for its freedom from artifice and adornment. Knowing my poor resources, I began it with fear; but what encouraged me to proceed was the fact that, if what is given were to bear an equal proportion to the receiver, there would be no one worthy of placing his works in your Excellency's hands; and oblivion would await the deeds achieved in these times by our Spaniards in the discovery, conquest, and conversion of the Filipinas Islands—as well as various fortunes which they have had from time to time in the great kingdoms and among the pagan peoples surrounding the islands: for, on account of the remoteness of those regions, no account has been given to the public which purports to treat of them from their beginnings down to the present condition. I entreat your Excellency to accept my good will, which is laid prostrate at your feet; and should this short treatise not afford that pleasure, which self-love—that infirmity of the human mind—leads me to expect, will your Excellency deal with me, as you are wont to deal with all, and read this book and conceal its imperfections with the exercise of your toleration and gentleness. For you are so richly endowed with these and other virtues—which, through the divine power, cause lofty things not to keep aloof from humble ones; and which, in addition to your own natural greatness, have placed your Excellency in your present office for the good of these realms, where you reward and favor the good, and correct and check the opposite. In such rule consists the welfare of the state; and this made the ancient philosopher, Democritus, say that reward and punishment were true gods. In order to enjoy this happiness, we need not crave any bygone time, but, contenting ourselves with the present, pray that God may preserve your Excellency to us for many years.

DON ANTONIO DE MORGA [2]

To the reader [3]

The greatness of the monarchy of the Spanish kings is due to the zeal and care with which they have defended, within their own hereditary kingdoms, the holy Catholic faith taught by the Roman church, against all enemies who oppose it, or seek by various errors to obscure its truth which the kings have disseminated throughout the world. Thus, by the mercy of God, they preserve their kingdoms and subjects in the purity of the Christian religion, meriting thereby their glorious title and renown of "Defenders of the Faith." Moreover, by the valor of their indomitable hearts, and at the expense of their revenues and possessions, they have ploughed the seas with Spanish fleets and men, and discovered and conquered vast kingdoms in the most remote and unknown parts of the world. They have led the inhabitants of these regions to a knowledge of the true God, and into the fold of the Christian church, in which those peoples now live, governed in civil and political matters with peace and justice, under the shelter and protection of the royal arm and power, which were wanting to them when weighed down by blind tyrannies and barbarous cruelties, on which the enemy of the human race had so long reared them for himself.

For this reason the crown and scepter of Espana have extended themselves wherever the sun sheds its light, from its rising to its setting, with the glory and splendor of their power and majesty, and the Spanish monarchs have excelled the other princes of the earth by having gained innumerable souls for heaven, which has been Espana's principal intention and its wealth. These, together with the great riches and treasures which Espana enjoys, and the famous deeds and victories which it has won, cause the whole world to magnify and extol its lofty name and the energy and valor of its subjects, who in accomplishing these deeds have lavished their blood.

Having won America, the fourth part of the earth, of which the ancients knew naught, they sailed in the course of the sun until they discovered an archipelago of many islands in the eastern ocean, adjacent to farther Asia, inhabited by various peoples, and abounding in rich metals, precious stones, and pearls, and all manner of fruit. There raising the standard of the Faith, they freed those peoples from the yoke and power of the demon, and placed them under the command and government of the Faith. Consequently they may justly raise in those islands the pillars and trophies of Non plus ultra which the famous Hercules left on the shore of the Cadiz Sea, which were afterward cast down by the strong arm of Carlos V, [4] our sovereign, who surpassed Hercules in great deeds and enterprises.

After the islands had been conquered by the sovereign light of the holy gospel which entered therein, the heathen were baptized, the darkness of their paganism was banished, and they changed their own for Christian names. The islands also, losing their former name, took—with the change of religion and the baptism of their inhabitants—that of Filipinas Islands, in recognition of the great favors received at the hands of his Majesty Filipo the Second, our sovereign, in whose fortunate time and reign they were conquered, protected, and encouraged, as a work and achievement of his royal hands.

Their discovery, conquest, and conversion were not accomplished without great expenditure, labor, and Spanish blood, with varying success, and amid dangers: these things render the work more illustrious, and furnish a spacious field of which historians may treat, for such is their office. Certainly the subject matter is not scanty, and contains both serious and pleasant elements sufficient to be worthy of attention, so that it will not depreciate historians to treat of Indian occurrences and wars, which those who have not experienced undervalue. For the people of those regions are valiant and warlike nations of Asia, who have been reared in continual warfare, both by sea and by land, and who use artillery and other warlike implements, which the necessity of defending themselves against great and powerful neighboring kingdoms, taught them to use skilfully; and—although somewhat imperfectly—they have gained dexterity and have completed their education in the school of Espana, which recently brought war to their gates—thus sharing the experience of other provinces of Europe, who also had formerly been ignorant and careless of the use of arms

Some painstaking persons, to whom—for lack of time and means—I have given and delivered many papers and relations which I possessed, have planned to write this history; and I hope that they will publish it in better shape than the fragmentary histories which we have hitherto received from some contemporary historians. [5]

I spent eight years in the Filipinas Islands, the best years of my life, serving continuously as lieutenant of the governor and captain-general, and, as soon as the royal Audiencia of Manila was established, in the office of auditor, which I was the first to fill. [6] And desirous that the affairs of those islands should be known, especially those which occurred during my connection with them, I have related these matters in a book of eight chapters, tracing them from their origin so far as was necessary. The first seven chapters contain an account of the discoveries, conquests, and other events in the islands and neighboring kingdoms and provinces, which occurred during the time of the proprietary governors [7] until the death of Don Pedro de Acuna. The eighth and last chapter contains a brief summary and account of the nature of these regions, their inhabitants, the manner of governing and converting them, and other details; moreover, it treats of the acquaintance, dealings, and intercourse which they maintain with their neighboring islands and pagan communities. As fearful am I for the imperfections which will be found in this work, as I am persuaded that they deserve forgiveness, since my design and chief intent has been to give each one his due and to present the truth without hatred or flattery, which has been injured in some current narratives. [8] The latter is a fault to be severely reproved in those who relate the deeds of others, inasmuch as it was prohibited by a penal law which Cato and Marcius, tribunes of the Roman people, established for those who, in relating their own deeds, overstepped the truth—although this seemed less worthy of punishment, on account of the self-love which intervenes in such a case.

There will not be wanting some person who will point out my oversights, but I shall have already answered him by confessing them; and should this not suffice to silence him, I shall stop up my ears like another Ulysses, and—considering the haste with which I have written—endure this inconvenience and difficulty, desiring only to please and serve whomsoever may read it; and this will be sufficient to protect me from greater dangers.

Notice is given that

In reading this history, one may find certain words—names of provinces, towns, magistrates, arms, and vessels—which it has seemed more suitable to write by their usual names in those regions. In the last chapter, which contains an account of the islands and their peculiarities, these words will be explained and defined.

¶

Chapter 1

Of the first discoveries of the eastern islands; the voyage thither by Adelantado Miguel Lopez de Legazpi; the conquest and pacification of the Filipinas during his governorship, and that of Guido de Labazarris, who afterward held the office.

According to ancient and modern cosmographers, that part of the world called Asia has adjacent to it a multitude of greater and lesser islands, inhabited by various nations and peoples, and as rich in precious stones, gold, silver, and other minerals, as they abound in fruit and grain, flocks, and animals. Some of the islands yield all kinds of spices which are carried away and distributed throughout the world. These islands are commonly designated in their books, descriptions, and sea-charts, as the great archipelago of San Lazaro, and are located in the eastern ocean. Among the most famous of them are the islands of Maluco, Celeves, Tendaya, Luzon, Mindanao, and Borneo, which are now called the Filipinas.

When Pope Alexander the Sixth divided the conquests of the new world between the kings of Castilla and of Portugal, the kings agreed to make the division by means of a line drawn across the world by the cosmographers, so that they might continue their discoveries and conquests, one toward the west and the other toward the east, and pacify whatever regions each might gain within his own demarcation.

After the crown of Portugal had conquered the city of Malaca, on the mainland of Asia, in the kingdom of Jor [Johore]—called by the ancients Aurea Chersonesus—a Portuguese fleet, in the year one thousand five hundred and eleven, on hearing of neighboring islands and especially of those of Maluco and Banda, where cloves and nutmegs are gathered, went to discover them. After touching at Banda, they went to Terrenate, one of the islands of Maluco, at the invitation of its king, to defend him against his neighbor, the king of Tidore, with whom he was at war. This was the beginning of the Portuguese settlement in Maluco.

Francisco Serrano, who after this discovery returned to Malaca, and thence went to India with the purpose of going to Portugal to give an account of the discovery, died before he had accomplished this voyage, but not, however, without having communicated in letters to his friend, Fernando de Magallanes, what he had seen; [9] for they had been together at the taking of Malaca, although the latter was then in Portugal. From this relation, Magallanes learned whatever was necessary for the discovery and navigation of these islands. [10]

At this time, Magallanes, who for certain reasons had entered the service of the king of Castilla, told the emperor Carlos V, our sovereign, that the islands of Maluco fell within the demarcation of the latter's crown of Castilla, and that their conquest belonged to him, according to the concessions made by Pope Alexander; moreover, he offered to make the expedition and navigation to the islands in the emperor's name, by sailing through that part of the demarcation belonging to Castilla, and by availing himself of a famous astrologer and cosmographer, named Ruy-farelo [sic], whom he had with him.

The emperor, moved by the importance of the undertaking, entrusted Fernando de Magallanes with this expedition and discovery, supplying him with the necessary ships and provisions therefor. Thus equipped, he set sail and discovered the strait to which he gave his name. Through this he entered the southern sea, and sailed to the islands of Tendaya and Sebu, where he was killed by the natives of Matan, which is one of these islands. His ships proceeded to Maluco, where the sailors fell into disputes and contentions with the Portuguese then stationed in the island of Terrenate. Finally, not being able to maintain themselves there, the Castilians left Maluco in a ship, called the "Victoria," the only remaining vessel of their fleet. As leader and captain, they chose Juan Sebastian del Cano, who made the voyage to Castilla by way of India, where he arrived with but few men, and informed his Majesty of the discovery of the great archipelago, and of his voyage.

The same enterprise was attempted at other times, and was carried out by Juan Sebastian del Cano, Comendador Loaisa, the Saoneses, and the bishop of Plasencia. [11] But these did not bear the fruits expected, on account of the hardships and perils of so long a voyage, and the opposition received by those who reached Maluco, from the Portuguese there.

After all these events, as it was thought that this discovery might be made quicker and better by way of Nueva Espana, in the year one thousand five hundred and forty-five, [12] a fleet, under command of Rui Lopez de Villalobos, was sent by that route. They reached Maluco by way of Sebu, where they quarreled with the Portuguese, and suffered misfortunes and hardships, so that they were unable to effect the desired end;

nor could the fleet return to Nueva Espana whence it had sailed, but was destroyed. Some of the surviving Castilians left Maluco by way of Portuguese India and returned to Castilla. There they related the occurrences of their voyage, and the quality and nature of the islands of Maluco and of the other islands that they had seen.

Afterward as King Don Felipe II, our sovereign, considered it inadvisable for him to desist from that same enterprise, and being informed by Don Luys de Velasco, viceroy of Nueva Espana, and by Fray Andres de Urdaneta of the Augustinian order—who had been in Maluco with the fleet of Comendador Loaisa, while a layman—that this voyage might be made better and quicker by way of Nueva Espania, he entrusted the expedition to the viceroy. Fray Andres de Urdaneta left the court for Nueva Espania, [13] for, as he was so experienced and excellent a cosmographer, he offered to go with the fleet and to discover the return voyage. The viceroy equipped a fleet and its crew with the most necessary things in Puerto de la Navidad, in the southern sea, under charge of a worthy and reliable man, Miguel Lopez de Legazpi, a citizen of Mexico and a native of the province of Guipuzcoa. On account of the viceroy's death, the Audiencia which was governing in his place completed arrangements for the despatching of Legazpi, and gave him instructions as to his destination, with orders not to open them until three hundred leguas at sea; for there were differences among members of the fleet, some saying that they would better go to Nueva Guinea, others to the Luzones, and others to Maluco. Miguel Lopez de Legazpi left Puerto de la Navidad in the year one thousand five hundred and sixty-four, with five ships and five hundred men, accompanied by Fray Andres de Urdaneta and four other religious of the Order of St. Augustine. After sailing westward for several days, he opened his instructions, and found that he was ordered to go to the islands of Luzones and there endeavor to pacify them and reduce them to the obedience of his Majesty, and to make them accept the holy Catholic faith. [14] He continued his voyage until reaching the island of Sebu, where he anchored, induced by the convenience of a good port and by the nature of the land. At first he was received peacefully by the natives and by their chief Tupas; but later they tried to kill him and his companions, for the Spaniards having seized their provisions, the natives took up arms against the latter; but the opposite to their expectations occurred, for the Spaniards conquered and subdued them. Seeing what had happened in Sebu, the natives of other neighboring islands came peacefully before the adelantado, rendered him homage, and supplied his camp with a few provisions. The first of the Spanish settlements was made in that port, and was called the city of Sanctisimo Nombre de Jesus [Most holy name of Jesus], [15] because a carved image of Jesus had been found in one of the houses of the natives when the Spaniards conquered the latter, which was believed to have been left there by the fleet of Magallanes. The natives held the image in great reverence, and it wrought miracles for them in times of need. The Spaniards placed it in the monastery of St. Augustine, in that city.

That same year the adelantado despatched the flagship of his fleet to Nueva Espana, with the relation and news of what had happened during the voyage, and of the settlement in Sebu. He requested men and supplies in order to continue the pacification of the other islands. Fray Andres de Urdaneta and his associate, Fray Andres de Aguirre, sailed in the vessel.

One of the ships which left Puerto de la Navidad in company with the fleet and under command of Don Alonso de Arellano, carried as pilot one Lope Martin, a mulatto and a good sailor, although a turbulent fellow. When the ship neared the islands, it left the fleet and went among them ahead of the other vessels. There they bartered for provisions, and, without awaiting the adelantado, returned to Nueva Espana by a northerly course—either because of their slight gratification at having made the voyage to the islands, or to gain the reward for having discovered the return passage. They soon arrived and declared that they had seen the islands and discovered the return voyage. They alleged various reasons for their coming, but brought no message from the adelantado, or news of what had happened to him. Don Alonso de Arellano was well received by the Audiencia which was governing, where the rewarding of him and his pilot was considered. This would have been done, had not the adelantado's flagship arrived during this time, after having made the same voyage. It brought an authentic account of events, of the actual state of affairs, and of the settlement of Sebu. Moreover, they related that Don Alonso de Arellano, without receiving any orders, and without any necessity for it, had preceded the fleet with his ship at the entrance of the islands, and was seen no more. They said also that, besides those islands which had peacefully submitted to his Majesty, there were many others, large and rich, well-inhabited, and abounding in food and gold. They hoped to pacify and reduce those islands with the reenforcements requested. They said that the adelantado had named all the islands Filipinas, [16] in honor of his Majesty. Reenforcements were immediately sent to the adelantado, and have been sent every year, as necessity has demanded, so that the land has been conquered and maintained.

The adelantado heard that there were other islands near Sebu, abounding in provisions, and accordingly sent some Spaniards thither to reduce the natives to peace, and bring back rice for the camp. Thus he relieved his necessity and maintained himself as well as possible until, having gone to the island of Panay, he sent Martin de Goiti, his master-of-camp, and other captains thence to the island of Luzon with what men he deemed sufficient, and under the guidance of a native chief of the latter island, called Maomat, to try to pacify it and reduce it to the obedience of his Majesty. When they reached the bay of Manila, they found its settlement on the seashore, near a large river, and under the rule and protection of a chief called Rajamora. Opposite, on the other side of the river, was another large settlement named Tondo, which was likewise held by another chief named Rajamatanda. [17] These settlements were fortified with palm-trees and stout arigues [18] filled in with earth, and very many bronze culverins and other pieces of larger bore. Martin de Goiti, having begun to treat with the chiefs and their people concerning the peace and submission which he demanded, found it necessary to come to blows with them. The Spaniards entered the land by force of arms, and took it, together with the forts and artillery, on the day of St. Potenciana, May nineteen, one thousand five hundred and seventy-one. [19] Upon this the natives and their chiefs made peace and rendered homage; and many others of the same island of Luzon did the same. [20]

When the news of the taking of Manila and of the Spanish settlement there reached Panay, Adelantado Legazpi set in order the affairs of Sebu and other islands which he had subdued, entrusted their natives to the most reliable soldiers, and having taken the most necessary precautions for the government of those provinces, which are commonly called Bicayas de los Pintados, [21] because the natives of them have all their bodies marked with fire, went to Manila with the remainder of his men. He was well received there, and established afresh with the natives and their chiefs the peace, alliance, and homage, which had been given. On the very site of Manila, of which Rajamora made a donation to the Spaniards for their settlement, the adelantado founded his town and colony, on account of its strength and its situation in a well-provisioned district, and in the midst of all the other islands. He left it its name of Manila which it had received from the natives. [22] Taking sufficient land for the city, the governor established therein his seat and residence, and fortified it with special care. He paid more attention to the above, in order to make this new settlement the seat of government, than to the temperature, and width of the site, which is hot and narrow from having the river on one side of the city and the bay on the other, while at the back are to be found large swamps and marshes, which make the place very strong.

From this post he continued to prosecute the pacification of the other provinces of this great island of Luzon and of surrounding districts. Some submitted voluntarily; others were conquered by force of arms or by the efforts of the religious, who have sown the good seed of the holy gospel therein. Various of them have labored valiantly in this, not only in the time and administration of Adelantado Miguel Lopez de Legazpi, but also in that of the governors that have succeeded him. The land was apportioned among its conquerors and colonizers. The capitals of provinces, the ports, and the settlements of cities and towns which had been founded, and other special encomiendas, were assigned to the royal crown, for the necessities that arise and the expenses of the royal exchequer. The affairs of government and the conversion of the natives were treated as was necessary. Ships were provided for the annual voyage to Nueva Espana, which return with the usual supplies. Thus the condition of the Filipinas Islands has reached its present known height in both spiritual and temporal matters.

Adelantado Miguel Lopez de Legazpi, as above-said, discovered the islands, colonized them, and made a good beginning in the work of pacification and subjugation. He founded the city of Sanctisimo Nombre de Jesus in the provinces of Pintados, and then the city of Manila in the island of Luzon. In this island he conquered the province of Ylocos, in whose settlement and port called Vigan, he founded a Spanish colony, to which he gave the name of Villa Fernandina. [23] He also pacified the province of Pangasinan and the island of Mindoro, fixed the amount of tribute that the natives were to pay throughout the islands, [24] and made many ordinances concerning their government and conversion, until his death in the year one thousand five hundred and seventy-four, at Manila, where his body was buried in the monastery of St. Augustine. [25]

At his death, there was found among his papers a sealed despatch from the Audiencia of Mexico, which was governing when the fleet left Nueva Espana, appointing a successor to the government, in case of the death of the adelantado. By virtue of this despatch, Guido de Labazarris, formerly a royal official, took the office and was obeyed. He continued the conversion and pacification of the islands with great wisdom, valor, and system, and governed them.

During his term the pirate Limahon came from China, and attacked Manila with a fleet of seventy large war-ships and many soldiers. He entered the city, and, after killing the master-of-camp, Martin de Goiti, with other Spaniards who were at his house, marched against the fort, in which the Spaniards, who were but few, had taken refuge, with the intention of seizing and subjecting the country. The Spaniards, reinforced from Vigan by Captain Joan de Salzedo and his soldiers—for Salzedo saw this pirate pass his coasts, and brought the reinforcement to Manila—defended themselves so bravely that, after having killed many of Limahon's men, they forced him to reembark, to leave the bay in flight, and to take refuge in Pangasinan River. The Spaniards went thither in search of him and burned his fleet. [26] For many days they besieged this pirate on land, but he, taking flight in small boats that he made there secretly, put to sea and abandoned the islands.

During the government of this same Guido de Labazarris, trade and commerce were established between Great China and Manila. Merchant ships came every year and the governor received them kindly, and as a consequence commerce has been growing ever since.

This same governor apportioned all the pacified land in the island of Luzon and surrounding islands, to the conquerors and settlers there. He assigned to himself the towns of Betis and Lubao in the province of Pampanga, besides others of some importance. The succeeding government dispossessed him of these towns; but afterward his Majesty, on account of his good services, granted them all to him, and he enjoyed them, together with the office of master-of-camp of the islands, as long as he lived.

Chapter 2

¶The administration of Doctor Francisco de Sande, and the events of the Filipinas Islands during his term.

When the news of the entrance and conquest of the Filipinas Islands by Miguel Lopez de Legazpi, and of his death, reached Espania, his Majesty appointed as governor and captain-general of the islands, Doctor Francisco de Sande, a native of Caceres, and alcalde of the Audiencia of Mexico. The latter journeyed thither, and took over his government in the year one thousand five hundred and seventy-five.

During this administration, the pacification of the islands was continued, especially that of the province of Camarines, by Captain Pedro Chaves, who often came to blows with the natives, until he conquered them and received their submission. A Spanish colony was founded there which was called the city of Caceres. Among other enterprises, the governor made in person the expedition to the island of Borneo with a fleet of galleys and frigates. [27] With these he attacked and captured the enemy's fleet, which had come out to meet him. He captured also the principal settlement, where the king of the island had his house and residence, but after a few days he abandoned it and returned to Manila, on account of sickness among the crews, and his inability to support and care for the Spaniards in that island. On the way back, and by his orders, Captain Estevan Rodriguez de Figueroa entered the island of Jolo; he came to blows with the natives and their chief, whom he conquered, and the latter rendered him acknowledgment and submission in the name of his Majesty. Thence he went to the island of Mindanao which he explored, reconnoitering its river and chief settlements. On his way he reduced other towns and natives of the same island, who had been pacified, to friendship and alliance with the Spaniards. The governor despatched the ship "San Juanillo" to Nueva Espana, under command of Captain Juan de Ribera, but it was lost at sea and never heard of again.

Doctor Sande remained until Don Gonzalo Ronquillo de Penalosa came from Espania as the new governor and captain-general. After his residencia the doctor returned to Nueva Espana to fill the office of auditor of Mexico.

¶

Chapter 3

Of the administration of Don Gonzalo Ronquillo de Penalosa, and of Diego Ronquillo, who filled the office because of the former's death.

Because of the many accounts that had reached the court of his Majesty concerning the affairs of the Filipinas, and because of their need of being supplied with settlers and soldiers to pacify them, an arrangement was made with Don Gonzalo Ronquillo de Penalosa, a native of Arevalo, and chief alguacil of the Audiencia of Mexico, who was residing at court, so that it might be done better and at less cost to the royal exchequer. By this arrangement he was to be governor of the Filipinas for life and was to take six hundred married and single men from the kingdoms of Castilla to the Filipinas. His Majesty granted him certain assistance and facilities for this purpose, together with other favors as a reward for this service.

Don Gonzalo prepared for the voyage, raised his people, and embarked them in the port of San Lucas Barremeda, but, as the fleet left the bar, one of his ships was wrecked. He returned in order to repair his losses, and, although he took less than at first, he made his journey to the mainland, and at Panama, embarked his people in the South Sea, and set sail for the Filipinas, where he arrived and took over the government, in the year one thousand five hundred and eighty.

Don Gonzalo Ronquillo founded a Spanish town in the island of Panay, in Oton, which he named Arevalo. During his term, the trade with the Chinese increased, and he built a market-place and Parian for them within the city, where the Chinese could bring and sell their merchandise. He tried to discover a return passage from the islands to Nueva Espana, by way of the south, for which purpose he sent his cousin, Captain Don Juan Ronquillo del Castillo. The latter could not effect this, for after sailing for some time, until finding himself near Nueva Guinea, he could go no farther, on account of many severe storms, and returned to the Filipinas. In like manner, Don Gonzalo sent another ship, under command of Don Gonzalo Ronquillo de Vallesteros, to Peru, with some merchandise, in order to obtain certain goods from those provinces which he said that the Filipinas needed. This vessel returned from Peru after the death of the governor. The latter imposed the two per cent duty on the merchandise exported to Nueva Espana, and the three per cent duty on the goods imported by the Chinese to the Filipinas. Although he was censured for having done this without his Majesty's orders, these duties remained in force, and continued to be imposed thenceforward.

During this same term, as his Majesty had succeeded to the kingdoms of Portugal, and had ordered the governor of Manila to maintain good relations with the chief captain of the fortress of the island of Tidore, in Maluco, and to assist him when necessary, he sent a fleet and soldiers thither from Manila, under command of Captain Don Juan Ronquillo del Castillo. This he did at the request of Diego de Azambuja, chief captain of Tidore, for the expedition and conquest of the island of Terrenate. But after reaching Maluco, the expedition did not succeed in its object. [28] Thenceforward supplies of men and provisions continued to be sent from the Filipinas to the fortress of Tidore.

During this same administration, the province of Cagayan in the island of Luzon, opposite China, was first pacified [29] by Captain Joan Pablos de Carrion, who founded there a Spanish colony, which he named Nueva Segovia. He also drove a Japanese pirate [30] from that place, who had seized the port with some ships, and fortified himself there.

A few days after Don Gonzalo Ronquillo had entered into the government, he sent Captain Gabriel de Ribera with a small fleet, consisting of one galley and several frigates, to explore the coast and settlements of the island of Borneo, with orders to proceed thence to the kingdom of Patan on the mainland, where pepper is produced. The captain having coasted along and reconnoitered Borneo, returned with his fleet to Manila, on account of the advanced season and lack of provisions. Thence the governor sent him to Espana, with authority from himself and from the islands, to confer with his Majesty upon several matters that he desired to see carried out, and upon others which would prove advantageous to the islands. [31] The captain found his Majesty in Portugal, gave him a few pieces of gold and other curiosities which he had brought for that purpose, and stated the matters of which he had come to treat. The result was that his Majesty, among other favors, appointed him marshal of Bonbon, for his hardships during this voyage, and the proper resolution was made in the matters of which he had come to treat.

It was during the administration of Don Gonzalo Ronquillo, that the first bishop of the Filipinas was appointed, in the person of Don Fray Domingo de Salazar, of the Dominican order, a man of great learning

27

and piety. As soon as he arrived in the islands, he took upon himself the management and jurisdiction of ecclesiastical affairs, which were at first in charge of the Augustinian friars who had come at the time of the conquest, and afterwards of the discalced Franciscan religious, who had arrived at the time of the conversion. The bishop erected his cathedral in the city of Manila, by apostolic bulls, with prebends paid by the royal exchequer, until there should be tithes and ecclesiastical revenues to maintain themselves. Moreover, he provided whatever else was necessary for the service and decoration of the church, and for the divine worship which is celebrated there with great solemnity and display. Don Fray Domingo de Salazar took Antonio Sedeno and Alonso Sanchez, both priests and grave members of the Society of Jesus, with him. They were the first to establish that order in the Filipinas, which, since that time, has been steadily growing, to the great profit and fruit of the teaching and conversion of the natives, consolation of the Spaniards, and the education and teaching of their children in the studies which they pursue.

Don Gonzalo Ronquillo was in such poor health from the day on which he entered upon his administration, that he died in the year one thousand five hundred and eighty-three, and his body was buried in the monastery of St. Augustine in Manila.

His kinsman, Diego Ronquillo, by virtue of his appointment through a decree of his Majesty, succeeded him in the governorship; this man continued what Don Gonzalo had commenced, especially in the assistance for Maluco and pacification for other islands.

During the same term of Diego Ronquillo, a fire broke out in the city of Manila, which started at midday in the church of the convent of St. Augustine, while the doors of the church were closed. The fire increased so rapidly that all the city was burned in a few hours, as it was built of wood. There was great loss of goods and property, and some persons were in danger. The city was rebuilt with great difficulty and labor, leaving the Spaniards very poor and needy. [32]

The main result of the matters treated at court by Mariscal Gabriel de Ribera was (although at that time the death of Governor Don Gonzalo Ronquillo was unknown) to order the establishment of a royal Audiencia in the city of Manila, whose president was to be governor and captain-general of all the Filipinas. In view of this, the necessary instructions were issued, and the presidency given to Doctor Sanctiago de Vera, alcalde of the Audiencia of Mexico, and a native of the town of Alcala de Henares. He went to the islands with the usual reenforcements from Nueva Espana, taking with him the royal seal of the Audiencia, the auditors whom his Majesty was sending, the fiscal, and other officials and assistants of the said Audiencia. The auditors and fiscal were Licentiates

Melchior de Avalos, Pedro de Rojas, and Gaspar de Ayala—[the latter] as fiscal. At the end of two years, Don Antonio de Ribera went as third auditor.

¶

Chapter 4

Of the administration of Doctor Sanctiago de Vera, and of the establishment of the Manila Audiencia, and until its suppression; and of events during his term.

The president and auditors arrived at the Filipinas in the month of May, in the year 1584, while Diego Ronquillo was governing. Doctor Sanctiago de Vera entered upon his office, and immediately established the Audiencia. The royal seal was received and deposited with all possible solemnity and festivity. Then they began to attend to the affairs both of justice and of war and government, to the great profit of the country. At this time new reenforcements were sent to Maluco for the conquests that the chief captain of Tidore intended to make of the island of Terrenate. Captain Pedro Sarmiento [33] went from Manila for this purpose, and on another occasion the captain and sargento-mayor, Juan de Moron; [34] but neither of these expeditions met with the desired result.

President Sanctiago de Vera also continued the pacification of several provinces of the islands, and did many things, which proved advantageous in every respect. He discovered a rebellion and insurrection which the native chiefs of Manila and Pampanga had planned against the Spaniards, and justice was done the guilty. [35] He built with stone the fortress of Nuestra Senora de Guia [Our Lady of Guidance], within the city of Manila on the land side, and for its defense he caused some artillery to be founded by an old Indian, called Pandapira, a native of the province of Panpanga. The latter and his sons rendered this service for many years afterward, until their deaths.

During the administration of President Sanctiago de Vera, the Englishman Thomas Escander, [36] entered the South Sea through the Strait of Magallanes; on the coast of Nueva Espana, close to California, he had captured the ship "Santa Ana," which was coming from the Filipinas laden with a quantity of gold and merchandise of great value. Thence he proceeded to the Filipinas; entering through the province of Pintados, he came in sight of the town of Arevalo and of the shipyard where a galleon was being built for the navigation of the Nueva Espana line. Wishing to burn this vessel, he made the attempt, but he was resisted by Manuel Lorenzo de Lemos, who was supervising its construction. The Englishman passed on, and went to India, whence he took his course to Inglaterra, having followed the same route which the Englishman Francisco Draque [Francis Drake] [37] had taken several years before. The latter had, in like manner, passed through the Strait of Magallanes to the Peruvian coast, where he made many prizes.

At this time, the Audiencia and the bishop thought it advisable that some person of sufficient and satisfactory qualities should be sent to Espana, to the court of his Majesty, to give a thorough and detailed account of the state of affairs in the Filipinas Islands, and to request that some necessary measures might be taken concerning them. The court was especially to be informed that, for the time being, the Audiencia could be dispensed with, for it was a heavy burden to all estates, because of the newness of the country. The person of Father Alonso Sanches, of the Society of Jesus, a learned man, and one well informed concerning the country, and very active in business, was chosen for this purpose. Instructions were given him, and authority to act for all estates, religious orders, and communities, as to what he was to treat and request in Espana, and at the court of his Holiness in Roma, where he was also to go. [38] This father reached Madrid, and after having conferred with his Majesty several times respecting those things of which he thought fit to treat and to make requests, went to Roma, where he introduced himself as the ambassador of all the estates of the Filipinas, and on their behalf he kissed the foot, and visited the pontiffs who ruled during that time, after the death of Sixtus the Fifth. Having received from them favors and indulgences with many relics, bulls, and letters for the Filipinas, he returned to Espana, where again he solicited a decision on the business which he had left under discussion when he went to Roma. His Majesty listened to the messages that he brought from the pontiffs, and lent him a favorable ear concerning the affairs of the islands. In private audiences the father made the king understand his requests, and decide them to his own satisfaction. But as soon as the despatches reached the Filipinas, much of their contents appeared outside the intention and expectation of both bishop and Audiencia, and the city, citizens, and encomenderos. They appeared even detrimental to the inhabitants of the islands, and therefore they expressed their displeasure toward Father Alonso Sanches, who was still in Espana. The father negotiated for the suppression of the Audiencia of Manila, and the appointment of a new governor; and in begging such an one, the same father, because of his friendly relations with him, proposed one Gomez Perez Dasmarinas, who had been corregidor of

Leon and later of Murcia, and who was at that time in the court, and corregidor-elect of Logrono and Calahorra. His Majesty appointed him governor and captain-general of the Filipinas, and increased the annual salary of his office to ten thousand Castilian ducados. Moreover, he made him a knight of the Order of Sanctiago, and gave him a large sum of money with which to meet the expenses of the voyage. He was provided with the necessary despatches, both for the exercise of his office, and for the suppression of the Audiencia of Manila, and the establishment of a camp of four hundred paid soldiers with their officers, at his Majesty's expense, for the garrison and defense of the land. His Majesty ordered him to sail immediately for Nueva Espana in the ships on which Viceroy Don Luis de Velasco sailed in the year one thousand five hundred and eighty-nine, who was going to govern that country.

Gomez Perez Dasmarinas left Mexico as soon as possible, and with what ships, soldiers, and captains he needed, sailed for the Filipinas, where he arrived in the month of May, in the year one thousand five hundred and ninety.

¶

Chapter 5

Of the administration of Gomez Perez Dasmarinas, and of Licentiate Pedro de Rojas, who was elected by the city of Manila to act as governor, on account of the former's death, until Don Luis Dasmarinas was received as the successor of Gomez Perez, his father.

As soon as Gomez Perez Dasmarinas reached the Filipinas, he was received as governor with universal acclaim. He suppressed the Audiencia, and the residencias of its president, auditors, fiscal, and other officials were taken by Licentiate Herver del Coral, whom Viceroy Don Luys de Velasco had sent for that purpose, by virtue of a royal decree received to that effect. The new governor inaugurated his rule by establishing the paid garrison, and by executing, with great enthusiasm and zeal, many and various things, for which he possessed royal orders and instructions, not shrinking from any kind of labor, or taking any care of himself. His first labor was the walling of the city, to which he attended so assiduously, that it was almost completed before his death. [39] He also built a cavalier on the promontory of Manila where the old wooden fort, which he called Sanctiago, formerly stood, and fortified it with some artillery. He razed to the ground the fort of Nuestra Senora de Guia, which his predecessor had built; he built of stone the cathedral of Manila, and encouraged the inhabitants of the city who had shortly before begun to build, to persevere in building their houses of stone, a work which the bishop was the first to begin in the building of his house. During his term he increased trade with China, and regulated better the navigation of Nueva Espana, and the despatch of vessels in that line. He built some galleys for the defense of the coast, pacified the Zambales, who had revolted, and ordered his son Don Luys Dasmarinas, of the habit of Alcantara, to make an incursion with troops from Manila into the interior of the island of Luzon, [40] by crossing the river Ytui and other provinces not yet explored or seen by Spaniards, until he arrived at Cagayan. He built also an artillery foundry in Manila, where, for want of expert founders, but few large pieces were turned out.

In the first year of his administration, he sent the president and auditors of the suppressed Audiencia to Espana. Licentiate Pedro de Rojas, the senior auditor, remained with the governor by order of his Majesty, as lieutenant-assessor in matters of justice, until some years later appointed alcalde in Mexico.

During Gomez Perez's administration, the relations and peace existing between the Japanese and the Spaniards of the Filipinas began to become strained; for hitherto Japanese vessels had gone from the port of Nangasaqui to Manila for some years, laden with their flour and other goods, where they had been kindly received, and despatched. But Taicosama, [41] lord of all Xapon, was incited through the efforts of Farandaquiemon—a Japanese of low extraction, one of those who came to Manila—to write in a barbarous and arrogant manner to the governor, demanding submission and tribute, and threatening to come with a fleet and troops to lay waste the country. But, between demands and replies, several years were spent, until at last Taico died. [42]

While Xapon was causing the governor some anxiety, the king of Camboja sent him an embassy by the Portuguese Diego Belloso, who brought a present of two elephants and offers of friendship and trade with his kingdom, and implored aid against Sian—which was threatening Camboja. The governor answered the king, and sent him a horse, with a few emeralds and other objects, but postponed until later what related to aid, and thanked him for his friendship. This was the origin of the events and the expeditions made later from Manila to the kingdoms of Sian and Camboja, on the mainland of Asia.

From the moment that Gomez Perez received his charge in Espana, he had cherished the desire to lead an expedition from Manila to conquer the fort of Terrenate in Maluco, on account of the great importance of this enterprise, and its outcome, in which no success had been attained on other occasions. He was constantly making necessary arrangements for undertaking this expedition, but so secretly that he declared it to no one, until, in the year ninety-three, seeing that the preparations for his intention appeared sufficient, he declared his purpose, and made ready to set out in person, with more than nine hundred Spaniards and two hundred sail, counting galleys, galliots, frigates, vireys, and other craft. He left the war affairs of Manila and of the islands, with a few troops—although insufficient for the city's defense—in charge of Diego Ronquillo, his master-of-camp; and those of administration and justice to Licentiate Pedro de Rojas. He also sent his son, Don Luys Dasmarinas, forward with the rest of the fleet, as his lieutenant in the office of captain-general, to the provinces of Pintados, whence they were to sail; while he himself remained in Manila making his final preparations and arming a galley of twenty-eight benches, in which he was to sail. This galley he manned with good Chinese rowers, with pay, [43] whom, in order to win their good will, he would not allow to be chained, and even winked at their carrying certain weapons. About forty Spaniards embarked on the galley, and the galley itself was accompanied by a few frigates and smaller vessels, in which private individuals embarked. The governor sailed from the port of Cabit, in the month of October, one thousand five hundred and ninety-three, for the provinces of Pintados, where they were to join the fleet which was awaiting them there, and to proceed to Maluco. In the afternoon of the second day of the voyage, they reached the island of Caca, [44] twenty-four leguas from Manila, and close to the coast of the same island of Luzon, at a place called Punta del Acufre [Sulphur Point], where there is a strong head wind. The galley tried to round this point by rowing, but being unable to make any headway until the wind should drop, they anchored and spread an awning, and stayed there that night. Some of the vessels sailing with the galley went in closer to the shore in sight of the galley, and awaited it there.

The governor and those who accompanied him passed the night playing on the poop, until the end of the first watch. After the governor had gone into his cabin to rest, the other Spaniards went also to their quarters [45] for the same purpose, leaving the usual guards in the midship gangway, and at the bow and stern. The Chinese rowers, who had three days before that conspired to seize the galley whenever a favorable opportunity presented itself—in order to avoid the labor of rowing on this expedition, and their covetousness of the money, jewels, and other articles of value aboard the vessel—thought that they should not lose their opportunity. Having provided candles, and white shirts with which to clothe themselves, and appointed chiefs for its execution, they carried out their plan that same night, in the last watch before dawn, when they perceived that the Spaniards were asleep. At a signal which one of them gave they all at the same time put on their shirts, lit their candles, and catan [46] in hand, attacked the guards and the men who slept in the quarters [ballesteras] and in the wales, and wounding and killing them, they seized the galley. A few of the Spaniards escaped, some by swimming ashore, others by means of the galley's tender, which was at the stern. When the governor heard the noise from his cabin, thinking that the galley was dragging and that the crew were lowering the awning and taking to the oars, he hurried carelessly out bareheaded through the hatchway of the cabin. Several Chinese were awaiting him there and split his head with a catan. Thus wounded he fell down the stairs into his cabin, and the two servants whom he kept there, carried him to his bed, where he immediately died. The servants met the same fate from the stabs given them through the hatch. The only surviving Spaniards in the galley were Juan de Cuellar, the governor's secretary, and Father Montilla of the Franciscan order, who were sleeping in the cabin amidships, and who remained there without coming out; nor did the Chinese, thinking that there were more Spaniards, dare to go in until next day, when they took the two men out and later put them ashore on the coast of Ylocos, in the same island of Luzon, in order that the natives might allow them to take water on shore, which they badly needed.

Although the Spaniards who were in the other vessels, close to the land, perceived the lights and heard the noise made in the galley from their ships, they thought that some work was being done; and when shortly afterward, they learned what was happening from those who had escaped by swimming, they could render no assistance and kept still, as everything was lost, and they were few and not in sufficient force therefor. They waited for the morning, and when it began to dawn, they saw that the galley had already set its bastard, and was sailing, wind astern toward China, and they were unable to pursue it.

The galley sailed with a favorable wind all along the coast of the island until leaving it. It took some water at Ylocos, where the secretary and the religious were abandoned. The Chinese tried to make for China, but not being able to fetch it, they ported in the kingdom of Cochinchina, where the king of Tunquin seized their cargo and two large pieces of artillery which were intended for the expedition of Maluco, the royal standard, and all the jewels, money, and articles of value; the galley he left to drift ashore, and the Chinese dispersed and fled to different provinces. Governor Gomez Perez met this unfortunate death, whereupon the expedition and enterprise to Maluco, which the governor had undertaken, ceased also. Thus ended his administration, after he had ruled somewhat more than three years.

Among other despatches which Gomez Perez Dasmarinas brought from Espana there was an order from his Majesty which authorized him to appoint the person whom he thought best to succeed him in case of death, until such time as his Majesty should appoint his successor. He showed this order to several of the most important persons of the island, giving each one to understand that he would be appointed, especially to Captain Estevan Rodriguez de Figueroa, an inhabitant of Pintados, a rich man of merit, and one of the first conquerors of the land. To him the governor showed an appointment drawn in his favor. He made use of the captain on all occasions and had him go with himself to Maluco. The news of the seizure of the galley was soon known in Manila. The citizens

36

and soldiers that had remained there, assembled at the house of Licentiate Pedro de Rojas, to discuss advisable measures. First of all they elected the latter governor and captain-general. Then they sent Captain Don Juan Ronquillo del Castillo and other captains with two frigates (for there were no other vessels) in pursuit of the galley, a fruitless attempt, for the galley was nowhere to be seen. The new governor also sent a message to Don Luis Dasmarinas and to the army and fleet who were awaiting Gomez Perez in Pintados, informing him of the latter's death and of what had happened, as well as of his own recent election to affairs of government. He also ordered them to return with all speed to Manila, for the city was left almost deserted, and without the necessary precautions for any emergency.

The news caused great grief in the fleet. Don Luys Dasmarinas and Captain Estevan Rodriguez de Figueroa, each in his own heart, was certain that he was to become governor, taking it for granted that the governor had nominated him for the office. With this hope, both of them with the best ships and crews of the fleet, set sail together for Manila with the utmost speed.

Licentiate Pedro de Rojas, anxious about this provision, which the governor would leave among his papers and drawers deposited in the monastery of St. Augustine in Manila, in the possession of Fray Diego Munoz, prior and commissary of the Holy Office, made the effort to gain possession of them. Although he seized some of them, he did not find the said provision, for the prior had anticipated him and set aside one of the drawers, in which the provision was supposed to be found, to await Don Luys Dasmarinas's arrival in the city. Juan de Cuellar, who had escaped from the galley, arrived from the province of Ylocos, and testified that an appointment for the succession to the governorship had been made by Gomez Perez, but he did not state whom; or among what papers the nomination could be found. Thereupon the licentiate Pedro de Rojas and those devoted to him became more anxious.

Forty days passed in this manner, at the end of which Don Luis appeared in the bay near the city, accompanied by Estevan Rodriguez and many men; and there he anchored, not choosing to enter the city, or to disembark. He caused a search to be made for the papers kept in St. Augustine, and among them was found the royal order and the nomination of Don Luys Dasmarinas to succeed to the governorship. One of his partisans announced the fact to the city magistrates, who, changing their ideas, and notwithstanding some opposition from the partisans of Licentiate Rojas, summoned Don Luys Dasmarinas to the municipal house and placed him in possession of the government. The same was done by the soldiers whom Don Luys had with him, and by the fleet. Each day brought a new disappointment to Licentiate Rojas, who returned to his office of lieutenant-assessor, after a rule of forty days.

If the death of Governor Gomez Perez Dasmarinas was an unfortunate event, both for the loss of his person and for the loss of a so good opportunity for the conquest of Terrenate, when all were certain of success, the return of the fleet and the arrival of the troops in the city was none the less a fortunate event, for, not many days after—having anticipated their usual time for the voyage—there arrived in Manila many Chinese ships which carried many men and little merchandise, and seven mandarins bearing the insignia of their office. This gave sufficient motive for suspecting that they had heard of the departure of the fleet for Maluco and of the city's lack of defense, and that they had therefore come on this occasion to try to seize the country. But they desisted from the attempt when they found the city with more troops than ever. They returned to China without showing any other particular motive for coming, and without either side showing that their motives were understood; except that Governor Don Luys was watchful and on his guard. He took the proper measures, especially those concerning the Chinese, and their settlement and Parian.

No ships went to Nueva Espana from the Filipinas that year, because Governor Gomez Perez, before starting on the expedition to Maluco, had sent there the vessels "San Felipe" and "San Francisco," both of which, on account of heavy storms, had to put back, the "San Felipe" to the port of Sebu and the "San Francisco" to Manila, and they were unable to resail until the following year. It was suspected in Nueva Espana that there were troubles in the islands because of the non-arrival of the ships, and persons were not wanting to affirm more than had really happened; nor was it possible at the same time—in the town of Mexico—to ascertain whence the news had emanated. This was very shortly known in Espana, by way of India, letters having been sent to Venecia [Venice], through Persia; and immediately they set about appointing a new governor.

In the first year of the government of Gomez Perez Dasmarinas, the need of an Audiencia began to be felt by many, upon their seeing all the power vested in one man, and that there was no one to whom they could apply for remedy for certain cases. [47] He who felt this most keenly was Bishop Fray Domingo de Salazar, who had had certain differences and disputes with the governor, which obliged him to start for Espana, notwithstanding his advanced age. The governor readily gave him leave for that year, and a vessel for the voyage, in order to rid himself of him; but at the same time and with full power from himself, he sent Fray Francisco de Ortega of the Augustinian order to court, to meet whatever the bishop might allege and to defend his side. Both reached Espana, and each spoke as his interests demanded. The chief thing insisted upon by the bishop was a request for the reestablishment of the Audiencia, and the foundation of other bishoprics in the Filipinas, besides that of Manila, as well as other things which he thought beneficial to the spiritual and temporal welfare. In all this he was opposed by Ortega. But the authority and piety of the bishop were of such weight, that, although at first the cause that made him, at his advanced age, leave his church, and travel five thousand leguas to Espana, seemed trivial, afterward he was favorably received by his Majesty and the Council and all his petitions and propositions were considered and discussed at length, and many consultations were held with his Majesty, in order to have a decision passed upon them.

In the same year of ninety-three in which Gomez Perez died in the Filipinas, the Council after consulting with his Majesty, resolved that the office of lieutenant-assessor in judicial matters, which had been filled by Licentiate Pedro de Roxas since the suppression of the Audiencia, should be made more important than formerly in order to facilitate matters; that the title of the office should thereafter be that of lieutenant-general; and that in judicial matters the holder of it should have authority to hear cases of appeal not exceeding the value of one thousand Castilian ducados. Thereupon Licentiate Pedro de Rojas was promoted to the office of alcalde of Mexico, and Doctor Antonio de Morga was appointed by his Majesty to take the latter's residencia, and to the office of lieutenant-general of the Filipinas. In the course of his journey the latter arrived at Nueva Espana in the beginning of the year ninety-four, and found that the ships which, as abovesaid, had failed to come from the Filipinas, had not arrived. Moreover the death of Gomez Perez, and the other events that had occurred, were unknown until the arrival of Don Juan de Velasco, in the month of November of the same year, in the galleon "Sanctiago," which had been sent to the islands the year before by Viceroy Don Luys de Velasco, with the necessary supplies. He brought news of the governor's death and of the succession to the office by the latter's son, Don Luys Dasmarinas. Men and fresh supplies for the islands were prepared immediately and together with many passengers and religious from Espana, Doctor Antonio de Morga embarked in the port of Acapulco, in the galleons "San Felipe" and "Santiago," with everything under his charge. He set sail March twenty-two of ninety-five, and arrived under fair weather in the port of Cabit, June eleven of the same year. He entered upon his office of lieutenant-general, and began to occupy himself with his duties and the other matters in his charge.

While Don Luys Dasmarinas was governing, the suspicions and fear of Xapon continued, which, together with the Chinese trouble, kept the people in continual anxiety. The governor sent his cousin, Don Fernando de Castro, with letters and despatches to the viceroy of Canton and to that of Chincheo, where many of the Chinese who had seized the galley and killed Governor Gomez Perez, were thought to be found. Supposing that they had gone there with the galley, the governor requested the Chinese authorities to deliver the culprits for punishment, and to restore the royal standard, artillery, and other things which had been seized. This was not obtained, for as the galley had gone to Cochinchina, and the Chinese had dispersed in so many directions, it could not be effected. However, after several days, some of the guilty Chinese were brought from Malaca to Manila, having been captured there by the chief captain, Francisco de Silva de Meneses. From these men more accurate information was derived concerning what had happened in the seizure of the galley and of the governor's death, and justice was dealt them.

In the year ninety-four, when Don Luys was governor, a large junk came to the Filipinas with some Cambodians and Siamese, several Chinese and three Spaniards—one a Castilian, named Blaz Ruyz de Hernan Gonzalez, and the other two Portuguese called Pantaleon Carnero and Antonio Machado. While they were in the city of Chordemuco, [48] in Camboja, with Prauncar [49] Langara, king of Camboja, the king of Sian attacked the former king with many soldiers and elephants, conquered the land, and seized the house and the treasures of the king, who, with his wife, mother, sister, and his one daughter, and two sons, fled inland to the kingdom of Lao. The king of Sian leaving some of his captains to guard Camboja returned to his home with the rest of the army, sending what booty he could not carry away by land, to Sian by sea in several junks. He captured the Portuguese and Castilians whom he found there [i.e., in Camboja], and embarked the above mentioned three with other Cambodian slaves on board this junk, besides many goods, and with a Siamese guard and a Chinese crew. While they were at sea, the three Spaniards, aided by the Chinese, took possession of the junk, and killed and imprisoned the Siamese guards. After that the Spaniards and the Chinese came to blows as to who should have the prize and where it was to be taken. The three Spaniards overcame the Chinese, and killing most of them, took the junk to Manila with all its cargo, and the vessel was adjudged to them. Liberty was granted to the Cambodians as well as to the Chinese who had survived the fray.

The king of Sian reached his court in the city of Odia [50] and waited for the arrival of the junk; but seeing that it delayed longer than was necessary, he suspected that it had been seized or lost, and desired to send someone to bring him news of it and the reason for the delay. Among the prisoners he had made in Camboja was the Portuguese, Diego Belloso, who had been sent to Manila in the time of Gomez Perez Dasmarinas by King Prauncar Langara, to request his friendship and assistance against Sian which was then threatening him, as abovesaid. On his return to Camboja with the governor's answer and present, Belloso found that the Siamese had seized the country and had occupied it. Accordingly they captured him, and the Siamese king seized the present which he carried off with the other captures to his country. This Diego Belloso, getting wind of the king's intention, had word sent to the latter that, if he were to send him on this business, he would go as far as Manila, since he knew that archipelago so well, and find out what had happened to the junk. At the same time he said that he would establish friendship and commerce in the king's name with the Spaniards, and would procure many European curiosities for him, which were to be found in Manila, especially a colored stone large enough to serve as a hilt for the two-handed sword which the king used—a thing which the king greatly desired on account of a smaller one that he had found among the presents, and which he carried before him when on his elephant. The king agreed to this and had a junk prepared; he sent in it a Siamese who was in his service, and all the other men necessary for the voyage, together with Diego Belloso. He sent two elephants to the governor of Manila, and a quantity of benzoin, ivory, and other merchandise for sale, with the proceeds of which they were to buy the curiosities mentioned by Belloso. Having set sail they encountered a storm, and the junk put in at Malaca, where they learned that the other junk of the Siamese king, for which they were looking, had been seized, and that the Spaniards who had embarked as prisoners at Camboja, had taken it with all its cargo to Manila, after killing the Siamese guards.

At this news the Siamese king's servant began to look less favorably upon the journey to Manila, and accordingly, although against Belloso's desire, began to discharge and sell the goods in Malaca with the intention of returning immediately to Sian. One morning this servant of the Siamese king, Aconsi [51] by name, was found dead in the junk, although he had retired safe and sound the night before. Thereupon Diego Belloso became master of the situation, and after again embarking the goods and elephants on the junk, left Malaca, and journeyed to Manila. There he found Don Luys Dasmarinas acting as governor, because of his father Gomez Perez's death. To him he gave the present of the elephants, which he brought from the king, and told him what else had been sent. The other goods and merchandise were offered for sale by another Siamese who represented his king's service in the same junk.

Belloso met Blas Ruys de Hernan Goncales and his two companions in Manila. Among them all they agreed to persuade Governor Don Luys to send a fleet to Camboja to aid King Langara who was living in exile and stripped of his kingdom. They alleged that it would be easy to restore the king to power, and that at the same time the Spaniards might gain a foothold on the mainland, where they could settle and fortify themselves, whence would follow other important and more considerable results. They called on the religious of the Order of St. Dominic to support them before the governor in this plan. These easily put the matter on such good footing—for the governor followed their advice in everything that it was decided to prepare a fleet with as many men as possible, under command of the captain and sargento-mayor, Juan Xuarez Gallinato, himself in a ship of moderate size. He was to be accompanied by two junks: one under command of Diego Belloso, and the other under that of Blas Ruyz de Hernan Goncalez, with one hundred and twenty Spaniards, some Japanese and native Indians, and all else that was necessary.

This resolution seemed inexpedient to the majority of people in the city, both because it took so many men away, and also, because the success of the expedition seemed very doubtful. Admitting reports that the country of Camboja was in the hands of the king of Sian, who held it with sufficient forces—and nothing else was known—the result of the expedition would be to make the king of Sian—from whom the governor had just received presents and a friendly embassy in the person of Belloso—their declared enemy. And without sending the king an answer they were about to take up arms against him in favor of one who was unknown to them, and from whom the Spaniards had received neither pledges nor obligations. Lieutenant-general Don Antonio de Morga and Master-of-camp Diego Ronquillo, together with other captains and influential persons, spoke of this matter to Don Luys, and even requested him in writing to desist from this expedition. But although he had no reasons on his side to satisfy them, he was so taken by the expedition, that, inasmuch as the said religious of St. Dominic upheld him, he would not change his plans. Accordingly he despatched the fleet to the kingdom of Camboja at the beginning of the year ninety-six, which is generally one week's voyage. On the other hand, he dismissed the Siamese who had accompanied Belloso, without any definite answer to the embassy of the king of Siam, to whom he sent in return for his presents, some products of the country, which he thought appropriate. The Siamese, seeing that they were being sent back to their country, were satisfied, and expected no other result of their coming.

A storm overtook the fleet, and the flagship which carried Juan Xuarez Gallinato and the majority of the Spaniards, took refuge in the strait of Sincapura near Malaca, where it remained for many days. The other two junks which carried Diego Belloso and Blas Ruyz with some Spaniards, Japanese, and natives of Manila, reached Camboja with great difficulty, and Blas Ruyz, preceding Belloso, went up the river Mecon as far as the city of Chordemuco. There they learned that the mandarins of Camboja had united against the Siamese whom they had conquered and driven from the kingdom; and that one of these mandarins, Anacaparan by name, had taken possession of the country, and was governing under the title of king, although against the will of the others. Diego Belloso, Blas Ruyz, and those with them thought that they had arrived in good season for the furtherance of their designs, since confusion reigned among the Cambodians, and the Siamese were out of the country. Expecting Gallinato and the flagship to arrive directly, they spent several days in Chordemuco with the permission of Anacaparan, who resided nine leguas away in Sistor. Although the latter knew of the entry of these ships and their men, and that many more were coming, whose intentions he knew; and although he thought that it would not be favorable to him: yet he dissembled with them, waiting to see what time would bring. At the same time six Chinese ships with their merchandise arrived in Chordemuco and, while they were discharging it, the Chinese being many and hating the Spaniards, behaved towards them with great arrogance and insolence. This obliged the Spaniards, for the sake of their reputation, and in order to avenge themselves for injuries received, to take up arms against the Chinese. This they did, killing many Chinese and seizing their ships and all their cargo. Anacaparan took offense at this, and was desirous for the Chinese to avenge themselves by his aid. To remedy this evil Fray Alonso Ximenez, [52] of the Dominican order, who accompanied the Spaniards, thought that he, together with Blas Ruys and Diego Belloso, and about fifty Spaniards, a few Japanese, and men from Luzon, should leave the rest to guard the ships in Chordemuco, and should go up in small boats to Sistor, in order to obtain an interview with Anacaparan and offer him excuses and satisfaction for the trouble that they had had with the Chinese. And in order to negotiate with him more easily, they made a letter of embassy in the name of the governor of Manila, because Gallinato carried with him the one given them by the governor. This device was of little service to them, because Anacaparan not only did not grant them audience, but after having seized their boats, kept them so hard pressed in a lodging outside the city, and so threatened that he would kill them, if they did not return the ships and what they had taken from them to the Chinese, that the Spaniards were quite anxious to return to Chordemuco and board their vessels for greater security. They decided to do so as best they could.

Their necessity, and beholding themselves in this danger, encouraged them, one night, although at great risk, to leave their lodgings, and find a passage where they could cross the river to the city side. They crossed the river, arms in hand, late at night, and as silently as possible. Finding themselves near the city, and their courage and determination increasing, they entered the city and went as far as the king's house. They set fire to it, to the magazines, and to other buildings on their way, and threw the Cambodians into so great confusion, that that night and the following morning they killed many people, among them King Anacaparan himself. After this they thought it unwise to advance or maintain their ground, and accordingly marched back to their ships as orderly as possible. Meanwhile a great number of Cambodians, with arms and several elephants, started to pursue the Spaniards and overtook them before the latter reached their ships. The Spaniards defended themselves valiantly, and continued their march until embarking without the loss of a single man, while the Cambodians returned to the city with some of their men killed and wounded.

Diego Belloso and Bias Ruiz had hardly boarded their ships, when Captain Gallinato entered Chordemuco with the flagship, by way of the river. They told him all that happened with the Chinese and Cambodians and of the favorable condition of affairs for continuing them, alleging that, since the usurper Anacaparan was dead, many Cambodians would immediately join the Spaniards in defense of the name and fame of Langara their legitimate king. But, although some of the Cambodians themselves came to visit the fleet, and assured Gallinato of the same, of the death of Anacaparan, and of the deeds of the Spaniards in Sistor, he appeared to give no credit to any of them, and could not be induced to believe them, or to continue the enterprise, or even to consider it. On the contrary he rebuked the Spaniards for what had taken place in his absence, and after depriving them of all that they had seized from the Chinese and Cambodians, put to sea in order to return to Manila. Belloso and Blas Ruiz persuaded him to go at least to Cochinchina, where the galley seized when Governor Gomez Perez was killed was said to have been taken, and where were the royal standard and the artillery carried aboard the galley, and for which he should ask. They promised, while Gallinato was making these negotiations, to go overland to the kingdom of Lao, where Langara, king of Camboja, was living, in order to restore him to his kingdom. Captain Gallinato consented to this, and sailed along the coast, until he entered the bay of Cochinchina, where, although he was apparently well received by the natives of the country, he would not disembark from his ships, but sent Gregorio de Vargas from them to visit the king of Tunquin, the chief king of that kingdom, and to treat with him concerning the galley, the standard, and the artillery. While he was thus engaged, Gallinato allowed Blas Ruyz and Diego Belloso to go ashore to endeavor to make the journey to Lao, for he agreed easily to their request because he thus got rid of them and left them busied in this matter, so that they could not do him any ill turn in Manila in regard to leaving Camboja.

Diego Belloso and Blas Ruyz went to the king of Sinua, son of the king of Tunquin, and begged him to help them in their journey. From him they received all that was necessary, and were well treated and served until they reached the city of Alanchan, [53] capital of the kingdom of Lao, where they were kindly received by the king of the country. They found that Prauncar Langara, king of Camboja, and his elder son and daughter had died, and that only his son Prauncar survived, and the latter's step-mother, grandmother, and aunts. They related the condition of affairs in Camboja, the arrival of the Spaniards, and the death of the usurper Anacaparan. The same news was brought by a Cambodian from Chor-demuco, who also added that since the death of Anacaparan, his younger son Chupinanu was reigning, that the country was entirely divided into factions, and that many upon seeing their natural and lawful king would leave Chupinanu and would join him and obey him.

The few difficulties for the departure having been overcome by the arrival at this time of the mandarin Ocuna de Chu at Lanchan, in Lao [54] from Camboja, who had been sent by order of other mandarins and grandees of Camboja with ten praus well equipped with artillery and weapons to fetch their lawful king, it was decided to go down to Cam-boja. Prauncar, his grandmother, aunt, and stepmother—he wife of Langara—together with Diego Belloso and Blas Ruyz, embarked and journeyed in the said boats and praus down the rivers flowing from Lao to Camboja. [55] There they found fresh disturbances in the provinces. But as soon as Prauncar arrived many went over to his side, especially two Moro Malays, Acuna La Casamana [56] and Cancona, who were in the country with a Malay army and a quantity of artillery and elephants. Prauncar was victorious on various occasions, and Chupinanu with his brothers and other rebels having died in battle, became master of almost all the provinces of his kingdom. He made Diego Belloso and Blas Ruyz chiefs in war affairs, and they managed war matters until they completely established Prauncar on the throne. When the war was almost entirely ended, the king made Belloso and Blas Ruyz great chofas [57] of his king-dom, gave them two provinces, and granted them other favors, although not so many as they expected, or as he had promised while still in Lao.

The chief reason for this was the stepmother, grandmother, and aunt of the king, who managed him, on account of his youth, and of his being addicted to wine, in excess even of his father Langara. The Moro Malay, Acuna Lacasamana, had great influence with these women. Being envious of the valor of the Spaniards, he was continually opposing them, and seeking their destruction, with whom, on this account, they were always at odds. It must be understood that this Moro held unlawful relations with the wife of Langara, the stepmother of King Prauncar.

Captain Gallinato's fleet remained in Cochinchina negotiating with the king of Tunquin for the royal standard and the artillery of the galley, as above stated, for the galley was lost upon that coast, and this king had the rest in his possession. The latter not only did not restore them, but entertaining Gallinato with flattering speech, was, on the contrary, planning to take from him his ships and their contents. Gallinato was secretly warned of this by one of the chief women of Cochinchina, who came to the fleet to see him, after which he kept a much more careful watch than before, and allowed no one to go ashore. But this order was of no avail with Fray Alonso Ximenez, one of the Dominican religious whom he had with him, and the chief promoter of the expedition. When the latter went ashore, they seized and kept him there. The Cochinchinese, imagining that the fleet was off its guard, sent some fire ships against it, followed by some galleys and warboats, in order to burn it, while many men armed with arquebuses annoyed the Spaniards from the neighboring shore. The fleet succeeded in getting away from the fire and put off from shore, and resisted the enemy's ships with artillery, musketry, and arquebuses, thus sinking some of them. After this the Spaniards waited no longer, but leaving Fray Alonso Ximenez on shore, and two lay companions, whom he took with him, put to sea and left the bay of Cochinchina, and ran toward the Filipinas.

While these things were happening in Camboja and Cochinchina, orders had arrived from Espana from his Majesty to conclude an agreement that Captain Estevan Rodriguez de Figueroa had made with Gomez Perez Dasmarinas, under which the former was to pacify and settle the island of Mindanao at his own expense, and receive the governorship of the island for two lives [58] and other rewards. The said agreement was effected, after certain difficulties that arose were settled. Don Estevan Rodriguez prepared men and ships, and what else was necessary for the enterprise, and with some galleys, galleots, frigates, vireys, barangays, and lapis, [59] set out with two hundred and fourteen Spaniards for the island of Mindanao, in February of the same year, of ninety-six. He took Captain Juan de la Xara as his master-of-camp, and some reli-

gious of the Society of Jesus to give instruction, as well as many natives
for the service of the camp and fleet.

He reached Mindanao River, after a good voyage, where the first
settlements, named Tancapan and Lumaguan, both hostile to the people
of Buhahayen, received him peacefully and in a friendly manner, and
joined his fleet. They were altogether about six thousand men. Without
delay they advanced about eight leguas farther up the river against Buhahayen, the principal settlement of the island, where its greatest chief had
fortified himself on many sides. Arrived at the settlement, the fleet cast
anchor, and immediately landed a large proportion of the troops with
their arms. But before reaching the houses and fort, and while going
through some thickets [cacatal] [60] near the shore, they encountered some
of the men of Buhahayen, who were coming to meet them with their
campilans, carazas [61] and other weapons, and who attacked them on
various sides. The latter [i.e., the Spaniards and their allies], on account of
the swampiness of the place and the denseness of the thickets [cacatal],
could not act unitedly as the occasion demanded, although the master-of-
camp and the captains that led them exerted themselves to keep the
troops together and to encourage them to face the natives. Meanwhile
Governor Estevan Rodriguez de Figueroa was watching events from his
flagship, but not being able to endure the confusion of his men, seized
his weapons and hastened ashore with three or four companions, and a
servant who carried his helmet, in order that he might be less impeded in
his movements. But as he was crossing a part of the thickets [cacatal]
where the fight was waging, a hostile Indian stepped out unseen from
one side, and dealt the governor a blow on the head with his campilan,
that stretched him on the ground badly wounded. [62] The governor's followers cut the Mindanao to pieces and carried the governor back to the
camp. Shortly after, the master-of-camp, Juan de la Xara, withdrew his
troops to the fleet, leaving behind several Spaniards who had fallen in the
encounter. The governor did not regain consciousness, for the wound
was very severe, and died next day. The fleet after that loss and failure
left that place, and descended the river to Tampacan, where it anchored
among the friendly inhabitants and their settlements.

The master-of-camp, Juan de la Xara, had himself chosen by the
fleet as successor in the government and enterprise. He built a fort with
arigues and palms near Tampacan, and founded a Spanish settlement to
which he gave the name of Murcia. He began to make what arrangements he deemed best, in order to establish himself and run things
independently of, and without acknowledging the governor of Manila,
without whose intervention and assistance this enterprise could not be
continued.

Chapter 6

Of the administration of Don Francisco Tello, and of the second establishment of the Audiencia of Manila; and of occurrences during the period of this administration.

Governor Don Luis Dasmarinas was awaiting news from Captain Juan Xuarez Gallinato, and from Governor Estevan Rodriguez de Figueroa concerning the voyage which each had made at the beginning of the year ninety-six, to Camboja and to Mindanao, when news reached Manila, in the month of June, that two ships had entered the islands by the channel of Espiritu Santo, and that they brought a new governor sent from Espana, namely, Don Francisco Tello de Guzman, knight of the Order of Sanctiago, a native of Sevilla, and treasurer of the India House of Trade. He arrived at Manila in the beginning of July and entered upon his office. It was also learned that Fray Ygnacio Sanctivanez, of the Order of St. Francis, a native of Sanctivanez, in the province of Burgos, had been nominated in Nueva Espana as archbishop of Manila, for Bishop Fray Domingo de Salazar had died in Madrid; and that Fray Miguel de Venavides, a native of Carrion and a religious of the Order of St. Dominic, who had gone to Espana with Bishop Fray Domingo de Salazar, had been appointed bishop of the city of Segovia in the province of Cagayan; also that Fray Pedro de Agurto, of the Order of St. Augustine, a native of Mexico, had been appointed in Mexico, bishop of the city of Sanctisimo Nombre de Jesus, and that these two bishops with another for the city of Caceres, in the province of Camarines, who was not yet named, had been lately added to the Filipinas and appointed as suffragans to the archbishop of Manila, at the instance of Bishop Fray Domingo. Also it was learned that the Audiencia which had been suppressed in Manila was to be reestablished there, as well as other things which the bishop had presented at court.

Shortly after Don Francisco Tello had taken over the governorship, news was brought of the death of Estevan Rodriguez de Figueroa in

Mindanao, by Brother Gaspar Gomez of the Society of Jesus. The latter brought the body for burial in the college of Manila, of which Don Estevan was patron. Juan de la Xara wrote that he had charge of affairs, that he had settled in Tampacan, that he intended to continue the pacification and conquest of the island as should seem most advisable, and that reenforcements of men and other things should be sent him. It was learned that he intended to make an ill use of the government, and would not remain dependent on, and subordinate to, the governor of the Filipinas; and that he was depriving the heirs of Estevan Rodriguez of what lawfully belonged to them. It was learned that, in order to make himself safer in this respect, he was sending his confidants to the town of Arevalo in Oton where Don Estevan had left his wife, Dona Ana de Osseguera, and his two small daughters, with his house and property, to persuade Dona Ana to marry him. This resolution appeared injurious in many respects, and the attempt was made to rectify matters. But in order not to disturb the affairs of Mindanao, the matter was left alone for the present, until time should show the course to be followed. And so it happened that when Juan de la Xara left the camp and settlements of Mindanao, and came hurriedly to Oton to negotiate his marriage in person—although the widow of Don Estevan had never been favorable to it—Don Francisco Tello sent men to arrest him. He was brought to Manila, where he died while his trial was being conducted.

After the imprisonment of Juan de La Xara, Don Francisco Tello immediately sent Captain Toribio de Miranda to Mindanao, with orders to take command of the camp and to govern, until some one should agree to continue the enterprise. When he arrived at Mindanao and the soldiers saw that Juan de La Xara's schemes had been defeated, and that the latter was a prisoner in Manila, with no hope of returning, they obeyed Toribio de Miranda and the orders that he brought.

In Manila the governor was considering carefully the necessary measures for continuing the war, since the island of Mindanao was so near the other pacified islands, and the island itself contained some provinces that professed peace and were apportioned as encomiendas, and had Spanish magistrates, such as the rivers of Butuan, Dapitan, and Caragan, so that it was desirable to pacify the whole island and subject it to his Majesty. The royal treasury was spent and could not bear the expense; and Estevan Rodriguez had bound himself by a legal writ, to carry the war to entire completion at his own expense, in accordance with the terms of his agreement. The guardian of his children and heirs brought the matter before the court, and refused to fulfil this obligation on account of Estevan Rodriguez's death. In order not to lose time, for what had been commenced had to be continued in one way or another, the governor decided to prosecute it, drawing the necessary funds from the royal treasury, either on its own account or on the account of Estevan Rodriguez's heirs, if such should be according to law. The governor then searched for a person to go to Mindanao, and selected Don Juan Ronquillo, general of the galleys. The latter was given the necessary reenforcements of men and other things, with which he reached Mindanao. He took command of the Spanish camp and fleet which he found in Tampacan. He confirmed the peace and friendship with the chiefs and people of Tampacan and Lumaguan, restored and set in better order the Spanish settlement and fort, and began to make preparation for the war against the people of Buhahayen. He spent many days in making a few incursions into their land and attacks on their forts, but without any notable result, for the enemy were many and all good soldiers, with plenty of arquebuses [63] and artillery, and had fortified themselves in a strong position. They had many other fortifications inland and went from one to the other with impunity, whenever they wished, and greatly harassed the Spaniards, who were little used to so swampy a country. The latter found themselves short of provisions without the possibility of getting them in the country on account of the war, inasmuch as the camp contained many men, both Spaniards and the native servants and boatmen, and it was not easy at all times to come and go from one part to another in order to provide necessities. [64]

Meanwhile Don Juan Ronquillo, seeing that the war was advancing very slowly and with little result, and that the camp was suffering, drew up a report of it, and sent letters in all haste to Governor Don Francisco Tello, informing him of the condition of affairs. He wrote that it would be better to withdraw the camp from Mindanao River, so that it might not perish; and that a presidio could be established on the same island in the port of La Caldera, which could be left fortified, in order not to abandon this enterprise entirely, and so that their friends of Tampacan and Lumaguan might be kept hostile to the people of Buhahayen. Meanwhile he and the rest of the camp and fleet would return to Manila, if permitted, for which he requested the governor to send him an order quickly. Upon the receipt of this despatch, Governor Don Francisco Tello resolved to order Don Juan Ronquillo, since the above was so and the camp could not be maintained, nor the war continued advantageously, to withdraw with his whole camp from Mindanao River. He was first to make a great effort to chastise the enemy in Buhahayen, and then to burn the Spanish settlement and fort and to go to La Caldera, fortify it, and leave there a sufficient garrison with artillery, boats, and provisions for its maintenance and service. Then he was to return to Manila with the rest of his men, after telling their friends in Tampacan that the

Spaniards would shortly return to the river better equipped and in greater numbers.

Silonga and other chiefs of Buhahayen were not neglecting their defense, since, among other measures taken, they had sent a chief to Terrenate to ask assistance against the Spaniards who had brought war into their homes. Thereupon the king of Terrenate despatched a numerous fleet of caracoas and other boats to Mindanao with cachils [65] and valiant soldiers—more than one thousand fighting men in all—and a quantity of small artillery, in order to force the Spaniards to break camp and depart, even could they do nothing else. When the news reached Buhahayen that this fleet was coming to their defense and support, they made ready and prepared to attack the Spaniards, who also having heard the same news were not careless. Consequently the latter turned their attention more to the main fort, and reduced the number of men in the smaller forts on Buquil River and other posts, mouths, and arms of the same river. These served to strengthen the garrison of the main fort and the armed galleys and other smaller craft, in order to use the latter to resist the expected attack of the enemy. The enemy having gallantly advanced to the very fort of the Spaniards with all their vessels and men, attacked and stormed it with great courage and resolution, in order to effect an entrance. The Spaniards within resisted valiantly, and those outside in the galleys on the river assisted them so effectively that together, with artillery and arquebuses, and at times in close combat with swords and campilans, they made a great slaughter and havoc among the men of Terrenate and those of Buhahayen, who were aiding the former. They killed and wounded a great number of them and captured almost all the caracoas and vessels of the enemy, so that very few boats escaped and they were pursued and burned by the Spaniards, who made many prisoners, and seized immense booty and many weapons from the enemy. As soon as possible after this, the Spaniards turned against the settlements and forts of Buhahayen where some of their results were of so great moment that the enemy, seeing themselves hard pressed and without anyone to help them, sent messages and proposals of peace to Don Juan Ronquillo, which were ended by their rendering recognition and homage, and the renewal of friendship with the people of Tampacan, their ancient enemy. In order to strengthen the friendship, they sealed it by the marriage of the greatest chief and lord of Buhahayen with the daughter of another chief of Tampacan, called Dongonlibor. Thereupon the war was apparently completely ended, provisions were now to be had, and the Spaniards with little precaution crossed and went about the country wherever they wished. The people of Buhahayen promised to dismantle all their forts immediately, for that was one of the conditions of peace.

51

Then the Spaniards returned to their fort and settlement at Tampacan, whence Don Juan Ronquillo immediately sent despatches to Governor Don Francisco Tello, informing him of the different turn that the enterprise had taken. In view of the present condition he requested the governor to issue new instructions as to his procedure, saying that he would wait without making any change, notwithstanding the arrival of the answer which he expected to his first report, for conditions had now become so much better than before that the governor's decision would be different.

The governor had already answered Don Joan Ronquillo's first despatch, as we have said above, when the second despatch arrived with news of the successes in Mindanao. Suspicious of the men in the camp who had constantly shown a desire to return to Manila, and little relish for the hardships of war, and fearing lest they would return at the arrival of the first order, executing that order and abandoning the enterprise which had reached such a satisfactory stage; and thinking that it would be unwise to abandon the river: the governor made haste to send a second despatch immediately by various roads, ordering them to pay no attention to his first orders, but to remain in Mindanao, and that he would soon send them what was necessary for further operations.

It seems that this message traveled slowly; for, the first having arrived, they obeyed it without any further delay, and camp was raised and the country abandoned. To their former enemy of Buhahayen they gave as a reason that the governor of Manila had summoned them; and to their friends of Tampacan, they said that they would leave men in La Caldera for their security, and that assistance would be sent them from Manila. This news caused as much sorrow and sadness to the latter, as joy to the people of Buhahayen. Then after burning their fort and settlement, the Spaniards embarked all their forces as soon as possible, left the river, and went to La Caldera, twenty-four leguas farther down in the direction of Manila. Having entered port, they built a fortress and left there a garrison of one hundred Spaniards, with some artillery, provisions, and boats for their use.

At this juncture, the governor's second message to General Don Joan Ronquillo arrived, to which the latter replied that he was already in La Caldera, and could not return to the river. Then, without any further delay, Don Juan Ronquillo went to Manila with the balance of his fleet, by way of the provinces of Oton, and Panay. The governor, having heard of his coming, sent to arrest him on the road before he entered the city, and proceeded against him by law for having withdrawn the camp and army from Mindanao River, without awaiting the orders he should have expected after the favorable turn that affairs had taken. Don Juan Ronquillo was set at liberty on showing a private letter from the governor, which the latter had sent him separately with the first instructions, to the effect that he should return to Manila with his troops in any event, for they were needed in the islands for other purposes; and because of this letter Don Juan had determined not to await the second order.

Captain and Sargento-mayor Gallinato crossed from Cochinchina to Manila in the flagship of his fleet, and informed Don Francisco Tello whom he found governing, of the events of his expedition; and that Blas Ruyz and Diego Belloso had gone by land to Lao from Cochinchina in search of King Langara of Camboja. Thus by their absence he avoided the blame of leaving Camboja, although there were not wanting many of his own followers who angrily gave information of the opportunity that he had lost by not showing himself or staying in Camboja when he had so good an opportunity; and they stoutly asserted that if he had done so, all that had been hoped in that kingdom would have been attained.

The other ship of his convoy, to which the balance of his fleet had been reduced, of which he made Alferez Luys Ortiz commander, could not pursue the voyage on account of heavy storms, and put in at Malaca. Some of the Spaniards remained there, and Ortiz with the rest of the crew, was able to set sail after a few months, and returned to Manila.

Coincident with the above, and at the beginning of Don Francisco Tello's administration, two Indian chiefs of the province of Cagayan, the more powerful of whom was called Magalat, were detained in Manila, because they, with their kinsmen, and others who followed their party and opinion, often incited the settlements of that province to rebellion; and it had cost no little trouble to subdue them; besides the daily murder of many Spaniards and other injuries inflicted upon the peaceful natives and their crops. Magalat was captain and leader of these men, and since he, with his brother and other natives, was in Manila, and unable to leave it, that province became more secure.

Some Dominican religious bound for Segovia, the capital of that province, where they give instruction, moved with pity, persuaded the governor to let Magalat and his brother return to their country with them. To such an extent did they importune the governor, that he granted their request. Having reached Cagayan, the chiefs went inland by the Lobo River and again incited the whole country to rebellion. With the help of other chiefs of Tubigarao, and other settlements, they so stirred up things, that it was impossible to go to those settlements or a step beyond the city. Magalat was the leader of the rebels, and he committed cruel murders and injuries even upon the natives themselves, if they refused to rise against the Spaniards. This reached such a point that the governor was obliged to send the master-of-camp, Pedro de Chaves, from Manila with troops, in order that he might suitably remedy the evil. In spite of many difficulties, the latter had so good fortune that he seized many insurgent leaders upon whom he executed justice and public punishment. As for Magalat himself, the governor caused him to be killed in his own house and land where he had fortified himself, by the hand of his own Indians, who had offered to do it for a reward; for in no other way did it appear possible. Had Magalat not been killed, the war would have dragged on for many years, but with his death the province became quiet and the peace secure.

In April of the year one thousand five hundred and ninety-five, Adelantado Alvaro de Mendana de Neira sailed from Callao de Lima in Peru, to colonize the Salomon Islands, which he had discovered many years before in the South Sea, [66] the principal one of which he had called San Christoval. He took four ships, two large ones—a flagship and an almiranta—a frigate, and a galliot, with four hundred men in all. He was also accompanied by his wife, Dona Ysabel Barreto and his three brothers-in-law. On the way he discovered other islands at which he did not stop; but not finding those which he had previously discovered, and as his almiranta had been lost, he anchored with the other ships at an island near Nueva Guinea, inhabited by blacks, to which he gave the name of Santa Cruz [Holy Cross]. There he settled—little to the satisfaction of his men. The adelantado, two of his brothers-in-law, and many of his people died there. Dona Ysabel Barreto abandoned the colony, on account of sickness and want, and embarked the survivors aboard her flagship, frigate, and galliot. But while they were sailing toward the Filipinas the frigate and galliot disappeared in another direction. The flagship entered the river of Butuan, in the island of Mindanao, and reached Manila after great want and suffering. There Dona Ysabel Barreto married Don Fernando de Castro, and returned to Nueva Espana in his ship, the "San Geronymo," in the year ninety-six. The events of this voyage have been only lightly touched upon here, so that it seems fitting to reproduce literally the relation, to which Don Pedro Fernandez de Quiros, chief pilot on this voyage, affixed his signature, which is as follows.

> Relation of the voyage of Adelantado Alvaro de Mendana de Neira for the discovery of the Salomon Islands
>
> On Friday, the ninth of the month of April, one thousand five hundred and ninety-five, Adelantado Alvaro de Mendana set sail with his fleet for the conquest and settlement of the western islands in the South Sea, sailing from the port of Callao de Lima, which lies in twelve and one-half degrees south latitude. Laying his course toward the valleys of Santa, Truxillo, and Sana, and collecting men and provi-

sions, he went to Paita. [67] There he took in water and numbered his forces, which amounted to about four hundred persons. Then with his four vessels, two large and two small, he left the said port, which is five degrees higher than the former port, and directed his course west-southwest in search of the islands that he had discovered. He took Pedro Merino Manrique as master-of-camp; his brother-in-law, Lope de la Vega, as admiral; and Pedro Fernandez de Quiros as chief pilot. Following the above-mentioned course he sailed to the altitude of nine and one-half degrees, whence he sailed southwest by west to fourteen degrees, where he changed his course to northwest by west. On Friday, the twenty-first of the month of July, having reached an altitude of ten long degrees, we sighted an island to which the general gave the name of Madalena. [68] From a port of this island, about seventy canoes came out, each containing three men, or thereabout, while some came swimming and others on logs. There were more than four hundred Indians, white and of a very agreeable appearance, tall and strong, large-limbed, and so well made that they by far surpassed us. [69] They had fine teeth, eyes, mouth, hands and feet, and beautiful long flowing hair, while many of them were very fair. Very handsome youths were to be seen among them; all were naked and covered no part. Their bodies, legs, arms, hands, and even some of their faces, were all marked after the fashion of these Bissayans. And indeed, for a barbarous people, naked, and of so little reason, one could not restrain himself, at sight of them, from thanking God for having created them. And do not think this exaggeration, for it was so. These people invited us to their port, and were in turn invited to our flagship, and about forty of them came aboard. In comparison with them we appeared to be men of less than ordinary size. Among them was one who was thought to be a palmo taller than the tallest man of our fleet, although we had in the fleet men of more than average height. The general gave some of them shirts and other things, which they accepted with much pleasure, dancing after their fashion and calling others. But being annoyed at the liberties that they took, for they were great thieves, the general had a cannon fired, in order to frighten them. When they heard it they all swam ashore, seized their weapons, and at the sound of a conch threw a few stones at the ships and threatened us with their lances, for they had no other weapons. Our men fired their arquebuses at them from the ships and killed five or six of them, whereat they stopped. Our fleet sailed on and we discovered three other islands. This island has a circumference of about six leguas. We passed it on its southern side. On that side it is high and slopes precipitously to the sea, and has mountainous ravines where the Indians dwell. There seemed to be many inhabitants, for we saw them on the rocks and on the beach. And so we continued our course to the other three islands. The first, to which was given the name San Pedro, is about ten leguas from Magdalena, and like it extends northwest by north. It has a circumference of about three leguas. The island is beautiful, and rich in woods and fine fields. We did not ascertain whether it was inhabited or not, for we did not stop there. To the southeast and about five leguas from it lies another island to which the general gave the name of Dominica. It is very sightly, and to all appearances thickly populated, and has a circumference of about fifteen leguas. To the south and a little more than one legua from it lies another island with a circumference of about eight leguas, which received the name of Sancta Cristina. Our fleet passed through the channel that separates the one island from the other, for all that we saw of these islands is clear sailing. On the west side of Sancta Cristina, a good port was found, and there the fleet anchored. [70] These Indians did not seem to me to resemble the first; but many beautiful women were seen. I did not see the latter, but some who did assured me that in their opinion, they are as beautiful as the women in Lima, but light complexioned and not so tall—and the women in Lima are very beautiful. The articles of food seen in that port were swine and fowl, sugar-cane, excellent bananas, cocoanuts, and a fruit that grows on high trees. Each of the last is as large as a good-sized pineapple, and is excellent eating. Much of it was eaten green, roasted, and boiled. When ripe it is indeed so sweet and good that, in my estimation, there is no other that surpasses it. Scarcely any of it, except a little husk, has to be thrown away. [71] There was also another fruit with a flavor like that of chestnuts, but much larger in size than six chestnuts put together; much of this fruit was eaten roasted and boiled. Certain nuts with a very hard shell, and very oily, were also found, which were eaten in great quantities, and which, according to some, induced diarrhoea. We also saw some Castilian pumpkins growing. Near the beach there is a fine cascade of very clear water, which issues from a rock at the height of two men. Its volume is about the width of four or five fingers. Then near by there is a stream, from which the boats drew a full supply of water. The Indians fled to the forests and rocks, where they fortified themselves and tried to do some mischief, by throwing stones and rolling down rocks, but they never wounded anyone, for the master-of-camp restrained them, by placing outposts. The Indians of this island, on seeing one of our negroes, made signs toward the south, saying that there were men like him there, and that they were wont to go there to fight; that the others were armed with arrows; and that they make the journey thither in certain large canoes which they possess. Since there was no interpreter, or much curiosity to learn more, no further investigations were made, although, in my opinion, this is impossible for Indians so remote, unless there be a chain of islands; for their boats and their customs in other things show that they have not come from any great distance.

This port lies in an altitude of nine and one-half degrees. The adelantado ordered three crosses to be planted, and on Saturday, August fifth, to weigh anchor and set sail southwest by west. We sailed with easterly and east southeasterly winds, now southwest by west and now northwest by west, for about four hundred leguas. One Sunday, August twenty, we sighted four low islands with sandy beaches, abounding in palms and other trees. On the southeast side, towards the north, was seen a great sandbank. All four islands have a circuit of about twelve leguas. Whether they were inhabited or not, we could not tell, for we did not go to them. That year appeared to be one of talk, of which I speak with anger. These islands lie in an altitude of ten and three-quarters degrees. They were named San Bernardo, [72] because they were discovered on that saint's day. Thenceforward we began to meet southeasterly winds, which never failed us, and which seem to prevail in those regions. With these winds we continued to sail al-

ways in the said direction, never going above eleven or below ten degrees, until Tuesday, August twenty-nine, when
we discovered a round islet, of about one legua in circumference, surrounded by reefs. We tried to land there, so
that the almiranta could take on wood and water, of which
there was great need, but could find no landing-place. We
gave it the name of La Solitaria [Solitary Island]. It lies in
an altitude of ten and two-thirds degrees, and is about one
thousand five hundred and thirty five leguas from Lima. [73]
From this island we continued to sail in the said course: a
thing which drew a variety of opinions from the men,
some saying that we did not know where we were going,
and other things which did not fail to cause some hard
feelings; but by the mercy of God, at midnight on the eve
of Nuestra Senora de Setiembre [Our Lady of September],
we sighted an island of about ninety or one hundred leguas
in circumference, which extends almost east southeast and
west northwest, and lies about one thousand eight hundred
leguas from Lima. [74] The whole island is full of dense forests, even to the highest ridges; and where it was not
cleared for the Indians' fields, not a palmo of earth could
be seen. The ships anchored in a port on the north side of
the island, in ten degrees of latitude. About seven leguas
north of that port, there is a volcano with a very well
shaped cone, which ejects much fire from its summit, and
from other parts. The volcano is high and about three
leguas in circumference. On the side toward the sea it is
very steep and quite bare, and offers no landing; and it
rumbles frequently and loudly within. Northeast of this
volcano are several small inhabited islets, surrounded by
many shoals. The distance to these islets is seven or eight
leguas. The shoals extend about northwest, and one who
saw them said that they were numerous. Around the large
island were several small ones, and as we sailed around
them, we found that they were all inhabited, even the large
one. Within sight of this large island, and to the southeast
of it, we saw another island of no great size. This must be
the connecting link with the other islands. [75] After having
put into port at the great island Sancta Cruz, as it had been
named, the adelantado ordered Captain Don Lorenzo, his
brother-in-law, to go with the frigate in search of the
almiranta, of which I have no favorable conjectures, and

which had disappeared on the night that we sighted the island. It was sought on this and on two other occasions, but nothing except the shoals above-mentioned were found. What was seen in the way of food in this bay and port was swine, fowl, bananas, sugar-cane, some two or three kinds of roots resembling sweet potatoes, which are eaten boiled or roasted and made into biscuits, buyos [i.e., betel], two kinds of excellent almonds, two kinds of pine-nuts, ring-doves and turtle-doves, ducks, gray and white herons, swallows, a great quantity of amaranth, Castilian pumpkins, the fruit which I mentioned as being in the first islands, chestnuts, and walnuts. Sweet basil, of great fragrance, and red flowers, which are kept in the gardens at that port, and two other kinds of different flowers, also red, are found. There is another fruit which grows on high trees, and resembles the pippin in its pleasing smell and savor; a great quantity of ginger grows wild there, as also of the herb chiquilite, from which indigo is made. [76] There are agave-trees, abundance of sagia [sago (?)], [77] and many cocoanuts. Marble is also to be seen, as well as pearl shells and large snail-shells, like those brought from China. There is a very copious spring and five or six rivers of small volume. There we settled close by the spring. The Indians endeavored to prevent us; but as the arquebus tells at a distance, upon seeing its deadly effects, their hostility was lukewarm, and they even gave us some of the things that they possessed. In this matter of procuring provisions, several cases of not over good treatment happened to the Indians; for the Indian who was our best friend and lord of that island, Malope by name, was killed, as well as two or three others, also friendly to us. No more of all the island than about three leguas about the camp was explored. The people of this island are black. They have small single-masted canoes for use about their villages, and some very large ones to use in the open sea. On Sunday, October eight, the adelantado had the master-of-camp stabbed. Tomas de Ampuero was also killed in the same way. Alferez Juan de Buitrago was beheaded; and the adelantado intended to have two others, friends of the master-of-camp, killed, but was restrained therefrom at our request. The cause of this was notorious, for these men tried to induce the adelantado to leave the land and abandon it.

There must have been other reasons unknown to me; what I saw was much dissoluteness and shamelessness, and a great deal of improper conduct. On October eighteen, after a total eclipse of the moon on the seventeenth, the adelantado died; [78] November two, Don Lorenzo, his brother-in-law, who had succeeded him as captain-general; the priest Antonio de Serpa, seven or eight days before; and November eight the vicar, Juan de Espinosa. Disease was rampant among our men and many died for lack of care, and the want of an apothecary and doctor. The men begged the governor Dona Ysabel Barreto to take them out of the country. All agreed to embark, and by the mercy of God, we left this port on Saturday, the eighteenth of the said month, and sailed southwest by west toward the island of San Cristoval or rather in search of it, to see whether we could find it or the almiranta, in accordance with the governor's orders. For two days nothing was seen; and at the request of all the men, who cried out that we were taking them to destruction, she ordered me to steer from our settlement, located in ten and one-half degrees of latitude, to Manila. Thence I steered north northwest to avoid meeting islands on the way, since we were so ill prepared to approach any of them, with our men so sick that about fifty of them died in the course of the voyage and about forty there in the island. We continued our course short of provisions, navigating five degrees south and as many north, and meeting with many contrary winds and calms. When we reached an altitude of six long degrees north latitude, we sighted an island, apparently about twenty-five leguas in circumference, thickly wooded and inhabited by many people who resembled those of the Ladrones, and whom we saw coming toward us in canoes. From the southeast to the north and then to the southwest, it is surrounded by large reefs. [79] About four leguas west of it are some low islets. There, although we tried, we failed to find a suitable place to anchor; for the galliot and frigates which accompanied our ship had disappeared some days before. [80] From this place we continued the said course until we reached an altitude of thirteen and three-quarters degrees, and in the two days that we sailed west in this latitude, we sighted the islands of Serpana [i.e., Seypan] and Guan in the Ladrones. We passed between the two and did not an-

60

chor there, because we had no cable for lowering and haul-
ing up the boat. This was the third of the month of
January, one thousand five hundred and ninety-six. On the
fourteenth of the same month we sighted the cape of
Espiritu Sancto, and on the fifteenth we anchored in the
bay of Cobos. [81] We reached there in such a state that only
the goodness of God could have taken us thither; for human strength and resources would hardly have taken us a
tenth of the way. We reached that place so dismantled and
the crew so weak that we were a most piteous sight, and
with only nine or ten jars of water. In this bay of Cobos
the ship was repaired and the men recuperated as much as
possible. On Tuesday, February second, we left the above
port and bay, and on the tenth of the same month we anchored in the port of Cabite, etc.

Besides my desire to serve your Grace, I am moved to
leave this brief relation for you, by the fact that if, perchance, God should dispose of my life, or other events
should cause me or the relation that I carry to disappear,
the truth may be learned from this one, which may prove a
matter of great service to God and to the king our sovereign. [82] Will your Grace look favorably upon my great
desire to serve you, of which I shall give a better proof, if
God permit me to return to this port. Will your Grace also
pardon my brevity, since the fault lies in the short time at
my present disposal. Moreover, since no man knows what
time may bring, I beg your Grace to keep the matter secret, for on considering it well, it seems only right that
nothing be said about the first islands until his Majesty be
informed and order what is convenient to his service, for,
as the islands occupy a position midway between Peru,
Nueva Espana, and this land, the English, on learning of
them, might settle them and do much mischief in this sea.
Your Grace, I consider myself as the faithful servant of
your Grace. May God our Lord preserve you for many
years in great joy and increasing prosperity, etc. Your
Grace's servant, PEDRO FERNANDEZ DE QUIROS
To Doctor Antonio de Morga, lieutenant governor of his
Majesty in the Filipinas.

When Governor Don Francisco Tello entered upon his office, in
the year ninety-six, he found the "San Geronymo," the ship in which
Don Fernando de Castro and his wife Dona Ysabel Barreto were return-

ing to Nueva Espana, preparing for the voyage in the port of Cabite. He also found there the galleon "San Felipe" laden with Filipinas goods, preparing to make its voyage to Nueva Espana. As soon as Governor Don Francisco Tello entered upon his administration, both ships were despatched and set sail. Although the "San Geronymo" sailed last, it made the voyage, reaching Nueva Espania at the end of the said year of ninety-six. The vessel "San Felipe," which was a large ship and heavily laden with merchandise and passengers, and whose commander and general was Don Mathia de Landecho, encountered many storms on the voyage, so that at one time it became necessary to throw considerable cargo overboard, and they lost their rudder while in thirty-seven degrees of latitude, six hundred leguas from the Filipinas, and a hundred and fifty from Xapon. Seeing themselves unable to continue their voyage, it was decided to put back to the Filipinas. They set about this and changed their course, but experienced even greater difficulties and trials. Many times they gave themselves up as lost, for the seas ran high, and as the vessel had no rudder, the rigging and few sails were carried away, and blown into shreds. They could not hold the vessel to its course, and it worked so often to windward that they were in great danger of foundering, and lost all hope of reaching the Filipinas. Xapon was the nearest place, but not sufficiently near to enable them to reach it or to venture near its coast which is very wild, and unknown to them even by sight; and even should they have the good fortune to reach it, they did not know how the Japanese would receive them. At this juncture arose confusion and a diversity of opinion among the men aboard. Some said that they should not abandon the course to Manila, in spite of the great peril and discomfort that they were experiencing. Others said that it would be a rash act to do so, and that, since Xapon was much nearer, they should make for it, and look for the port of Nangasaqui, between which and the Filipinas trade was carried on. There they would be well received and would find means to repair their ships, and of resuming the voyage thence. This opinion prevailed, for some religious in the ship adopted it, and the rest coincided with them, on the assurance of the pilots that they would quickly take the ship to Xapon. Accordingly they altered their course for that country, and after six days sighted the coast and country of Xapon, at a province called Toca; [83] and although they tried by day to reach the land, at night, when they lowered the sails, the tide carried them away from it. Many funeas [84] came to the ship from a port called Hurando, and the Spaniards, persuaded by the king of that province, who assured them of harbor, tackle, and repairs, entered the port, after having sounded and examined the entrance, and whether the water was deep enough. The Japanese, who were faithless, and did this with evil intent, towed the ship into the port, leading and guiding it onto a shoal, where, for lack of water, it touched and grounded. Therefore the Spaniards were obliged to unload the ship and take all the cargo ashore close to the town, to a stockade which was given them for that purpose. For the time being the Japanese gave the Spaniards a good reception, but as to repairing the ship and leaving port again, the latter were given to understand that it could not be done without permission and license from Taicosama, the sovereign of Japon, who was at his court in Miaco, one hundred leguas from that port. General Don Matia de Landecho and his companions, in order to lose no time, resolved to send their ambassadors to court with a valuable gift from the ship's cargo for Taicosama, to beg him to order their departure. They sent on this mission Christoval de Mercado, three other Spaniards, Fray Juan Pobre, of the Franciscan order, and Fray Juan Tamayo, of the Augustinian order, who were aboard the vessel. They were to confer concerning this affair with Taico in Miaco, and were to avail themselves of the Franciscan fathers who were in Miaco. The latter had gone as ambassadors from the Filipinas to settle matters between Xapon and Manila, and were residing at court in a permanent house and hospital, with Taico's sufferance. There they were making a few converts, although with considerable opposition from the religious of the Society of Jesus established in the same kingdom. The latter asserted other religious to be forbidden by apostolic briefs and royal decrees to undertake or engage in the conversion of Japon. The king of Hurando, although to all appearances friendly and kind to the Spaniards in his port, took great care to keep them and their merchandise secure. He immediately sent word to court that that ship of foreigners called Nambajies [85] had been wrecked there, and that the Spaniards had brought great riches. This kindled Taicosama's greed, who, in order to get possession of them, sent Ximonojo, one of his favorites and a member of his council, to Hurando. Ximonojo, upon his arrival, took possession of all the merchandise, and imprisoned the Spaniards within a well-guarded palisade, after having forced them to give up all their possessions and what they had hid, under pain of death. Having exercised great rigor therein, he returned to court, after granting permission to the general and others of his suite to go to Miaco. The ambassadors who had been sent before to Miaco with the present, were unable to see Taico, although the present was accepted; nor did they succeed in making any profitable arrangement, although father Fray Pedro Baptista, superior of the Franciscan religious residing there, employed many methods for the purpose of remedying the grievance of the Spaniards. These attempts only served to intensify the evil; for the favorites, who were infidels and hated the religious for making converts at court, on seeing Taico so bent upon the riches of the ship and so unwilling to listen to any restitution, not only did not ask him to do so, but in order to make the matter easier, and taking advantage of the occasion, set Taicosama against the Spaniards; telling him that the religious and the men from the ship were all subjects of one sovereign, and conquerors of others' kingdoms. They said that the Spaniards did this by first sending their religious to the kingdoms, and then entered after with their arms, and that they would do this with Xapon. They were aided in this purpose by the fact that when the favorite, who went to seize the property of the ship, was in Hurando, its pilot, Francisco de Sanda, had shown him the sea-chart in which could be seen all the countries which had been discovered, and Espana and the other kingdoms possessed by his Majesty, among which were Piru and Nueva Espana. When the favorite asked how those distant kingdoms had been gained, the pilot replied that the religious had entered first and preached their religion, and then the soldiers had followed and subdued them. It is true that the said pilot imprudently gave those reasons, which Ximonojo noted well and kept in mind, in order to relate them to Taicosama whenever a suitable opportunity should present itself, which he now did.

All this, together with the persistency with which the religious begged Taico to restore the merchandise to the Spaniards, resulted in angering him thoroughly, and like the barbarous and so avaricious tyrant that he was, he gave orders to crucify them all and all the religious who preached the religion of Namban [86] in his kingdoms. Five religious who were in the house at Miaco were immediately seized, together with another from the "San Felipe" who had joined them, and all the Japanese preachers and teachers. [87] It was also understood that the persecution would extend to the other orders and Christians in Japon, whereupon all received great fear and confusion. But later Taico's wrath was moderated, for, allowing himself to be entreated, he declared that only the religious who had been found in the house at Miaco, and their companions, the Japanese preachers and teachers, who were arrested, would be crucified; and that all the others, together with the Spaniards of the ship, would be allowed to return to Manila. Fonzanbrandono, brother of Taracabadono, governor of Nangasaqui, was entrusted with the execution of the order. He placed all those who were taken from the house of the Franciscan religious at Miaco on ox-carts, under a strong guard; namely, Fray Pedro Baptista, Fray Martin de Aguirre, Fray Felipe de las Casas, Fray Goncalo, Fray Francisco Blanco, Fray Francisco de San Miguel, and twenty-six [sic] Japanese preachers and teachers with two boys who were in the service of the religious. Their right ears were cut off, and they were paraded through the streets of Miaco and through those of the cities of Fugimen,

Usaca, and Sacai, [88] to the great grief and sorrow of all Christians who saw their sufferings. The sentence and cause of their martyrdom was written on a tablet in Chinese characters, which was carried hanging on a spear; and read as follows.

> Sentence of the Combaco, [89] lord of Xapon, against the discalced religious and their teachers, whom he has ordered to be martyred in Nangasaqui.
>
> Inasmuch as these men came from the Luzones, from the island of Manila, in the capacity of ambassadors, and were allowed to remain in the city of Miaco, preaching the Christian religion, which in former years I have strictly forbidden: I order that they be executed together with the Japanese who embraced their religion. Therefore these twenty-four [sic] men will be crucified in the city of Nangasaqui. And whereas I again forbid the teaching of this religion henceforward: let all understand this. I command that this decree be carried out; and should any person dare to violate this order, he shall be punished together with his whole family. Given on the first of Echo, and second of the moon. [90]

Thus these holy men were taken to Nangasaqui. There, on a hill sown with wheat, in sight of the town and port, and near a house and hospital called San Lazaro, established in Nangasaqui by the said religious on their first coming from the Filipinas, before going up to the capital, they were all crucified in a row. The religious were placed in the middle and the others on either side upon high crosses, with iron staples at their throats, hands, and feet, and with long, sharp iron lances thrust up from below and crosswise through their sides. [91] Thus did they render their souls to their Creator for whom they died with great resolution, on the fifth of February, day of St. Agueda, of the year one thousand five hundred and ninety-seven. They left behind in that ploughed field, and through it in all that kingdom, a great quantity of seed sown, which they watered with their blood, and from which we hope to gather abundant fruit of a numerous conversion to our holy Catholic faith. Before these holy men were crucified, they wrote a letter to Doctor Antonio de Morga, in Manila, by the hand of Fray Martin de Aguirre, which reads word for word as follows.

> To Doctor Morga, lieutenant-governor of Manila, whom may God protect, etc., Manila.

65

Farewell, Doctor! farewell! Our Lord, not regarding my sins, has, in His mercy, been pleased to make me one of a band of twenty-four [sic] servants of God, who are about to die for love of Him. Six of us are friars of St. Francis, and eighteen are native Japanese. With hopes that many more will follow in the same path, may your Grace receive the last farewell and the last embraces of all this company, for we all acknowledge the support which you have manifested toward the affairs of this conversion. And now, in taking leave, we beg of you—and I especially—to make the protection of this field of Christendom the object of your special care. Since you are a father, and look with favor upon all things which may concern the mission of the religious in this conversion, so may your Grace find one who will protect and intercede for you before God in time of need. Farewell sir! Will your Grace give my last adieu to Dona Juana. May our Lord preserve, etc. From the road to execution, January twenty-eight, one thousand five hundred and ninety-seven.

This king's greed has been much whetted by what he stole from the "San Felipe." It is said that next year he will go to Luzon, and that he does not go this year because of being busy with the Coreans. In order to gain his end, he intends to take the islands of Lequios [92] and Hermosa, throw forces from them into Cagayan, and thence to fall upon Manila, if God does not first put a stop to his advance. Your Graces will attend to what is fitting and necessary. [93]

FRAY MARTIN DE LA ASCENCION

The bodies of the martyrs, although watched for many days by the Japanese, were removed by bits (especially those of the monks) from the crosses as relics by the Christians of the place, who very reverently distributed them around. Together with the staples and the wood of the crosses they are now scattered throughout Christendom.

Two other religious of the same band, who were out of the house at the time of the arrest, did not suffer this martyrdom. One, called Fray Geronimo de Jesus, [94] hid himself and went inland, in order not to leave the country; the other, called Fray Agustin Rodriguez, was sheltered by the fathers of the Society, who sent him away by way of Macan. General Don Mathia and the Spaniards of the ship, naked and stripped, left Japon. They embarked at Nangasaqui and went to Manila in various ships which make that voyage for the Japanese and Portuguese. The first news of this event was learned from them in the month of May of ninety-seven. Great grief and sadness was caused by the news, in the death of the holy religious, and in the disturbances which were expected to take place in future dealings between Japon and the Filipinas; as well as in the loss of the galleon and its cargo en route to Nueva Espana. The value of the vessel was over one million [pesos?], and caused great poverty among the Spaniards. After considering the advisable measures to take under the circumstances, it was ultimately decided that, in order not to allow the matter to pass, a circumspect man should be sent to Japon with letters from the governor to Taicosama. The letters were to set forth the governor's anger at the taking of the ship and merchandise from the Spaniards, and at the killing of the religious; and were also to request Taicosama to make all the reparation possible, by restoring and returning the merchandise to the Spaniards, and the artillery, tackle, and spoils of the vessel that were left, as well as the bodies of the religious whom he had crucified; and Taicosama was so to arrange matters thenceforth, that Spaniards should not be so treated in his kingdom.

The governor sent Don Luis Navarrete [95] Fajardo as bearer of this message, and a present of some gold and silver ornaments, swords, and valuable cloth for Taicosama. He also sent him an elephant well caparisoned and covered with silk, and with its naires [i.e., elephant keepers] in the same livery, a thing never before seen in Xapon. According to the custom of that kingdom, Don Luis was to make the present to Taico when he presented his embassy, for the Japanese are wont to give or receive embassies in no other manner. When Don Luys de Navarrete reached Nangasaqui, Taicosama readily sent from the court for the ambassador and for the present which had been sent him from Luzon, for he was anxious to see the gifts, especially the elephant, with which he was greatly delighted. He heard the embassy and replied with much ostentation and display, exculpating himself from the death of the religious upon whom he laid the blame, saying that after he had forbidden them to christianize, or teach their religion, they had disregarded his orders in his own court. Likewise, the seizure of the ship and its merchandise, which entered the port of Hurando in the province of Toza, had been a justifiable procedure, according to the laws of Japon, because all ships lost on its coast belong to the king, with their merchandise. Nevertheless, he added that he was sorry for all that had happened, and that he would return the merchandise had it not been distributed. As to the religious, there was no remedy for it. But he begged the governor of Manila not to send such persons to Xapon, for he had again passed laws forbidding the making of Christians under pain of death. He would deliver whatever had remained of the bodies of the religious and would be glad to have peace and friendship with the Luzon Islands and the Spaniards, and for his part, would endeavor to secure it. He said that if any other vessel came to his kingdom from Manila, he would give orders that it be well received and well treated. With this reply and a letter of the same purport for the governor, Don Luys Navarrete was dismissed. He was given a present for the governor consisting of lances, armor, and catans, considered rare and valuable by the Japanese. The ambassador thereupon left Miaco and went to Nangasaqui, whence by the first ship sailing to Manila, he sent word to Governor Don Francisco concerning his negotiations. But the message itself was taken later to Manila by another person, on account of the illness and death of Don Luis in Nangasaqui. Taicosama rejoiced over his answer to the ambassador, for he had practically done nothing of what was asked of him. His reply was more a display of dissembling and compliments than a desire for friendship with the Spaniards. He boasted and published arrogantly, and his favorites said in the same manner, that the Spaniards had sent him that present and embassy through fear, and as an acknowledgment of tribute and seigniory, so that he might not destroy them as he had threatened them at other times in the past, when Gomez Perez Dasmarinas was governor. And even then the Spaniards had sent him a message and a present by Fray Juan Cobo, the Dominican, and Captain Llanos.

The Japanese Faranda Quiemon sought war with Manila, and the favorites who aided him did not neglect to beg Taico not to lose the opportunity of conquering that city. They said that it would be easy, since there were but few Spaniards there; that a fleet could be sent there quickly, which Faranda would accompany. The latter assured Taico of success, as one who knew the country and its resources. They urged him so continually that Taico entrusted Faranda with the enterprise, and gave him some supplies and other assistance toward it. Faranda began to prepare ships and Chinese for the expedition, which he was never able to carry out; for, being a man naturally low and poor, he possessed neither the ability nor the means sufficient for the enterprise. His protectors themselves did not choose to assist him, and so his preparations were prolonged until the enterprise was abandoned at the death of Taico, and his own death, as will be stated later.

Meanwhile news was constantly reaching Manila that a fleet was being equipped in Japon, completely under the supervision of Faranda, and it naturally caused some anxiety among the people in spite of their courage and determination to resist him, for the enemy was arrogant and powerful. Although the city was thoroughly resolved and determined to resist him, yet the governor and city would never show openly that they were aware of the change which Taico was about to make, in order not to precipitate the war or give the other side any reason for hastening it. Trusting to time for the remedy, they so disposed affairs in the city, that they might be ready for any future emergency. They sent the Japanese who had settled in Manila—and they were not few—back to Xapon, and made those who came in merchant ships give up their weapons until their return, which they endeavored to hasten as much as possible; but in all other respects, they treated them hospitably. And because it was heard that Taico intended to take possession of the island of Hermosa, a well-provisioned island off the Chinese coast, very near Luzon, and on the way to Xapon, in order to make it serve as a way-station for his fleet, and thus carry on more easily the war with Manila, the governor sent two ships of the fleet under command of Don Juan de Camuzio, to reconnoiter that island and all its ports, and the nature of the place, in order to be the first to take possession of it. At least, if means and time should fail him, he was to advise China, and the viceroys of the provinces of Canton and Chincheo, so that, since the latter were old-time enemies of Xapon, they might prevent the Japanese from entering the island, which would prove so harmful to all of them. In these measures and precautions several days were spent in the matter. However, nothing was accomplished by this expedition to Hermosa Island beyond advising Great China of Xapon's designs.

Several days after the imprisonment of Father Alonso Ximenez in Cochinchina where Captain and Sargento-mayor Juan Xuarez Gallinato had left him, the kings of Tunquin and Sinua permitted him to return to Manila. He took passage for Macan in a Portuguese vessel. Not only did he arrive unwearied by his voyages, hardships, and imprisonment, but with renewed energy and spirits proposed to set on foot again the expedition to Camboja. Although little was known of the state of affairs in that kingdom, and of the restoration of Prauncar to his throne, he together with other religious of his order, persuaded Don Luys Dasmariñas, upon whom he exercised great influence, and who was then living in Manila, taking no part in government affairs, and inclined him to broach the subject of making this expedition anew and in person and at his own expense, from which would ensue good results for the service of God and of his Majesty. Don Luys discussed the matter with Governor Don Francisco Tello, and offered to bear all the expense of the expedition. But a final decision was postponed until the receipt of news from Camboja, for their only information was that Blas Ruyz and Diego Belloso, leaving Captain Gallinato and his ships in Cochinchina, had gone to Lao.

At the departure of Don Juan Ronquillo and his camp from Min-danao River, the people of Tampacan were so disheartened, and the spirit of those of Buhahayen so increased that, in spite of the friendship that they had made, and the homage that they had rendered, they became declared enemies [to the former]. Matters returned to their former state, so that, not only did the inhabitants of Buhahayen not dismantle their forts, as they had promised to do, but they repaired them and committed other excesses against their neighbors of Tampacan. They would have altogether broken into open war, had they not feared that the Spaniards would return better prepared and in larger number, as they had left the garrison at La Caldera with that intention. Thus they let matters stand, neither declaring themselves fully as rebels, nor observing the laws of friendship toward the men of Tampacan and other allies of the Span-iards.

Near the island of Mindanao lies an island called Jolo, not very large, but thickly populated with natives, all Mahometans. They number about three thousand men, and have their own lord and king. When Governor Francisco de Sande was returning from his expedition to Bor-neo, he sent Captain Estevan Rodriguez de Figueroa to Jolo. He entered the island and reduced the natives to his Majesty's rule as above related. The natives were apportioned to Captain Pedro de Osseguera for his lifetime, and after his death, to his son and successor, Don Pedro de Osseguera. He asked and collected for several years what tribute they chose to give him, which was but slight, without urging more, in order not to make a general disturbance. While Don Juan Ronquillo was with his camp in Mindanao, the men of Jolo, seeing Spanish affairs flourish-ing, were willing to enjoy peace and pay their tribute; but at the departure of the Spaniards, they became lukewarm again. Captain Juan Pacho, who commanded the presidio of La Caldera in Don Juan Ronquillo's absence, having sent some soldiers to barter for wax, the Joloans maltreated them and killed two of them. Juan Pacho, with the intention of punishing this excess of the Joloans, went there in person with several boats and thirty soldiers. As he landed, a considerable body of Joloans descended from their king's town, which is situated on a high and strongly-fortified hill, and attacked the Spaniards. Through the number of the natives and the Spaniards' inability to make use of their arquebuses, on account of a heavy shower, the latter were routed, and Captain Juan Pacho and twenty of his followers killed. The rest wounded and in flight took to their boats and returned to La Caldera.

This event caused great grief in Manila, especially because of the reputation lost by it, both among the Joloans, and their neighbors, the people of Mindanao. Although it was considered necessary to punish the

Joloans in order to erase this disgrace, yet as this should be done signally and just then there was not sufficient preparation, it was deferred until a better opportunity. Only Captain Villagra was sent immediately as commander of the presidio of La Caldera, with some soldiers. Having arrived there, they spent their time in pleasure, until their provisions were consumed, and the garrison suffering. They were maintained and supported because of the slight protection that the people of Tampacan felt, knowing that there were Spaniards on the island, and hoped for the arrival of more Spaniards, as Don Juan had promised them, and for punishment and vengeance upon the men of Jolo.

While affairs in the Filipinas were in this condition, ships from Nueva Espana arrived at Manila, in the month of May, one thousand five hundred and ninety-eight. These ships brought despatches ordering the reestablishment of the royal Audiencia, which had been suppressed in the Filipinas some years before. Don Francisco Tello, who was governing the country, was named and appointed its president; Doctor Antonio de Morga and Licentiates Christoval Telles Almacan and Alvaro Rodriguez Zambrano, auditors; and Licentiate Geronymo de Salazar, fiscal; and other officials of the Audiencia were also appointed. By the same ships arrived the archbishop, Fray Ignacio de Sanctivanes, who enjoyed the archbishopric only for a short time, for he died of dysentery in, the month of August of the same year. The bishop of Sebu, Fray Pedro de Agurto came also. On the eighth of May of this year-five hundred and ninety-eight, the royal seal of the Audiencia was received. It was taken from the monastery of San Agustin to the cathedral upon a horse caparisoned with cloth of gold and crimson, and under a canopy of the same material. The staves of the canopy were carried by the regidors of the city, who were clad in robes of crimson velvet lined with white silver cloth, and in breeches and doublets of the same material. The horse that carried the seal in a box of cloth of gold covered with brocade was led on the right by him who held the office of alguacil-mayor, who was clad in cloth of gold and wore no cloak. Surrounding the horse walked the president and auditors, all afoot and bareheaded. In front walked a throng of citizens clad in costly gala dress; behind followed the whole camp and the soldiers, with their drums and banners, and their arms in hand, and the captains and officers at their posts, with the master-of-camp preceding them, staff in hand. The streets and windows were richly adorned with quantities of tapestry and finery, and many triumphal arches, and there was music from flutes, trumpets, and other instruments. When the seal was taken to the door of the cathedral of Manila, the archbishop in pontifical robes came out with the cross, accompanied by the chapter and clergy of the church to receive it. Having lifted the box containing the seal from the horse under the canopy, the archbishop placed it in the hands of the president. Then the auditors went into the church with him, while the band of singers intoned the Te Deum laudamus. They reached the main altar, upon the steps of which stood a stool covered with brocade. Upon this they placed the box with the seal. All knelt and the archbishop chanted certain prayers to the Holy Spirit for the health and good government of the king, our sovereign. Then the president took the box with the seal, and with the same order and music with which it had been brought into the church it was carried out and replaced upon the horse. The archbishop and clergy remained at the door of the church, while the cortege proceeded to the royal buildings. The said box containing the royal seal was placed and left in a beautifully-adorned apartment, with a covering of cloth of gold and crimson, on a table covered with brocade and cushions of the same material, which stood under a canopy of crimson velvet embroidered with the royal arms. Then the royal order for the establishment of the Audiencia was publicly read there, and the nominations for president, auditors, and fiscal. Homage was done them and the usual oath administered. The president proceeded to the Audiencia hall, where the court rooms were well arranged and contained a canopy for the royal arms. There the president, auditors, and fiscal took their seats and received the ministers and officials of the Audiencia. Then the ordinances of the Audiencia were read in the presence of as many citizens as could find room in the hall. This completed the establishment of the Audiencia on that day. Thenceforth it has exercised its functions, and has had charge and disposition in all cases, both civil and criminal, of its district. The latter includes the Filipinas Islands and all the mainland, of China discovered or to be discovered. In charge of the president who acts as governor of the land, were all government affairs according to royal laws, ordinances, and special orders, which were acted on and brought before the Audiencia.

A few days after the Chancilleria of the Filipinas had been established in Manila, news arrived of events in the kingdom of Camboja after the arrival of Prauncar—son and successor of Prauncar Langara, who died in Laos—together with Diego Belloso and Blas Ruyz de Hernan Gonzalez, and of his victories and restoration to the throne, as has already been related. [The news came] in letters from King Prauncar to Governor Don Francisco Tello and Doctor Antonio de Morga. They were signed by the king's hand and seal in red ink. The letters were written in Castilian so that they might be better understood. Since they were alike in essence, I thought it proper to reproduce here the letter written by King Prauncar to Doctor Antonio de Morga, which reads word for word as follows:

72

Prauncar, King of Camboja, to Doctor Antonio de Morga, greeting; to whom I send this letter with great love and joy. I, Prauncar, King of the rich land of Camboja, I, sole lord of it, the great, cherish an ardent love for Doctor Antonio de Morga, whom I am unable to keep from my thoughts, because I have learned through Captain Chofa Don Blas, the Castilian, that he, from the kindness of his heart, took an active part and has assisted the governor of Luzon to send to this country Captain Chofa Don Blas, the Castilian, and Captain Chofa Don Diego, the Portuguese, with soldiers to find King Prauncar my father. Having searched for him in vain, the two chofas and the soldiers killed Anacaparan, who was reigning as sole great lord. Then they went with their ships to Cochinchina, whence the two chofas went to Lao, to find the king of this land. They brought me back to my kingdom, and I am here now through their aid. The two chofas and other Spaniards who have come, have helped me to pacify what I now hold. I understand that all this has come to me because the doctor loves this country. Hence I shall act so that Doctor Antonio de Morga may always love me as he did my father Prauncar, and assist me now by sending fathers for the two chofas and the other Spaniards and Christians who dwell in my kingdom. I shall build them churches and permit them to christianize whatever Cambodians choose to become Christians. I shall provide them with servants and I shall protect them as did formerly King Prauncar my father. I shall provide Doctor Antonio de Morga with whatever will be useful to him from this country. The two chofas have received the lands which I promised them. To Captain Don Blas, the Castilian, I gave the province of Tran, and to Captain Chofa Don Diego, the Portuguese, the province of Bapano. These provinces I grant and bestow upon them for the services which they have rendered me and in payment for the property they have spent in my service, so that they may possess and enjoy them as their own, and do what they will with them while in my service.
96

73

Together with the king's letter Blas Ruis de Hernan Gonzalez wrote another detailed letter to Doctor Morga, informing him of all the events of his expeditions. The letter reads as follows.

To Doctor Antonio de Morga, Lieutenant-governor of the Filipinas Islands of Luzon, in the city of Manila, whom may our Lord preserve.

From Camboja: Your Grace must have already heard of events in this kingdom of Camboja, from my arrival until the captain withdrew the fleet. These accounts will undoubtedly vary according to what each man thought fit to say in order to gild his own affairs: some according to their bent and opinion, and others according to their passion. Although the matter has been witnessed and thoroughly known by many persons, I am about to relate it as well as possible to your Grace, as to a person who can weld all the facts together and give to each circumstance the weight which it may possess and deserve. I shall also give an account among other things of all that happened to Captain Diego Belloso and myself on the journey to Lao, and the vicissitudes and wars in this kingdom, from our arrival until the condition of affairs now in force. Since Spaniards have taken part in all these events it will please your Grace to know the manner and retirement with which I have lived in this kingdom ever since my arrival here from Manila, sustaining the soldiers and other men whom I brought in my ship at my own expense, keeping them in a state of discipline and honor, and never allowing them to abandon themselves to sensual pleasures; although I had no credentials for this, for Gallinato had those which the governor was to give me. I shall not discuss the why and wherefore of most of the Chinese matters, because Fray Alonso Ximenez and Fray Diego [97] witnessed some of the events and heard of others and will have informed your Grace of everything, including the war against the usurper, and Gallinato's abandonment of this kingdom when affairs had practically been settled. Had he continued to follow up matters, half of the kingdom would today justly belong to his Majesty, and the whole of it would be in the power and under the rule of the Spaniards; and perhaps the king himself with most of his people would have embraced Christianity. As to Chinese matters which require most explanation I only ask your Grace to consider the kingdom which we came to help, that the Chinese had no more right there than we had, and that we had to try to gain reputation, not to lose it. Since we came with a warlike attitude, and it was the first time that an armed Spanish force set foot on the mainland, was it right for us to endure insults, abuse, contempt, and open affronts from a so vile race as they are, and before all these pagans? [Was it right to endure] the further action of their arguments before the usurping king, to induce him to kill us; their many evil and infamous reports to him concerning us, in order to induce him to grant their request; and above all their impudence in killing and disarming Spaniards and going out in the streets to spear them? All this I endured very patiently in order not to disturb the land by breaking with them, until one day when they actually tried to kill some of our men in their Parian, and the numbers being very unequal, they had already wounded and maltreated them. We came out at the noise and the Chinese drew up in battle array, armed with many warlike instruments, challenging us to battle, with insults and expressions of contempt. At this juncture, what would have become of our reputation had we retired when the advantage was on their side? Then, too, after attacking and killing many of them what security had we in this tyrannical kingdom, which showed itself not at all friendly to us, with only one ship, [98] which was at the time aground, and with the artillery and provisions ashore; while they had six ships and many rowboats all provided with one or two culverins and many men, both in the ships and those living in the port? [99] Would it have been right, after war had broken out, to have them with all their resources while we had none? Had they taken our lives, what reputation would the Spaniards have left in these kingdoms? For this reason I thought it better for us to overpower them, rather than to be at their mercy, or at that of the king. Accordingly, in order to assure our lives we were obliged to seize their ships and to strengthen ourselves by means of them, since the Chinese began the war. After this, father Fray Alonso Ximenez and we thought that, by making an embassy with presents to the king, and by exculpating ourselves in this matter, before him, everything would turn out well; and that if we had peace with him, and our persons in safety in a fort, or under his word and safe-conduct, we would give the Chinese their ship and property. All this was written out and signed by us. In order to carry this out, a letter was written in the name of the governor of that city [i.e., Manila], and we went to deliver it nine leguas away at the residence of the king, leaving the vessels guarded. But when he found us there, the king deprived us of the boats in which we had gone, and refused to receive the letter, which went under form of embassy, or to hear us unless we first restored the ships. Then he immediately began to prepare arms and to assemble many men, with the intention, unless we restored the ships, of killing us, or reducing us by force to such straits as to compel us to restore them; and after their restoration, of making an end of us all without trouble or risk to his own men. For he trusted us in nothing, since we were going in search of, and bringing help to, him whom he had dispossessed. All this was told us by some Christians among them, especially by a young mestizo from Malaca who lived among them and knew their language. Therefore considering that we were already separated from our companions, and that, if we restored the ships, they could easily take ours by means of them and kill the men left in them, and then us who were in that place; also that if we waited for them to collect and attack us, they could very easily kill us: we decided to seek the remedy by first attacking them instead of waiting to be attacked; and try to rejoin our men and assure our lives or end them by fighting. Accordingly we attacked them, and such was our good fortune that we killed the king in the fight. Then we retired to our ships with great difficulty, without the loss of a single Spaniard. We did not allow the king's house to be sacked, so that it might not be said that we had done this to rob him. At this juncture, the captain and sargento-mayor, our leader, arrived. He belittled and censured what we had done, and ridiculed our statement and that of some of the Cambodians, namely, that we had killed the usurper. All that he did was simply to collect whatever silver and gold certain soldiers seized during these troubles, and everything valuable in the ships, and then to burn the latter. Then he drew up a report against us and dispossessed us of our ships and command, thus formulating suspicion and distrust. After that he gave orders for the departure from the kingdom, paying no heed to many Cambodians who came to speak to us when we went ashore, and told us that we might build a fortress there, for they had a legitimate king before, but that he who was their king lately had driven him to Lao, and thus they had no king; that they would gather wherever the most protection could be found; and that we should continue the war. Nor did the captain accept any of our suggestions, when we told him that the usurper had imprisoned a kinsman of the lawful king; that we should go to his rescue; that the latter would raise men in favor of the legitimate king; and that with his support we would take possession of the kingdom, and then go to get the king. But he was deaf to all this and accordingly abandoned the kingdom, and this great opportunity was lost. The only thing that we could obtain from him by great entreaty after putting to sea, was to go to Cochinchina to inquire about the galley, since they had intended to send from Manila for that purpose. I also offered to go to Lao by land at my own expense, in search of the king of Camboja, for I knew that that way led thither. Accordingly, as soon as we arrived in Cochinchina, the captain sent Diego Belloso and myself to Lao, and Captain Gregorio de Vargas to Tunquin. Meanwhile he held an auction among the soldiers of everything valuable from the Chinese ships, and of what else he had taken from the soldiers; but the men were all without a real, and so he had everything bought for himself, at whatever price he was pleased to give. The king of Sinoa, a province of Cochinchina, equipped us for the voyage with a good outfit, by giving us an embassy for that country, and men to accompany us on the road. Thus we made the entire journey well provided and always highly honored and feared and much looked at, as the like had never before been seen in those kingdoms.

We were all sick on the road; but in all our troubles we were greatly comforted by the love which the people showed towards us, and: by the kind reception that we met at the hands of all. Finally we reached Lanchan, the capital and the royal seat of the kingdom. This kingdom has a vast territory, but it is thinly populated because it has been often devastated by Pegu. It has mines of gold, silver, copper, iron, brass, [sic] and tin. It produces silk, benzoin, lac, brasil, wax, and ivory. There are also rhinoceroses, many elephants, and horses larger than those of China. Lao is bounded on the east by Cochinchina and on the northeast and north by China and Tartaria, from which places came the sheep and the asses that were there when I went. Much of their merchandise is exported by means of these animals. On its west and southwest lie Pegu and Sian, and on the south and southeast, it is bounded by Camboja and Champan. [100] It is a rich country, and everything imported there is very expensive. Before our arrival at Lanchan, a cousin of the exiled king, on account of the usurper's death, had fled thither from Camboja, fearing lest the latter's son who was then ruling would kill him. He related what we had done in Camboja, in consequence of which the king of Lao received us very cordially, and showed great respect for us, praising our deeds and showing amazement that they had been accomplished by so few. When we arrived the old king of Camboja, together with his elder son and daughter, had already died, and there was left only the younger son with his mother, aunt, and grandmother. These women rejoiced greatly over our deeds and arrival, and more attention was given them thenceforth. Before our arrival at the city, we met an ambassador, whom the usurping king, Anacaparan, had sent from Camboja, in order that he might reach Lanchan before we did, and see what was going on there. He feigned excuse and pretext of asking for the old queen, who was the step-mother of the dead king Prauncar, and whom Anacaparan claimed to be his father's sister. The king of Lao was sending her, but at our arrival, and on our assuring him of Anacaparan's death, he ordered her to return, and the ambassador, for fear of being killed, fled down the river in a boat to Camboja. Then we declared our embassy, and asked for the heir of the kingdom in order to take him to our ships and thence to his own country. We were answered that he [i.e., the younger son] was the only one, and that they could not allow him to go, especially through a foreign country, and over such rough roads and seas. The youth wished to come, but his mothers [101] would not consent to it. Finally it was decided that we should return to the fleet and proceed with it to Camboja. We were to send them advices from there, whereupon they would send him under a large escort. His mothers gave me letters directed to that city [i.e., Manila], making great promises to the Spaniards on behalf of the kingdom, if they would return to Camboja to pacify the land and restore it to them. The king of Lao entrusted me with another embassy, in which he petitioned for friendship and requested that the fleet return to Camboja, adding that, should Gallinato be unwilling to return, he would send large forces by land to our assistance, under command of the heir himself. Thus we took leave and went to Cochinchina. While these things were happening in Lao, the following occurred in Camboja. As soon as the fleet had departed, the news of Anacaparan's death was published. When it was heard by Chupinaqueo, kinsman of the lawful king, who was in prison, he escaped from his prison, incited a province to rise, collected its men, and having proclaimed Prauncar as the lawful king, came to get us with about six thousand men, in order to join us and make war upon the sons of the usurper, who were now ruling. Not finding us in Chordemuco, where our ships had been lying, he sent boats to look for us as far as the bar. Seeing that we were nowhere to be found he seized all the Chinese and other people there, and returned to his province where he had gathered his forces, and there he fortified himself. Meanwhile the men at Champan, who had gone thither to take it, returned, whereupon the commander of the camp, called Ocuna de Chu, took sides with the sons of the usurper and had one of them—the second—Chupinanu by name, proclaimed king, because he was the most warlike. For this reason, the elder brother, called Chupinanon, and those of his party were angered, and consequently there was continual strife between them. Then all having united, together with the army from Chanpan, pursued Chupinaqueo, who came out to meet them with many of his men. They fought for many days, but at last it was Chupinaqueo's fate to be conquered and cruelly killed. Thus for the time being Chupinanu ruled as king, and the camp was disbanded, each man going to his own home. At this time a ship arrived from Malaca on an embassy, bringing some Spaniards who came in search of us, and a number of Japanese. Chupinanu would have liked to have killed them all, but seeing that they came on an embassy, and from Malaca, he let them go immediately. A large province, called Tele, seeing the cruelty with which the king treated them, revolted, and declaring themselves free, proclaimed a new king; then they marched against Chupinanu, and defeated and routed him, took from him a large number of elephants and artillery, and sacked his city. In the battle, most of the Spaniards and Japanese who had come from Malaca were killed. Chupinanu retreated with all his brothers, six in number, to another province, always accompanied by Ocuna de Chu. There they began to make plans and to collect men. They also invited two Malays, leaders of all the other Malays on whom Chupinanu relied strongly, who on the break-up of the camp after Chupinaqueo's death, had gone to the lands of which they were magistrates. But in order that what follows may be understood, I will tell who these Malays are. When this country was being ravaged by Sian, these two went to Chanpan, taking with them many of their Malays, as well as many Cambodians; and because the ruler of Champan did not show them all the honors that they desired, they caused an insurrection in the city when he was away. They fortified themselves there, and then plundered the city, after which they returned to this kingdom with all the artillery and many captives. When they arrived here the usurper Anacaparan was ruling. Congratulating one another mutually for their deeds, the usurper gave them a friendly welcome, and they gave him all the artillery and other things which they had brought. Then the usurper gave them lands for their maintenance, and made them great mandarins. These two Malays made it easy for him to capture Champan, and offered to seize its king. Since the latter had been so great and long-standing an enemy of the Cambodians, Anacaparan immediately collected an army, which he sent under command of Ocuna de Chu. When we killed Anacaparan, these forces were in Chanpan, and, as abovesaid, they returned after his death. These men presented themselves before the new king, Chupinanu, with all their Malays and it was at once decided to attack the insurgents of Tele. At this juncture arrived the ambassador who had fled from Lao as we reached Lanchan. He said that we had remained there and that our purpose was to ask for the lawful heir of Camboja in order to take him to our ships and transport him to his kingdom; that the king of Cochinchina was going to help us in this undertaking; that we had entered Lao with that report; and that the king of Lao was about to send the heir with great forces by river and by land, while we and the men of Cochinchina would go by sea and join them in Camboja, where we would declare war and inflict severe punishment upon whomsoever would not render homage. When the new king and his followers heard this news they were frightened, and consequently each thought only of himself. A few days later it was reported from the bar that four Spanish ships had entered, accompanied by many galleys from Cochinchina. This report was either a vision that some had seen, or was a fiction; and we have been unable to clarify the matter to this very day. At any rate, on hearing this news, these people confirmed as true the entire report of the ambassador who had fled. The mandarins of Camboja, taking into consideration the war which was now waging with the men of Tele, and the new one threatened by the Spaniards, Cochinchina, and Lao, decided to depose the new king and render homage to the one who was coming from Lao. For this purpose they communicated with the two Malays and together with them attacked the king with his brothers and turned them out of the realm. The two elder brothers fled separately, each to the province where he thought to find more friends. After this the mandarins ordered a fleet of row-boats to proceed toward Lao to receive their king, who they said was already coming. They sent Ocuna de Chu as leader of the fleet and also his two sons. Other boats were sent to the bar to receive the Spaniards, and make friendly terms with them, sending for that purpose certain Spaniards there. Two Cambodian mandarins and the two Malays were to remain to guard the kingdom, and to act as governors. The Spaniards went to the bar, but, finding nothing, returned. Ocuna de Chu took the road to Lao, but seeing that he did not meet his king, or hear any news of him, resolved to go to Lanchan and ask for him. He continued his march, but suffered some pangs of hunger, for he had left the kingdom unprovided, and the way was long. On account of this some of his men deserted, but at last he reached Lanchan with ten armed praus. All the kingdom of Lao was thrown into great confusion. Imagining that he was coming to make war, they abandoned their villages and property, and fled to the mountains. But on seeing that he was coming on a peaceful mission, they lost their apprehension. At his arrival we were already on the road to Cochinchina, whereupon the king ordered us to return to Lanchan immediately. The king [of Lao], on learning what was happening in Camboja, despatched there a large fleet by sea, and forces by land, and sent for the king of that country. He despatched me to Cochinchina with news of what was happening, and to take the ships to Camboja; but, while on the way, I heard of the battle fought by our fleet, whereupon I returned to Camboja with the king. When we reached the first village of the kingdom, we learned from the spies who had preceded us, that, as the news of the ships had been untrue, and Cuna de Chu was delaying so long, the provinces where the two brothers sought shelter had proclaimed them kings, and were at war with one another; that the people of Tele had come to fight with the governors, who were divided into factions; and that each man obeyed whom he pleased. But they said that Ocuna Lacasamana, one of the Malay headmen, had the greatest force of artillery and praus; and that a Japanese junk—the one that had been in Cochinchina when our fleet was there—had arrived, and was supporting Chupinannu. The sea and land forces were collected together at the point where this news had been received, and it was found that they were not sufficient to make a warlike entry. A fort was built there, and a request for more men sent to Lao. In the meantime, secret letters were despatched to probe the hearts of the leading men. The men from Lao delayed, and no answers were received to the letters. Feeling insecure in that place, they deliberated upon returning to Lao, but at this juncture news arrived from Ocuna Lacasamana, one of the Malays who had fortified himself in his own land, saying that he was on their side, although he had rendered homage to Chupinanu—a feigned promise because he had seen the king's delay—but that as soon as the king entered the land he would join his party. Soon after news came from another Cambojan governor, to the effect that, although he had rendered homage to Chupinanu, yet, if the king would come to him, he would attack Chupinanu, and depose or kill him. For that he said that he had four thousand men fortified with himself on a hill. He sent one of his relatives with this message. All trusted in this man, and immediately we set out for that place. When the above-mentioned man learned of the king's approach, he attacked the other king and routed him; then he came out to receive us, and thus we entered. That province and many others were delivered to us immediately. Chupinanu withdrew to some mountains. Immediately the two Malays, each with his forces, joined us; the Japanese did the same. The king then gave orders to pursue Chupinanu until he was taken and killed. Then he seized another man who was acting as judge in another province and put him to death. Soon after war began against the eldest of the brothers and against the people of Tele who also refused homage. At this juncture, a ship arrived from Malaca with fourteen Spaniards of our fleet, who had put into Malaca. The king was delighted thereat, and honored and made much of them, when he learned that they were some of the men who had killed the usurper. They were esteemed and respected in an extraordinary manner by the whole kingdom. Captain Diego Belloso tried to assume charge of them by virtue of an old document from Malaca; this I forbade, alleging that the right of this jurisdiction should proceed from Manila, since the restoration of this kingdom proceeded from that place, and that those men were Castilians and had nothing to do with his document or with Malaca. The king, before whom this matter was brought, replied that the matter lay between us two, and refused to mingle in those affairs. Some of the newcomers coincided with Belloso's opinion, and others with mine; and thus we have gone on until now. This has been the cause of my not asking the king for a fort to secure our personal safety. It would have been a footing for some business, [102] and what I shall relate later would not have happened to us. After the arrival of the Castilians, the king sent an embassy to Cochinchina—a Spaniard and a Cambodian—to get father Fray Alonso Ximenez and certain Spaniards, who, as we heard, had remained there. The ruler of Chanpan seized them, and they have not returned. The wars continued, in all of which the Spaniards and Japanese took part. Whatever we attacked, we conquered with God's assistance, but where we did not go, losses always resulted. Consequently we gained great reputation and were esteemed by our friends and feared by the enemy. While we were making an incursion, Ocuna de Chu, who was now called manbaray—the highest title in the kingdom—tried to revolt. In this he was aided by one of the Malay chiefs called Cancona. The king summoned me and ordered me to bring with me the Spaniards of my party. He ordered Diego Belloso to remain, for both of us were leaders and still are, in any war in which any of us is engaged. I came at his bidding, and he told me that those men were trying to kill him and deprive him of his kingdom, and asked me to prevent such a thing. The mambaray was the one who ruled the kingdom, and since the king was young and addicted to wine, he held the latter in little esteem and considered himself as king. At last, I, aided by Spaniards, killed him; then his sons were captured and killed. Afterward the Malay Cancona was seized and killed, and the king was extricated from this peril by the Spaniards. Then we returned to the war. I learned that another grandee who was head of a province was trying to rebel and join Chupinannon; I captured him and after trying him, put him to death. Therefore the king showed great esteem for us, and the kingdom feared us; that province was subdued and we returned to the king. At this time a vessel arrived from Sian, and ported here on its way to an embassy at Manila. On board this vessel were father Fray Pedro Custodio and some Portuguese. The king was greatly delighted at the arrival of the father and wished to build him a church. We all united and continued the war. Again we returned, after having reduced many provinces to the obedience of the king, and left Chupinanon secluded on some mountains, thus almost ending the war. Hereupon many Laos arrived under the leadership of one of their king's relatives, for hitherto they had done nothing nor uttered any sound. I do not know whether it was from envy at seeing us so high in the king's favor and that of the people of the kingdom, or whether they decided the matter beforehand in their own country; they killed a Spaniard with but slight pretext. When we asked the king for justice in this matter, the latter ordered his mandarins to judge the case. Meanwhile we sent for the Japanese who were carrying on the war in another region, in order to take

vengeance if justice were not done. The Laos, either fearing this, or purposing to make an end of us, attacked our
quarters at night and killed the father and several Spaniards
who had accompanied him and who were sick; they also
killed some Japanese, for their anger was directed against
all. The rest of us escaped and took refuge on the Japanese
vessel, where we defended ourselves until the arrival of the
Japanese. The Laos made a fort and strengthened themselves therein. There were about six thousand of them.
They sent a message to the king saying that they would not
agree to any act of justice which he might order to be carried out. The king was very angry for the deaths that they
had caused, and for the disrespect with which they treated
him; but, in order not to break with their king, he refused
to give us forces with which to attack them, although we
often requested him to do so; nor did we attack them ourselves, as we were without weapons. The king sent word of
this affair to Lao, and we remained for the time, stripped,
without property, without arms, without justice or revenge,
and quite angry at the king, although he was continually
sending us excuses, saying that if the king of Lao did not
do justice in this matter, he himself would do it, and would
not let them leave the country on that account; he also
sent us food, and some clothes and weapons. At this juncture a ship was despatched on an embassy to Malaca in
which we wished to embark, but neither the king nor his
mothers would allow Diego Belloso or me to leave. Some
of the Spaniards embarked in it, some returned to Sian,
and others remained with us; and the king from that time
on made us more presents than ever. The Japanese gathered in their ship, and refused to continue the war. When
the enemy learned that we were in confusion, they collected large forces and regained many undefended regions.
The king requested the Laos to go to war, since they had
thrown into confusion those who were defending his
country. They went, lost the first battle, and returned
completely routed, leaving many dead and wounded on the
field. Chupinanon followed up the victory and came within
sight of the king's residence, only a river separating them.
Thereupon the king quite disregarded the Laos, and persuaded us and the Japanese to take up arms again and
defend him. By this time we had all reequipped ourselves

with arms and ammunition, and after much entreaty from him and his mothers, we went to war and relieved a fortress which Chupinanon was besieging. We won two battles and forced him to withdraw, thus taking from him all he had just regained, as well as other lands which had remained in those regions. We captured a quantity of rice and provisions from the enemy—with which the king's forces recuperated themselves, for they were suffering famine—and we went into quarters. This we did, I, the Spaniards, and the Japanese who were on my side. Diego Belloso and his men went to Tele, killed its king, and returned after having conquered part of the province. At this time a Portuguese ship arrived from Macao, [103] laden with merchandise; on which account, and on beholding our deeds, the Laos were filled with great fear of us, and without leave from the king, departed in boats to their country. Thereupon we went to the king, and requested him not to let them go without doing justice, unless he wished to break friendship with Luzon and Malaca. He replied that he did not dare detain them, but that if we wished to pursue and dared to fight them, he would secretly give us men. Accordingly we all negotiated for ten praus, and followed them. But since they were far ahead of us and under the spell of fear, we could not overtake them for many days. For this reason Belloso turned back with some Spaniards and Japanese. I followed with great difficulty—on account of certain strong currents, for we dragged the praus part way with ropes—although with but few men, until I overtook many of the Laos, and seized their praus and possessions, from which we all received compensation and gained still more in reputation, which at present we enjoy to a higher degree than was ever enjoyed by any nation in foreign lands. We are greatly esteemed by the king and his men, and by those native here; and greatly feared by foreigners. Accordingly we receive great respect in all parts of the kingdom. They have bestowed upon Captain Diego Belloso and myself the title of grandee, the highest in their kingdom, so that we may be more respected and feared, and better obeyed. Two of the best provinces in the kingdom are entered in our names, and will be made over to us as soon as the turmoils of war are settled and assemblies have been held to take the oaths to the king, which has not yet been done. In the meantime we are making use of other people whom the king orders to be given us. There is no opportunity in the kingdom for any one else to possess entire power and command, beyond Ocuna Lacasamana, leader of the Malays, whom the king favors on account of his large forces, and because he needs him for the wars in which he is engaged. The Spaniards have some encounters with his men, for which reason we hold aloof from one another. I have informed your Grace so minutely of these wars and affairs, in order that it may be judged whether his Majesty has any justifiable and legal right to seize any portion of this kingdom, since his forces killed the man who was quietly in possession of it; and since its heir, who was driven away where he had lost hope of ever again possessing it, has afterward reconquered it through his Majesty's subjects, who have guarded and defended his person from his enemies. For the hope that the king will give it up voluntarily will never be realized, as he rather fears having so many Spaniards in his country, even while he esteems them; for he dreads lest they deprive him of his kingdom, since he sees that this only requires the determination therefor. Some of our enemies impress this fact upon him, especially the Moros. I beg and entreat your Grace, who can do so much in this matter, to see that we do not lose our hold on this land, since so much has been accomplished in it, and it has been brought to a so satisfactory state. Moreover it is very important to possess a fortress on the mainland, since it is the beginning of great things. For if a fortress be built here, and the king see a large force in this land, he would have to do what he knows to be just, even if ill-disposed. I say this on account of his mother, aunt, and grandmother, who rule and govern, for he only does as they tell him. He is a child and is addicted to wine more than his father; he only thinks of sports and hunting, and cares nothing for the kingdom. Therefore should he see many Spaniards, and that nobody could harm them, he would do whatever they wished, because, as above-said, he loves them; neither would our opponents dare to offer any opposition. If perchance there should be so few men in the Filipinas at present that no great number of them can be sent, at least send as many as possible with the fathers, so as not to lose this jurisdiction and our share in anything; for Diego Belloso sent to Malaca for religious, men, and documents, so that by that means he may become chief justice of this land, and make over this jurisdiction to Malaca. Since this kingdom has been restored by that kingdom [i.e., the Philippines], your Grace should not allow others to reap the fruits of our labors. If some soldiers should come, and the Cambodians should refuse them the wherewithal to maintain themselves because of their small number, and not fearing them, I would do here whatever your Grace bade me, so long as it were reasonable; and until more soldiers came, I could manage to make the Cambodians give it, however much against their inclination. These men should come bound hard and fast by documents, so that, as the country is very vast, they should not be tempted to avail themselves of license, for lack of discipline was the cause of our encounter with the Laos. It has been very difficult for me to despatch this vessel, because little is given to the king for any purpose, and because there were many opponents to prevent it—for it is evident that the mandarins, whether native or foreign, are not pleased to see men set over them in the kingdom—and as I am poor, for I have lived hitherto by war, and subsisted from its gains by many wars, for the king also is very poor. The Spaniard whom I entrust with this mission is poor and an excellent soldier; and to enable him to go, I have assisted him from my indigence. Will your Grace please assist both him and the Cambodian, in order that the latter may become acquainted with some of the grandeur of his Majesty. I would rejoice to be the bearer of this, so as to give your Grace a long account of these affairs and of other notable things, and of the fertility of these kingdoms; but neither the king nor his mothers have allowed me to go, as the bearer will state, among other things. Your Grace may believe him, for he is a person disinterested in all respects, having just arrived from Macan. On account of the many wars, the king does not possess many things to send your Grace. He sends two ivory tusks, and a slave. Your Grace will forgive him; he will send many things next year, if the pacification of his country is accomplished, for he still has something to do in it. I have spoken to him and persuaded him to send to that city [i.e., Manila] to request soldiers, in order to complete the pacification of the country; but his mothers would not have it on any account, I am sure that they act thus in order not to promise them lands for their maintenance, or that they may not seize the land. But when they were in Lao, they promised very vast lands. But if what is done is not sufficient to provide for them, let the mercy of God suffice. When this embassy was despatched, Diego Belloso and myself told the king that if he did not give us the lands that he had promised us, we intended to go to Luzon, because we did not now possess the wherewithal with which to maintain ourselves. Many things occurred with respect to this request, but finally he gave us the lands, as is stated in the embassy; he gave them to us on condition of our holding them in his service and obedience. By this means I shall have more resources for your Grace's service. I spent all my possessions in meeting the expenses that I incurred in that city [i.e., Manila], and in maintaining my men in this kingdom. For that purpose I took the silver of the common seamen of my vessel, and although I paid the latter with some silver which we found in the [Chinese] ships, Gallinato would not consent to it, but took it all for himself. In Malaca they made me pay it out of the property on my ship, and would not consent to their being paid out of the prizes, since the war was considered a just one. [104] For this reason I am now destitute of any property, and therefore do not possess the means of serving your Grace as I ought and as I should have desired. Recollecting your Grace's unique armory I send you a bottle and a small flask of ivory. Your Grace will forgive the trifle for I promise to compensate for it next year. Your Grace may command me in any service for I shall take great pleasure therein. Will your Grace do me the favor to protect my affairs, so that they may gain some merit by your favor. Trusting to this, may our Lord preserve your Grace, and give you increase in your dignity, as this servant of your Grace desires in your affairs. From Camboja, July twenty, one thousand five hundred and ninety-eight.

Your Grace's servant,

BLAS RUYZ DE HERNAN GONCALES

Through this news and despatch from Camboja we learned in Manila of the good result attained by the stay of Diego Belloso and Blas

Ruys in that land. Don Luys Dasmarinas gaining encouragement in the enterprise that he had proposed, discussed it with greater warmth. But since difficulties were still raised as to the justification with which an entrance could be made into Camboja with armed forces for more than the protection of, and completion of establishing, Prauncar in his kingdom, and to leave preachers with him—it was said on Don Luys's behalf that after accomplishing the above, he would, with the necessary favor of the same king of Camboja, proceed to the neighboring kingdom of Champan and take possession of it for his Majesty. He would drive thence a usurper, the common enemy of all those kingdoms, who lorded over it, and who, from his fortress near the sea, sallied out against all navigators, plundering and capturing them. He had committed many other crimes, murders, and thefts, on the Portuguese and other nations, who were obliged to pass his coasts in their trading with, and voyages to, China, Macan, Xapon, and other kingdoms, concerning all of which sufficient testimony had been given. On account of all these reports, the theologians and jurists decided that the war against the ruler of Champan and the conquest of his lands was justifiable, and that this position was of no less importance to the Spaniards than that of Camboja.

The governor and president, Don Francisco Tello, held a consultation with the Audiencia and others—religious and captains—as to what in their opinion was the most advisable measure to take in this matter. It was resolved that, since Don Luys offered to make this expedition at his own expense with those men who chose to follow him, the plan should be carried out. [105] Accordingly, an agreement was made with him on the above basis. He was to take the men at his own expense, with commission and papers from the governor for affairs of government and war, and provisions from the Audiencia for the administration of justice. He began preparing ships, men, and provisions, in order to sail as soon as possible.

In the meanwhile, Governor Don Francisco Tello despatched Don Joan de Camudio with a moderate-sized ship to Great China to obtain leave from the viceroy of Canton for the Spaniards to communicate and trade with his province. He was also to fetch saltpeter and metals which were wanted for the royal magazines of Manila. Don Joan reached his destination with good weather, and after stationing himself off the coast of Canton, sent certain of his company to the city with despatches for the tuton or viceroy. When the viceroy heard of the arrival of the Spaniards and the reason thereof, he gave them audience, and treated them cordially. The Portuguese residing in Macan near the city of Canton, made many efforts to prevent the viceroy, the conchifu, and other mandarins from admitting the Castilians of Manila into their country, alleging that the latter were pirates and evil-doers, who seized upon whatever kingdom and province they visited. They told them so many things that it would have sufficed to destroy them, had not the viceroy and mandarins looked at the matter dispassionately; for they knew the declaration of the Portuguese to be hate and enmity, and that these passions moved them to desire that the Castilians have no trade with China, for their own interests. The affair went so far, that, having been brought before a court of justice, silence was imposed upon the Portuguese of Macan, under penalty of severe corporal punishment; while the Castilians were given and assigned a port on the same coast, named El Pinal [Pine Grove], twelve leguas from the city of Canton, where they might then and always enter and make a settlement of their own; and they were given sufficient chapas [i.e., edicts or passports of safety] and provisions therefor. Thereupon Don Joan de Camudio, entered El Pinal with his ship and there he was furnished with everything needful by the Chinese at a moderate price while the Spaniards went to and fro on the river upon their business to Canton in lorchas [106] and champans. While the Spaniards were detained, in the said port they were always well received in the city and lodged in houses within its walls. They went about the streets freely and armed, a thing which is new and unique in China in respect to foreigners. This caused so great wonder and envy to the Portuguese (who are not so treated) that they tried with might and main to prevent it, even going so far as to come by night in boats from Macan to El Pinal to fire the ship of the Castilians. This did not succeed, however, for, having been heard, the necessary resistance was made, and after that a good watch was always kept on board, until the ship having accomplished its business and object departed thence, much to the satisfaction of the Chinese, who gave the Spaniards chapas and documents for the future. The ship reached Manila at the beginning of the year one thousand five hundred and ninety-nine.

After Don Luys Dasmarinas had equipped two moderate-sized ships and a galliot, and collected two hundred men who chose to follow him in this enterprise to Camboja—they were part of the unemployed in Manila—with the necessary provisions, ammunition, and equipment on his ships; and accompanied by Fray Alonso Ximenez and Fray Aduarte of the Order of St. Dominic and Fray Joan Bautista of the Order of St. Francis, some Japanese, and native Indians of Manila: he set sail with his fleet from the bay, in the middle of July, [107] of the year ninety-eight. The weather was somewhat contrary as the seasons of the vendavals had set in, but his desire to accomplish his voyage, lose no time, and leave Manila, which was the greatest difficulty, caused him to disregard the weather; he thought that, once at sea, he would be able to stop on the coast in the port of Bolinao.

This plan did not succeed so well as Don Luis had anticipated, for, as soon as the fleet of these three ships left the bay it was so buffeted by the weather that it could not fetch the port of Bolinao or hold the sea. The flagship sprung a leak, and the ships returned to the mouth of the bay above Miraveles, [108] where they stayed several days refitting. When the weather moderated they set sail again, but again they were buffeted so violently that the ships were separated from one another, and the galliot—the weakest of them—with difficulty made the port of Cagayan. Quite dismantled and very necessitous, it entered by the bar of Camalayuga to the city of Segovia, which is at the head of the island of Luzon opposite Great China. There the alcalde-mayor of that province furnished it the necessary provisions and tackle. Captain Luis Ortiz, who commanded this galliot, together with twenty-five Spaniards and some Indians, hastened preparations for their departure and again left that port to rejoin the fleet which he had to follow, according to his instructions, making for the bar of the river of Camboja which was their destination. He had scarcely left Cagayan, when the almiranta entered the port in the same distress as the galliot. It was also detained some days to refit. Then it left again to rejoin the flagship and the galliot. The flagship being a stronger vessel kept the sea with difficulty; and as the storm lasted a long time, it was compelled to run in the open toward China. The storm continued to rage so steadily that, without being able to meliorate its voyage, the ship was obliged to sail, amid high seas and cloudy weather, to certain small uninhabited islands on the coast of China below Macan. There it was many times in danger of shipwreck, and parts of the cargo were thrown away daily. The almiranta, after having been refitted, left Cagayan, made the same voyage in the same storm, and anchored near the flagship, where it was lost with some men and its entire cargo. [109]The flagship did its best to rescue those who escaped from the almiranta, and although the former kept afloat several days, at length it grounded near the coast. There it began to leak so badly that, with that and the strong sea which struck it broadside, the vessel went to pieces. The ship's boat had already been lost, and in order to save their lives before the ship was completely wrecked they were obliged to make rafts and prepare framework and planks on which Don Luis and the religious and crew—in all one hundred and twenty Spaniards—went ashore. They brought away from the said ship a few of the most valuable objects, the weapons, and the most manageable pieces of artillery, abandoning the rest as lost. All of the Spaniards were so soaked and in so ill a plight that some Chinese who came to the coast, from some neighboring towns, both from compassion felt for their loss and on account of having been given certain things that had been brought away from the wreck, provided them with food and with a native vessel of small burden in which to leave that place and make for Macan and Canton, which were not far.

As soon as Don Luis and his men sighted Macan, the former sent two soldiers of his company in Chinese vessels to the city and settlement of the Portuguese to announce their arrival and hardships, in order to obtain some help from them. He sent two other soldiers to Canton to ask the viceroy or tuton for assistance and protection, so that they might equip themselves in, and sail from, China, in prosecution of their voyage. The people of Macan and their chief captain Don Pablo of Portugal received the Castilians so ill that they were thrown into prison and not allowed to return to Don Luis. To the latter they sent word warning him to leave the coast immediately, as they would treat them all no less ill. When the Portuguese learned that Captain Hernando de los Rios [110] and one of his companions had gone to Canton for the same purpose, they at once sent two Portuguese, members of their council and magistracy [camara and regimiento] to oppose their entry into China, by saying that they were robbers and pirates, and evil-doers, as they had said before of Don Joan de Camudio, who at this time was with his ship in the port of El Pinal, as abovesaid.

In Canton, Captain Hernando de los Rios and his companion met Alferez Domingo de Artacho and other companions belonging to Don Joan's ship, who, on learning of the disaster of Don Luis's fleet and that it had been wrecked near by, came together and defended themselves against the calumnies and pretensions of the Portuguese. The result was that, as the main difficulty had been already overcome in the case of Don Joan, and the viceroy and mandarins were informed that all were from Manila, who Don Luis Dasmarinas was, and that he was going to Camboja with his fleet, they received him with the same good-will with which they had received Don Joan de Camudio, and gave him permission to enter the port of El Pinal with him. There the two met, with much regret by the one at Don Luis Dasmarinas's loss, and with much satisfaction by the other at finding there Don Joan de Camudio and his men, who provided them with certain things that they needed. With Don Joan's assistance, Don Luis at once bought a strong, moderate-sized junk, on which he embarked with some of his men, and the artillery and goods which had been saved. He enjoyed the same advantages in that port as the Spaniards of Don Joan de Camudio's ship. He intended to remain there until, having sent news to Manila, ships and the other necessary things for pursuing his voyage thence to Camboja, should be sent him, in respect to which Don Luis would never allow himself to show any discouragement or loss of resolution.

Don Joan de Camudio left El Pinal, leaving Don Luis Dasmarinas and his men in that port, at the beginning of the year ninety-nine, and reached Manila in twelve days. After him, Don Luis sent Alferez Francisco Rodrigues with three companions to Manila in a small champan to beg the governor and his supporters for help and assistance in his present emergency, a vessel, and what was needful to continue the expedition that he had begun. In Manila the news of Don Luis's loss and of the conditions to which he was reduced, was learned both from Don Joan de Camudio and from Alferez Francisco Rodrigues, who reached Manila after the former. Seeing that it was impossible for Don Luis to continue the voyage to Camboja, and that there was neither property nor substance with which to equip him again, nor the time for it, a moderate-sized ship was purchased and despatched from Manila to E1 Pinal with provisions and other things, under command of the same Alferez Francisco Rodrigues, who was accompanied by some soldiers of whom he was captain and leader. Through them Don Francisco Tello sent orders to Don Luis to embark his men and return to the Filipinas, without thinking for the present of the expedition to Camboja or of anything else.

Captain Hernando de los Rios, who attended to Don Luis's affairs in Canton, wrote a letter at this time to Doctor Antonio de Morga; and in order that what happened in this respect may be better understood, the letter reads word for word as follows.

> Fernando de los Rios Coronel, to Doctor Antonio de Morga, of his Majesty's council, and his auditor in the royal Audiencia and Chancilleria of the Filipinas, whom may our Lord preserve, in Manila. The hardships which have befallen us within the short time since we left Manila, have been so many, that, if I were to give your Grace an account of them all, it would weary you; moreover the short time in which Don Joan is to depart does not allow of it. And since he will relate everything fully, I will relate only what occurred to us after reaching this land; for our Lord was pleased to change our intentions, which were to remain in Bolinao until the bad weather which we were having had terminated. In sight of the port we were overtaken by a storm which greatly endangered our lives and forced us to come to this kingdom of China, where we expected at least that the Portuguese would allow us to refit our ship. As it was the Lord's will that we should lose it,

we have suffered hardships enough, for scarcely anything
was saved. I lost my property and a portion of that of others, because I was not present at the time of the wreck, as
my general ordered myself and a coast-pilot the day before
to go to look for fresh provisions. This coast is so wretchedly laid down on the charts that we did not know where
we were, and on account of bad weather I could not return
to the ship. Consequently I was obliged to go to Canton,
where the Sangleys, who conveyed me and those who left
the ship with me, accused us of having killed three
Sangleys. And had we not found there Alferez Domingo
de Artacho and Marcos de la Cueva, who were pleading
against the Portuguese, we would have fared very ill. It was
God's will, that, with their aid, we settled the case in court;
and, although without proofs, and without taking our
depositions, they condemned us to a fine of fifty taes of
silver. There we learned that for one and one-half months
they [i.e., the men of Juan Zamudio's vessel] had been defending themselves against the Portuguese, who, as soon
as the Spaniards had arrived, went about saying that they
were robbers and rebels, and people who seized the kingdoms into which they entered, and other things not worth
writing. But in the end, all their efforts, good and evil—
and indeed very evil—profited them nothing, because, by
means of great assiduity and a quantity of silver, the Spaniards negotiated a matter which the Portuguese had never
imagined, namely, the opening of a port in this country, in
order that the Spaniards might always come safely, and the
granting of houses in Canton, a privilege which was never
extended to the Portuguese, on account of which the latter
are, or will be, even more angered. Besides, silence was
imposed upon the Portuguese, although this was no part
of the negotiations, so that they might not attempt by
other means to do us all the injury possible (as the
Sangleys who were among them tell us). It is impossible to
tell how much the Portuguese abhor the name of Castilians, unless it be experienced as we have done for our sins,
for they have placed us in great extremity, as Don Joan will
relate fully. For, when our general wrote to them that we
had been wrecked, and were dying of hunger among infidels, and in great peril, and that he was not coming to
trade, but was engaged in the service of his Majesty, the

welcome given him by the Portuguese was to seize his messengers and keep them up to the present time in a dungeon. Lastly, while we have been in this port, undergoing the difficulties and perils which Don Joan will relate, although they are so near, not only do they leave us to suffer, but, if there are any well-disposed persons, they have forbidden them to communicate with us or to give us anything, under both temporal and spiritual penalty. In truth, to reflect upon this cruelty, and still more to experience it as we are doing, exhausts all patience. May God in His mercy give us patience and consolation because these infidels [i.e., the Chinese] are the people who have corrupted the natural light more than any other people in the world. Hence angels and not men are required to deal with them. Since there are historians who record events in these regions, I shall not go into details respecting them. I only say, in order that you may understand in what a country we are, that it is the true kingdom of the devil, where he seems to rule with full power. Hence each Sangley appears to be the devil incarnate, for there is no malice or deceit which they do not attempt. Although outwardly the government, with all its order and method, seems good as far as its preservation is concerned, yet, in practice, it is all a scheme of the devil. Although here they do not rob or plunder the foreigners openly, yet they do it by other and worse methods. Don Joan has worked hard, and gratitude is certainly due him, for he has accomplished a thing so difficult, that the Portuguese say only the devil or he could have done it. However, it is true that it has cost him, as I have heard, about seven thousand pesos, besides the risk to which he has been exposed; for the Portuguese attempted to burn him in his ship; and although their schemes came to naught, it is impossible to describe the bitterness which they feel at seeing us come here to trade, because of the signal injury they receive thereby. However, if one considers it thoroughly, the truth is that, if this business were established on the basis of a fair agreement, the Portuguese would rather gain by it, because they would dispose of innumerable articles that they possess, and the majority of them, especially the poor, would profit by selling the work of their hands, and what they get from India, for which they always obtain a good price. As far as raising the price of [Chinese] merchandise to them is concerned, once established, and if the Sangleys understood that ships would come every year, they would bring down much more merchandise: and so much the more as Canton possesses such a large quantity of it, that there is more than enough for twice as many as are here, as we have seen with our own eyes. I can testify that, if they wish to load a ship with only one kind of goods, they can do so, even if it be needles; the more so, since the greater part of what the Chinese consume is not included among our articles of purchase, the great bulk of our purchases being raw silk. Therefore I believe that the continuation of this would be of great advantage to that city [i.e., Manila] for the following reasons which present themselves to me. The first is that, if orders were given for a ship to come authorized to invest the bulk of the money of that city [i.e., Manila], much more and better goods could be bought with much less money, and in articles which would prove more profitable; since, in short, we would save what the people of Chincheo gain with us [at Manila]—a goodly sum.

The second reason is that that city [i.e., Manila] would be provided with all necessaries, because one can find in the city of Canton anything that can be desired.

The third is that by this means we would avoid the excessive commerce of the Sangleys in that city [i.e., Manila], who cause the harm which your Grace knows, and even that which we do not know. They are people who, the less they are admitted, the better will it be for us in every respect. Hence there is no need of there being more of them than the number required for the service of the community; and then they would neither raise the price of provisions, nor retail what remains in the country, as they do now. Thus many pernicious sins which they commit and teach to the natives would be avoided. Although there seems to be some difficulty in establishing this and in smoothing down the Portuguese, still it might be accomplished.

The fourth reason is that, if the purchase is made here, it will reach that city [i.e., Manila] by Christmas, and each man would store his property in his house, and prepare and arrange it; and then, even should the ships from Castilla arrive early, no loss would be suffered as at present—

97

when, if those ships arrive before the goods purchased from China [reach Manila] the merchandise rises a hundred per cent.

The fifth reason is that the ships might easily take in cargo any time in the month of May, and take advantage of the first vendavals, which sometimes begin by the middle of June or before. By sailing then, they run less risk, and will reach Nueva Espana one month or even two months earlier. Then, they can leave that country in January and come here [i.e., to the Filipinas] by April without any of the dangers which beset them among these islands if they sail late, as we know.

The sixth reason is that the many inconveniences now existing at the time of the purchase [in Manila] would be avoided—inconveniences with which your Grace is acquainted—and the citizens would have less trouble. Also in respect to the lading and its allotment [i.e., of shipping room] a better system could certainly be followed, and it would be known who is to share in it. Things would be better remedied, because neither the money of Mexico nor that of companies would be allowed to be employed. The strict prevention of this alone would be sufficient to assure prosperity to Manila in a short time; for, if only the inhabitants were to send their invested property, it is certain that all the machinery of the money of the Mexicans would have to be employed on the goods sent from here—I mean from Manila—if they do not allow the Mexicans to purchase in that city [i.e., Manila]. And if less merchandise is sent from here [i.e., China, and consequently Manila] and there are more buyers there [i.e., in Mexico], the goods would be worth double. This is self-evident, and if, as your Graces have already begun to remedy this matter, the measure be rigorously carried still farther, that city [i.e., Manila] must prosper greatly. For, by not sending to Nueva Espana any other produce except that from that city [i.e., Manila] mainly purchased in this country [i.e., China], Manila would prosper as greatly as one could desire. If we consider the benefit and favor which his Majesty confers upon us in this matter, we would esteem it much more than we do now. But I believe that we shall regret it, when, perchance, we are deprived of it. Perhaps some one would say, in opposition to what I have said about coming to purchase here, that his Majesty would be defrauded of the customs and duties which the Sangleys now pay, and of their tribute. But there is a remedy for all this, for with the freight duties alone his Majesty would save much more; as also by buying ammunitions here and other articles which he needs for the conservation of that country [i.e., the islands] twice as cheaply and abundantly, and without depending on the Chinese to bring them at their leisure, who at times—and indeed every year—leave us without them, since we are forced to go to get them. As far as the tribute is concerned, I believe that his Majesty would be better served if there were no Sangleys there at all, than by receiving the tribute. And it might happen, through this way, if our Lord ordered it, that a door might be opened for the preaching of the gospel and for the conversion of the people, a thing desired so earnestly by his Majesty, and especially aimed at by him. After all, things require a beginning, and the road would be opened, although at present it seems shut; for, if we hope that the Portuguese attempt this, I do not know when they will do it, considering that they have not tried to do so, for so long as they have been settled here. Even the Sangleys say that the Portuguese began like ourselves. At first they went to and fro; then two sick men remained; the next year they built four houses; and thus they continued to increase. I know that there is no other difficulty for us to do likewise than that which the Portuguese offer. To return to the Portuguese opposition, it is something amazing, for not only are they vexed at our coming here, but also at our going to Camboja or to Sian. They assert that those districts are theirs, but I cannot see why they so designate them—for it is just the contrary—unless it be because we have allowed them, through our negligence, to seize our possessions near the strait of Malaca, and enter the line of demarcation falling to the crown of Castilla, as I would make them fully understand if an opportunity were presented. One can read in Historia de las Indias [111] [i.e., History of the Indias] in the one hundred and second chapter, and before and after it, that, at the request of the Portuguese, his Holiness drew the said line from three hundred and seventy leguas west of the islands of Caboverde, which were called the Espericas. The one hundred and eighty degrees of longitude falling to the Portuguese terminate and end as abovesaid, near the above-mentioned strait. All the rest belongs to us. Furthermore, since we are subjects of one king, how do we suffer them to forbid us all our trade? Why do they bar us from Maluco, Sian, Camboja, Cochinchina, China, and all the rest of this archipelago? What are we to do then, if they wish to seize everything? Surely this is a very unreasonable proceeding. I have dwelt on this matter in order to express my feelings. Not until our departure shall I write to your Grace about the fertility and nature of the country, and of its greatness. Then I shall endeavor to give a full account of the land, and to mark out this coast, for nothing is put down correctly.

This is the best coast [112] of all that have been discovered, and the most suitable for galleys, if God should ordain that they come hither. I have already discovered where the king keeps his treasure. The country is very rich, and the city of Canton well supplied, although there is nothing to be said in regard to its buildings, of which the whole city possesses few of any importance, according to the information received from a Theatin [113] Sangley with whom I found much pleasure in talking—though I was able to do so for only one afternoon. He was a man of intelligence and reason, and it is said that he is a scholar. He told me that in Paquien [i.e., Pekin], where the king resides, and in Lanquien [i.e., Nankin] the fathers of the Society enjoy the quiet possession of three houses. There are seven fathers, among whom is one called Father Ricio, [114] an associate of Father Rugero who went to Roma. He is an excellent mathematician and has corrected the Chinese calendar which contained many errors and false opinions, and their fantastic idea of the world, which they believed to be flat. He made them a globe and a sphere, and with this and the sound arguments and reasons which they give them, the fathers are considered as people descended from heaven. He says that in those regions the people would be very favorable to conversion, if there were ministers; and that there [i.e., in Pekin] the foreigners are not looked upon with wonder as they are here [i.e., in Canton]. He says that the people are much more sensible and reasonable, so much so that they call the people of this country barbarians. He adds that Lanquien lies in the latitude of Toledo, namely thirty and two-thirds degrees, and that from there to Paquien is a twenty-five days' journey, so that the latter city must lie in more than fifty degrees of latitude. [115] The above-mentioned brother comes down annually to collect the stipend given them by the people here for their three houses. Now they are expecting a great friend of theirs who is said to be the second person nearest to the king. One can travel through all this land by water, and therefore it abounds in everything, for articles are conveyed over the rivers and there is no need of beasts of burden, which is its special greatness.

He who wishes to depict China without having seen the land, must draw a country full of rivers and towns, and without a palmo of ground left lying idle. I wish I had more time in which to describe some of the things of China which I have observed and inquired about with special care, and of which, if God please, I shall be the messenger. The affairs of Camboja are in a good condition, and we shall arrive there at a seasonable time, if it be our Lord's will that we leave this place with good auspices. The king sent a ship to Manila at the end of August to ask for assistance. I do not know whether it has arrived or whether it returned to put in port, for it left very late. Bias Ruis sent fifty picos [116] from Camanguian. According to report, the king has apportioned and given him nine thousand vassals, and as many more to Belloso.

At present we ourselves are enduring the necessity of which Don Juan Camudio will inform you. I entreat your Grace to help us, since it is of so great importance. I kiss many times the hand of my lady Dona Joana. May our Lord preserve your Grace for many years in the prosperity and tranquillity which we your servants desire. From the port of El Pinal, frozen with cold, the twenty-third of December, ninety-eight.

If my brother should come before I return, I beseech your Grace, since it is so natural in your Grace to do good to all—especially to those of that land—to show him the goodness which your Grace has always shown me,

FERNANDO DE LOS RIOS CORONEL

After Don Juan de Camudio's departure from El Pinal, where Don Luis Dasmarinas remained with his junk awaiting the assistance that he expected from Manila and which he had requested through Don Joan and Alferez Francisco Rodrigues, Don Luis thought that, since some time had passed, the answer was being delayed, while his people were suffering great want and cold there. Therefore he tried to put out to sea in the junk, and to make for Manila. But the weather did not permit this, nor was the vessel large enough to hold all of Don Luis's men for the voyage. He stopped near the fort where the Portuguese of Macan again sent him many messages and requests to leave the coast at once, warning him that they would seize him and his companions, and would send them to India, where they would be severely punished. Don Luis always answered them that he had not come to harm or offend them, but that he was going to the kingdom of Camboja for the service of God and of his Majesty; that he had been shipwrecked and had suffered many hardships, the severest of which had been due to the Portuguese of Macan themselves, subjects of his Majesty; that he was expecting help from Manila in order that he might return thither; and that he begged and requested them to aid and protect him, and to free the two Castilians whom they had seized. Finally he declared that if, in spite of all this, they should attempt to do him any harm or injury, he would defend himself to the best of his ability; and he protested that any losses resulting therefrom would lie at their door. Thenceforward Don Luis Dasmarinas kept strict watch on his ship. He kept his weapons ready and the artillery loaded, and was on his guard day and night. And he was not mistaken, for the people of Macan resolved to attack him in order to seize him. To this end the chief captain himself came one day, with some fustas and other vessels, and with men armed with javelins, guns, and artillery, when they thought the Castilians would be off their guard, to attack Don Luis Dasmarinas. The latter, suspecting what was about to happen, awaited them arms in hand; and as he saw the Portuguese fleet attacking him, he began to play upon them with his muskets, arquebuses, and a few pieces of artillery, with such rapidity that he inflicted a very severe loss upon his enemy and upon the ship which carried the chief captain, killing one of his pages who stood behind him, and other persons. The chief captain retired with all the other vessels, and they made for the high sea, having been defeated by Don Luis, who did not attempt to follow them but remained on the watch. As the Portuguese did not dare attack him again they made for Macan, and Don Luis Dasmarinas put into the port of El Pinal, where he thought he would be in greater security. There Don Luis remained until Captain Francisco Rodrigues arrived with the ship from Manila, and joined him. They distributed their men between the two ships and made some purchases with what this last ship had brought from Manila, in the very city of Macan, for the Portuguese, for the sake of their own interests, gave and sold them goods, in spite of a certain apprehension of the law. They returned to Manila leaving a few men in El Pinal who had died of sickness, among whom was Fray Alonso Ximenez, the principal promoter of this enterprise. His associate, Fray Diego Aduarte, did not choose to return to Manila, but went to Macan and thence to Goa, in order to go to Espana. Don Luis reached Manila with both ships, and his expedition to Camboja and his conduct of the said enterprise remained in this state.

It has been already related that the galliot, one of the ships of Don Luis Dasmarinas's fleet, in which Luis Ortiz and twenty-five Spaniards had sailed, after having put into Cagayan and refitted there, sailed again during fairly good weather to find the fleet. This ship although so inadequate to resist storms at sea, was permitted, through God's mercy, to encounter those which it met without being wrecked. It made its way along the coast of Cochinchina and Champan, inside the shoals of Aynao, and reached the bar of Camboja. Expecting to find all or some of the ships of its convoy within the bar, it ascended the river as far as the city of Chordemuco. There they found Diego Belloso and Blas Ruys de Hernan Goncalez, with some Castilians who had joined them, and other Portuguese who had come by way of Malaca, and with whose assistance many battles had been won in favor of King Prauncar, who had been restored to his kingdom, although some of his provinces had not been entirely pacified. It was learned there that neither Don Luis Dasmarinas nor any other of his fleet had reached Camboja. Those in the galliot said that Don Luis was coming in person with a large force of ships, men, arms, and some religious, to accomplish what he had always desired to do in that kingdom; that he would not be long in coming; and that their galliot and crew belonged to his fleet. Blas Ruis and his Castilian companions greatly rejoiced over so opportune news. The former thought that everything was turning out well, and that now, according to the present state of affairs, matters would be accomplished and settled as they wished. Diego Belloso and his party, although they did not show their regret, were not so pleased, for they much preferred the happy termination and reward of this expedition to be for the Portuguese and the government of India. They had had certain quarrels and disputes with Blas Ruis over this. But seeing that the affair had reached this state, they conformed to the times. Thereupon all joined together, Portuguese and Castilians, and informed Prauncar and his mandarins of the arrival of Alferez Luis Ortiz with his galliot and companions, saying that they were part of a large fleet which would shortly arrive, and that Don Luis Dasmarinas was coming in it in person, with religious and men to aid and serve the king, in conformity to what he himself had requested in his letter to Manila, several months before. The king seemed pleased at this, and so did some of his mandarins who liked the Spaniards, and recognized what benefits they had derived from them hitherto. These believed that the matter would turn out as it was represented to them. But the king's stepmother, and other mandarins of her party, especially the Moro Malay Ocuna Lacasamana, were vexed at the arrival of the Spaniards, for they thought that the latter, being valiant men, numerous, and so courageous, as they already knew, would dominate everything, or at least would take the best; moreover they alone wished to deal with King Prauncar. Thus their aversion for Spanish affairs became known to be as great as the favor with which Prauncar, on the contrary, regarded them. The latter immediately assigned the Spaniards a position with their ship near the city, at the place which Blas Ruiz and Diego Belloso occupied.

Before Don Luis Dasmarinas left Manila with his fleet, Captain Joan de Mendoca Gamboa requested Governor Don Francisco Tello to allow him to go to the kingdom of Sian with a moderate-sized ship, in order to trade. For the greater security of his voyage and business, he asked the governor to give him letters to the king of Sian, in which the latter should be informed that he was sent as the governor's ambassador and messenger to continue the peace, friendship, and commerce which Joan Tello de Aguirre had contracted with Sian the year before. Seeing that Don Luis Dasmarinas, who was on the way to Camboja, had left in Manila for another occasion some ammunition and other things of use to his fleet, Don Joan, in order better to facilitate the granting of his request, offered to take these stores on board his ship and sail round by way of Camboja, where he supposed that he would find Don Luis Dasmarinas, and deliver them to him. The governor thought the two proposals timely, and having furnished him with the necessary despatches, Don Joan de Mendoca left Manila with his ship, taking as pilot Joan Martinez de Chave, who had been Joan Tello's pilot when the latter went to Sian. He took as companions some sailors and Indian natives. He had a quantity of siguei [117] and other goods to barter, and the ammunition and provisions which he was to convey to Don Luis. With him embarked Fray Joan Maldonado [118] and an associate, both religious of the Order of St. Dominic. The former was a grave and learned man and a very intimate friend of Don Luis Dasmarinas, to whom his order took great pleasure in sending him as a companion. They left Manila, without knowing of Don Luis's shipwreck two months after the latter had set sail. Crossing over the shoals they shortly reached the bar of Camboja and ascended to the capital, where they found the galliot of the fleet and learned that its other ships had not arrived. The king received them cordially and lodged them with Diego Belloso, Blas Ruiz, Luis Ortiz, and their companions. They passed the time together, and would not let Joan de Mendoca leave Camboja with his ship until something was heard of Don Luis Dasmarinas. A few days later, they learned through Chinese ships, and by other means, that the latter had put into China with difficulty and in distress, and that he was there preparing to continue his voyage. Although this event caused them sorrow, they still hoped that in a short time Don Luis would be in Camboja with the two ships of his fleet.

At this same time, a mestizo, named Govea, son of a Portuguese and a Japanese woman, who lived in Japon, collected some mestizo companions, as well as Japanese and Portuguese, on a junk which he owned in the port of Nangasaqui, with the intention of coasting along China, Champan, and Camboja, to seek adventures and to barter, but mainly to make prizes of what they might meet at sea. With them embarked a Castilian who had lived in Nangasaqui after the wreck of the galleon "San Felipe," while on its way to Nueva Espana in the year ninety-six. His name was Don Antonio Malaver, and he had been a soldier in Italia. He came to the Filipinas from Nueva Espana as captain and sargento-mayor of the troops brought that year by Doctor Antonio de Morga in the fleet from Nueva Espana to Manila. Don Antonio Malaver, who had no wish to return to the Filipinas, thinking that by that way he could go to India and thence to Espana, and that on the road there might fall to him some share of the illgotten gains of that voyage, embarked with Govea and his company. After they had run down the coast and heard some news of the entry of Spaniards into Camboja, Don Antonio persuaded Govea to enter the river of Camboja, where they would find Spaniards, and affairs in such a state that they might take some effective action in that kingdom, and thrive better than at sea. They went up as far as Chordemuco, joined the Castilians and Portuguese and were received into their company and list. As they all—and they were a considerable number of men—saw the delay of Don Luis Dasmarinas, they proclaimed as leaders Fray Joan Maldonado, Diego Belloso, and Blas Ruis. Then they began to treat with King Prauncar on their own account concerning their establishment and comfort, and to request lands and rice for their maintenance and other things which had been promised them, alleging that they did not derive the necessary usufruct and profit out of his concessions to Belloso and Blas Ruis. Although the king gave them good hopes for everything he brought nothing to a conclusion, being hindered in this by his stepmother and the mandarins of her party, who would have liked to see the Spaniards out of the kingdom; and in this they gained more animus every day by the non-arrival of Don Luis Dasmarinas. Consequently, the Spaniards spent the time in going to and fro between their quarters and the city to negotiate with the king, with whose answers and conversations they sometimes returned satisfied and at other times not so much so.

Ocuna Lacasamana and his Malays had their quarters near those of the Spaniards, and since they were Moros, so opposed in religion and pretension, the two parties had no affinity. Once a quarrel arose between Spaniards and Malays, and several men were severely wounded on both sides. Among them Alferez Luys Ortiz, commander of the galliot, had both legs run through and was in great danger. King Prauncar was angry at this, but did not dare to inflict any punishment or make any reparation for these injuries. While matters were at such a heat and the Malays were ill-disposed toward the Spaniards, one day while Fray Joan Maldonado, Diego Belloso, and Blas Ruyz were in the city, and Luys de Villafane was in command of the quarters, on account of the wounds and illness of Luys Ortiz, another quarrel arose in the quarters with the Malays. Luys de Villafane, taking advantage of this opportunity, determined, with a few Spaniards who followed him, to unite with Govea and his men, and attack the Malays, their quarters, and the goods that they possessed, and sack them. Incited by anger and still more by covetousness, they carried this out, and after having killed many Malays and taken a quantity of property from them, they retired and fortified themselves in their own quarters and in the Japanese ship. The king and his mandarins were very angry at this, and not less so were Fray Joan Maldonado, Belloso, and Blas Ruyz, who were in Chordemuco; but Ocuna Lacasamana was far the angriest, at seeing the injury and insult done him, and at the breaking of the peace so recently made in reference to former quarrels. Although Fray Joan Maldonado, Belloso, and Blas Ruiz went at once to the quarters to remedy the matter, they found it so complicated that not even King Prauncar, who tried to intervene, could compose it. The latter warned the Spaniards to look to their personal safety, for he saw their party fallen and in great danger, without his being able to help it. Fray Joan Maldonado and his companion, although facing the matter in company with Diego Belloso and Bias Ruis, yet took refuge in Joan de Mendoca's ship for greater security, and some Spaniards did the same. Diego Belloso, Blas Ruiz, and the others relying on the king's friendship, and their services in the country, remained on shore, although they took every precaution and kept the closest possible guard over their safety. [119]

The Malay Lacasamana, aided by his men and the mandarins of his party, and supported by the king's step-mother, lost no more time, nor the present opportunity, but attacked the Castilians, Portuguese, and Japanese, at once, both by land and sea. Finding them separated—

although some offered as much resistance as possible—he killed them all, including Diego Belloso and Blas Ruiz de Hernan Goncales. Then he burned their quarters and vessels except that of Joan de Mendoca, who, fearing the danger, descended the river toward the sea and defended himself against some praus that had followed him. He took with him Fray Joan Maldonado, the latter's associate, and some few Spaniards. On shore there remained alive only one Franciscan religious, five Manila Indians, and a Castilian named Joan Dias, whom the king, who grieved exceedingly for the deaths of the Spaniards, had hid carefully in the open country. Although the king advised the friar not to appear in public until the Malays were appeased, that religious, imagining that he could escape their fury, emerged with two Indians in order to escape from the kingdom. But they were found and killed like the others. Joan Dias and three Indians remained many days in concealment, and the king maintained them, until, after other events, they could appear. Thus the cause of the Spaniards in Camboja came to an end, and was so entirely defeated that the Moro Malay and his partisans remained complete masters. They managed the affairs of the kingdom with so little respect for King Prauncar, that finally they killed him also. Thereupon a fresh insurrection broke out, the provinces revolted, each man seized whatever he could, and there was more confusion and disturbance than before.

The Spanish garrison left in La Caldera, at the withdrawal of Don Joan Ronquillo's camp from the river of Mindanao, passed into command of Captain Villagra at the death of Captain Joan Pacho in Jolo, and was suffering for lack of provisions; for neither the people of the river could give them to the Spaniards, nor would the Joloans furnish any on account of the war declared upon them. Therefore the garrison urgently requested Governor Don Francisco Tello either to aid their presidio with provisions, soldiers, and ammunition, or to allow them to retire to Manila—a thing of which they were most desirous—since there they gained no other special result than that of famine, and of incarceration in that fort, and of no place wherein to seek their sustenance. The governor, in view of their insistence in the matter; and having but little money in the royal exchequer, with which to provide for and maintain the said presidio—and for the same reason the punishment that was to be inflicted upon the Joloans for their outrages upon the Spaniards, and their insurrection was deferred—and thinking that the return to Mindanao matters would be a long question, he was inclined to excuse the difficulty and anxiety of maintaining the presidio of La Caldera. In order to do it with a reasonable excuse he consulted the Audiencia and other intelligent persons, and requested them to give him their opinion. But he first communicated his wishes to them and gave them some reasons with which he tried to persuade them to give him the answer that he desired. The Audiencia advised him not to remove or raise the garrison of La Caldera, but to reenforce and maintain it, and to attend to the affairs of Jolo and the river of Mindanao as soon as possible, even if what was necessary for those two places should be withdrawn from some other section. They said that this was the most urgent need, and the one which required the greatest attention in the islands, both in order to pacify those provinces and to keep them curbed; lest, seeing the Spaniards totally withdrawn, they should gain courage and boldly venture still farther, and come down to make captures among the Pintados and carry the war to the very doors of the Spaniards. [120] Notwithstanding this reply the governor resolved to raise and withdraw the garrison, and sent orders to Captain Villagra immediately to burn the fort which had been built in La Caldera, to withdraw with all his men and ships, and return to Manila. This was quickly done, for the captain and the soldiers of the garrison waited for nothing more than to dismantle the fort and leave. When the Joloans saw the Spaniards abandoning the country, they were persuaded that the latter would return to Mindanao no more, and that they had not sufficient forces to do so. Thereupon they gained fresh resolution and courage, and united with the people of Buhahayen on the river, and equipped a number of caracoas and other craft, in order to descend upon the coast of Pintados to plunder them and make captives. The people of Tampacan, who lost hope of receiving further help from the Spaniards, and of the latter's return to the river, since they had also abandoned the fort of La Caldera and left the country, came to terms with and joined the people of Buhahayen, their neighbors, in order to avoid the war and injuries that they were suffering from the latter. Then all turned their arms against the Spaniards, promising themselves to make many incursions into their territory and gain much plunder. Accordingly they prepared their fleet, and appointed as leaders and commanders of it two of the experienced chiefs, of the river of Mindanao, called Sali and Silonga. They left the Mindanao River in the month of July of the year ninety-nine, in the season of the vendavals, with fifty caracoas, containing more than three thousand soldiers armed with arquebuses, campilans, carasas, other weapons with handles, and many culverins, and steered toward the islands of Oton and Panay, and neighboring islands. They passed Negros Island and went to the river of Panay, which they ascended for five leguas to the chief settlement, where the alcalde-mayor and some Spaniards were living. They sacked the settlement, burned the houses and churches, captured many native Christians—men, women, and children—upon whom they committed many murders, cruelties, and outrages. They pursued these in boats more than ten leguas up the river, and destroyed all the crops. For the alcalde-mayor, and those who could, fled inland among the mountains, and accordingly the enemy had a better opportunity to do what they pleased. After they had burned all the vessels in the river, they left the river of Panay with their boats laden with pillaged goods and captive Christians. They did the same in the other islands and towns which they passed. Then they returned to Mindanao, without any opposition being offered, with a quantity of gold and goods and more than eight hundred captives, besides the people whom they had killed. In Mindanao they divided the spoil, and agreed to get ready a larger fleet for the next year, and return to make war better prepared. [121]

This daring attack of the Mindanaos worked great injury to the islands of Pintados, both on account of their deeds there and also on account of the fear and terror with which they inspired the natives; because of the latter being in the power of the Spaniards, who kept them subject, tributary, and disarmed, and neither protected them from their enemies, nor left them the means to defend themselves, as they used to do when there were no Spaniards in the country. Therefore many towns of peaceful and subjected Indians revolted and withdrew to the tingues, [122] and refused to descend to their houses, magistrates, and encomenderos. As was reported daily, they all had a great desire to revolt and rebel, but they were appeased and reduced again to subjection by a few promises and presents from their encomenderos and religious who showed great pity and sadness over their injuries. Although in Manila people regretted these injuries, and still more those which were expected in the future from the enemy, they did nothing but regret them—since the governor was ill provided with ship and other necessities for the defense—and reckon them with the loss which they had suffered for having raised the camp on the river of Mindanao and dismantled the presidio of La Caldera.

As soon as the weather permitted, the Mindanaos and Joloans returned with a large fleet of more than seventy well-equipped ships and more than four thousand fighting men, led by the same Silonga and Sali, and other Mindanao and Jolo chiefs, to the same islands of Pintados, with the determination of taking and sacking the Spanish town of Arevalo, which is situated in Oton. Captain Joan Garcia de Sierra, alcalde-mayor of that province, having heard of this expedition and of the designs entertained by the enemy, took the most necessary precautions, and, gathering into the town all the Spaniards who lived there and in its neighborhood, shut himself up in it with all of them. Then, having repaired, as well as possible, a wooden fort there, he gathered there the women and their possessions. He and the Spaniards—about seventy men—armed with arquebuses, awaited the enemy. The latter, who intended to attack the river of Panay again, passed Negros Island and made for the town of Arevalo, where they anchored close to the native settlement. Then they landed one thousand five hundred men armed with arquebuses, campilans, and carasas, and, without stopping on the way marched against the Spanish town which was the object of their attack. The Spaniards, divided into troops, sallied forth and opened fire with their arquebuses upon the enemy with such vehemence that they forced them to retreat and take refuge on board their caracoas. So great was the enemy's confusion that many Mindanaos were killed before they could embark. Captain Joan Garcia de Sierra, who was on horseback, pursued the enemy so closely to the water's edge that the latter cut off the legs of his mount with their campilans and brought him to the ground where they killed him. The enemy embarked with a heavy loss of men, and halted at the island of Guimaraez, [123] in sight of Arevalo. There they counted their men, including the dead and the wounded, who were not a few, and among whom was one of the most noted chiefs and leaders. Then they sailed for Mindanao, making a great show of grief and sorrow, and sounding their bells and tifas. [124] They made no further delay at the Pintados, deriving little profit or gain from the expedition, but much injury, and loss of men and reputation, which was felt more deeply upon their arrival in Jolo and Mindanao. In order to remedy this disaster, it was proposed to renew their expedition against the Pintados at the first monsoon with more ships and men, and it was so decided.

When the affairs of Japon were discussed above, we spoke of the loss of the ship "San Felipe" in Hurando, in the province of Toca; of the martyrdom of the discalced Franciscan religious in Nangasaqui; and of the departure of the Spaniards and religious who had remained there, with the exception of Fray Geronymo de Jesus, who, changing his habit, concealed himself in the interior of the country. We related that Taicosama, after he had given an answer to the governor of Manila, through his ambassador, Don Luis Navarrete, excusing himself for what had happened, was induced, at the instigation of Faranda Quiemon and his supporters, to send a fleet against Manila; that he had supplied Faranda with rice and other provisions in order to despatch it; and that the latter had begun preparations, but not having managed to bring the matter to the point that he had promised, the enterprise was dragged on and left in that condition. What happened after these events is that Taicosama was seized with a severe sickness in Miaco and died, not without having first had time to dispose of the succession and government of his kingdom, and to see that the empire should be continued in his only son, who was ten years old at that time. For this purpose he fixed his choice on the greatest tono in Japon, called Yeyasudono, lord of Quanto—which are certain provinces in the north—who had children and grandchildren, and more influence and power in Japon than any other man in the kingdom. Taicosama summoned Yeyasudono to court, and told him that he wished to marry his son to the latter's granddaughter, the daughter of his eldest son, so that he might succeed to the empire. The marriage was celebrated, and the government of Japon left, until his son was older, to Yeyasudono, associated with Guenifuin, Fungen, Ximonojo, and Xicoraju, his special favorites and counselors, [125] to whose hands the affairs of his government had passed for some years, in order that thus united they might continue to administer them after his death, until his son, whom he left named and accepted by the kingdom as his successor and supreme lord of Japon, was old enough to rule in person. After the death of Taicosama in the year one thousand five hundred and ninety-nine, [126] the five governors kept his son carefully watched in the fortress of Usaca, with the service and pomp due his person, while they remained at Miaco at the head of the government for some time. Consequently the pretensions of Faranda Quiemon to make an expedition against Manila ceased altogether, and nothing more was said about the matter. Since the affairs of Japon are never settled, but have always been in a disturbed condition, they could not last many days as Taico left them. For, with the new administration and the arrival at court, from other provinces of Japon, of tonos, lords, captains, and soldiers, whom the combaco in his lifetime had kept busy in the wars with Coray [i.e., Corea] and the king of China, in order to divert them from the affairs of his kingdom, the men began to become restless and corrupt. The result was that the four governors entertained suspicions of, and quarreled with, Yeyasudono, for they feared from his manner of governing and procedure that he was preparing, on account of his power, to seize the empire for himself, and to exclude and take no notice of Taico's son, who had been married to his granddaughter. The flame burned still higher, for many tonos and lords of the kingdom felt the same way about the matter; and now, either because they desired the succession of Taico's son, or because they liked to see matters in disorder so that each one might act for his own interest— which was the most likely motive, and not the affection for Taicosama, who, being a tyrant, had been feared rather than loved—they persuaded the governors to oppose Yeyasudono and check his designs. Under this excitement, the opposition became so lively, that they completely declared themselves, and Yeyasudono found it convenient to leave the kingdom of Miaco and go to his lands of Quanto, in order to insure his own safety and return to the capital with large forces with which to demand obedience. The governors, understanding his intentions, were not idle, but collected men and put two hundred thousand soldiers in the field. They were joined by most of the tonos and lords of Japon, [127] both Christian and pagan, while the minority remained among the partisans and followers of Yeyasudono. The latter came down as speedily as possible from Quanto to meet the governors and their army, in order to give them battle with one hundred thousand picked men of his own land. The two armies met, and the battle was fought with all their forces. [128] In the course of the struggle, there were various fortunes, which rendered the result doubtful. But, finally, after a number of men had deserted from the camp of the governors to that of Yeyasudono, it was perceived that the latter's affairs were improving. Victory was declared in his favor, after the death of many soldiers and lords. Those who remained—for but few escaped—including the four governors, surrendered to Yeyasudono. After he had beheaded the majority of the tonos, and deprived others of their seigniories and provinces, which he granted again to men devoted to his party; and after his return to the capital, triumphant over his enemies, and master of the whole kingdom: he inflicted special punishment upon the governors, by having them crucified immediately, and their ears cut off, and then carried through the streets of the principal cities of Usaca, Sacay, Fugimen, and Miaco, in carts, until they died on the crosses in the midst of other tortures. Since these were the men through whose zeal and advice Taico had, a few years before, inflicted the same punishment upon the discalced friars whom he martyred, we may infer that God chose to punish them in this world also with the same rigor.

Thus Yeyasudono remained the supreme ruler of Japon as Taico had been, but failed to withdraw the son from the fortress of Usaca; on the contrary he set more guards over him. Then, changing his own name, as is usual among the seigniors of Japon, he styled himself Daifusama for the sake of greater dignity.

Fray Geronymo de Jesus, associate of the martyrs, who kept hidden in Japon on account of the tyrant Taicosama's persecution, lived in disguise in the interior of the country among the Christians. Consequently, although he was carefully sought, he could not be found, until, after Taicosama's death and Daifu's seizure of the government, he came to Miaco. He found means to reveal himself to one of Dayfu's servants, to whom he told many things about the Filipinas, the king of Espana, and the latter's kingdoms and seigniories, especially those of Nueva Espana and Peru, of which the Filipinas were a dependency and with whom they had communication, and the importance to Daifu of gaining the friendship and commerce of the Spaniards. The servant found an opportunity to relate all these things to Daifu, who for some time had desired to have the trade and commerce which the Portuguese had established in Nangasaqui in his own kingdoms of Quanto, of which he was the natural lord, in order to give it more importance. Thinking that this could be accomplished through the means which Fray Geronymo had suggested, he had the latter summoned. Having asked him his name, Fray Geronymo told the king that after the martyrdom of his associates, he had remained in Japon, that he was one of the religious whom the governor of Manila had sent when Taicosama was alive, to treat of peace and friendship with the Spaniards, and who had died as was well known, after having made converts to Christianity and established several hospitals and houses at the capital and other cities of Japon, where they healed the sick and performed other works of piety, without asking any other reward or advantage than to serve God, to teach the souls of that kingdom the faith and path of salvation, and to serve their neighbors. In this work, and in works of charity, especially to the poor, as he and his fellow religious professed, they lived and maintained themselves, without seeking or holding any goods or property upon the earth, solely upon the alms which were given them therefor. After this, he told him who the king of Espana was, that he was a Christian, and that he possessed great kingdoms and territories in all parts of the world; and that Nueva Espana, Piru, Filipinas, and India, belonged to him; and that he governed and defended them all, attending above all else to the growth and conservation of the faith of our Lord Jesus Christ, the true God, and Creator of the universe. The religious explained to the king, as well as he could, other things concerning the Christian religion, and said that if he wished friendship with his Majesty and the latter's subjects of Manila, as well as with his viceroys of Nueva Espana and Piru he [i.e., Fray Geronymo] would be able to compass it, for it would be very useful and profitable to the king and to all his Japanese kingdoms and provinces. This last motive, namely, the profit and benefit to be derived from friendship and commerce with the Spaniards, was more to the taste of Daifusama than what he had heard concerning their religion. Although he did not reject the latter or say anything about it, yet at this interview and at others with Fray Geronymo—whom Daifu had given permission to appear in public in his religious habit, and to whom he furnished the necessary support— he treated only of friendship with the governor of Manila, of the Spaniards' coming yearly with ships from Manila to trade at Quanto, where the Japanese had a port, and an established commerce with the Spaniards. Also his Japanese were to sail thence to Nueva Espana, where they were to enjoy the same amity and trade. As he understood the voyage to be long and Spanish ships necessary for it, Daifu proposed that the governor of Manila send him masters and workmen to build them. He also proposed that in the said kingdom and principal port of Quanto, which, as above-said, lies in the north of Japon, and is a mountainous country, abounding in silver mines, which were not worked because no one knew how, Fray Geronymo and whatever associates he might choose from among the Spaniards who came there, should establish their house and dwelling, just as the religious of the Society of Jesus had theirs with the Portuguese in Nangasaqui. Fray Geronymo, who desired by any means to restore the cause of his religious, and of the conversion of Japon through their labor, as they had begun to do when the martyrs were alive—for this aim alone moved him—did not doubt that he could once and many times facilitate Daifusama's desires, and even assured him that they would certainly be realized through his help, and that there would be no difficulty whatever to prevent this. Thereupon Daifu appeared favorable and more inclined to the affairs of Manila than Taico, his predecessor, had been. He assured the religious that he would give the Spaniards a good reception in Japon, and that the ships, which should happen to put in there in distress or in any other way, would be equipped and despatched with all necessities; and that he would not allow any Japanese to go to plunder or commit any injury on the coasts of the Filipinas. In fact, because he learned that six ships of Japanese corsairs had sailed that year from the island of Zazuma [Satsuma] and other ports of the lower kingdoms, and had seized and plundered two Chinese merchantmen on the way to Manila, and had done other mischief on its coast, he immediately had them sought out in his kingdom. Having imprisoned more than four hundred men, he had them all crucified. Likewise he ordered that, in the future, the annual ships from Nangasaqui to Manila laden with flour and other goods should not be so numerous, but only enough to supply Manila, and that they should have the permission and sanction of its governor, so that they might not be the cause of loss or injury to that place.

Since Daifu pressed Fray Geronymo more and more every day for the fulfilment of what he had taken upon himself, the latter told him that he had already written and would write again about those matters to the governor and royal Audiencia of Manila. He requested Daifu to send a servant of his household with these letters and the message, in order that they might have more credit and authority. Daifu approved of this and despatched them through Captain Chiquiro, a pagan Japanese and a servant of his, who took a present of various weapons to the governor and the letters of Fray Geronymo. There was no special letter from Daifu, except that Fray Geronymo said that he wrote and petitioned in the name of Daifu. He explained the better condition of peace and friendship now existing between the Filipinas and Japon, and what Daifu promised and assured. He wrote that, in order to facilitate the above, Daifu had promised him that the Spaniards could go with their ships to trade at Quanto, and that the governor should send him masters and workmen to build ships for the voyage from Japon to Nueva Espana. There was also to be commerce and friendship with the viceroy of that country. He said that Daifu had already given leave for religious to go to Japon, to christianize and to found churches and monasteries, and had given him a good site for a monastery in Miaco, where he was, and that the same would be done in other parts and regions of Japon in which they might wish to settle. Fray Geronymo insidiously and cunningly added this last to Daifu's promise in order that he might incite the religious of the Filipinas to push the matter more earnestly before the governor and Audiencia, that they might agree to this more easily, in order not to lose the great results that Fray Geronymo said were set afoot.

During the same administration of Don Francisco Tello, in the year one thousand six hundred, toward the end of the month of October, a ship came from the province of Camarines with news that two ships, a flagship and its almiranta, well armed and with foreign crews, had entered and anchored in one of its northern bays, twenty leguas from the channel and cape of Espiritu Sancto. Under pretense of being friends of the Spaniards they asked, and bartered with, the natives for rice and other provisions that they needed. Then they weighed anchor and went away, making for the channel through which they entered, after having left certain feigned letters for Governor Don Francisco Tello, in which they declared themselves friends, and that they were coming to Manila to trade by permission of his Majesty. From this, and from a negro who escaped from these ships by swimming to the island of Capul, and also through an Englishman, [129] seized by the natives while on shore, we learned that these ships were from Holanda, whence they had sailed in a convoy of three other armed vessels, with patents and documents from Count Mauricio de Nasao who called himself Prince of Orange, in order to make prizes in the Indias. [130] Having entered the South Sea through the strait of Magallanes, three of the five ships had been lost, and these two, the flagship and the almiranta coasted along Chile, where they captured two vessels. Then, having turned away from the coast of Lima, they put out to sea and pursued their voyage, without stopping anywhere, in the direction of the Filipinas, among which they entered with the intention of plundering whatever might come their way. Having learned that a galleon, named "Santo Tomas" was expected from Nueva Espana with the money derived from the merchandise of two years' cargoes which had been sent there from Manila; that in a few days merchant ships would begin to arrive from China, by which they could fill their hands; and that there were no galleys or armed ships at that season which could do them any harm: they determined to go as far as the mouth of Manila

Bay, and stay there, supplying themselves with the provisions and re-freshments which might enter the city; and accordingly, they carried out this resolution. The flagship named "Mauricio," with one hundred men and twenty-four pieces of bronze artillery with ladles [131] was under the command of Oliber de Nort [i.e., Oliver van Noordt] of Amstradam. This ship was one of those which the count of Leste had several years before at the taking of the city of Cadiz. [132] The almiranta named "Con-cordia," with forty men and ten pieces of artillery, was under command of Captain Lamberto Viesman of Roterdam. When these ships were seen on the coast of Chile, Viceroy Don Luis de Velasco, who was governor in Piru, despatched a fleet of vessels well equipped with artillery and brave soldiers to follow and pursue them along the coast of Piru and Nueva Espana, as far as California. The fleet left Callao de Lima, under command of Don Joan de Velasco, but was unable to find the enemy, as they had left the coast, put out to sea, and steered for the Filipinas. Moreover the Piru fleet, having been overtaken by a storm on its way back from California, lost its flagship with all hands aboard and was never seen again.

Governor Don Francisco Tello, seeing that this corsair was making incursions among the islands, according to the information given him by certain captains and soldiers whom he had sent by land along the coasts of the island of Luzon, in order to prevent the enemy from landing men and from injuring the settlements, and from the information given by certain small single boats which had kept in sight of the enemy, discussed plans for meeting this necessity. This it appeared very difficult to do on that occasion, not only because the governor found himself without any kind of rowing vessels or ships with high freeboard, with which to put to sea, but also because he had few soldiers in the camp, for the majority of them were with Captain and Sargento-mayor Joan Xuarez Gallinato in the Pintados provinces, together with galleys, galliots, and other craft, for the purpose of defending the natives against the ships of the Mindanaos and Joloans, who were continually making plundering expeditions against them, and of preparing for the expedition which it was thought would be made from Jolo at the first monsoon, and which could no longer be de-ferred. When the governor saw himself hard pressed by this difficulty, and that the Dutch enemy could cause so much harm, take so many prizes, and then depart with them, leaving the country ruined, he sum-moned the Audiencia and communicated the state of affairs to them, requesting the auditors to assist him in person in any advisable course. They discussed what should be done, namely, to put the port of Cabit, which is inside the bay, into a state of defense, in order to prevent the enemy from seizing it, together with the magazines, artillery, and shipyard; then to endeavor to equip several ships with which to put to sea and offer some resistance to the enemy—even if no more could be done—so that he might not firmly establish himself in the land, and that he might be induced to leave the islands. For, if the enemy found everything so defenseless and if no resistance were offered him, he would remain there until he attained his designs. The execution of these measures was entrusted to Doctor Antonio de Morga. Licentiate Telles de Almacan was ordered to remain in the city with the governor and president for its defense, and to supply thence the port of Cabit and Doctor Antonio de Morga with what was necessary for the latter's commission. On the same day, the last of October of the year six hundred, Doctor Antonio de Morga left Manila with some soldiers and ammunition and went to the port of Cabit, which he put in a state of defense with one hundred and fifty men, both arquebusiers and musketeers, who kept continual watch day and night over the port, by means of sentinels and outposts at the necessary points. He collected at the settlement all the vessels in port, and stationed them as near as possible to the shipyards, where a galizabra was being built, and where lay a ship of Sebu with a small Portuguese patache, the latter of which had come from Malaca laden with merchandise. For the defense of these he placed and planted on shore twelve pieces of moderate-sized bronze cannon with ladles, besides two of greater range, which were placed on a point at the entrance of the port. These altogether commanded the port and the vessels in it. Farther on along the beach, a rampart was made with stakes and planks, filled in with earth, behind which, in case the enemy should enter, the soldiery could cover and defend themselves with their artillery. After the auditor had thus put the said port in a state of defense, he planned to complete the galizabra, although much work was still needed, to launch it, and fit it with sails, and at the same time to refit the Sebu ship. He attended to these works with so great haste that within thirty days he hoisted the yards on the galizabra and on the Sebu ship, and furnished each of the two with eleven pieces of artillery, both of large and moderate size, which had been sent from Manila, in addition to the artillery in the port.

The corsair reached the mouth of the bay, eight leguas from the port of Cabit, but did not dare to make a dash into the port, as he had planned, for he learned from some Sangleys who were going out to sea with their champans, that it was already defended. However, he was not informed that the Spaniards were arming to attack him, or that there was any preparation or forces at that season for that purpose. Accordingly he contented himself with remaining at the mouth of the bay, moving about with both ships and their boats, and going from one side to another on various days, in order to seize the vessels coming to the city with provisions, and not allowing one to escape him. At night he anchored under shelter of the land. All this took place four leguas from the mouth of the bay, and he went no farther from it, in order to be ready for any occasion that might present itself.

Doctor Antonio de Morga kept several very small and swift vessels within sight of the enemy, under shelter of the land, which informed him daily of the enemy's position and doings. They reported that he had quietly stationed himself, and that every evening he placed his guard on deck with drums and flags, and firing of musketry. The corsair's forces could be estimated from that and it could be seen that the larger and better contingent was aboard the flagship, which was a good and swift ship. The auditor also took the precaution not to let any champan or ship leave the bay, in order not to give the corsair an opportunity to learn what was going on. When affairs reached this point, he informed the governor of what had been done, and suggested that, if the latter thought it advisable, the Portuguese vessel might also be equipped, in order to sally out with the two ships—the galizabra and the "Sant Antonio" of Sebu—for he had laid an embargo on it, and had fitted it for that purpose. Ammunition and some provisions of rice and fish were providedfor the two ships, and it remained only to man them with sailors and soldiers who were to go out in them. Of such there was little supply; the sailors were hiding and feigning sickness, and one and all showed little desire to undertake an affair of more risk and peril than of personal profit. The captains and private soldiers of the city, who were receiving neither pay nor rations from the king, but who could go on the expedition, did not offer their services to the governor; and if anyone were ready to do so, he dissembled until knowing who was to be commander of the fleet. For, although some land captains might fill the place, the governor was not inclined to appoint any of them, nor were the others willing to go under their command. Each one claimed and boasted himself capable of being the leader, and none other of his neighbors was to have command. The governor was prevented from going out in person, and learned that all the people of the city were willing to go with Doctor Antonio de Morga if he had command of the fleet, and would not mind any dangers that might present themselves. When the governor learned the desire of those who were able to embark, and understood that there was no other means by which to realize the aim in view, and that each day's delay was of very great detriment, he summoned the auditor to the city and set the matter before him. In order that the latter might not refuse, the governor issued an act and had the auditor immediately notified by the secretary of the government and ordered, on behalf of his Majesty, to embark as general and commander of the fleet and to follow and pursue the corsair, because, as matters stood, the suitable result could not be attained otherwise. The auditor, thinking that, if he failed to take up the matter, he would receive the blame of losing so pressing an occasion for the service of God and his Majesty, and for the welfare of the whole country; and, since war affairs both of sea and of land had been under his charge and management, that it might be reckoned ill against him if he turned his back at this juncture, when he had been sought for it and served especially with papers from the governor, appointing him to the charge: obeyed for the discharge of his conscience the orders set forth in the governor's act, which together with his answer reads word for word as follows.

> Edict of Governor Don Francisco Tello, and reply of Doctor Antonio de Morga
>
> In the city of Manila, on the first of December, one thousand six hundred, Don Francisco Tello, knight of the Order of Santiago, governor and captain-general of these Filipinas Islands, and president of the royal Audiencia resident therein, declared: That, whereas, because of the coming to these islands of two hostile English [sic] ships, the preparation of a fleet to attack them was immediately discussed with the resolution and advice of the royal Audiencia, and for this effect it was resolved that Antonio de Morga should go to the port of Cabit to attend to the fitting and despatch of the said war-vessels and the defense of that port, as appears, by the act and resolution made thereon, in the book of the government matters pertaining to this said Audiencia, on the last day of the month of October, of this present year, and to which we refer; and whereas, in execution of the said resolution, he has attended until now, to the defense of the said port, and the fitting and equipping of the said fleet, consisting of the vessel "San Diego," [133] of Sebu, the galleon "San Bartolome," which he caused to be finished in the shipyard and launched, an English [134] patache from the city of Malaca, a galliot which was fitted up, and other smaller craft; and whereas, the said fleet, because of his diligence and care, is in so good condition that it can shortly sail, and the said enemy is still near this city, on the coast of the island of Miraveles [i.e., Corregidor]; and whereas, many captains, knights, and chief men of this community have heard that

119

the said auditor was to make the said expedition, they have offered to go with him to serve the king, our sovereign, in it at their own expense; and whereas, a great preparation of men and provisions has been made with this intent, which would fail and be of no effect did the said auditor not sail with the said fleet in pursuit of the said enemy, and would not have the result aimed at—a matter so greatly to the service of God our Lord, and the welfare of this country— and whereas, moreover, the said auditor is (as is a fact) experienced in matters of war, and has been general of his Majesty's fleets by the latter's own appointment at other times, and lieutenant of the captain-general in this kingdom for several years, in which he has fulfilled his duties well; and whereas he is highly esteemed and liked by the soldiers; and whereas he is the most suitable man, according to the condition of affairs; and for other just considerations that move the governor thereto, so that the said expedition may be effected and not fall through, or at least, so that it may not be delayed with loss and trouble: therefore he ordered—and he did so order—the said auditor, since he has fostered this affair, and has personally put it in its present good shape, and since all the men—and they are many—who receive no pay, have prepared in consideration of him, to prepare himself to go as general and commander of the said fleet in pursuit of the enemy, with all possible haste. For this the governor said that he would give him the necessary messages and instructions, for thus is it advantageous to the service of the king our sovereign. In the name of the latter, the governor orders him to do and accomplish the above. He [i.e., the governor] as president of the said royal Audiencia, grants him leave and absence for the above during the time that he shall occupy himself therein, from attendance on his duties in the said royal Audiencia. He gave him the commission in due legal form, and authority for the said absence. Thus he provided and ordered, and affixed his signature thereto.

DON FRANCISCO TELLO

Before me:
GASPAR DE AZEBO

In the city of Manila, on the first of December, of the year one thousand six hundred, I, the government notary, served the above act upon Doctor Antonio de Morga, auditor of the royal Audiencia. He declared that, from the first day of the month of November just expired, by commission of the royal Audiencia of these islands, he has busied himself in everything mentioned in the said act, and has done his utmost toward its execution; that the expedition is on the good footing and in the condition that is known; that if, for its good result and for what is expected from it, his person and property are suitable and fitting for the service of the king our sovereign, he is ready to employ everything in it and to do what has been ordered and commanded him by the said president; and that consequently he has no other wish or desire than for what might be to the service of God and of his Majesty. Thereupon may your Lordship order and provide what may be found most expedient, and as such he will fulfil it. He affixed his signature to this writ.

DOCTOR ANTONIO DE MORGA
GASPAR DE AZEBO

Doctor Antonio de Morga provided himself with all that was requisite for the expedition without asking or taking anything from the king's exchequer. He aided several needy soldiers who came to offer their services, and many other persons of importance who had done the same, so that, within one week, there were already enough men for the expedition, and an abundance of provisions, ship's stores, and arms; whereupon all embarked. With the volunteers and regulars whom the governor had in camp under Captain Augustin de Urdiales, and whom he gave to the auditor, there were men enough to man both ships each with about one hundred soldiers in addition to gunners, sailors, and common seamen, of the last mentioned of whom there was a smaller supply than was needed. As admiral of this fleet the governor appointed Captain Joan de Alcega, an old soldier, and one well acquainted with the islands; as captain of the paid soldiers who were to sail in the almiranta, Joan Tello y Aguirre; as sargento-mayor of the fleet, Don Pedro Tello, his kinsman; the necessary other offices and positions; and the nomination and title of general of the fleet to Doctor Antonio de Morga. He gave the latter closed and sealed instructions concerning what he was to do in the course of the voyage and expedition, with orders not to open them until he had put to sea, outside of the bay of Manila. The instructions read as follows.

* * * * *

Instructions given by the governor to Doctor Antonio de Morga

What Doctor Antonio de Morga, auditor of the royal Audiencia of these Filipinas Islands, and captain-general of the fleet which is about to pursue the English [sic] enemy, has to do, is as follows.

First, inasmuch as we have been informed that the English [sic] enemy, against whom this fleet has been prepared, lies in the bay of Maryuma, [135] it is ordered that, lest perchance the enemy hearing of our fleet should try to escape without receiving any injury, the fleet sail as quickly as possible in his pursuit, in order to engage and fight him until, through the grace of our Lord, he be taken or sunk.

Item: If, in fighting the said enemy both with artillery and in grappling—and this shall be attempted with all the diligence and care possible—whichever the weather may better and more conveniently permit, the latter should take to flight at sight of the fleet, he shall be pursued until the desired result is attained.

Item: If, at the time that the fleet sails to attack the said enemy he shall have left this coast and news is received that he has coasted to any other of these islands, the fleet shall follow and pursue him until he is taken or sunk. If the enemy has left these islands, the fleet shall pursue him as far as possible; but this is left to your own discretion so long as the object be attained.

Item: Inasmuch as the opinion was expressed in a council of war held on the second day of the present month and year, by the master-of-camp and the captains who were present, that, if there were no certain information of the course and direction taken by the enemy, the said fleet should follow the coast of Ilocos, and make for the strait of Sincapura, through which it is presumed that the enemy will pass in order to pursue his voyage: notwithstanding the said council of war, if the said general should not receive any information as to the course taken by the enemy, then he shall do what he thinks most expedient, as the one in charge of the affair, and as the enemy and the occasion allow, endeavoring to obtain the desired object, namely, the overtaking and destruction of the enemy.

Item: If the fleet should encounter any other hostile pirates or any others going about these islands or who shall have left them after doing them injury, whether they be English, Japanese, Terrenatans, Mindanaos, or others, it shall endeavor to chastise and injure them, so that should this occur a good result might also be obtained therefrom.

Item: If the enemy be captured, as is hoped through the grace of God our Lord, the survivors and ships shall be brought in by the fleet.

Item: Any spoil found in the said ships shall be divided as is customary, among the victors.

Item: Great care shall be exercised to keep the men of the fleet peaceable and well disciplined; concerning this, the course taken on similar occasions shall be followed.

Item: A good system in regard to the provisions and ammunition carried shall be observed, and the use of them all well moderated, especially should the fleet leave sight of these islands.

Item: If perchance, after having engaged the said enemy or pursued him, he should leave these islands, then, the object having been accomplished, you shall endeavor to return as speedily as possible to the islands. If the weather do not permit a return until the monsoon sets in, you shall endeavor to keep the fleet together and to supply and provide it with everything necessary, at the expense of his Majesty, so that you may pursue your voyage with the greatest speed and safety possible. Given in the city of Manila, the tenth of December of the year one thousand six hundred.

DON FRANCISCO TELLO
By order of the governor and captain-general:
GASPAR DE AZEBO

The auditor went to the port with all his men and put them aboard the two ships. As flagship he took the "Sant Antonio" of Sebu, on account of its having more room to accommodate the assistants [gente de cumplimiento] who embarked with him. He left the Portuguese patache because the governor had taken off the embargo, in order to allow the Portuguese to return with it to Malaca without loss of time. Then he equipped two caracoas for the service of the fleet with Indian crews and two Spaniards to direct them. After they had confessed and taken communion, they left the port of Cabit and set sail on the twelfth day of the month of December of the year one thousand six hundred, with Alonzo Gomez as chief pilot. They also took Father Diego de Santiago and a lay brother of the Society of Jesus, and Fray Francisco de Valdes of the Order of Augustine, aboard the flagship; and Fray Joan Gutierrez [136] and another associate of the same order aboard the almiranta, so that they might attend to whatever required their ministry.

At night of the same day both ships of this fleet anchored near the settlement and anchorage of the island of Miraveles at the mouth of the bay. Immediately at daybreak a barangai approached the ships from shore with the sentinels whom the auditor had hastily sent the day before to obtain some reliable news of the corsair's position. They told him that, as soon as the fleet sailed from the port of Cabit, the enemy, who lay in the direction of the port Del Fraile [of the Friar], [137] had also weighed anchor, and having stowed their small boats, both ships had crossed to the other and sea side, and that they had seen him anchor after nightfall opposite the point of Valeitegui, [138] where he still was. Upon hearing this, the auditor thought that perhaps the corsair had been informed of the preparation of the fleet and of its departure, and had consequently weighed anchor from his position; and that, since he had stowed his small boats aboard the ships, he was about to put to sea to avoid the fleet. He immediately sent the same news to the admiral, and opened the instructions given him by the governor. Seeing that he was ordered thereby to seek the enemy with all diligence, pursue him, and endeavor to fight him, he thought best to shorten the work before him, and to lose no time and not allow the enemy to get farther away. With this object in view, the fleet spent the thirteenth of December, St. Lucy's day, in making waist-cloths, arranging the artillery, getting ready the weapons, alloting men to their posts, and preparing themselves to fight on the next day, on which it was thought that they would fall in with the corsair. The auditor sent special instructions in writing to the admiral concerning what he was to do and observe on his part. These instructions specified chiefly that upon engaging with the enemy, both ships were to grapple and fight the corsair's flagship—in which were carried all the forces—and other things which will be understood from the instructions given to the admiral. These were as follows.*

At the same time the auditor notified the admiral that the fleet would weigh anchor from its anchorage shortly after midnight, and would go out of the bay to sea, crowding all sail possible, so that at dawn

---

* These instructions are given in VOL. XI of this series, pp. 145-148.

it might be off the point of Baleitigui to windward of the point where the enemy had anchored on Tuesday night, according to the sentinels' report.

At the appointed hour both vessels—the flagship and the almiranta—weighed anchor from Miraveles, and, favored by a light wind, sailed the rest of the night toward Baleitigui. The two caracoas used as tenders could not follow because of a choppy sea, and a fresh north-wester; they crossed within the bay, and under shelter of the land to the other side. At the first streak of light both vessels of the fleet found themselves off the point; and one legua to leeward, and seaward, they sighted the corsair's two vessels riding at anchor. As soon as the latter recognized our ships and saw that they flung captain's and admiral's colors at the masthead, they weighed anchor and set sail from their anchorage, after having first reenforced the flagship with a boatload of men from their almiranta, which stood to sea, while the flagship hove to, and awaited our fleet, firing several pieces at long range. The flagship of our fleet being unable to answer the enemy with its artillery because the gun-ports were shut, and the vessel was tacking to starboard, determined to close with him. It grappled his flagship on the port side, sweeping and clearing the decks of the men on them. Then the colors with thirty soldiers and a few sailors were thrown aboard. They took possession of the forecastle and after-cabin and captured their colors at masthead and quarter, and the white, blue, and orange standard with the arms of Count Mauricio flung at the stern. The main- and mizzen-mast were stripped of all the rigging and sails, and a large boat which the enemy carried on the poop was captured. The enemy, who had retreated to the bows below the harpings, upon seeing two ships attacking him with so great resolution, sent to ask the auditor for terms of surrender. While an answer was being given him, Admiral Joan de Alcega, who, in accordance with the instructions given him the day previous by the auditor, ought to have grappled at the same time as the flagship, and lashed his vessel to the enemy, thinking that the victory was won, that the corsair's almiranta was escaping, and that it would be well to capture it, left the flagship and followed astern of Lamberto Viezman, crowding all sail and chasing him until he overtook him. Oliber de Nort, seeing himself alone and with a better ship and artillery than the auditor's, waited no longer for the answer to the terms for which he had asked at first, and renewed the fight with musketry and artillery. The combat between the two flagships was so obstinate and bitter on both sides that it lasted more than six hours, and many were killed on both sides. But the corsair had the worst of it all the time, for not more than fifteen of his men were left alive, and those badly maimed and wounded. [139] Finally the corsair's ship caught fire, and the flames rose high by the mizzen-mast and in the stern. The auditor, in order not to endanger his own ship, found it necessary to recall his colors and men from the enemy's ship, and to cast loose and separate from it. This he did, only to discover that his ship, from the pounding of the artillery during so long a combat, as it was but slightly strengthened, had an opening in the bows and was filling so rapidly that being unable to overcome the leak, it was foundering. The corsair seeing his opponent's trouble and his inability to follow him, made haste with his few remaining men to extinguish the fire on board his ship. Having quenched it, he set his foresail, which was still left. Shattered in all parts, stripped of rigging, and without men he reached Borneo and Sunda, where he was seen so enfeebled and distressed that it seemed impossible for him to navigate, or to go farther without shipwreck. The Spanish flagship, which was fully occupied in trying to remedy the extremity to which it was reduced, could not be assisted, because it was alone and far from land, and consequently sank so rapidly that the men could neither disarm themselves, nor get hold of anything which might be of help to them. The auditor did not abandon the ship, although some soldiers, in order to escape therein, seized the boat at the stern, and asked him also to get into it. Thereupon they made off and went away, in order to prevent others from taking it away from them. When the ship sunk, the auditor swam constantly for four hours, with the quarter colors and the enemy's standard which he took with him. He reached a very small desert island, two leguas away, called Fortuna, where a few of the ship's men who had more endurance in the sea, also arrived in safety. Some perished and were drowned, for they had not even disarmed themselves, and whom this predicament had overtaken when exhausted by the long fight with the enemy. Those who met death on this occasion were fifty in all. The most important among them were Captains Don Francisco de Mendoca, Gregorio de Vargas, Francisco Rodriguez, and Gaspar de los Rios, [140] all of whom died fighting with the enemy. Among those drowned at sea were Captains Don Joan de Camudio, Augustin de Urdiales, Don Pedro Tello, Don Gabriel Maldonado, Don Cristoval de Heredia, Don Luis de Belver, Don Alonso Locano, Domingo de Arrieta, Melchior de Figueroa, Chief-pilot Alonso Gomez, father Fray Diego de Santiago, and the brother who went with him. Admiral Joan de Alcega, having overtaken Lamberto Viezman slightly after midday, captured him with little resistance; and although he afterward saw the so battered ship of Oliber del Nort pass by and escaping at a short distance, he did not pursue him. On the contrary, without stopping longer, he returned with his almiranta to Miraveles, leaving the prize with some of his own men, whom he had put aboard it, to follow him. He neither looked for his flagship nor took any other step, imagining that if any mishap had occurred, he might be blamed for leaving the flagship alone with the corsair and pursuing Lambert Biezman without orders from the auditor, and contrary to the instructions given him in writing; and fearing lest if he were to rejoin the auditor after having left him, ill would befall himself. The auditor took the wounded and the men who had escaped from the islet of Fortun, at nightfall, in his ship's boat which he found at that port, as well as the corsair's boat and a caracoa which arrived there. And on the following day, he landed them in Luzon, at the bar of Anazibu, in the province of Balayan, [141] thirty leguas from Manila, where he supplied them with provisions as quickly as possible. Moreover he explored the coast and neighboring islands with swift boats, in search of his almiranta and the captured corsair. This prize was taken to Manila, with twenty-five men alive and the admiral, ten pieces of artillery, and a quantity of wine, oil, cloth, linen, weapons, and other goods which it carried. The admiral and the Dutchmen of his company were garroted by orders of the governor. [142] Thus ended the expedition. Thereby was averted the injury which it was thought that the corsair would inflict in these seas, had he been allowed to remain there with the aim that he cherished, although so much to the detriment of the Spaniards by the loss of their flagship, which would not have happened had the orders of the auditor been observed. Governor Don Francisco Tello presented an attestation of this event to the auditor, which is as follows.

* * * * *

Attestation of Governor Don Francisco Tello of events in the expedition against the Dutch corsair

Don Francisco Tello, knight of the Order of Santiago, governor and captain-general in these Filipinas Islands, and president of the Audiencia and royal Chancilleria resident therein, etc.: I certify to whomever may see this present, that last year, one thousand six hundred, a squadron of Dutch war-vessels under command of Oliber del Nort, after passing through the strait of Magallanes to the South Sea, reached these islands, in the month of October of the said year, with two armed ships. They entered among these islands, making prizes and committing depredations, and at length stationed themselves off the entrance of the bay of the city of Manila, with the design of lying in wait for the merchant ships from China, and for the galleon "Santo Tomas," expected from Nueva Espana with the silver of two years belonging to the merchants of this kingdom. By a decision of the said royal Audiencia, on the thirty-first of October of the said year, Doctor Antonio de Morga, senior auditor of the said Audiencia, was commissioned and charged to go immediately to the port of Cabit, and place and hold it in a state of defense, and to prepare and equip a fleet to attack the corsair. In this matter the said auditor busied himself in person. Having, with great assiduity and industry, fortified and put the said port in a state of defense, he completed in the shipyard and then launched, a moderate-sized ship, armed and equipped another belonging to private persons then in the port, both of which he equipped with yards and rigging—all inside of forty days. In order that the expedition might be made more quickly, and with a supply of soldiers and the most necessary equipment, inasmuch as affairs were such that it could be done by no one else, on the first of December of the same year, I nominated and appointed the said auditor to sail as general of the fleet in pursuit of the enemy, and to fight him until destroying and driving him from these islands. The said auditor performed and accomplished this in the following manner. On the twelfth of the said month of December, he sailed with the two ships of his fleet from the port of Cabit; on the fourteenth of the same month, at dawn, he sighted the corsair outside of the bay of this city, off the promontory of Baleitigui, with his two ships— flagship and almiranta. He pursued the enemy until he came close to him; and both fleets having prepared for action, engaged one another. The said auditor in his flagship attacked the corsair's flagship with great gallantry and resolution, and grappled it. The latter was a large and strong ship, carrying a quantity of artillery and many fighting men. The auditor immediately threw on board the enemy the infantry colors with thirty arquebusiers and a few volunteers and sailors, who captured the forecastle, after-cabin, and the colors of the vessel. At the end of the action, these men retreated to our ship on account of the violent fire which at the last began to rage aboard the enemy's ship. Thereupon the action and fight continued on both sides, and lasted more than six hours, during which the artillery, musketry, and arquebuses were repeatedly discharged in all quarters. In another direction the enemy's almiranta, commanded by Lamberto Viezman, was defeated and captured, with the crew, artillery and other things aboard it. The two flagships having cast loose and separated on ac-

count of the fire which had broken out, and the quantity
of water that poured in our bows, the enemy took to flight
with only the foremast standing, with nearly all his men
killed, and having lost his boat, the standard and the colors
at his masthead and quarter. Stripped of his yards, sails,
and rigging, and the ship leaking in many places, the enemy
ran before the wind. It has been heard from various
sources that he passed Borneo with only fifteen or sixteen
men alive, and most of them maimed and wounded, and
that a few days later, he was entirely wrecked not far from
the Sunda. [143] The said auditor and his companions suffered great hardship and danger; for besides several men of
note who died fighting, the ship which was leaking at the
bows as abovesaid, because of being weak and not built
for a war vessel, and as they were unable to stop or overcome the leak, foundered that same day, and part of the
men on board were drowned on account of being wearied
with fighting and not even yet having disarmed. When the
ship sunk, the said auditor, who would never leave or
abandon it, took to the water with the rest of the men, and
escaped by swimming, with some of the enemy's colors
about him, to an uninhabited islet, called Fortun, two
leguas from the place where the fight had taken place. The
next day he took away the people from that place in several small boats which he found, and landed them in safety
on this island. In all the above, the said auditor acted with
great diligence and valor, exposing himself to all the risks
of the battle and afterward of the sea. He did not receive
any reward for his services, nor any salary, expenses, or any
other recompense. On the contrary, he contributed and
spent his own property to provide all the necessary equipment for the said expedition, and also assisted some
volunteers who went with him. Of the booty taken from
the corsair's almiranta, which was brought to this city, he
refused to take nor did he take anything; on the contrary,
the share which should have fallen to him, he ceded and
passed over to the king, our sovereign, and to his royal exchequer. Thus our aim and object, namely, the destroying
and defeating of the said corsair, has been accomplished,
so much to the service of God and of his Majesty, and to
the welfare of this kingdom, as is more minutely set forth
by acts, depositions, and other inquiries concerning this

expedition. At the request of the said Doctor Antonio de Morga, I gave him the present, with my signature attached, and sealed with the seal of my arms. Given in Manila, August twenty-four, one thousand six hundred and one.

DON FRANCISCO TELLO

* * * * *

In the same year of one thousand six hundred, two merchantships left Manila for Nueva Espana: the flagship the "Sancta Margarita," with Juan Martinez de Guillestigui as general, who had arrived the year before in the same capacity; and the "San Geronimo," under Don Fernando de Castro. On their way, both ships met with storms in the latitude of thirty-eight degrees and at six hundred leguas from the Filipinas, and suffered great hardship. At the end of nine months at sea, after many of the men had died and much of the merchandise had been thrown overboard and lost, the "San Geronimo" put back to the Filipinas, off the islands of Catenduanes, outside of the channel of Espiritu Santo, and there was wrecked, although the crew were saved. The flagship "Sancta Margarita," after the death of the general and most of the crew, ported at the Ladrones Islands and anchored at Zarpana. There natives who went to the ships, seeing it so abandoned and battered, boarded and took possession of it, and of its goods and property. The few men whom they found alive, they took away to their settlements, where they killed some and apportioned others to various villages, where they maintained them and gave them better treatment. The Indians wore the gold chains and other things of the ship around their necks, and then hung them to the trees and in their houses, like people who had no knowledge of their value. [144]

In the month of May of the year six hundred and one, the galleon "Santo Tomas" arrived at the Filipinas from Nueva Espana with passengers, soldiers, and the return proceeds of the merchandise which had been delayed in Mexico. Its general was Licentiate Don Antonio de Ribera Maldonado, who had been appointed auditor of Manila. A small patache had sailed in company with the galleon from the port of Acapulco, but being unable to sail as rapidly as the "Santo Tomas," after a few days' voyage, it dropped behind. When they arrived off the Ladrones Islands, some natives went out, as usual, to meet the ship in their boats, and brought with them five Spaniards of the crew of the ship "Sancta Margarita," which had been lost there the year before. The loss of that vessel was learned from those men; also that as many as twenty-six Spaniards were living in the towns of those islands; and that if the ship would wait, the natives would bring them.

130

The religious and men with the general tried to persuade him, since the weather was calm, to wait in that place, in order to take these men from those islands, where they had lingered for a year. Certain more courageous persons even offered to go ashore to get them either in the galleon's boat or in the vessels of the Ladrones themselves. But the general would not allow this, believing that time would be lost, and his expedition exposed to peril. Without leave from the general, Fray Juan Pobre, a lay-brother, who was in charge of the discalced religious of St. Francis, who were coming on that occasion to the Filipinas, jumped into one of the Ladrones' vessels, and was taken by the Indians to the island of Guan, where he remained with the Spaniards whom he found. The galleon "Santo Tomas," without further delay, pursued its voyage, to the great grief and regret of the Spaniards on shore, who saw themselves left among those barbarians, where some of them died later of illness and other hardships. The galleon reached the Filipinas, making for the cape of Espiritu Santo and the harbor of Capul, at the conjunction of the moon and change of the weather. The land was so covered with thick fogs, that the ship was upon it before it was seen, nor did the pilots and sailors know the country or place where they were. They ran toward the Catenduanes, and entered a bay, called Catamban, [145] twenty leguas from the channel, where they found themselves embayed and with so much wind and sea astern of them, that the galleon ran upon some rocks near the land and came very near being wrecked that night with all aboard. At daybreak, the general went ashore with the small boat and had the ship made fast to some rocks. As the weather did not improve, and the ship was hourly in greater danger of being wrecked, and the cables with which it was made fast had given way, he determined to disembark the cargo there, and as quickly as possible, by means of the boat. They went to work immediately and took off the people, the silver, and the greater part of the goods and property, until, with native boats, the Spaniards and Indians of that province carried everything to Manila over a distance of eighty leguas, partly by sea and partly by land. They left the ship—a new and handsome one—wrecked there, without being able to derive any profit whatever from it.

The daring and audacity of the Mindanaos and Joloans in making incursions with their fleets into the islands of Pintados had reached such a state that it was now expected that they would come as far as Manila, plundering and devastating. In order to check them, at the beginning of the year six hundred and two, Governor Don Francisco Tello, deriving strength from weakness, determined that the expedition against Jolo should be made at once, without more delay, in order to punish and pacify it, with the forces and men whom Captain and Sargento-mayor Joan

Xuarez Gallinato held in Sebu and in the Pintados, together with more men, ships, and provisions, which were sent him, accompanied by the necessary documents and instructions for him to enter the island, chastise its king and inhabitants, and pacify and reduce it to the obedience of his Majesty. By this means, until there should be an opportunity to settle the affairs of Mindanao, which is quite near Jolo, the audacity of the enemy would be checked; and by bringing the war into his own country, he would not come out to commit depredations. Captain Gallinato set out on this expedition with two hundred Spanish soldiers, ships, artillery, enough provisions for four months—the time which it was thought the expedition would last—and with Indians as rowers for the ships and for other services that might arise. When he arrived at Jolo, at the bar of the river of this island, which is two leguas from the principal town and dwellings of the king, he landed his men, artillery, and the necessary provisions and left his ships under a sufficient guard. The islanders were all in the town and dwellings of the king, which are situated on a very high hill above some cliffs, and have two roads of approach through paths and roads so narrow that they can be reached only in single file. They had fortified the whole place, intrenched it with palms and other woods, and a number of culverins. They had also collected provisions and water for their sustenance, besides a supply of arquebuses and other weapons. They had neither women nor children with them, for they had taken them out of the island. They had requested aid from the people of Mindanao, Borney, and Terrenate, and were awaiting the same, since they had been informed of the fleet which was being prepared against them in the Pintados. Gallinato determined to pitch his camp near the town, before this aid should arrive, and to attack the fort. After he had quartered himself at a distance of one-half legua, in a plain facing the ascent, he sent interpreters with messages to the king and chiefs of the island, calling on them to surrender, and telling them that good terms would be given them. While waiting for an answer, he fortified his quarters in that spot, intrenching himself wherever necessary. He mounted the artillery in the best position for use, and kept his men ready for any emergency. A false and deceptive answer was returned, making excuses for the excesses that had been committed, and for not complying just then with what had been asked of them, and making loud promises to do so later. All this was with the object of detaining the captain in that place, which is very unhealthy, until the rains should set in, his provisions run short, and the arrival of the expected aid. After this answer had been received the Joloans, thinking that the Spaniards had become more careless on account of it, swarmed down quickly from the said fort in a large body of probably somewhat over one thousand; and armed with arquebuses and other weapons with handles, campilans, and caracas, attacked and assaulted the quarters and camp of the Spaniards. This could not be done so secretly as not to be seen by the Spaniards, and allow them opportunity to prepare to receive the Joloans before their arrival. This the Spaniards did, and having permitted the natives to come all together in a body to the very inside of the quarters and trenches, as soon as the Joloans had discharged their arquebuses, the Spaniards opened fire upon them, first with their artillery, and then with their arquebuses, killing many, and forcing the rest to retire in flight to the fort. The Spaniards pursued them, wounding and killing to the middle of the hill. But seeing that farther on the paths were so narrow and rough, they retreated before the heavy artillery fire from the heights, and the large stones hurled down upon them, and returned to their quarters. Upon many other days, efforts were made to reach the fort, but without any result. Thereupon Gallinato, in consideration of the war being prolonged beyond what had been expected, built two forts, one where he kept his ships in order to defend them and the port; and the other one-half legua farther on in a suitable place where they could take refuge and communicate with the camp. The forts were built of wood and fascines, and fortified with the artillery from the ships. The Spaniards shut themselves up in these forts, whence from time to time they sallied, making incursions as far as the enemy's fort. The latter always remained shut up in their fort without ever choosing to come down or to yield; for he was convinced that the Spaniards could not remain long in the island. When Gallinato saw that the rains were fast setting in, that his men were becoming ill, and that his provisions were failing, without his having accomplished the desired task, and that it could not be accomplished with his remaining resources; and that the enemy from Mindanao with other allies of theirs were boasting that they were gathering a large fleet in order to drive the Spaniards from Jolo: he sent news of all that had occurred to the governor of Manila, with a plan of the island and fort and a relation of the difficulties which the enterprise presented. He sent this in a swift vessel, by Captain and Sargento-mayor Pedro Cotelo de Morales, toward the end of May of the year six hundred and two, in order to obtain instructions as to his procedure, and the necessary reenforcements of men and provisions. The captain was charged to return quickly with the answer.

When the Moro Ocuna Lacasamana and his followers killed Diego Belloso, Blas Ruyz de Hernan Goncales, and the Castilians and Portuguese with them in the kingdom of Camboja, we said that Joan de Mendoca Gamboa with father Fray Joan Malclonado, and his associate, Don Antonio Malaver, Luys de Villafane, and other Spaniards who escaped by embarking with him in his vessel, descended the river with his vessel toward the sea, defending themselves against some Cambodian and Malayan praus which pursued them until they crossed the bar. Joan de Mendoca pursued his voyage along the coast to Sian, where his main business lay. Having reached the bar he ascended the river to the city of Odia, the court of the king, and the latter received the letter and message of Governor Don Francisco Tello, although with less pomp and courtesy than Joan de Mendoca wished.

Then he bartered his merchandise, and was so stingy in the regular custom of making some presents and gifts to the king and his favorites that he even bargained closely over the presents offered. The king was even inclined to seize the artillery of his ship, for which he had a great longing. Joan de Mendoca, fearing this, sunk it in the river with buoys, so that he could recover it at his departure, and for appearances left in the ship only one iron gun and some culverins. There was a Portuguese of the Order of St. Dominic in Odia, who had been residing in that court for the last two years, administering to the Portuguese who carried on trade in that region. Among these Portuguese were some whom the king had brought from Camboja and Pigu, when at war with both kingdoms. These and other Portuguese had had some quarrels with Siamese in the city, and had killed one of the king's servants. The king, being little inclined to clemency, had fried some of the delinquents and had forbidden the other Portuguese and the religious to leave the city or kingdom, although they had urgently asked leave and permission to do so. On seeing themselves deprived of liberty, less well treated than before, and threatened daily, they conspired with Fray Joan Maldonado to be smuggled aboard his vessel at its departure, and taken out of the kingdom. The religious took the matter upon himself. After Joan de Mendoca had concluded his business, although not as he had desired, since the king gave him no answer for the governor, putting it off, and his merchandise had not yielded much profit, he determined, at the advice of Fray Joan Maldonado, to recover his artillery some night, and to descend the river as rapidly as possible. On that same night the Portuguese religious and his companions, about twelve in number, were to leave the city secretly and wait eight leguas down the river in an appointed place, where they would be taken aboard. This plan was carried out, but when the king heard that Don Joan de Mendoca had taken his ship and departed without his leave and dismissal, and that he was carrying away the friar and the Portuguese who had been kept at his court, he was so angered that he sent forty praus with artillery and many soldiers in pursuit of him with orders to capture and bring them back to court or to kill them. Although Joan de Mendoca made all possible haste to descend the river, the ship, being without oars and its sails not always to be depended upon, and the distance to cover more than seventy leguas, he was overtaken by the Siamese in the river. When they drew near, Joan de Mendoca assumed the defensive, and gave them so much trouble with his artillery and musketry, that they did not dare to board him. Nevertheless, they approached him several times, and managing to break through, tossed artificial fire aboard, which caused the Spaniards much trouble, for the combat lasted more than one week, day and night. Finally, when near the bar, in order that the ship might not escape them, all the praus surviving the previous engagements attacked with one accord and made the last effort in their power. Although the Siamese could not carry out their intentions, and suffered the more killed and wounded, the Spaniards did not escape without severe losses; for the pilot, Joan Martinez de Chave, the associate of Fray Joan Maldonado, and eight other Spaniards died in the conflict. Fray Joan Maldonado was badly wounded by a ball from a culverin, which shattered his arm, and Captain Joan de Mendoca also received dangerous wounds. Thereupon the Siamese reascended the river, and the ship put to sea badly misused. As the weather was not favorable for crossing by way of the shoals to Manila or Malaca, which lay nearer to them, they steered for Cochinchina, where they put in and joined a Portuguese vessel lying there, for which they waited until it should sail to Malaca, in order to sail in its company. There Fray Joan Maldonado and Captain Joan de Mendoca grew worse of their wounds, and both died. Fray Joan Maldonado left a letter, written a few days before his death, for his superior and the Order of St. Dominic, in which he related his journeys, hardships and the cause of his death; and informed them of the nature and condition of the affairs of Camboja (whither he had been sent), of the slight foundation and motives for them troubling themselves with that enterprise, and the slight gain which could be hoped from it. He charged them upon their consciences not again to become instruments of a return to Camboja. The ship went to Malaca with its cargo, where everything was sold there by the probate judge. Some of the Spaniards still living returned to Manila sick, poor, and needy, from the hardships which they had undergone.

The affairs of Maluco continued to assume a worse appearance, because the ruler of Terrenate was openly waging war against his neighbor of Tidore and against the Portuguese who were with the latter. He had allowed some ships which had come to Terrenate from the islands of Holanda and Zelanda by way of India to trade with him, and through them had sent a message to Inglaterra and to the prince of Orange, concerning peace, trade, and commerce with the English and the Dutch. To this he had received a favorable answer, and he expected shortly a large fleet from Inglaterra and the islands, with whose help he expected to accomplish great things against Tidore and the Filipinas. Meanwhile, he kept some Flemings and Englishmen in Terrenate who had remained as pledges, and a factor engaged in purchasing cloves. These people had brought many fine weapons for this trade, so that the island of Terrenate was exceedingly well supplied with them. The king of Tidore and the chief captain wrote yearly to the governor of the Filipinas, informing him of what was going on, so that it might be remedied in time, and aid sent to them. Once, Cachilcota, [146] brother of the king of Tidore, a brave soldier and one of the most famous of all Maluco, came to Manila for that purpose. They always received men, provisions, and some ammunition; but what they most desired was that an expedition should be made opportunely against Terrenate, before the English and Dutch came with the expected fleet. This could not be done without an order from his Majesty, and great preparation and equipment for such an enterprise. The same message was always sent from Tidore. At last, during this administration of Don Francisco Tello, Captain Marcos Dias de Febra returned with this request, and brought letters to the governor and to the Audiencia from the king [of Tidore], and from the chief captain, Rui Goncales de Sequeira, in which were detailed contemporaneous events, and the necessity of at least sending succor to Tidore. The king wrote specially about this to the king [of Espana] and to Doctor Antonio de Morga, with the latter of whom he used to correspond, the following letter, which was written in Portuguese and signed in his own language.

> To Doctor Morga, in the Filipinas Islands, from the king of Tidore.
> I greatly rejoiced in receiving a letter from your Grace written on the eighth of November last, because by it I particularly understand your great sincerity in remembering me and my affairs; for this, may God reward your Grace with long life and prosperity for the service of the king, my sovereign. For I understood that he keeps your Grace in these islands with the hope of their increase, and I am aware that your being there will serve as a remedy for this fortress and island of Tidore. I have written to the governor and to the Audiencia in Manila, concerning the succor for which I beg, for I have asked it so often, on account of the great necessity of it; for through its means the injury may be checked; otherwise it may later cost much to the king our sovereign. I beg your Grace to favor me in this, or at least in what may be necessary for the future, for thus it will render a great service to God and to the king, my

sovereign. May God preserve your Grace with life for many years. From this island of Tidore, today, March eight, one thousand six hundred and one.

THE KING OF TIDORE

The bearer, namely, Marcos Dias, will give your Grace a flagon and a little flask of Moorish brass workmanship. I send them in order that your Grace may remember this your friend. [147]

Marcos Dias returned to Tidore at the first monsoon, in the beginning of the year six hundred and two, bearing an answer to his message, and taking the reenforcements that had been asked, of provisions, ammunition, and a few soldiers. He was satisfied therewith, until a fitting opportunity should offer for making the desired expedition from Manila.

Chapter 7

Of the government of Don Pedro de Acuna, governor and president of the Filipinas, and of what happened during his administration, until his death in June of the year six hundred and six, after his return to Manila from Maluco, where he had completed the conquest of the islands subject to the king of Terrenate.

In the month of May of six hundred and two, four ships came to Manila from Nueva Espana, with a new governor and president of the Audiencia, named Don Pedro de Acuna, knight of the Order of St. John, comendador of Salamanca, and lately governor of Cartagena in Tierra Firme. He was received into the government to the great satisfaction of the whole country, on account of the need there of one who would be as skilled in matters of war as watchful and careful in the government. Don Francisco Tello, his predecessor, awaiting his residencia which was to be taken, had to remain in Manila until the following year, six hundred and three, and in the month of April he died of an acute illness. The new governor, upon seeing things in so great need of stability, and so limited resources in the royal treasury for the purpose, found that his lot was not so good as he had imagined when he had been appointed; since the state of affairs obliged him to risk a part of his reputation without his being able to remedy matters as quickly as was to be desired. He took heart as much as possible, however, and without sparing himself any personal labor in whatever presented itself, he began with what was to be done in Manila and its environs. He began to construct galleys and other vessels in the shipyard, for there was great need of these, in order to defend the sea, which was full of enemies and pirates from other islands, especially from Mindanao. He discussed going immediately in person to visit the provinces of Pintados, in order to supply more quickly the needs of that region, which was causing the greatest anxiety. But he had to postpone that several months to arrange for the despatch of Japon and Jolo matters, and for the ships which were to make the voyage to Nueva Espana, all of which came at once and had to be seen to.

Chiquiro, the Japanese, having arrived in Manila, delivered his message and present to Governor Don Pedro de Acuna, who had been in the government but a few days. The matter and its determination, together with the reply, were immediately considered. It required the greatest amount of thought to decide how this was to be made, in the most fitting manner possible. For, although friendship with Daifusama was held to be a good thing and of great profit, and a necessity to obtain and conclude, even should certain difficulties have to be overcome; and although the sailing to Quanto and its commerce were not of much account to the Spaniards; nevertheless those things would be fulfilled by sending a ship there with some goods for exchange. But the rest, namely, the trade and friendship with Nueva Espana, and the sending of masters and workmen to build ships in Japon for that navigation, which Daifu insisted upon, and which Fray Geronymo had assured him would be done, was a serious matter and impossible to be carried out, as it was very harmful and prejudicial to the Filipinas. For their greatest security from Japon had ever been the Japanese lack of ships and their ignorance of navigation. As often as the latter had intended to attack Manila, they had been prevented by this obstacle. Now to send the Japanese workmen and masters to make Spanish ships for them and show them how such vessels were made, would be to give them the weapons that they needed for their own [i.e., the Filipinas'] destruction, while their navigation to Nueva Espana, and making long voyages, would cause very great troubles. [148] Each matter singly was of great importance and consideration, and such that the governor could not decide them, and they could not be decided in Manila, without informing his Majesty and the latter's viceroy of Nueva Espana, who was so much concerned, thereof. In order to take measures in the matter, and not to delay the Japanese from returning with his reply, a moderate present of Spanish articles was sent to Daifu, in the same ship which had come, in return for what it had brought. These Fray Geronymo was to give Daifu in person. The former was written to tell Daifu with what pleasure the governor received the good-will that he manifested to him, and the peace and friendship with the Spaniards, and all the other things that he was doing for them; and that he, the governor, would keep it and observe it in so far as he was concerned, and that very year he would send a Spanish ship to trade at Quanto according to Daifu's desire, and that he would despatch it quickly. As to the navigation which the latter wished to undertake to Nueva Espana and his desire to have masters sent him for that purpose, to build ships for that voyage, that was a matter which—although the governor would do his best to effect, and to please him in everything—was not within his control, without first informing his Majesty and the latter's viceroy in Nueva Espana thereof; for he, the governor, had no power or authority outside of the affairs of his government of the Filipinas. He said that he would write and would treat of it immediately, and hoped that it would be properly settled there. Until the reply came from Espana, which would necessarily have to be delayed three years, because that country was so far, he begged Daifu to be patient and suffer it, since it was not in his control, and nothing else could be done. The governor wrote Fray Geronymo to humor Daifu in everything, with the best words he could use to please him, but not to embarrass himself thenceforward by promising him and expediting such things for him. With this despatch, Chiquiro sailed for Japon with his ship, but was so unfortunate on the voyage that he was wrecked off the head of Hermosa Island, and neither the vessel nor its crew escaped. News thereof was not received in Manila or in Japon until many days afterward.

Upon the arrival of the letters from Fray Geronymo de Jesus, and the news of the changed conditions which he wrote existed in Japon, and the permission which he said that Daifu had given him to make Christians and build churches, not only the discalced religious of St. Francis but those of the other orders of St. Dominic and St. Augustine, set about going to Japon without loss of time; and, in order to be taken, each one made use of the Japanese ships and captains which were then at Manila, having come with flour, and which were about to return. In particular, the Order of St. Dominic sent to the kingdom of Zazuma four religious, under Fray Francisco de Morales, [149] Prior of Manila, in a ship about to go to that island and province. They said that they had been summoned by its king, the only one who had not yet rendered homage to Daifusama. The Order of St. Augustine sent two religious to the kingdom of Firando in a ship which had come from that port, under Fray Diego de Guebara, [150] Prior of Manila, because they had heard that they would be well received by the king of that province. The Order of St. Francis, in the ships about to sail to Nangasaqui, sent Fray Augustin Rodrigues, [151] who had been in Japon before, in company with the martyrs, and a lay-brother, with orders to go to Miaco, to become associates of Fray Geronymo de Jesus. Although some difficulties presented themselves to the governor in regard to the departure of these religious from Manila, and their going to Japon so hastily, yet on account of the great pressure which they brought to bear upon him, these were not sufficient to cause him to refuse them the permission which they requested. The religious reached the provinces to which they were going and were received there, although more coolly than they had expected, and with fewer conveniences than they needed for their support, and less inclination than they desired for the matters of the conversion, in which they had imagined that they were to have great and immediate results, for very few of the Japanese became Christians. In fact, the kings and tonos of those provinces kept them in order, by means of them, to open intercourse and commerce in their lands with the Spaniards—which they desired for their own interests rather than for the religion, to which they were not inclined.

The governor, Don Pedro de Acuna, in fulfilment of his letter, namely, that he would send a ship to Quanto, prepared and then sent out a medium-sized ship, named "Santiago el Menor" [i.e., St. James the Less], with a captain and the necessary seamen and officers, and some goods consisting of red wood, [152] deerskins, raw silk [153] and other things. This ship set out with orders to go to Quanto, where it would find discalced Franciscan religious and there to sell its goods and return with the exchange—and with the permission of Daifusama—to Manila. Thus Japanese matters were provided for, as far as seemed necessary, according to the state of affairs.

Daifusama, sovereign of Japon, who was awaiting Chiquiro, his servant, whom he had sent to Manila with the letters from Fray Geronymo de Jesus, pressed the latter so closely concerning the things which he desired and about which he had treated with him, that Fray Geronymo, seeing that Chiquiro was slow in returning, and that few arguments were of avail with Daifu, in order to satisfy him the better, requested permission of him to go to Manila in person, there to communicate and conclude matters with the governor by word of mouth, and bring a reply to him. He said that he would leave at the court Fray Augustin Rodriguez and another companion, who had lately come to him, as hostages for his return. The king granted the permission and gave him provision, so that Fray Geronymo came quickly to Manila, where he learned of the message which Chiquiro had taken. Then he began to treat with Governor Don Pedro de Acuna, about his business, saying that Chiquiro had not yet arrived in Xapon, which gave rise to the suspicion that he had been wrecked. The ship sent by the governor being unable to double the head of Xapon in order to pass to the north side, put into the port of Firando, where the religious of St. Augustine had had a station for a short time, and anchored there. Thence the captain advised the court of Miaco that he had been unable to reach Quanto. He sent also the letters for the religious and what was to be given to Daifu. The religious, Fray Geronymo's associates, gave Daifu the presents which were for him, and told him that the governor was sending that ship at his disposition and command, but that the weather had not allowed it to reach Quanto. Daifusama received the presents, although he did not believe what they told him, but that they were compliments to please him. He ordered the ship to get its trading done immediately, and to return with some things which he gave them for the governor, and thenceforward to go to Quanto as promised him. Thereupon it returned to Manila.

Fray Geronymo de Jesus reached the Filipinas so quickly, as has been said, that he had opportunity to treat with Governor Don Pedro de Acuna, about the matters under his charge, from whom he received the promise that ships would continue to be sent to Quanto to please Daifusama. Taking with him a good present, given him by the governor, consisting of a very rich and large Venetian mirror, glass, clothes from Castilla, honey, several tibores, [154] and other things which it was known would please Daifu, he returned immediately to Japon. He was well received there by Daifu, to whom he communicated his message, and that his servant Chiquiro had been well sent off by the new governor, and that nothing less than shipwreck was possible, since he had not appeared in so long a time. He gave Daifu what he had brought, which pleased the latter greatly.

During the first days of the governor's administration he found in the shipyard of Cabit two large ships which were being finished to make their voyage that year to Nueva Espana. One of them, belonging to Don Luys Dasmarinas, by an agreement which the latter had made with the governor's predecessor, Don Francisco Tello, was to go with a cargo of merchandise. The other, called the "Espiritu Santo," built by Joan Tello de Aguirre and other residents of Manila, was to make the voyage with the merchandise of that year credited to the builders, but was to pass into possession of his Majesty on its arrival in Nueva Espana, according to an agreement and contract made with the same governor, Don Francisco Tello. Don Pedro de Acuna made so great haste in despatching both ships that, with the cargo which they were to carry, he sent them out of port at the beginning of July of the aforesaid year six hundred and two, with Don Lope de Ulloa in the "Espiritu Santo" as general, and Don Pedro Flores in charge of the "Jesus Maria." Both ships went on their way, and in thirty-eight degrees met such storms that they were many times on the point of being wrecked, and threw overboard a quantity of their merchandise. The ship "Jesus Maria" put back into Manila with difficulty after having been more than forty days in the island of the Ladrones, whence it was unable to depart. During this time they had opportunity to pick up all the surviving Spaniards from among those left by the ship "Santa Margarita," among them, Fray Joan Pobre, who had jumped into one of the boats of the natives from the galleon "Santo Tomas," when it passed that way the year before. Five other Spaniards were in other islands of the same Ladrones, but although every effort was made to bring them, they could not come. The natives brought Fray Joan

Pobre and the others to the ship in their own boats, with great friendship and good will. After they had been entertained on board the ship, which they entered without fear, and after iron and other presents had been given to them, they returned without the Spaniards, weeping and showing great sorrow. The ship "Espiritu Santo," with the same difficulty, put into Japon, as it could do nothing else, with its mainmast gone, and entered a port of Firando, twenty leguas from a station of the religious of St. Augustine, who had gone there the same year from Manila, and where also the ship bound for Quanto had entered. The harbor could be sounded [i.e., it formed a good anchorage], but to enter and leave it were very difficult, because its channel had many turns, with rocks and high mountains on both sides. However, as the Japanese natives with their funeas towed and guided the ship so that it might enter, it had less difficulty. When it was inside, a Japanese guard was placed on the ship, and those who went ashore were not allowed to return to the ship. The supplies furnished them did not suffice for all their necessities, and the price was not suitable. On this account, and because a large number of soldiers had assembled quickly at the port from the whole district, and had asked the general for the sails of the ship, which he had always declined to give them, he feared that they wished to seize the ship and its merchandise, as was done in Hurando, with the ship "San Felipe," in the year ninety-six. He acted with caution, and kept much closer watch thenceforward, without leaving his ship or allowing his men to leave it alone, or any of the merchandise to be unloaded. At the same time he sent his brother, Don Alonso de Ulloa, and Don Antonio Maldonado to Miaco with a reasonable present for Daifusama, that he might have provision given them and permission to go out again from that harbor. [155] These men made the journey by land. Meanwhile, those on the ship were greatly troubled by the Japanese who were in the port, and by their captains, who were not satisfied with the presents which were given them to make them well disposed, but forcibly seized whatever they saw, giving out that everything was theirs and that it would soon be in their power. Fray Diego de Guebara, the Augustinian superior in Firando, came to the ship and told the general that he had put into a bad harbor of infidels and wicked people, who would take his ship and rob it, and that he should endeavor with all his might to get it out of there and take it to Firando where he [the father] was living. Meanwhile he told him to be on the watch and guard to the best of his ability. As the father was returning to his house with some pieces of silk, given him on the ship for his new church and monastery at Firando, the Japanese took it away from him and did not leave him a thing, saying that it was all theirs, and he went away without it. About a dozen and a half of the Spaniards of the ship were ashore, where they were kept in confinement and not allowed to go on board again, and although the general warned them that he had determined to leave the port as soon as possible, and that they should make every effort to come to the ship, they could not all do so, but only four or five of them. Without waiting any longer he drove the Japanese guard from the ship, bent the foresail and spritsail, loaded the artillery, and, with weapons in hand, one morning set the ship in readiness to weigh anchor. The Japanese went to the channel at the mouth of the harbor with many funeas and arquebusiers, stretched a thick rattan cable which they had woven, and moored it on both banks in order that the ship might not be able to sail out. The general sent a small boat with six arquebusiers to find out what they were doing, but at their approach, a number of the Japanese funeas attacked them with the purpose of capturing them. However, by defending themselves with their arquebuses they returned to the ship and reported to the general that the Japanese were closing the exit from the harbor with a cable. Taking this to be a bad sign, the ship immediately set sail against the cable to break it, and a negro, to whom the general promised his freedom, offered to be let down over the bow with a large machete in order to cut the cable when the ship should reach it.

With the artillery and the arquebuses he cleared the channel of the funeas there, and when he came to the cable, with the impetus of the vessel and the strenuous efforts of the negro with the machete, it broke, and the ship passed through. It still remained for it to go through the many turns which the channel made before coming out to the sea and it seemed impossible for a ship which was sailing fast to go through them, but God permitted it to pass out through them as though it had had a breeze for each turn. But the Japanese, who had assembled in great numbers on the hills and rocks within range of where the ship was passing, did not fail to annoy the ship with many volleys, with which they killed one Spaniard on the ship and wounded others. The ship did the same, and with their artillery they killed several of the Japanese. The Japanese failed to obstruct the ship's passage, and accordingly were left without it. The general, finding himself on the sea and free from the past danger, and seeing that it was beginning to blow a little from the north, thought it best to venture on his voyage to Manila rather than to seek another harbor in Japon. Having raised a jury-mast [156] in place of the main-mast, and with the wind freshening daily from the north, he crossed to Luzon in twelve days, via the cape of Bojeador, and reached the mouth of the bay of Manila, where he found the ship "Jesus Maria," which was also putting in in distress through the Capul Channel; and so the two ships together, as they had gone together out of the port of Cabit five months before, made harbor there again in distress after having suffered many damages and losses to the exchequer.

Don Alonso de Ulloa and Don Francisco Maldonado, while this was going on in the harbor where they had left the ship "Espiritu Santo," reached Miaco and delivered their message and present to Daifusama. The latter, upon being informed who they were, that their ship had entered Japon, and that they were from Manila, received them cordially, and quickly gave them warrants and chapas [i.e., safe-conducts], in order that the tonos and governors of the provinces where the ship had entered should allow it and its crew to depart freely. They were to be allowed to refit, and to be given what they needed; and whatever had been taken from them, whether much or little, was to be returned.

While this matter was being attended to, news reached Miaco of the departure of the ship from the harbor, and the skirmish with the Japanese over it, and of this they complained anew to Diafu. He showed that he was troubled at the departure of the ship and the discourtesy to it, and at the outrages committed by the Japanese. He gave new chapas for restitution of all the goods to be made; and sent a catan from his own hand with which justice should be performed upon those who had offended in this matter, [157] and ordered that the Spaniards who remained in the port should be set free, and that their goods be returned to them. With this warrant the Spaniards left that port and recovered what had been taken from them. The ambassadors and the others returned to Manila in the first vessels which left, taking with them eight chapas of the same tenor from Daifusama, in order that in the future ships coming from Manila to any port whatever of J apon, might be received courteously and well treated, without having any harm done them. These, upon their arrival in Manila, they handed over to the governor, who gives them to the ships sailing to Nueva Espana, to provide for any incidents on the voyage.

At the same time that Governor Don Pedro de Acuna entered upon his administration, the captain and sargento-mayor, Pedro Cotelo de Morales, arrived from Jolo with the advices and report of Joan Xuarez Gallinato concerning the state of affairs in that island, whither he had gone with the fleet at the beginning of that same year. The governor, on account of the importance of the matter, wished to make every effort possible, and determined to send him supplies and a reenforcement of some men, which he did as soon as possible. He was ordered to at least make an effort to punish that enemy, even if he could do nothing more, and, whenever the opportunity presented itself, to go to do the same thing in the river of Mindanao, and return to the Pintados. When this commission reached Jolo, Gallinato was already so worn out, and his men so ill, that the reenforcements only made it possible for him to get away from there; accordingly without seeing to another thing, he broke camp, burned the forts which he had built, embarked, and went to Pintados, leaving the people of that island of Jolo and their neighbors, those of Mindanao, emboldened more than ever to make raids against the Pintados, and the islands within, which they did.

The governor, without delaying any longer in Manila, hastily started for the island of Panay and the town of Arevalo, in a galliot and other small vessels, to see their needs with his own eyes, in order to provide for them. He left war matters in Manila, during his absence, in charge of Licentiate Don Antonio de Ribera, auditor of the Audiencia.

As soon as the governor left Manila, the auditor had plenty to look after, because a squadron of twenty caracoas and other vessels from Mindanao entered the islands as far as the island of Luzon and its coasts, making captures. Having taken some ships bound from Sebu to Manila, they captured ten Spaniards in them, among them a woman and a priest and Captain Martin de Mandia, and they took them off with them. They entered Calilaya, burned the church and all the town, and captured many persons of all classes among the natives. Thence they passed to the town of Valayan [Balayan] to do the same, but the auditor, having received news of the enemy in Manila, had it already in a state of defense with fifty Spaniards and a captain and some vessels. Consequently, they did not dare to enter the town or its bay, but crossed over to Mindoro, where, in the principal town, they captured many men, women, and children among the natives, seizing their gold and possessions, and burning their houses and church, where they captured theprebendary Corral, curate of that doctrina. They filled their own ships, and others which they seized there, with captives, gold, and property, staying in the port of Mindoro as leisurely as though in their own land, notwithstanding that it is but twenty-four leguas from Manila. Captain Martin de Mendia, prisoner of these pirates, offered for himself and the other Spanish captives that, if they would let him go to Manila, he would get the ransom for all, and would take it, or would send it within six months, to the river of Mindanao, or otherwise he would return to their power. The chief in command of the fleet agreed thereto, with certain provisions and conditions, and caused the other captives to write, to the effect that what had been agreed upon might be fulfilled, and then he allowed the captain to leave the fleet. The latter came to the city, and upon receiving his report, the auditor sent munitions, ships, and more men to Valayan than there were there already, with orders to go in pursuit of the enemy without delay, saying that they would find him in Mindoro. Captain Gaspar Perez, who had charge of this in Valayan, did not start so quickly as he should have done in order to find the enemy in Mindoro, for when he arrived he found that he had left that port six days before, laden with ships and booty, to return to Mindanao. Then he went in pursuit of him, although somewhat slowly. The enemy put into the river of a little uninhabited island to get water and wood. Just at that time Governor Don Pedro de Acuna, who was hastily returning to Manila, from the town of Arvalo, where he had learned of the incursion of those pirates, passed. He passed so near the mouth of this river, in two small champans and a virrey, with very few men, that it was a wonder that he was not seen and captured by the enemy. He learned that the enemy was there, from a boat of natives which was escaping therefrom, and then he met Gaspar Perez going in search of the enemy with twelve vessels, caracoas and vireys, and some large champans. The governor made him make more haste and gave him some of his own men to guide him to where he had left the pirates the day before, whereupon they went to attack them. But the latter espied the fleet through their sentinels whom they had already stationed in the sea, outside the river. Accordingly they left the river in haste, and took to flight, throwing into the sea goods and slaves in order to flee more lightly. Their flagship and almiranta caracoas protected the ships which were dropping behind and made them throw overboard what they could and work with all the strength of their paddles, assisted by their sails. The Spanish fleet, the vessels of which were not so light, could not put forth enough strength to overtake all of them, because, furthermore, they went into the open without fear of the heavy seas which were running, inasmuch as they were fleeing. Yet some of the ships of Captain Gaspar Perez, being lighter, got among the enemy's fleet, sunk some caracoas, and captured two, but the rest escaped, although with great danger of being lost. Without accomplishing anything else, the fleet returned to Manila where the governor had already entered, very much disturbed that things should have come to such a pass that these enemies, who had never dared to leave their houses, should have been so daring and bold as to come to the very gates of the city, doing great damage and making captures.

Some years before this his Majesty had ordered an expedition to be prepared in Portuguese India for the capture of the fort of Terrenate in Maluco, which was in the power of a Moro who had rebelled and subjected it in a tyrannical manner, and had driven out the Portuguese there. The necessary preparations of ships, munitions, and men were made for this undertaking in India, and a hidalgo, named Andrea Furtado de Mendoca, [158] was chosen general of this expedition. He was a soldier skilled in the affairs of India, who had won many victories of great importance and fame on sea and land in those parts, and had lately had a very notable one at Jabanapatan. [159] He sailed from Goa with six galleons of the kingdom, fourteen galliots and fustas, and other ships, and one thousand five hundred fighting men, and with supplies and munitions for the fleet. On account of the storms which he met, his fleet was so scattered before reaching Amboino that the galleys and fustas could not keep up with the galleons or follow them, and only three of them, in convoy of the galleons, reached Amboino. The other vessels put back into Goa and other forts on the line of that voyage. The island of Amboino was in rebellion and the Portuguese fort there was in great need, so that, while the galliots, fustas, and other vessels of his fleet which had fallen off on the voyage were gathering, and while help was coming which he had sent to ask of the fort of Malaca, it seemed best to Andrea Furtado de Mendoca to stop in Amboino, which is eighty leguas from Maluco, in order to pacify the island and some towns of the neighborhood, and reduce them to the crown of Portugal. He was more than six months in this, having encounters with the enemy and with the rebels, in which he always came out victorious, and from which he obtained the desired result, and left everything reduced and pacified. His ships did not arrive, however, and the help which he had requested did not come from Malaca, and yet it was necessary for him to go to Terrenate, as that was the principal purpose for which he had been sent. Considering this, and yet seeing that he had fewer men than he needed for it, and that the greater part of the munitions and supplies which he had brought were spent, he determined to send word to the governor of the Filipinas of his coming with that fleet, of what he had done in Amboino, that he was to proceed to attack Terrenate, and that, because a part of his ships had been scattered, and because he had stopped so many months for those undertakings, he had fewer men than he wanted and was in need of some things, especially supplies. He requested the governor, since this matter was so important and so to the service of his Majesty, and since so much had been spent on it from the royal treasury of the crown of Portugal, to favor and help him, by sending him some supplies and munitions and some Castilians for the undertaking. He asked that all of this should reach Terrenate by January of six hundred and three, for he would then be off that fort and the help would come to him very opportunely. This message and his letters for the governor and the Audiencia he sent to Manila from Amboino in a light vessel in charge of Father Andre Pereira of the Society of Jesus, and Captain Antonio Fogoca, one of his own followers. They found Governor Don Pedro de Acuna in Manila, and presented the matter to him, making use of the Audiencia and of the orders, and making many boasts of the Portuguese fleet and the illustrious men who were in it, and of the valor and renown of its general in whatever he undertook. They asserted at the same time the success of the capture of Terrenate at that time, especially if they received from Manila the succor and help for which they had come, and which, in justice, should be given them, as it was given from the Filipinas whenever the king of Tidore and the chief captain of that fort requested it, and as his Majesty had ordered—and with more good reason and foundation on such an occasion. [160]

Although Don Pedro de Acuna, from the time of his appointment to the government, had the intention and desire to make an expedition against Terrenate, and when he was in Mexico on his way, had treated of this matter with those there who had any information about Maluco, and sent Brother Gaspar Gomez of the Society of Jesus from Nueva Espana to his Majesty's court—who had lived in Manila many years, and also in Maluco in the time of Governor Gomez Perez Dasmarinas—to treat of the matter in his name with his Majesty; and although he was in hopes of making this expedition: nevertheless it seemed to him best, without declaring his own desires, to aid in what Andrea Furtado asked, and even more, not only on account of the importance of the matter, but also because by thus helping, he would keep the general and his messengers, in case they were unsuccessful, from excusing themselves by saying that they had asked for help and reenforcement from the governor of the Filipinas, and the latter had not given it, and so that it might not be understood that he had failed to do so because he himself was arranging for the expedition. Don Pedro de Acunia consulted about this matter with the Audiencia, which was of the opinion that the aforesaid reenforcement, and more besides, should be sent to the Portuguese at the time for which it was asked. When this was decided upon, they put it into execution, very much to the satisfaction of Father Andrea Pereira and Captain Fogaca. At the end of the year six hundred and two they were despatched from the Filipinas, taking with them the ship "Santa Potenciana" and three large frigates, with one hundred and fifty well armed Spanish soldiers, ten thousand fanegas of rice, one thousand five hundred earthen jars of palm wine, two hundred head of salt beef, twenty hogsheads of sardines, conserves and medicines, fifty quintals of powder, cannon-balls and bullets, and cordage and other supplies, the whole in charge of the captain and sargento-mayor, Joan Xuarez Gallinato—who had now returned from Jolo and was in Pintados—with orders and instructions as to what he was to do, namely, to take that help to Terrenate, to the Portuguese fleet which he would find there, and to place himself at the orders and command of its general. [161] Thither he made his voyage in a fortnight, and anchored in the port of Talangame, in the island of Terrenate, two leguas from the fort, where he found Andrea Furtado de Mendoca with his galleons at anchor, awaiting what was being sent from Manila. He and all his men were very much pleased with it.

In the month of March of this year six hundred and three, there entered Manila Bay a ship from Great China, in which the sentinels reported that three great mandarins were coming, with their insignia as such, on business in the service of their king. The governor gave them permission to leave their ship and enter the city with their suites. In very curious chairs of ivory and fine gilded woods, borne on the shoulders of men, they went straight to the royal houses of the Audiencia, where the governor was awaiting them, with a large suite of captains and soldiers throughout the house and through the streets where they passed. When they had reached the doors of the royal houses they alighted from their chairs and entered on foot, leaving in the street the banners, plumes, lances and other very showy insignia which they brought with them. The mandarins went into a large, finely-decorated hall, where the governor received them standing, they making many bows and compliments to him after their fashion, and he replying to them after his. They told him through the interpreters that their king had sent them, with a Chinaman whom they had with them in chains, to see with their own eyes an island of gold, called Cabit, which he had told their king was near Manila, and belonged to no one. [162] They said that this man had asked for a quantity of ships, which he said he would bring back laden with gold, and if it were not so that they could punish him with his life. So they had come to ascertain and tell their king what there was in the matter. The governor replied briefly, saying only that they were welcome, and appointed them quarters in two houses within the city which had been prepared for them, in which they and their men could lodge. He said that the business would be discussed afterwards. Thereupon they left the royal houses again, and at the doors mounted in their chairs on the shoulders of their servants, who were dressed in red, and were carried to their lodgings, where the governor ordered them to be supplied fully with whatever they needed during the days of their stay.

The coming of these mandarins seemed suspicious, and their purpose to be different from what they said, because it seemed a fiction for people, of so much understanding as the Chinese, to say that their king was sending them on this business. Among the Chinese themselves who came to Manila at the same time in eight merchant ships, and among those who lived in the city, it was said that these mandarins were coming to see the land and study its nature, because the king of China wished to break relations with the Spaniards and send a large fleet, before the end of the year, with one hundred thousand men to take the country.

The governor and the Audiencia thought that they ought to be very careful in guarding the city, and that these mandarins should be well treated, but that they should not go out of the city nor be allowed to administer justice, as they were beginning to do among the Sangleys, at which the mandarins were somewhat angry. He asked them to treat of their business, and then to return to China quickly, and he warned the Spaniards not to show that they understood or were suspicious of anything other than what the mandarins had said. The mandarins had another interview with the governor, and he told them more clearly, making some joke of their coming, that he was astonished that their king should have believed what that Chinaman whom they had with them had said, and even if it were true that there was so much gold in the Filipinas, that the Spaniards would not allow it to be carried away, since the country belonged to his Majesty. The mandarins said that they understood very well what the governor had communicated to them, but that their king had ordered them to come and that they must needs obey and bring him a reply, and that when they had performed their duty, that was all, and they would return. The governor, to cut short the business, sent the mandarins, with their servants and the prisoner, to Cabit, which is the port, two leguas from the city. There they were received with a great artillery salute, which was fired suddenly as they landed, at which they were very frightened and fearful. When they had landed, they asked the prisoner if that was the island of which he had spoken to the king, and he replied that it was. They asked him where the gold was, and he replied that everything there was gold and that he would make his statement good with the king. They asked him other questions and he always replied the same thing. Everything was written down in the presence of some Spanish captains who were there with some confidential interpreters. The mandarins ordered a basketful of earth to be taken from the ground, to take to the king of China, and then, having eaten and rested, they returned to Manila the same day, with the prisoner. The interpreters said that the prisoner, when hard pressed by the mandarins to make suitable answers to their questions, had said that what he had meant to tell the king of China was that there was much gold and wealth in the hands of the natives and Spaniards of Manila, and that if they gave him a fleet with men, he offered, as a man who had been in Luzon and knew the country, to capture it and bring the ships back laden with gold and riches. This, together with what some Chinamen had said at the beginning, seemed very much to have more meaning than the mandarins had implied, especially to Don Fray Miguel de Benavides, archbishop-elect of Manila, who knew the language. Thereupon the archbishop and other religious warned the governor and the city, publicly and privately, to look to its defense, because they felt sure of the coming of the Chinese fleet against it shortly. Then the governor dismissed the mandarins and embarked them on their ship, with their prisoner, after giving them some pieces of silver and other things with which they were pleased. Although, in the opinion of the majority of those in the city, it seemed that it was beyond all reason that the Chinese should attack the country, the governor began covertly to prepare ships and other things suitable for defense, and made haste to complete extensive repairs which he had begun to make on the fort of Sanctiago at the point of the river, and for the defense of the fort he built on the inside a wall of great strength, with its wings, facing toward the parade ground.

At the end of April of this year six hundred and three, on the eve of Sts. Philip and James [Santiago] a fire started in a little field house [casilla de zacate] used by some Indians and negroes of the native hospital in the city, at three o'clock in the afternoon, and passed to other houses so quickly, with the force of the rather fresh wind, that it could not be stopped, and burned houses of wood and stone, even the monastery of St. Dominic—house and church—the royal hospital for the Spaniards, and the royal warehouses, without leaving a building standing among them. Fourteen people died in the fire, Spaniards, Indians, and negroes, and among them Licentiate Sanz, canon of the cathedral. In all two hundred and sixty houses were burned, with much property which was in them, and it was understood that the damage and loss amounted to more than one million [pesos].

After Ocuna Lacasamana, the Moro Malay, with the help of the mandarins of Camboja who sided with him, and of the stepmother of King Prauncar, had killed and put an end to Bias Ruyz de Hernan Goncales and Diego Belloso, and the Castilians, Portuguese, and Japanese on their side who were in the kingdom, his boldness went so far that he even killed the king himself, whereby the whole kingdom was divided into factions and suffered greater disturbances than it had ever known before. God permitted this for His just judgments, and because Prauncar did not deserve to enjoy the good fortune which he had had in being placed on his father's throne, since he lost it at the same time that he did his life. Nor did Bias Ruiz de Hernan Gonzales and Diego Belloso, and their companions, deserve the fruit and labor of their expeditions and victories, since they were converted into disastrous and cruel death at the time when they seemed most secure and certain, for perchance their pretensions and claims were not so well adjusted to the obligations of conscience as they ought to have been. But God did not wish the Moro Malay to remain unpunished.

When this Malay thought that he was going to get the better part of the kingdom of Camboja, because he had killed the Castilians and Portuguese, their captains, and the legitimate and natural king himself who favored them, he was more mistaken than he thought, because the disorders and uprisings in the provinces gave opportunity for some powerful mandarins in the kingdom, who held and maintained the saner course, to join, and avenge the death of King Prauncar by force of arms. So they turned against Ocuna Lacasamana and his Malays, and, meeting them in battle on different occasions, conquered and routed them, so that the Moro was forced to flee from Camboja, with the remaining remnant of his men, and pass to the kingdom of Champa, which bordered on it, with the purpose of disturbing it and making war on the usurper who held it, and of seizing it all, or as much as he could. This also did not turn out well for him, for, although he brought war into Champa, and all the disturbances which it brings, and caused the usurper and his men a great deal of trouble, at last he was routed and killed and came to pay wretchedly for his sins at the usurper's hands.

Seeing themselves rid of the Malay, but finding that the kingdom was still disturbed, as he had left it, and without a male descendant in the line of Prauncar Langara, who died in Laos, the mandarins of Camboja turned their eyes toward a brother of his whom the king of Sian had captured and taken with him in the war which he had made against Langara, and whom he held in the city of Odia, as they thought that he had the best right to the kingdom of Camboja, by legitimate succession, and that it would be more easily pacified in his presence. They sent an embassy to Sian, asking him to come to reign, and asking the king of Sian, who held him captive, to allow him to go. The king thought well of it, and, with certain provisions and conditions which he made with his prisoner, gave him his liberty and six thousand fighting men to serve and accompany him. With these he came immediately to Camboja and was readily received in Sistor and other provinces, and placed on the throne, and from those provinces he went on pacifying and reducing the more distant ones.

This new king of Camboja who, from being a captive of the king of Sian, came to the throne by such strange events and varying chances—for God held this good fortune in store for him, and holds still more of greater worth, if he can carry on what he has begun—caused search to be made for Joan Diaz, a Castilian soldier, who survived from the company of Blas Ruyz de Hernan Goncales. He bade him go to Manila and, in his behalf, tell the governor that he was on the throne, and also what had happened in regard to the death of the Spaniards and of his nephew Prauncar, in which he [the new king] was in no wise to blame. He said that he recognized the friendship which they—Langara, his brother, and the latter's son—received from the Spaniards in the time of their troubles; that he himself was well disposed to continue this friendship and understanding; and he again asked the governor, if he were willing, to send him some religious and Castilians to reside at his court and to make Christians of those who wished to become so.

With this message and embassy, and many promises, Joan Diaz came to Manila, where he found Don Pedro de Acuna in the government, and treated of the matter with him. The governor thought it unwise to close the door to the preaching of the holy gospel in Camboja, which God had opened again in this way, and he agreed to do what the king asked. So, at the beginning of the year six hundred and three, he sent a frigate to Camboja, with four religious of the Order of St. Dominic with Fray Ynigo de Santa Maria, prior of Manila, at their head with five soldiers to accompany them, among them Joan Diaz himself. They were to give the king the reply to his message, in confirmation of the peace and friendship for which he asked, and, according to the circumstances which they found there, the religious were to stay in his court and advise what seemed best to them. This frigate reached Camboja after a ten days' voyage with favoring winds, and the religious and the soldiers in their company ascended the river to Chordemuco, where the king received them with great satisfaction. He immediately built them a church, and gave them rice for their support, and granted them liberty to preach and christianize. This seemed to the religious to be the work of Heaven, and a matter in which a great many workers could be employed. They sent immediate word of their good reception and condition to Manila in the same frigate, after asking permission of the king that it might return. The king granted it and gave them the necessary supplies for their voyage, and at the same time sent a servant of his with a present of ivory tusks, benzoin, and other curious things for the governor, with a letter thanking him for what he was doing and asking for more religious and Castilians. Fray Ynigo de Santa Maria [163] with a companion embarked on this frigate, in order to come to give a better report of what he had found, but he sickened and died on the voyage. His companion and those aboard the frigate reached Manila in May of six hundred and three and gave an account of events in Camboja.

At the end of the same month of May, there came to Manila two ships from Nueva Espana, in command of Don Diego de Camudio, with the regular reenforcements for the Philipinas. It brought news that Fray Diego de Soria, [164] of the Order of St. Dominic, bishop of Cagayan, was in Mexico, and was bringing the bulls and pallium to the archbishop-elect of Manila, and Fray Baltasar de Cobarrubias, [165] of the Order of St. Augustine, appointed bishop of Camarines by the death of Fray Francisco de Ortega. In the same ships came two auditors for the Audiencia of Manila, Licentiates Andres de Alcaraz, and Manuel de Madrid y Luna.

The captain and sargento-mayor, Joan Xuarez Gallinato, with the ship "Santa Potenciana" and the men whom he had taken in it to Maluco in aid of the Portuguese fleet which Andrea Furtado de Mendoca had brought to assault the fortress of Terrenate, found this fleet in the port of Talangame. As soon as this help arrived, Andrea Furtado landed his men, Portuguese and Castilians, with six pieces of artillery, and marched with them along the shore, toward the fort, to plant the battery. He took two days to reach the fort, passing through some narrow places and gullies which the enemy had fortified. When he had reached the principal fort, he had all that he could do to plant the artillery, for the enemy sallied out frequently against the camp and hindered the work. Once they reached the very gate of the quarters, and would have done a great deal of damage had not the Castilians nearest the entrance stopped them and pressed the Moros so hard that, leaving some dead, they turned and fled and shut themselves up in the fort. At the same time five pieces were placed within cannon-shot of it. The enemy, who had sufficient men for their defense, with a great deal of artillery and ammunition, did much damage in the camp, whereas the pieces of the battery had no considerable effect, having but a short supply of powder and ammunition. Consequently what Gallinato and his men had heard, when they joined the Portuguese fleet, of the scant supply and outfit which Andrea Furtado had brought for so great an enterprise, was seen and experienced very quickly. That they might not all be killed, Andrea Furtado, having asked the opinion of all the officers of his camp and fleet, withdrew his pieces and camp to the port of Talangame. He embarked his men on his galleons and returned to the forts and islands of Amboino and Vanda, where he had first been, taking for the support of the fleet the supplies brought him by Gallinato, to whom he gave permission to return to Manila, with the Castilians. The latter did so, in company with Ruy Goncales de Sequeira, until recently chief captain of the fort of Tidore, who, with his household and merchandise, left that fortress in another ship, and they reached Manila at the beginning of the month of July of this year six hundred and three, bearing the following letter from Andrea Furtado de Mendoca to Governor Don Pedro de Acuna.

* * * * *

A letter which General Andrea Furtado de Mendoca wrote to Don Pedro de Acuna from Terrenate on the twenty fifth of March of the year one thousand six hundred and three.

> There are no misfortunes in the world, however great they
> may be, from which some good may not be gained. Of all
> those through which I have passed in this undertaking, and

they have been infinite, the result has been that I have learned the zeal and courage which your Lordship shows in the service of his Majesty, on account of which I envy your Lordship and hold you as master, affirming that the thing which I would like most in this life would be for your Lordship to hold the same opinion of me, and, as one that is very particularly your own, that your Lordship should command me in what is for your service.

The help sent me by your Lordship came in time, by the favor of God, and was what gave this fleet to his Majesty and our lives to all of us alive today. By what happened in this expedition, his Majesty will understand how much he owes to your Lordship and how little to the captain of Malaca, for the latter was partly the cause that the service of his Majesty was not accomplished. When the ship sent me by your Lordship arrived, this fleet was without any supplies because it had been two years since it had left Goa, and they had all been consumed and spent on the occasions which had presented themselves. Admitting this in order that it may not be imagined that it was on my account that the service of his Majesty was not carried out, I went on shore, which I gained, inflicting great losses on the enemy, and I placed my last trenches a hundred paces from the enemy's fortification. I landed five heavy pieces for battering, and in ten days of bombarding, knocked to pieces a large part of a bastion where all the enemy's force was concentrated. In these days all the powder in the fleet was spent, without a grain being left with which its artillery could be loaded even once, and if I should happen to run across a Dutch squadron, of which I have little doubt, I should be forced to fight with them. This was the principal cause for which I raised the siege, when I had the enemy in great distress through hunger and also through having killed many of his captains and other men in the course of the fighting. From this your Lordship may judge of the state of suffering and grief in which I must be. God be praised for everything, since it is His will, and may He permit that His greatest enemies in these regions may become the vassals of his Majesty.

I am leaving for Amboino to see if I can get help there, and if I find sufficient, and if there is not elsewhere in the south anything in such urgent need that I must attend to it,

I am going to return to this undertaking, and I will inform your Lordship of it at length. If I do not find there the help which I expect, I shall go to Malaca to refit, and from whatever place I am in, I shall always inform your Lordship. I am writing to his Majesty, giving him a long account of the affairs of this enterprise, and stating that it cannot be accomplished or preserved in the future, unless it is done by the order of your Lordship, and helped and increased by that government, since India is so far that it could not receive help from there within two years. In conformity with this, your Lordship should inform his Majesty, that he may be undeceived in this regard about Maluco, and I trust to God that I may be one of your Highness's soldiers.

I do not know with what words I can praise or thank your Lordship for the kind things which you have done for me. These were made plain to me by Antonio de Brito Fogaca, as well as by Tomas de Araux, my servant. These are things which can not be rewarded or paid except by risking life, honor, and property on every occasion which offers itself in your service. If such an occasion should be presented to me, it will be seen that I am not ungrateful for the favors which I have received; the greatest of which, and the one which I esteem most highly, was that, with this help, your Lordship sent me Joan Xuarez Gallinato, Don Tomas de Acuna, and the other captains and soldiers. If I were to mention to your Lordship the deserts of each and every one of these, I should never end.

Joan Xuarez Gallinato is a person whom your Lordship should esteem highly on every occasion, because he deserves it all. In this expedition and enterprise he conducted himself with so great satisfaction, courage, and prudence, that it is very clear that he was sent by your Lordship and had fought under the banners of so distinguished captains. Consequently, I shall be glad to know that your Lordship has shown him many kindnesses, on account of his services to his Majesty in these regions, and on my own account. The thing which pleased me most in this undertaking, and which is worthy of being remembered, is that, contrary to the proverb of the old Portuguese women, in the course of this war there was not one harsh word between the Spaniards and Portuguese, though they ate together at one mess. But your Lordship may attribute this to your good fortune, and to the intelligence and experience of Joan Xuarez Gallinato.

Don Tomas conducted himself in this war, not like a gentleman of his age, but like an old soldier, full of experience. Your Lordship should greatly esteem this relative, for I trust that your Lordship may be a second father to him.

The sargento-mayor conducted himself in this war like an excellent soldier, and he is a man whom your Lordship should regard favorably, for I give my word that the Manilas do not contain a better soldier than he, and I shall be greatly pleased if your Lordship honor him and show him very particular favors on my account. Captain Villagra fulfilled his duty well and Don Luys did the same. In short all the soldiers, to a man, great and small, did likewise in this enterprise, so that for this reason I am under so great obligations to them that, if I were now before his Majesty, I would not leave his feet till I had heaped them all with honors and favors since they also deserve them. So for this reason I shall always be particularly glad if your Lordship confers honors and favors on them all in general. May our Lord preserve your Lordship for many years, as I, your servant, desire. From the port of Talangame, in the island of Terrenate, on the twenty-fifth of March, of the year one thousand six hundred and three.

ANDREA FURTADO DE MENDOCA

(To be continued)

Appendix A:
Expedition of Thomas Candish

Thomas Candish or Cavendish, was a native of "Trimley in the country of Suffolke." His fleet, consisting of three vessels, "The Desire," of 120 tons, "The Content," of 60 tons, and "Hugh Gallant," of 40 tons, left Plymouth July 21, 1586, with one hundred and twenty-three men in all, and provisions for two years. Steering a general southwest course they reached the Strait of Magellan January 6, 1587. In the strait they found the melancholy remains of a Spanish colony started three years before— Twenty-three people out of the four hundred settlers, two of whom were women. One named Hernando they took with them. This place the Englishmen appropriately named Port Famine. Shortly after leaving the strait they found at an Indian settlement, under the Spanish, some "guinie wheat, which is called Maiz." The first capture was May 1—a boat of three hundred tons from Guaianel laden with timber and food. Prizes after that were thick and fast, and the vessels were generally burned after being despoiled of valuables. On July 9, near the coast of New Spain, a ship of one hundred and twenty tons was taken, from one of the crew of which, Michael Sancius from Marseilles, they first heard of "the great shippe called The Santa Anna, vvhich vve aftervvard tooke comming from the Philippinas." After coasting along New Spain and California committing various depredations, among them the defacing of the Spanish churches, and various other piratical deeds, they met on the fourth of November with the "Santa Ana." They pursued it for three or four hours and finally overtaking fought with and captured it. The fight is described as follows:

> "In the afternoone we gat vp vnto them, giuing them the broad side with our great ordnance, and a volee of small shot, and presently laid the ship aboord, whereof the King of Spaine was owner, which was Admirall of the South-sea, called the S. Anna, and thought to be seuen hundred

tvnnes in burthen. Now as we were readie on their ships
side to enter her, beeing not past fiftie or sixty men at the
vttermost in our ship, we perceived that the Captain of the
said ship had made fights fore and after, and laid their
sailes close on their poope, their mid-ship, with their forecastle, and hauing not one man to be seene, stood close
vnder their fights, with Lances, Iauelings, Rapiers and Tar-
gets, and an innumerable sort of great stones, which they
threw ouer boord vpon our heads, and into our ship so
fast, and beeing so many of them, that they put vs off the
shippe againe, with the losse of two of our men which
were slaine, and with the hurting of foure or fiue. But for
all this we new trimmed our sailes, and fitted euery man his
furniture, and gaue them a fresh incounter with our great
Ordnance, and also with our small shot, raking them thorough and thorough, to the killing and maiming of many of
their men. Their Captaine still like a valiant man with his
companie, stood very stoutly vnto his close fights, not
yeelding as yet. Our General incouraging his men afresh
with the whole noyse of trumpets, gaue them the third encounter with our great Ordnance, and all our small shot to
the great discomforting of our enemies, raking them
through in diuerse places, killing and spoyling many. They
beeing thus discomforted, and their shippe beeing in haz-
ard of sinking by reason of the great shot which were
made, whereof some were vnder water, within fiue or sixe
houres fight, set out a flagge of truce, and parled for mercie, desiring our Generall to saue their liues, and to take
their goods, and that they would presently yeeld. Our
Generall promised them mercy, and willed them to strike
their sayles, and to hoyse out their boat, & to come
aboord: which newes they were full glad to heare, and
presently stroke their sailes, hoysed their boat out, and one
of their chiefe marchants came aboord vnto our Generall:
and falling downe vpon his knees, offered to haue kissed
his feete, and craued mercie: the Captaine and their Pilote,
at their comming vsed the like duetie and reuerence as the
former did. The Generall promised their liues and good
vsage. They declared what goods they had within boord, to
wit, an hundreth and two and twenty thousand pezos of
gold: and the rest of the riches that the ship was laden
with, was in Silkes, Sattens, Damasks, with Muske and

160

diuers other marchandize, and great store of all manner of victualls, with the choice of many conserues of all sorts for to eate, and of sundry sorts of very good wines. These things beeing made knowne, they were commanded to stay aboord the Desire, and on the sixt day of Nouember following, we went into an harbour, which is called by the Spaniards, Aguada Segura, or Puerto Seguro."

During the division of the booty, a mutiny broke out, especially in the ship "Content," but was quelled. The Spaniards, to the number of one hundred and ninety men and women, were set ashore. Ammunition and arms were left them, and the English departed: taking with them however from the Spanish boat two clever young Japanese, three boys born in Manila, a Portuguese, and one Thomas de Ersola, a pilot from Acapulco. The "Santa Ana" was burned on the nineteenth of November, and the English turned toward home. That same night the "Content" vanished and was seen no more. January 3, 1588, the Ladrones were reached. They had the experiences with the natives that are so often described by the Spaniards, iron being the usual article bartered by the English. The natives are described as "of a tawny colour, and maruellous fat, and bigger ordinarily of stature then the most part of our men in England, wearing their haire maruellous long: yet some of them haue it made vp, and tyed with a knot on the Crowne and some with two knots, much like vnto their Images which we faw carued in wood, and standing in the head of their boats, like vnto the Images of the deuill." January 14, they reached the Philippines at Cabo del Santo Espiritu, "which is of very great bignesse and length .... and it is short of the chiefest Island of the Philippinas called Manilla, about sixtie leagues. Manilla is vvel planted and inhabited with Spaniards, to the number of sixe or seuen hundred persons: vvhich dvvell in a tovvne vnvvalled, which hath three or foure Blocke-houses, part made of vvood, and part of stone, being indeed of no great strength: they haue one or tvvo small Gallies belonging to the Tovvne. It is a very rich place of Gold, and many other commodities; and they haue yeerely traffique from Alcapulco in Nueva Espanna, and also twenty or thirtie shippes from China, and from the Sanguelos, which bring them many sorts of marchandize. They bring great store of gold vvith them, vvhich they traffique and exchange for siluer, and give vveight for vveight. These Sanguelos are men of maruellous capacity, in deuising and making all manner of things, especially in all handiecrafts and sciences: and euery one is so expert, perfect, and skilfull in his facultie, as fevv or no Christians are able to go beyond them in that vvhich they take in hand. For drawing and imbroidering vpon Satten, Silke, or

Lavvne, either beast, fovvle, fish, or vvorme, for liuelinesse and perfect-
nesse, both in Silke, Siluer, Gold, and Pearle, they excell. Also the
fourteenth day at night we entred the Straits between the Island of Lucon, and the Island of Camlaia." The natives imagining them Spaniards
willingly traded their food with them. At an anchorage Thomas Ersola,
the Spanish pilot, was hanged for trying to inform the Spanish of the
English. The following on the customs of the inhabitants as seen at the
island of Capul is interesting, and accords, with slight differences, with
the Spanish records:

> "We roade for the space of nine dayes, about this Island of
> Capul, where we had diuerse kinds of fresh victualls, with
> excellent fresh water in euery bay, and great store of wood.
> The people of this Island go almost all naked, and are
> tawny of colour. The men weare onely a stroope about
> their wastes, of some kind of linnen of their owne
> weauing, which is made of Plantan-leaues, and another
> stroope comming from their backe vnder their twistes,
> Which couereth their priuy parts, and is made fast to their
> girdles at their nauels; which is this. Euery man and man-
> child among them, hath a nayle of Tynne thrust quite
> through the head of his priuie part, being split in the lower
> ende, and riuetted, and on the head of the nayle is as it
> were a Crowne: which is driuen through their priuities
> when they be yong, and the place groweth vp ag tine [sic],
> without any great paine to the child: and they take this
> nayle out and in as occasion serueth; and for the truth
> thereof, we our selues haue taken one of these nayles from
> a Sonne of one of the Kings, which was of the age of
> tenne yeeres, who did weare the same in his priuy member.
> This custome was granted at the request of the women of
> the Country, who finding their men to be giuen to the fov-
> vle sinne of Sodomie, desired fome remedie against that
> mischiefe, and obtained this before named of the Magis-
> trates. Moreouer all the males are circumcised, hauing the
> fore skinne of their flesh cut avvay. These people vvholly
> vvorshippe the Deuill, and oftentimes haue conference
> vvith him, vvhich appeareth vnto them in moft vgly and
> monstrous shape."

In this island Candish, or Cavendish, announced their nationality to
the natives—whom he had made pay tribute in "Hogges, Hennes, Potatoes, and Cocos"—and their hostility to the Spaniards. The natives

promised "both themselues and all the Islands thereabout, to ayde him, whensoeuer hee should come againe to ouercome the Spaniards." Their tribute money was returned to them in token of the Englishmen's hostility to the Spaniards. January 24 the English coasted along Luzon, and ran northwest between that island and Masbat.

> "The eight and twentieth day, in the morning about seuen of the clocke, riding at an anchor betwixt two Islands, wee espyed a Frigat vnder her two Coarses, comming out betweene two other Islands, which (as wee imagined) came from Manilla, sayling close aboord the shore, along the maine Island of Panama. Here wee rode at anchor all that night, and perceiued that certaine Spaniards (which came from Manilla to Ragaun, to fetch a new shippe of the Kings, there builded) had disperfed their Band into two or three parts, and kept great Watch in seuerall steedes, with Fires, and shooting off their Pieces. This Island hath much plaine Ground in it, in many places, and many faire and straight Trees doe grow vpon it, fit for to make excellent good Masts for all sorts of shippes. There are also Mynes of very fine Gold in it, which are in the custodie of the Indians. And to the South-ward of this place, there is another very great Island, which is not subdued by the Spaniards, nor any other Nation. The people which inhabit it, are all Negros, and the Island is called the Island of Negros; and is almost as bigge as England, standing in nine degrees: The most part of it seemeth to be very lowe Land, and by all likelyhood is very fruitfull.
> "The nine and twentieth day of January, about six of the clocke in the morning wee set sayle, sending our Boat before, vntill it was two of the clocke in the afternoone, passing all this time as it were through a Strait, betwixt the laid two Islands of Panama, and the Island of Negros; and about sixteene Leagues off, wee espyed a faire opening, trending South-west and by South: at which time our Boat came aboord, and our Generall sent commendations to the Spanish Captaine, which wee came from the Euening before, by a Spaniard which wee had taken, and willed him to provide a good store of Gold; for hee meant for to see him with his company at Manilla within few yeeres; and that hee did but want a bigger Boat to haue landed his men; or

else hee would haue seene him then; and so caused him to be let on shore."

Thence the expedition passed through the Moluccas. At one of the islands where they reprovisioned two Portuguese came to inquire of "Don Antonio their King, then in England." These Portuguese declared "that if their King Don Antonio, would come vnto them, they would warrant him to haue all the Malucos at commandment, besides China, Sangles, and the Isles of the Philippinas, and that he might be assured to have all the Indians on his side that are in the countrey." The sixteenth of May the Cape of Good Hope was sighted. August 23, the Azores Islands hove in sight, and on September 9, they put into Plymouth. A letter from the commander contains the following:

"The matter of most profit vnto me, was a great ship of the Kings vvhich I tooke at California, vvhich ship came from the Philippinas, beeing one of the richest of merchandize that euer passed those Seas, as the Kings Register and marchants accounts did shew: for it did amount in value to * in Mexico to be sold. Which goods (for that my Ships vvere not able to containe the least part of them) I vvas inforced to set on fire. From the Cape of California, being the vthermost part of all Nueua Espanna, I nauigated to the Islands of the Philippinas, hard vpon the Coast of China; of which Countrey I haue brought such intelligence as hath not been heard of in these parts. The statlinesse and riches of vvhich Countrey I feare to make report of, least I should not be credited: for if I had not knovvn sufficiently the incomparable vvealth of that Countrey, I should haue beene as incredulous thereof, as others vvill be rhat [sic] haue not had the like experience."
166

Appendix B:
Early Years of the Dutch in
the East Indies

The voyages of the Dutch into the East Indies had important results for both Spain and Portugal. While they concerned themselves principally with Java and the islands of the Moluccas, they made incursions among the Philippines, where they were a constant menace for many years. The first two expeditions—that of Houtman, June 11, 1596-August 14, 1597; and that of van Neck and van Warwyck, May 1, 1598-May 30, 1600—did little but establish the custom and make beginnings in the East India trade. The first was concerned mainly with Java, but the second entered (with four of its eight vessels) the Moluccas, and brought back a load of cloves. These two expeditions also marked the beginning of troubles with the Portuguese and natives. They were both by way of the Cape of Good Hope.

VOYAGE OF OLIVER VAN NOORDT
The first voyage of great importance was that of Oliver van Noordt. In 1598 a commercial company contracted with him to conduct five vessels through the Strait of Magellan for traffic on South American coasts. This fleet sailed on September 13, 1598, going first to Plymouth, England, where an English pilot, who had been with Candish on his expedition, was engaged. After various fortunes along the eastern South American coasts, during which about one hundred men were lost, the fleet entered the Strait of Magellan November 5, 1599. Contentions between van Noordt and his vice-admiral resulted in the latter's being marooned, and the elevation to his place of Captain Pierre de Lint, while Lambert Biesman was made captain of the "Concordia." The vice-admiral and his ship were lost on March 14, 1600, which with other losses, reduced the fleet to but two vessels. On debouching from the strait the fleet cruised along the Chilean coast, alternately trading and

committing depredations, and seizing prizes, and finally determined to go to the Philippines by way of the Ladrones. On September 15, the latter islands were sighted. There they met the same experience as the Spaniards from the thievishness of the natives.

"These people, both men and women, seem amphibious, and to be able to live on water as well as on the land, so well do they swim and dive. Five pieces of iron were thrown into the sea to them for the pleasure of seeing them exercise themselves. One of them was skilful enough to get all five of them, and in so short a time that one can regard it as marvelous.... Their canoes are so well made ... and are fifteen or twenty feet long. They are quite roomy and good sailers. They do not turn about to tack, but place the helm in what was the bow, and leave the sail, which is made of reed mats and resembles a mizzen-sail, in its same position without changing it." Thence the route to the Philippines was continued. "They are called also the Manillas, from the name of the chief port, and the city built by the Spaniards.

"Some call them the islands of Lucon, because their chief island is so named. It is said to be quite one hundred leagues in circumference. There is located the city of Manille or Manilhe, the capital of all these islands. They were formerly part of the crown of China, which abandoned them for some slight pretext. After that their laws and civilization were so poorly observed that they seemed deadened when the Spaniards landed there. In fact, the inhabitants there lived like beasts. Each one enslaved his neighbor, if he could, and their chief occupation was mutual oppression.

"Such a nature gave the Spaniards great facility in subduing them, which was rendered greater, since these people were simple and very stupid. As soon as one mentioned baptism to them, they ran to get it in droves, and became Christians to the extent desired. However the Ilocos and others, too, who are called Pintados did not cease to give trouble to their new masters.

"All these islands are densely populated and produce abundance of rice and wine made from nypa. Deer, buffaloes, bulls, cows, swine, goats, and other live-stock are found, although formerly they had none. But now the care exercised by the Spaniards has made them so abundant, that they yield in no way to Nouvelle Espagne.

"There are also many civet-cats, and all sorts of fruit as in China. They yield considerable quantities of honey and wax. They even have gold, but although the islanders pay their tribute to the Spaniards in gold, the latter have not as yet—that is in the year 1600—been able to ascertain where they get it, notwithstanding their efforts. They are commencing to sow wheat there. Flour was formerly brought from Japon. The islands also supplied quantities of ebony and bamboo.

"The Chinese engage extensively in trade there. They take all kinds of merchandise there from China, namely, silks, cottons, china-ware, gunpowder, sulphur, iron, steel, quicksilver, copper, flour, walnuts, chestnuts, biscuits, dates, all sorts of stuffs, writing-desks, and other curiosities.

"The Spaniards load all this merchandise in Manila and export it to Nouvelle Espagne, whence more than one and one-half millions of silver in money and in bars is taken annually to the Philippines. This silver is exchanged for gold, giving four livres of silver for one of gold. But this traffic is not extensive, since there is enough gold in Perou and Chili. They prefer to traffic with the Chinese, for their returns reach one thousand per cent.

"The city of Manille is located in fourteen degrees of north latitude. There is situated the residence of the Spanish governor, who rules all the islands. The archbishop also lives there. He has supreme authority in the ecclesiastical affairs of all the same islands, where there are also three bishops suffragan to himself."

On October 14, 1600, the Dutch sighted the cape of Espiritu Santo, whence they steered toward Manila. On the sixteenth their first encounter with the Spanish in the islands occurred, but the Dutch reassured the latter by flying a Spanish pennant, and declaring themselves to be French commissioned by the Spanish monarch. Consequently they were allowed to buy provisions freely, in return for which the natives demanded money.

"The majority of these Indians were naked. Some wore a cloth garment, while some were even clad like Spaniards.

The chiefs, who belong to the former race of commanders of the country, and who yet remember that fact, have their skin cut or pricked very skilfully and singularly. These cuts or pricks have been made with iron and never fade.

"Besides this is a wretched race, who have no weapons, so that the Spaniards tyrannize over them at will. They make them pay a tribute of three reals [sic], that is, a trifle less than three Dutch florins, per head, all men or women above twenty years.

"There are very few Spaniards in each district. They have a priest, whom the inhabitants of the place revere greatly, so much so that only lack of priests prevents them from holding all these islands in servitude; for even in places where there are neither priests nor Spaniards they have made the people pay tribute."

The Spaniards at last became suspicious of the strangers and demanded to see their commission, upon which the one given by the prince of Orange was produced, whereat great consternation reigned, and the Dutch were forbidden more provisions. The latter continuing their course entered the Manila strait on October 24, anchoring near Capul. On landing near here, one of the crew, Jean Caleway [i.e., John Calleway], an Englishman, and a musician, was somehow left behind, and it was conjectured that the natives had seized him. November 1, the vessels left Capul for Manila, sailing among the various islands, and committing some depredations on Spanish, native, and Chinese vessels. From a Chinese pilot, van Noordt gained certain information concerning Manila.

"The houses of the city of Manila are built close together. The city is surrounded by a rampart supported by a wall. More than fifteen thousand Chinese live outside its walls. They engage in their business together, and are given to various industries. In addition more than four hundred vessels go there annually from China, from the city and province of Chincheo, laden with silks and all sorts of merchandise. They take back silver money in return. They come at a certain fixed time, namely, after the month of December or between Christmas and Easter. At the beginning of this present month of November ... two Japanese vessels also generally sail to Manila, laden with iron, flour, bacon, and other food...."

"The walls of the city of Manila and the houses are built of stone, in the modern fashion. It is so large and extensive that the Spaniards have had a second wall built inside the city of less size than the first, within which to retire in case of need.... It was made especially in consideration of the Japanese, of whom the Spaniards are very suspicious.

"The governor of all the islands, who resembles a viceroy, lives in Manille, as does also the archbishop. Besides the cathedral there are several other beautiful churches. All the inhabitants of these islands are either Christians or pagans. As for the Moros or Mahometans, they have all been exterminated."

The Dutch continued their depredations, and sent a letter by an Indian to the governor, notifying him that they were going to visit him. Biesman was sent on a scouting expedition, from which he finally returned, after having been considered lost by some of the Dutch.

"The island of Manille, called Lucon by its inhabitants, is larger than England and Scotland together. [167] There are other various islands about it, also very large."

From a Japanese vessel some provisions were obtained, and the vessel was allowed to continue its course to Manila. The depredations of the Dutch were called to a sudden halt by the two Spanish vessels sent out under Dr. Morga on the fourteenth of December, 1600, when ensued the fight described in Morga. [168] Van Noordt inspired his men with new courage by threatening to blow up the vessel unless they fought more bravely. The Dutch found "a little silver box containing little tickets filled with prayers and devotions to various saints, to obtain their protection in times of peril," on the dead body of a Spaniard. "The two Spanish vessels had about five hundred men, both Spaniards and Indians, and ten pieces of cannon." The Dutch flagship finally returned to Holland by way of Borneo, and Cape of Good Hope, reaching Rotterdam August 26, 1601. [169]

* * * * *

Etienne van der Hagen's expedition (April 6, 1599—July 12, 1601) reached the island of Amboina, where they besieged the Portuguese fort there for two months, but were unable to take it. They made an alliance with the natives before leaving against the Portuguese. The Dutch fleet consisted of three vessels, and was sent out by the Dutch East India Company for trading purposes.

The first expedition of Paul van Caerden (the Blancardo of the Spanish accounts) occupied December 21, 1599—October 11, 1601, and was sent out by the Nouvelle Compagnie des Brabancons. The fleet—four vessels in all—left Holland in charge of Admiral Pierre Both. In their company sailed four vessels of the old company, but they separated almost immediately. They all went by way of the Cape of Good Hope. At Bantam in Java two vessels of the four were sent, under command of van Caerden, to trade for pepper. The two ships coasted the shore of the island of Sumatra, stopping at various places, without much success, on account of the tricks of the natives in their trade, until they reached Achem in the northern part of the island. There they had trouble with the natives which was instigated by a Portuguese priest, and after seizing some pepper, which act they justified, returned to Bantam in Java, where their cargo was completed. Van Caerden lost twenty-seven men on this voyage, but brought back ten others who had been held prisoners at Achem.

The second voyage of van Neck, or Nek (June 28, 1600—July 15, 1604), followed, as the preceding expedition, the African route to Bantam, where it met two Dutch vessels of the new trading company. The fleet of six vessels had separated by common consent, October 10, 1600, in order to facilitate their trade. Van Neck in the vessels with him, skirted Celebes, and went to Ternate, where he was cordially received by the natives. There the usual troubles with the Portuguese began, which ended in an indecisive naval battle. Shortly after, the Dutch left for China, leaving six men to watch their interests among the natives. "On the nineteenth [of August] they anchored near the island of Coyo, one of the Philippines. There they sent a small boat ashore. Its crew learned that the inhabitants were savages, who paid tribute to the Spaniards. On the twenty-second they anchored near another large island of the Philippines, whose name cannot be found on the maps. It was called Langhairs-eiland, or Longhair Island, because its inhabitants wore their hair long, and hanging below the shoulders." September 20 they reached the Chinese coast, and on the twenty-seventh sighted "a large city, built almost like Spanish cities," which they found to be Macao. There unfortunate encounters with the Portuguese lost the Dutch some men; and failing in their efforts there, they went to Patane, where they traded some pepper. Thence the return voyage to Holland by way of the Cape of Good Hope was made. The other three vessels of his fleet arrived six weeks later. As consorts to van Neck's six vessels two other vessels had left Holland on the same date, also sent by the new trading company. After several mutinies they reached Sumatra, whence after troubles with the king of Achem, the two vessels left, leaving twelve of their men prisoners. The efforts of the latter to escape were fruitless and even the efforts (in 1602) of one of the vessels of Admiral Heemskerk, commander of a Dutch trading fleet, were unable to rescue the prisoners.

April 5, 1601, a Dutch fleet of five vessels, under Wolphart Harmansan, set out with another fleet under Jaques van Heemskerk. On May 8, the two fleets separated, the former reaching the Bantam channel December 26, 1601. Several naval encounters with the Portuguese fleet under Andrea Furtado de Mendoza resulted in partial victory for the Dutch, who, after refitting at Bantam, took their course through the Moluccas, and then returned to Bantam and Holland, reaching that country, April 4, 1603.

Georges Spilberg left Holland May 5, 1601, with three vessels. Rounding the cape, he cruised along until reaching Ceylon, whence he went to Sumatra in September of 1602. At Sumatra he joined some English vessels, and all remained together, and opposed the Portuguese. April 3, 1603, the Dutch and English left Sumatra and went to Java. At Bantam they were joined by Admiral Wybrant Waarwyk with nine vessels. On June 30, Admiral Heemskerk anchored at the same place with a Portuguese prize. After effecting their trade, the vessels returned to Holland, and Spilberg reached that country May 24, 1604.

Corneille de Veen, in command of nine vessels, sailed from Holland June 17, 1602, and was joined at sea by three others. April 15, 1603, Sumatra was sighted, and the fleet anchored at Bantam in Java on the twenty-ninth. Thence part of the fleet sailed for China. The fleet captured near Macao a Portuguese vessel richly laden. They also fought with a Siamese vessel, mistaking it for an enemy. Leaving Bantam finally on their homeward trip, on January 27, 1604, they reached Holland the thirtieth of August.

The expedition under Wybrandt van Waarwyk marked a new progression in Dutch trading in Eastern seas. His expedition established Bantam in Java more fully as the chief Dutch trading-post and base of supplies. The number of vessels at his command (fifteen) enabled him to despatch them in different directions to pursue their trade. The hostility to, and competition with, the Portuguese became more marked, and the entrance into India (through Ceylon), Siam, and China, more pronounced. This expedition left Holland July 17, 1602, being joined on the nineteenth by other vessels. Near the Cape of Good Hope three vessels separated with orders to proceed directly to Achem in Sumatra. At that place they met three vessels, which had left Holland May 30, 1602, and whose commander Sebald de Weert received commission from Waarwyk as vice-admiral of the six vessels. After negotiations at Achem, the six vessels established relations and promised assistance against the Portuguese, in Ceylon, but they almost ended by the massacre of the vice-admiral and a number of his men. Engagements with the Portuguese through these seas, and more or less successful attempts at trading and establishing themselves marked the progress of these vessels, until the return of three of them to Holland in the latter part of 1604. The main body of the fleet had experiences about similar to the above vessels, singly and in company, cruising through the East Indian seas, trading for pepper, cinnamon, silks, and other products. The Moluccas and the Philippines were generally given a wide berth, the Dutch seeking to establish themselves fully on portions of the mainland and in Sumatra and Java. Francois Wittert, who was later commander of a fleet, was made chief commissary at Bantam and given detailed instructions. The admiral finally reached Holland June 4, 1607, with several vessels.

The expedition in charge of Etienne van der Hagen (or Haagen), that set out from Holland late in 1603 and early in 1604, had also decisive results that more completely established the Dutch power in the East Indies. This expedition was destined to come more intimately in contact with the Portuguese and Spaniards than any former expedition. From this time and even before, the Dutch expeditions overlapped, and Dutch vessels in the Eastern seas were by no means rare. This fleet (the second voyage of van der Hagen) comprised twelve vessels and twelve hundred men. Its course was by way of Goa, Calicut, Cochin, and Ceylon, to Sumatra and Java, reaching the post at Bantam December 31, 1604. There, shortly after, some English vessels were met. On January 17, 1605, the principal vessels of the fleet left for the Moluccas. February 21, they anchored at Amboina, where they were about to storm the Portuguese fort, when the commander capitulated. "After several conferences between the Portuguese commander's deputies and the admiral, it was resolved that all the unmarried Portuguese should retire, and that those married could be free to remain, if they took the oath of allegiance to the States-general and to Prince Maurice. Each one was allowed to take his gun or musket, but all the cannon, ammunition, and arms of the king were to remain in the fort." The admiral and fifty men went to the captured fort, where they ran up the Dutch colors. The fort and island had contained six hundred Portuguese. Forty-six Portuguese families remained and took the oath. "This victory was considerable, not only because of its slight cost, no blood having been shed, but because this place and this island were of great importance." Thence five Dutch vessels went to Tidore, where the Portuguese lost two vessels in a sea fight. Then the Portuguese fort was attacked, which was taken May 19, 1605, with a loss of two

Dutchmen and seventy-three Portuguese. The Portuguese, five hundred in number, took the boats offered them and set out for the Philippines. "By this last victory, the Portuguese were driven from all the Moluccas, and had nothing more there, except a small fort in the island of Soler, near Timer." The conquered fort was destroyed. Meanwhile other vessels of the fleet cruised about Sumatra, Java, Malacca, and neighboring places, trading and seeking to check the Portuguese. Shortly after June of 1607, the Spaniards, two hundred and fifty in number, attacked one of the Dutch and Ternatan forts, but were repulsed. On the desertion of the Tidore fort by the Dutch, seven hundred Spaniards returned to it. Thus the Dutch continued to strengthen their hold throughout the Indies.

The expedition under command of Admiral Corneille Matelief (1605-1608) was remarkable chiefly for its siege of Malacca, and later its manipulations in the Moluccas and in China. The fleet was composed of eleven vessels and one thousand three hundred and fifty-seven men, and cost 1,952,282 livres. Great trouble was experienced by the admiral in the intoxication and excesses of his men, which led to insubordination, during the entire course of the expedition. Also in all parts he met a great unwillingness among the natives for work and the coming to definite conclusions, the latter exercising duplicity and at times treachery in their dealings with the Dutch. On March 22, 1606, the fleet sighted Sumatra, after hearing of the successes in Amboina and Tidore. Going to the mainland they made agreements or treaties with the king of Johore, clause ten of which reads: "Neither of the two parties shall make peace with the king of Spain, without the consent of the other." The succeeding siege of Malacca resulted in failure, and on August 24, 1606, the Dutch retired after losing two of their ships. The Portuguese were in charge of Andrea Furtado de Mendoza. On the return of the Dutch to Sumatra and Java, they met the great Portuguese fleet consisting of eighteen galleons, four galleys, one caravel, and twenty-three fustas, with over three thousand men—the largest fleet ever seen in the Indias—and in the combat captured and destroyed four galleons, although with some considerable loss to themselves. The Portuguese prisoners taken formed lengthy material for debates between the Portuguese and Dutch. On December 6, 1606, the admiral determined to go to the Moluccas with six vessels, and to send the others to Achem to load cargo for Holland. Reaching those islands after anchoring at Bantam, the Dutch negotiated with the natives for their aid against the Spaniards garrisoned in Ternate and Tidore. At Amboina, the admiral "learned that the soldiers of the garrison were living there in great debauchery, and that they became intoxicated, and nearly every man had his concubine. On that account the inhabitants were greatly shocked and were losing all their affection for the Dutch. They said that the Portuguese married women among them, by which the two nations were united. But since there were no marriages with the Dutch, the two races could not be bound by affection." Besides the natives wished settlers and not new men continually, whom they did not know. In consequence the Dutch were permitted to marry the native women. Skirmishes with the Spaniards resulted in little gain for the Dutch, and finally the fleet sailed for China, after passing among a few of the Philippines, where they entered into various relations and had various adventures, trying ever to establish a fixed trade. Thence the vessels went in different directions and on different missions toward the Dutch base at Bantam. At Bantam Admiral Paul van Caerden anchored on January 5, 1608, to whom Matelief communicated the necessity of first attending to Molucca affairs, giving him also information and advice concerning those islands and the Dutch and Spaniards there. Shortly after Admiral Matelief returned to Holland, where he anchored on September 2, 1608. Admiral Matelief drew up while on this expedition a good resume of Dutch aspirations in the East Indies that shows the compelling motive in their expeditions thither. This memorial is as follows.

* * * * *

Memoir by Admiral C. Matelief, on the subject of the condition and the commerce of the Indies

When I consider the condition of our country, and the wars that afflict it, on the part of an enemy so powerful as Albert of Austria, who is sustained by the house of Austria, and by his own house of Spain, it seems to me that one cannot be more assured of the prosperity of affairs in the Indias, than by leaving them solely in the hands of the directors [of the trading company].

The Spaniards and the Portuguese are our adversaries. More than a century ago they began to establish themselves there. They have gained an entrance into several countries, where they have fortresses, many men, and an established government. Consequently they are enabled to attend to their business with greater certainty and by more convenient methods than we, for we have to bring men from Holland, who become weakened by the fatigues of the voyage, while the subjects of the Portuguese, who live in the country, are fresh and full of health.

For, although the Portuguese have an insufficient number of men in the Indias, to attend to all matters that arise, and at the same time defend themselves against our nation,

they can send men there much easier than we. Vessels
from Portugal are obliged to go only as far as Goa, where
their men disembark and rest. Then they form their fleets
from them; and the other Spaniards who come from the
Manilles do the same.

If, then, we would also establish ourselves advantageously
and solidly in the Indias, we must necessarily have some
station, where we may be received and free, on our arrival
from Holland. This would be the means of great profits.
Refreshments could be found there ready for the crews
and for the vessels. That would increase our reputation
among the Indian princes, who as yet have not dared re-
pose entire confidence in us. The natives are sufficiently
convinced that the Dutch are a good race, and more gentle
and tractable than the Spaniards. "But," they say, "what
good does that do us? The Dutch come here in passing,
and only while on their journey. As soon as their vessels
are laden, they return. After that we are abandoned to the
Spaniards and Portuguese, against whom we are powerless
to defend ourselves. They come to pounce upon us, because we have traded with the Dutch, their enemies. On
the other hand, if we attach ourselves to the Spanish, they,
at least, protect us in our needs. On the contrary, although
the Dutch should come with forces sufficient to protect
us, we fear nothing from them; they do not treat us as
enemies. Even though we trade with the Portuguese, the
Dutch allow us to live quietly, and we have only to be careful of those who molest us. Consequently our best plan is
to favor the Portuguese, lest they annihilate us."

Such are the reflections of all the Indians. Besides the Portuguese do their best to persuade them that we have no
forces, that we are but a rabble, who scarcely have fixed
habitations in our own country, and quite far from being
able to make lasting settlements in the Indias. As for them,
they are established there with men who wish to live there.
Therefore it is necessary for us to seek means by which to
gain the Indians, and make them understand that we have
forces, and wish also to become established among them.
If not, one must recognize that our affairs will prosper ill.

The commerce of the Indias consists chiefly: 1. In pepper,
which is loaded at Bantam, Jahor, Patane, Queda, and
Achin; 2. in cloves, which are loaded at Amboina and the

Moluccas; 3. in nutmeg and mace, or the rind of the nut-meg, which are loaded at Banda; 4. in the commerce of Cambaie; 5. in the commerce of the Coromandel coast; 6. in the commerce of both the Chinese and Japanese coasts.

If the commerce of each of these is not managed by one nation, whether the Portuguese or others, it will happen that one will destroy the other. It will cause the price of merchandise in the Indias to advance, and a low price will be paid for them in Europe.

However, in regard to pepper, it is impossible for us to get the commerce all to ourselves; for, besides the Portuguese, the English have also undertaken the navigation to Ban-tam. They have their trading-posts and houses, and are trading there peacefully, while we are at war against the Portuguese. We defend Bantam and the English together, while they enjoy there the profits that cost them neither defenses, blood, nor any annoyance.[*]

Besides we are at peace with the English, and it would be unjust to try to find means to exclude them from a com-merce which they have already commenced. But measures can easily be taken to prevent them from entering into the commerce of other spices. In regard to pepper, we would have to make it serve as a ballast. By this means we could give it so cheaply that the other nations, finding scarcely any profit in it longer, would be obliged to cease trading in it themselves, without counting on our part our profits from the other merchandise.

For, according to my opinion, we could easily attract all the commerce of nutmegs and mace. For this purpose, in-stead of seizing Banda, and building a fort there, which would cost considerable, and give us a bad reputation among the Indian princes, the following is what I think that we should do.

As the king of Macassar is a powerful prince, whose coun-try is densely populated, and well supplied with rice and all manner of food; and as he furnishes them to Malacca and Banda: it would be necessary to make a treaty with him, and to send him three vessels with two hundred men for

[*] The king of Bantam is too young to negotiate with, and too much money would be spent uselessly. For the natives throughout the Indies would not hesi-tate to violate any treaty in any peril or to their own profit.

176

his country. This number, together with the Macassar men, would be sufficient to attack Banda, and we would promise the king to deliver it into his hands, without claiming any recompense for this aid, except that no other nation but our own could load merchandise there, and that the nutmegs and mace would be taken annually at a fixed price, namely, at the selling price at the time of the expedition.

[Matelief is certain that the king of Macassar will acquiesce, and would also probably be willing to build a trading-house for the Dutch. Other conditions for the security of Banda might also be imposed in the treaty.]

Of the clove-trade, it is very difficult for us to render ourselves masters. We have the product of Amboina, Luho, and Cambelo; but not that yielded by the Moluccas. The only means of obtaining it is to drive the Spaniards from Ternate, and it can easily be imagined that the task is not easy. However I shall not hesitate to write here my thought concerning the matter.

The thing does not appear impossible to me, if one wishes to build on a firm foundation. This would require a return to the Malacca affair. For had the Portuguese lost Malacca, they could not easily go from Goa to reenforce the Moluccas; and I do not think there would be much trouble in preventing the sending of supplies to Ternate from the Manilles.

First, we should have to send three or four vessels to the king of Mindanao, whose country is densely inhabited, and who, as report runs, can launch fifty caracoas. All this fleet would go to Panama or Panati [i.e., Panay] which is near the Manilles, and where there is a place named Otting [i.e., Oton], guarded by but eighteen Spanish soldiers with about the same number of other inhabitants, so that in all there are but forty whites. This place would be destroyed, or if the blacks of Mindanao wished to keep it, it would be given them, for it is a country abounding in rice and several other foods, which are transported to Ternate.

Thence I would suggest going directly to the Manilles to destroy all the vessels in their ports, so that they could not aid Ternate. Immediately a vessel of one hundred and sixty or two hundred tons would be sent back to Mindanao, which would cross with the king's caracoas to the strait of

Tagima, to capture the vessels that should try still to go to Ternate, because there is no other route. After capturing one or two of them, no other vessels would dare to try it, so that Ternate would perish from famine. For did we try at present to overpower the island by force, I believe that the Spaniards could fortify it so strongly, and have so many men there, that large armies would be required to drive them out.

It would be difficult for them to provide Ternate with cloth, for the little taken there now is brought by the Chinese to the Manilles. This want of cloth would not fail to trouble the inhabitants, and it would have to be sent from Malacca, and that could not be done easily. If a galley could also be taken to Ternate, it would greatly annoy the Spaniards....

The commerce of China depends moreover upon Malacca. If the Portuguese were driven from that place, the Chinese would have to give up that traffic....

The commerce of cotton stuffs at Coromandel is of great importance, for all the inhabitants of the Indias dress in those stuffs, and must have them at any price. There are different styles for each nation, according to their taste, and they make them so in different places ... If Malacca were taken from the Portuguese, they would have no further favorable opportunity for the trade in cloth....

If no means are found to besiege Malacca again, the Portuguese might make use of their fustas to hinder our trade with Coromandel. For, since this entire coast is low, and the fustas draw but little water, they could always station themselves between the shore and our vessels. Besides it is very dangerous for vessels to anchor there. If the enemy is spry, he could carry the news to Goa in one week, whence they could easily despatch their fleets against us.

It is certain that, if the Portuguese could be driven from Malacca, they would have to renounce trade on the Coromandel coast; for they would have no safe course, should they wish to get cloth, and they could gain nothing, for the expense would overbalance the profit. Consequently, I believe that all the commerce of the Portuguese in the East Indies depends on Malacca, and that, in order to cut it, one must take that place.

After that, there is no doubt that the inhabitants of Bantam would not be reasonable, when they would see us in fixed establishments, and would understand that since the English had no other commerce in the Indias than that of pepper, they would not care to make frequent voyages, or great expenses. The pepper of Jambeo, Andragyri, and other points, that is taken to Bantam, would be taken to Malacca, where, also, cloth for the return cargo would be found.

I have not learned whether the Portuguese have any strength at Bengale. All whom I have heard speak of that country say that a good commerce can be obtained there....

It would be advisable to send two vessels to Arracan to try to trade. Besides the king is very anxious for us to go there. A Portuguese, one Philippe de Britto, has a fort there, with a garrison of eighty men. This fort is fifty leagues inland, and Britto holds the entire country in check. Although the king of Arracan is powerful, he has been unable as yet to find means for driving out this Portuguese. This alarms all the kingdom of Pegu, especially since it is annoyed by civil wars. That country has immense wealth, especially in precious gems.

I do not believe that anything can be done with Cambaie while the Portuguese have forts on the Malabar coast, and while the king is not better disposed toward us. We must wait until he knows us better, and until his mind is disabused concerning the Spaniards. For, until he gives us permission to trade in his ports, we would always encounter great danger, since large vessels can not enter. Besides that country is so near Goa, that the Portuguese would be notified as soon as we arrived there, and would pounce upon us with their forces, so that we could hope for neither help nor protection.

All the above points to Malacca's importance, for the establishment that we wish to make in the Indias. Therefore, for that reason, we should reflect on it well. For, in short, it is time now for us to assure ourselves of a fixed place and of a retreat. And this place or that place that one might select, would cost immense sums before it could reach the present condition of Malacca. Besides it will be very difficult to find a place so advantageous.

* * * * *

The second expedition of Paul van Caerden (1606-1609) consisted of eight vessels, equipped at a cost of 1,825,135 livres. Its chief result was the capture of the Spanish fort at Machian and the two captures of the commander, who finally died in prison at Manila. The expedition sailed April 20, 1606, and shortly afterward began to have trouble with the Portuguese. After rounding the cape they besieged and took a Portuguese trading-post, after which they cruised past Goa, Calcutta, and other places, finally sighting Sumatra, January 5, 1607, and anchoring at Bantam, January 6. There they met the Matelief expedition. With a half-hearted following of Matelief's advice, van Caerden anchored at Amboina in March, whence on May 10, he started for Ternate. His capture by the Spanish of Ternate, the taking of the Spanish fort at Machian—the place "most abounding in cloves of all the Moluccas"—and other operations on land and sea followed. The expedition finally left Ternate on August 3, 1608, and by way of Bantam, reached Holland August 6, 1609, with a portion of its vessels.

The few years succeeding, events came thick and fast. Dutch interests in the Indias multiplied. The taking of Malacca was again considered. Resistance to Portuguese and Spanish interests became even more pronounced, while the English and the Dutch came to definite agreements, between their respective trading companies as to trade in the Indias. The Dutch opened trade communication with Japan. They became thoroughly established in the Moluccas, in Amboina, and in the islands of Banda. The Spanish under Governor Juan de Silva of Manila, took the offensive, and opposed the Dutch vigorously, maintaining certain forts in Ternate, from which the efforts of the Dutch failed to dislodge them. A Dutch fleet of thirteen vessels, with Pierre Verhoeven as Admiral, and Francois Wittert as vice-admiral, left Holland in 1607. Their course carried them along the shores of India, before Malacca, and among the islands of Sumatra, Java, and others. They had communication with vessels of other Dutch commanders, among them those of the ill-fated van Caerden, who was exchanged by the Spaniards March 23, 1610, proclaimed general of all the Moluccas July 1, 1610, and shortly after captured again by the Spaniards. They had certain negotiations also with the English. At Borneo, Amboina, Banda, Ternate, and their neighboring islands many important negotiations were carried on, looking ever to the strengthening and prepetuation of Dutch power. The war with the Banda islanders was at length settled satisfactorily, although it required a number of years. In this period came the twelve years' truce between Spain and Holland, or the States-general, but notwithstanding active hostilities between the two nations occurred afterward, the defeat and capture of

Wittert's vessels near Manila Bay occurring after news of the truce had reached the Indias. In September of 1610 two vessels returning to Holland met seven vessels under Admiral Both, in which were the first Dutch women sent to the Indias. About 1613 the Spanish force in the Moluccas is stated as follows:

"... The Spaniards have control of the city of Gammalamma, in the island of Ternate, which they took from the inhabitants. They call it Nuestra Signora di Rosario. It has a wall and bastions built of stone. It is abundantly provided with cannon and war-supplies, which are sent from the Manilles.

"It is at present garrisoned by 200 Spaniards and 90 Papaugos [i.e., Pampangos (?)] who are inhabitants of the Philippines, who are well disciplined in arms, and serve as Spanish soldiers. There are also 30 Portuguese families, 60 or 80 Chinese families, who engage in different trades, and 50 or 60 Christian Molucca families.

"They have another fort between Gammalamma and Malaia, called Sts. Peter and Paul, located on an elevation, and mounted with six pieces of cannon. There are thirty-three cast-iron cannon in the first fort. The garrison of the latter consists generally of 27 Spaniards, 20 Papaugos, and some other people from the Manilles.

"They possess all the island of Tidore, where they have three forts, namely, that of Taroula, located in the large city where the king lives. It is stronger than the other two by its situation, which is on an elevation. Its garrison is usually 50 Spaniards, and 8 or 10 Papaugos. It has ten large cast-iron cannon.

"The second fort is the old Portuguese castle taken by Corneille Bastiaansz, which the Spaniards have retaken. It has 13 Spaniards, with several islanders, and 2 pieces of cannon.

"The third is named Marieco, and is in sight of Gammalamma....Its garrison consists of 14 Castilians and a few Papaugos, and it has two pieces of cannon....The wars have somewhat depopulated the country "*

---

* The Spaniards also possessed several forts in Gilolo: Sabougo, taken from the Dutch by Juan de Silva in 1611; Gilolo, also taken from the Dutch by the same governor; and Aquilamo. All these forts contained light garrisons. On the island

The Dutch power in the Moluccas was as follows:

"We have three forts at Ternate: that of Malaia, or Orange, commenced by Admiral Matelief, where the king of Ternate lives; that of Toluco, or Hollande, lying at the east end of the island, on an elevation, one-half legua north of that of Malaia, built of stone; for fear lest the Spaniards occupy this post, and for the same reason to send there to live a portion of the superfluous men at Malaia.

"Our third fort is that of Tacomma or Willemstad, lying at the northwest. It was constructed by Admiral Simon Jansz Hoen...."*

By 1627 affairs were still more flourishing and Batavia in Bantam, on the island of Java, had already been made a base of supplies. Spain still maintained forts at Ternate in that year. Signs of a desire to attack the Spaniards in the Philippines began to be manifest.

In regard to Wittert's expedition, defeat, and death, the following has been translated and condensed from Journal de l'amiral Wittert, 1607-10 (Liege, 1875), a small pamphlet in the library of Columbia University, New York.

"In the year 1607, the Company of the East Indies despatched thirteen vessels to find the Portuguese fleet, and probably to attack it, off Mosambique or in neighboring waters. Pierre Willemsz, of Amsterdam, was appointed admiral of this fleet; and Francois de Wittert, of the ancient baronial family of that name—seignior of Hoogeland, Emeeclaar, etc.—was made vice-admiral and president of the council-in-ordinary, with full power to take the place of the admiral, who was very old and infirm." The flagships of these officers were of eight

---

of Moro, the Spaniards had the forts Jolo, Isiau, and Joffougho. They usually maintained in the sea a number of vessels. Juan de Silva is described as a brave, energetic, and diplomatic man. The second capture of van Caerden proved a decided blow to the Dutch, because of the loss of certain important papers.

* In the island of Machian, they possessed the fort of Taffalo and Tabillola. In Bachian they had a fort called Gammedource. All these forts were adequately garrisoned.

hundred and one thousand tons, respectively. The entire fleet carried two thousand eight hundred to two thousand nine hundred men, forty-two pieces of brass artillery and two hundred and eighty-three of iron, one hundred stone-mortars, with the necessary munitions, and provisions for more than three years. This armament cost ten million eight hundred livres. The fleet set sail from the Texel on December 22, 1607, and reached "the fort of Mosam-bique" on the twenty-eighth of July following. The Dutch besieged the fort, but were obliged to retreat (August 13). "In this siege 30 of our men were killed, and 85 wounded. We fired 2,250 cannon-shots at this fortress, which is the most important one possessed by the Portuguese in the East Indies; it has four bastions and three ramparts. But after this siege, it was almost entirely ruined, and the Por-tuguese power is destroyed, especially as regards the puissant empire of the Abissinians, whose emperor is named Preter-Jan [i.e., Prester John]." On November 5, 1608, the Dutch fleet reached Sumatra, where a naval bat-tle with some Portuguese vessels ensued. In January, 1609, Wittert went, with some of the ships, to Johor, and aided the king of that state to resist the Portuguese. On February 15, the fleet anchored at Bantam, and on April 8, at Nera, one of the isles of Banda, where they built a fort. Here, on May 22, the admiral and many of his officers were treach-erously assassinated by the natives. Here the journal ends. Another and later entry reads: "Letters from Moluque [Maluco] bring the news that on June 12, 1610, the admiral Francois Wittert, while having some junks unloaded at Manila, was surprised by the Spanish and slain in the com-bat. He was attacked by more than 12 vessels at once, but defended himself for a long time. The 'Amsterdam' was fi-nally captured by four ships which attacked it at once—one of which, however, the Dutch blew up—and was taken to Manila with 51 dead on board, including the ad-miral; the yacht 'Faucon' had 34 dead, and all its officers were slain except two—Pierre Gervits, master of the yacht, and Pierre Hertsing— who were wounded. The 'Faucon' also was carried away, with 22 dead. [170] The Spaniards made 120 prisoners on the two ships. As for the other ves-sels in their company the yacht 'Aigle' was blown up; the 'Paon' and the shallop 'Delft' escaped. It is not exactly known whither these vessels have gone; but it is believed that they went to Patan."

With the increase of Dutch power in the Indias, complications naturally multiplied. The year spent by Pierre van den Broeck in the eastern seas, saw conflicts on the Indian coast, in Java, against the English and Javanese, and also with the Portuguese. Van den Broeck was in the service of the Dutch Trading Company for over seventeen years. He went first to the Indias in the expedition under Gerard Reyust, which left Holland May 3, 1613. On June 1, 1615, he embarked with Admiral Verhagen for the Moluccas. He played an important part in the establishment of Batavia in 1619, and in the troubles with the English and Javanese. The truth of the inadequacy of the natives against the more progressive races was proved again, as it had previously been proved by the experiences of Portuguese and Spanish. A siege of Batavia in 1629, by the Javanese failed in its purpose. Van den Broeck returned to Holland June 6, 1630.

The second Dutch voyage to the East Indies under command of Georges Spilberg sailed from Holland August 8, 1614, with six vessels. Its object was chastisement of the Spanish. Reaching the Strait of Magellan, March 28, 1615, after many adventures with the Portuguese along the Brazilian coast, the fleet made the passage, and debouched into the South Sea on May 6. Thence they coasted the western shores of South America, and as far as Acapulco in New Spain. Near Lima a sea fight with the Spanish occurred, in which the latter were worsted, and three ships destroyed. When some of the Spanish who were in the water called piteously for help, after saving the first and second pilot, and a few sailors, "we left the remainder to the mercy of the waves." The chronicle adds "Nevertheless some of the sailors killed several who were swimming, and struggling against death—which they did in disobedience to their orders." At Acapulco, the Spanish received the Dutch well and some change of prisoners was effected. On November 18, 1615, the fleet turned westward, and sighted the Ladrones by January 1, 1616. On February 9, the cape of Espiritu Santo was sighted, and on the 19th, under the guidance of native pilots, they sailed toward Manila Bay, and anchored that same day near Luzon. "Our intention was to make some Spaniard prisoner, in order to gain more detailed information of what had been told us at Capul, namely, that a fleet had been awaiting us for many days at the Manilles, and we wished eagerly to learn more particular news of it." It was learned that the Spanish fleet under Juan de Silva had gone to the Moluccas to aid the Spanish there. Consequently, the Dutch fleet, after an ineffectual attempt to exchange prisoners at Manila, went (March 10) to the Moluccas. On the way they received assurance of the hatred in and about Mindanao for the Spaniards, and their willingness to join the Dutch.

Reaching the Moluccas they cruised about for some time, and finally two of the vessels were sent back to Holland, reaching that country, July 1, 1617. With them they took the celebrated Jacques le Maire who had attempted to find a new passage to the South Sea, below the Strait of Magellan. As his voyage was not for the trading company which enjoyed the monopoly of trade in the Indies, his ship was confiscated. He died on the passage home. [171]

Although the Dutch were later in their explorations and conquests throughout the Indies and neighboring regions than other nations, their activity carried them to all the places visited or conquered by the latter. As years went on the contests of the Dutch with the Spanish tended to lessen, while those with the natives increased. Women went to the new colonies in greater number, and life gradually assumed a more settled aspect. The strenuous efforts of the Dutch sent them into Formosa, China, Japan, and other countries. Expeditions of more or less ships multiplied. The names of the Dutch famous in the annals of the eastern seas are numerous. Their efforts, first and foremost, were the establishment of a sound commerce. The above, with the exception of the extract concerning Francois de Wittert, is translated and condensed from Recueil des voyages ... de la Compagnie des Indes Orientales (Amsterdam, 1725). See also, Histoire des voyages (Paris, 1750); Isabelo de los Reyes y Florentino: Articulos varios, (Manila, 1887), pp. 71-86, "Triunfos del Rosario o Los Holandeses en Filipinas;" and Ferdinand Blumentritt: Hollaendische Angriffe auf die Philippinen (Leitmeritz, 1880).
Morga's Philippine Islands

Volume II

Preface

In the present volume is concluded the notable work by Morga, Sucesos de las Islas Filipinas, which was begun in VOL. I. The reader is referred to the preface of that volume for some account of the book, and of the manner in which it is presented in this series.

Continuing his narrative, Morga describes his voyage to Mexico, whither he goes (1603) to be a member of the Audiencia there. He then relates the events of the Chinese uprising in Luzon in that year, which has been fully described in previous volumes of this series; and his picturesque although plain narrative casts new light upon that episode. Many Spaniards in Manila are so alarmed by this danger that they remove, with all their households and property, to Nueva España; but one of the ships carrying them is lost at sea, and the other is compelled, after great injury and loss, to return to Manila—a serious calamity for the colony there. The governor does his best to fortify the city, and reenforcements and supplies are provided for him from Nueva Espana. Bishop Benavides dies (1605). Friars from the islands go to Japan, but the emperor of that country is offended at their preaching, and advises Acuna to restrain them. In the summer of 1605 arrive supplies and men from Nueva Espana, and Acuna proceeds with his preparations for the expedition against the Dutch in the Moluccas. In the following spring he sets out on this enterprise, conducting it in person; Morga describes this naval campaign in detail. Ternate is captured by the Spaniards without bombardment, and with little loss to themselves. The fugitive king of the island is persuaded to surrender to the Spaniards and become a vassal of Felipe. Several other petty rulers follow his example and promise not to allow the Dutch to engage in the clove trade. Acuna builds a new fort there, and another in Tidore, leaving Juan de Esquivel as governor of the Moluccas, with a garrison and several vessels for their defense, and carrying to Manila the king of Ternate and many of his nobles, as hostages. During Acuna's absence a mutiny occurs among the Japanese near Manila, which is quelled mainly by the influence of the friars. The governor dies, apparently from poison, soon after his return to Manila. The trade of the islands is injured by the restrictions laid upon it by the home government; and the reduction of Ternate has not sufficed to restrain the Moro pirates. The natives of the Moluccas are uneasy and rebellious, especially as they have a prospect of aid from the Dutch, who are endeavoring to regain their lost possessions there. Morga cites a letter from a Spanish officer at La Palma, recounting the purpose and outcome of van Noordt's expedition to the Indian archipelago.

The historical part of Morga's account ends here; and the final chapter is devoted to a description of the islands and their people, the customs and religious beliefs of the natives, and the condition at that time of the Spanish colony and the city of Manila. He describes the principal islands of the Philippine group, beginning with Luzon; the various races of inhabitants—Moros, Negritos, and Visayans: their mode of dress, their occupations and industries, their habits of life; their weapons, their ships and boats; the trees and fruits of the islands; the animals and birds, both wild and tame; the reptiles, fishes, and other creatures; and various plants. Among these is the buyo (or betel); the habit of chewing it has become universal among the Spaniards, of all classes, and poison is often administered through its medium. Various means and methods of poisoning are described, as well as some antidotes therefor. Some account is given of the gold mines and pearl fisheries, and of other products of the country which form articles of commerce. Morga describes the two great lakes of Luzon (Bombon and Bai), Manila and its harbor and approaches, and other principal ports, with some neighboring islands; and gives some account of the Visayan people and the larger islands inhabited by them, and of the tides in the archipelago. Then follows an interesting and detailed account of the Filipino peoples, their language, customs, beliefs, etc. The language used in Luzon and other northern islands is different from that of the Visayas; but all the natives write, expressing themselves fluently and correctly, and using a simple alphabet which resembles the Arabic. Their houses, and their mode of life therein, are fully described; also their government, social organization, and administration of justice. The classes and status of slaves, and the causes of enslavement are recounted. Their customs in marriages and dowries, divorces, adoption, and inheritance are described; also in usury, trading, and punishment for crimes. The standard of social purity is described by Morga as being very low; yet infamous vices were not indigenous with them, but communicated by foreigners, especially by the Chinese. The natives of Luzon appear to be superior, both intellectually and morally, to the Visayan peoples. Their religious beliefs and practices are recounted by Morga, who naturally ascribes these to the influence of the devil. He also narrates the entrance of Mahometanism into the islands, and how it was checked by the coming of the Spaniards.

Morga next sketches the condition at that time of Spanish colonies in the islands. He describes the city of Manila in detail, with its fortifications, arsenals, government and municipal buildings, cathedral, and convents; also the seminary of Santa Potenciana, and the hospitals. There are six hundred houses, mostly built of stone, within the walls, and even more in the suburbs; "and all are the habitations and homes of Spaniards." All the people, both men and women, are clad and gorgeously adorned in silks; and nowhere is there greater abundance of food, and of other necessaries of human life, than in Manila. Morga enumerates the dignitaries, ecclesiastical and civil, who reside in the city; and mentions it as the center and metropolis of the archipelago. He then briefly describes the other Spanish settlements in the Philippines; and mentions in their turn the various orders and their work there, with the number of laborers in each. He praises their efforts for the conversion, education, and social improvement of the Indians. He defines the functions of both the civil and the ecclesiastical authorities, and the policy of the government toward the natives; and describes the application and results in the Philippines of the encomienda system imported thither from America. He deprecates the permission given to the Indians for paying their tributes in kind or in money, at their option; for it has led to their neglecting their former industries, and thus to the general damage of the country. Slavery still exists among them, but the Spaniards have been forbidden to enslave the natives. Personal services of various sorts are due from the latter, however, to their encomenderos, to the religious, and to the king, for all of which they receive a moderate wage; and all other services for the Spaniards are voluntary and paid. Close restrictions are laid upon the intercourse of the Spaniards with natives. Various information is given regarding appointments to office, residencias, elections, town government, and finances; also of the ecclesiastical organization, expenses, and administration, as well as of the incomes of the religious orders. Morga recounts the numbers, character, pay, and organization of the military and naval forces in the islands. The bulk of the citizens are merchants and traders, commerce being the chief occupation and support of the Spanish colony. Manila is a market for all the countries of Eastern Asia, from Japan to Borneo. The China trade is restricted to the inhabitants of the Philippines; Morga describes its nature and extent, and the manner in which it is conducted, as well as the character and methods of the Chinese traders. A similar account is given of the trade carried on with the Philippines by the Japanese, Borneans, and other neighboring peoples, and of the shipment to Nueva Espana of the goods thus procured. This

190

last commerce is "so great and profitable, and easy to control, that the Spaniards do not apply themselves to, or engage in, any other industry," and thus not only they neglect to avail themselves of and develop the natural resources of the country, but the natives are neglecting and forgetting their former industries; and the supply of silver in the country steadily flows out of it and into the hands of infidels. Morga enumerates the officials, revenues, and expenditures of the colonial government. As its income is too small for its necessary expenses, the annual deficit is made up from the royal treasury of Nueva Espana. But this great expense is incurred "only for the Christianization and conversion of the natives, for the hopes of greater fruits in other kingdoms and provinces of Asia."

The large extent of the Chinese immigration to the islands is disapproved by Morga, as unsafe to the Spaniards and injurious to the natives. Some Chinese are needed for the service of the Spaniards, for all the trades are carried on by them; but the number of Chinese allowed to live in the islands should be restricted to those who are thus needed. Morga describes the character, dress, mode of life, and settlements of the Chinese near Manila; they are cared for in religious matters by the Dominican friars. The Christian Chinese live apart from the heathens, in a settlement of some five hundred people; Morga has but a poor opinion of even these converts. Some account is also given of the Japanese who have settled in Manila; Morga commends them, and states that they prove to be good Christians.

He ends his work by a detailed account of the navigation and voyage to and from the Philippines. The Mexican port of departure for this route has been removed from Navidad to Acapulco. Morga describes the westward voyage; the stop at the Ladrone Islands, and the traffic of the natives with the ships; and the route thence, and among the Philippine Islands. The return route to Mexico is much more difficult and dangerous; for the winds are varying and not always favorable, and the ship must change its course more frequently, and go far north to secure favoring winds, there encountering cold weather. These severe changes cause much suffering, and even death; and the vessel makes this voyage without once touching land until it reaches Acapulco, a period of five or six months. Morga also describes the voyage to Spain by way of Goa and the Cape of Good Hope, which also is long and dangerous.

THE EDITORS
January, 1907

191

Chapter 7 (cont.)

On the tenth [of July] [173] of the same year, the vessels "Espiritu-Santo" and "Jesus Maria" left the port of Cabit en route for Nueva Espana—in the wake of two smaller vessels, which had been despatched a fortnight before—with the Filipinas merchandise. Don Lope de Ulloa was their commander, while Doctor Antonio de Morga left those islands in the almiranta, the "Santo Espiritu," to fill the office of alcalde of the court of Mexico. Before leaving the bay, both vessels were struck head on by a storm, and went dragging upon the coast, buffeted by the heavy seas and winds, and amid dark and tempestuous weather, from three in the afternoon until morning of the next day, notwithstanding that they were anchored with two heavy cables in the shelter of the land, and their topmasts struck. Then they grounded upon the coast, in La Pampanga, ten leguas from Manila. The storm lasted for three more consecutive days. Consequently it was regarded as impossible for those vessels to sail and make their voyage, inasmuch as the season was now well advanced, and the vessels were very large and heavily laden, and were deeply imbedded in the sand. Advice was immediately sent overland to Manila, whence were brought several Chinese ships, cables, and anchors. By dint of the great efforts exerted, both vessels, each singly, were fitted with tackle and cables, which were rigged at the stern. There awaiting the high tide, the ships were drawn, by force of capstan and men, stern first for more than one legua through a bank of sand, upon which they had struck, until they were set afloat, on the twenty-second of July, St. Magdelen's day. Immediately they set sail again, as the vessels had sustained no injury, nor sprung any leak; and they made their voyage and navigation, under light winds, to the coast of Nueva Espana. A violent south-southwest gale, accompanied by heavy showers, hail, and cold, struck the ship "Espiritu Sancto" on the tenth of November, in forty-two degrees, and within sight of land. The wind was blowing obliquely toward the shore, upon which the vessel was almost wrecked several times. The vessel suffered distress and lost its rigging, while the crew was worn out by the voyage and with the cold. The storm lasted until November twenty-second. On the morning of that day, while the ship was in the trough of the waves, and with topmasts shipped, it was struck by a squall of rain and hail, accompanied by great darkness. A thunderbolt, descending the mainmast, struck the vessel amidships. It killed three men besides wounding and maiming eight others; it had entered the hatches, and torn open the mainhatch, with a blaze of light, so that the interior of the ship could be seen. Another thunderbolt fell down along the same mast among the entire crew, and stunned sixteen persons, some of whom were speechless and unconscious all that day. It left the vessel by the pump-dale. The next day, the wind veered to north-northeast, whereupon the ship set sail, and went coasting along the land, with sufficient winds until the nineteenth of the month of December, when it made port at Aca-pulco. There were found the two smaller vessels that had sailed first from Manila. Three days later, General Don Lope de Ulloa entered the same port of Acapulco, in the ship "Jesus Maria." That vessel had sustained the same storms as the ship "Espiritu Sancto." From the time when the two vessels had separated, on sailing out of the channel of Capul, in the Filipinas Islands, they had not sighted one another again during the entire voyage.

In the same year six hundred and three, Governor Don Pedro de Acuna sent the ship "Sanctiago" from Manila to Japon, with merchandise. It was ordered to make its voyage to Quanto, in order to comply with the desire and wish of Daifusama. As news had been already received of the death of Fray Geronimo de Jesus, four of the most important religious of his order in Manila—namely, Fray Diego de Bermeo [174] (who had been provincial), Fray Alonso de la Madre de Dios, Fray Luys Sotello, [175] and one other associate—sailed on that vessel for the said kingdom.

As soon as the ships "Jesus Maria" and "Espiritu Sancto" sailed for Nueva Espana, and the ship "Sanctiago" with the religious for Japon, there was more time to discuss further the matter started by the coming of the Chinese mandarins. For finding themselves unoccupied with other matters, fear of the Sangleys became universal, and the suspicions that were current that the Sangleys were about to commit some mischievous outbreak. This the archbishop and some religious affirmed and told, publicly and privately. At this time, a considerable number of Chinese were living in Manila and its environs. Some of them were baptized Christians living in the settlements of Baibai and Minondoc, [176] on the other side of the river, opposite the city. Most of them were infidels, occupied and living in these same settlements and in the shops of the parian in the city; [they were employed] as merchants and in all other occupations. The majority of them were fishermen, stonecutters, charcoal-burners, porters, masons, and day-laborers. Greater security was always felt in regard to the merchants, for they are the better class of people, and those who are most interested, because of their property. So great security was not felt about the others, even though they were Christians; because, as they are a poor and covetous people, they would be inclined to any act of mean-ness. However, it was always thought that it would be difficult for them to cause any commotion, unless a strong fleet came from China, on which they could rely. Talk continued to increase daily, and with it suspi-cion; for some of the Chinese themselves, both infidels and Christians, in order to prove themselves friends of the Spaniards, and clean from all guilt, even told the Spaniards that there was to be an insurrection shortly, and other similar things. Although the governor always considered these statements as fictions and the exaggerations of that nation, and did not credit them, yet he was not so heedless that he did not act cautiously and watch, although with dissembling, for whatever might happen. He took pains to have the city guarded and the soldiers armed, besides flattering the most prominent of the Chinese and the merchants, whom he assured of their lives and property. The natives of La Pampanga and other prov-inces near by were instructed beforehand to supply the city with rice and other provisions, and to come to reenforce it with their persons and arms, should necessity arise. The same was done with some Japanese in the city. As all this was done with some publicity, since it could not be done secretly, as so many were concerned, one and all became convinced of the certainty of the danger. Many even desired it, in order to see the peace disturbed, and to have the opportunity to seize something. [177] From that time, both in the city and its environs, where the Sangleys were living scattered, these people began to persecute the Sangleys by word and deed. The natives, Japanese and soldiers of the camp took from them their possessions and inflicted on them other ill-treatment, calling them dogs and traitors, and saying that they knew well that they meant to rebel. But they said they would kill all the Sangleys first, and that very soon, for the governor was preparing for it. This alone was suf-ficient to make it necessary for the Sangleys to do what they had no intention of doing. [178] Some of the most clever and covetous set them-selves to rouse the courage of the others, and to make themselves leaders, telling the Sangleys that their destruction was sure, according to the determination which they saw in the Spaniards, unless they should anticipate the latter, since they [the Sangleys] were so numerous, and at-tack and capture the city. They said that it would not be difficult for them to kill the Spaniards, seize their possessions, and become masters of the country, with the aid and reenforcements that would immediately come to them from China, as soon as the auspicious beginning that they would have made in the matter should be known. In order to do this when the time came, it was advisable to build a fort and quarters in some retired and strong place near the city, where the people could gather and unite, and where arms and supplies could be provided for the war. At least such a fort would be sufficient to assure there their lives from the outrages that they were expecting from the Spaniards. It was learned that the chief mover in this matter was a Christian Sangley, an old-time resident in the country, named Joan Bautista de Vera. [179] He was rich and highly esteemed by the Spaniards, and feared and respected by the Sangleys. He had often been governor of the latter, and had many godchildren and dependents. He had become an excellent Spaniard, and was courageous. He himself, exercising duplicity and cunning, did not leave the city, or the houses of the Spanish during this time, in order to arouse less suspicion of himself. From there he managed the affair through his confidants; and in order to assure himself better of the result, and to ascertain the number of men of his race, and to make a census and list of them, he cunningly had each of them ordered to bring him a needle, which he pretended to be necessary for a certain work that he had to do. These needles he placed, as he received them, in a little box; and when he took them out of it, he found that he had sufficient men for his purpose. They began to construct the fort or quarters immediately at a distance of slightly more than one-half legua from the village of Tondo, among some estuaries and swamps, and in a hidden location. [180] They stored there some rice and other provisions, and weapons of little importance. The Sangleys began to gather there, especially the masses—the common people and day-laborers; for those of the parian, and the mechanics, although urged to do the same, did not resolve to do it, and remained quiet, guarding their houses and property. The restlessness of the Sangleys daily continued to become more inflamed. This, and the advices given to the governor and the Spaniards, kept the latter more anxious and apprehensive, and made them talk more openly of the matter. The Sangleys, seeing that their intention was discovered, and that delay might be of so great harm to them, determined, although the insurrection was planned for St. Andrew's day, the last of November, to anticipate that day, and to lose no more time. On Friday, the third day of the month of October, the eve of St. Francis, they collected very hurriedly in the above-mentioned fort; consequently, by nightfall, there were two thousand men in it. Joan Bautista de Vera—a thief in the role of an honest man, since he was the leader and organizer of the treason—went immediately to the city and told the governor that the Sangleys had risen, and that they were collecting on the other side of the river. The governor, suspecting the mischief, had him immediately arrested and carefully guarded; and he was afterward executed. Then, without tap of drum, the governor ordered the companies, both of the camp and the city, to be notified, and all to hold their arms in readiness. Very shortly after night-fall, Don Luys Dasmarinas, who was living near the monastery and church of Minondoc, on the other side of the river, came hurriedly to the city to advise the governor that the Sangleys had revolted. He asked for twenty soldiers to go to the other side [of the river], where he would guard the said monastery. Cristoval de Axqueta, sargento-mayor of the camp, went with these men, together with Don Luys. As the silence of night deepened, the noise made by the Sangleys grew louder, for they were continuing to assemble and were sounding horns and other instruments, after their fashion. Don Luys remained to guard the monastery, with the men brought from Manila, where he had placed in shelter many women and children of Christian Sangleys, with the religious. The sargento-mayor returned immediately to the city, where he told of what was being done. The call to arms was sounded, for the noise and shouts of the Sangleys, who had sallied out to set fire to some houses in the country, was so great that it was thought that they were devastating that district. The Sangleys burned, first, a stone country-house belonging to Captain Estevan de Marquina. The latter was living there with his wife and children; and none of them escaped, except a little girl, who was wounded, but who was hidden in a thicket. [181] Thence the Sangleys went to the settlement of Laguio, [182] situated on the shore of the river, and burned it. They killed several Indians of that settlement, and the rest fled to the city. There the gates were already shut and all the people, with arms in hand, manned the walls and other suitable posts, ready for any emergency, until dawn. The enemy, who now had a greater number of men, retired to their fort, to make another sally thence with more force. Don Luys Dasmarinas, who was guarding the church and monastery of Minondoc, expected hourly that the enemy was about to attack him, and sent a messenger to the governor to beg for more men. These were sent him, and consisted of regulars and inhabitants of the city, under Captains Don Tomas Brabo de Acuna (the governor's nephew), Joan de Alcega, Pedro de Arzeo, and Gaspar Perez, by whose counsel and advice Don Luys was to be guided on this occasion. All was confusion, shouting, and outcry in the city, particularly among the Indians, and the women and children, who were coming thither for safety. Although, to make certain of the Sangleys of the parian, their merchants had been asked to come into the city, and bring their property, they did not dare to do so; for they always thought that the enemy would take the city because of their great force of numbers, and annihilate the Spaniards, and they would all be in danger. Consequently they preferred to remain in their parian, in order to join the victorious side. Don Luys Dasmarinas thought it advisable to go in search of the enemy immediately with the reenforcements sent him by the governor, before they should all assemble and present a strong front. He left seventy soldiers in Minondoc, in charge of Gaspar Perez; while with the rest, about one hundred and forty of the best picked arquebusiers, he went to the village of Tondo, in order to fortify himself in the church, a stone building. He arrived there at eleven o'clock in the morning. The Chinese, in number one thousand five hundred, arrived at the same place at the same time, bent on the same purpose. An hour's skirmish took place between the two sides, as to which one would gain the monastery. Captain Gaspar Perez came up with the reenforcement of the men left at Minondoc. The enemy retired to his fort, with a loss of five hundred men. Gaspar Perez returned to his post, where Pedro de Arzeo was also stationed. Don Luys Dasmarinas, exultant over this fortunate engagement, determined immediately to press forward in pursuit of the enemy with his men, notwithstanding the heat of the sun and without waiting to rest his followers. He sent Alferez Luys de Ybarren to reconnoiter. The latter brought word that the enemy was in great force, and near by. Although Juan de Alcega and others requested Don Luys to halt and rest his men, and await the governor's orders as to what was to be done, his desire not to lose the opportunity was so great that, rousing his men with harsh words, in order to make them follow him, he marched forward until they reached a swamp. After leaving the swamp, they came suddenly into a large clearing, where the enemy was stationed. The latter, upon seeing the Spaniards, surrounded them in force on all sides, armed with clubs, some with catans, and a few with battle-axes. Don Luys and his men, not being able to retreat, fought valiantly, and killed a number of Sangleys. But finally, as the latter were in so great force, they cut all the Spaniards to pieces, only four of whom escaped, badly wounded; and these carried the news to Manila. [183] This result was of great importance to the Sangleys, both because so many and the best Spanish soldiers were killed in this place, and because of the weapons that the Sangleys took from them, and which they needed. With these arms they flattered themselves that their object was more certain of accomplishment. Next day, October five, the Sangleys sent the heads of Don Luys, Don Tomas, Joan de Alcega, and other captains to the parian; and they told the Sangleys there that, since the flower of Manila had been killed, they should revolt and join them, or they would immediately come to kill them. The confusion and grief of the Spaniards in the city was so great that it prevented them from taking the precautions and exercising the diligence demanded by the affair. But the sight of their necessity, and the spirit of their governor and officials made them all remain at their posts on the walls, arms in hand. They fortified as strongly as possible the gates of the parian and of Dilao, and all that part of the wall where the enemy might make an assault. They mounted a piece of artillery above each gate, and stationed there the best men, among whom were religious of all the orders. Upon that day, Sunday, the enemy, flushed with the victory of the preceding day and their army swelled by the additional men that joined them, attacked the city. Burning and destroying everything in their path, they went to the river, for there was no vessel with which to resist them, as all those of the fleet were in the provinces of the Pintados. They entered the parian, [184] and furiously assaulted the city gate, but were driven back by the arquebuses and muskets, with the loss of many Sangleys. They went to the church of Dilao, and there assaulted the gate and walls (which were there lower), by means of scaling-ladders, with the same determination. But they experienced the same resistance and loss, which compelled them, on the approach of night, to retire with great loss to the parian and to Dilao. That whole night the Spaniards spent in guarding their wall, and in preparing for the morrow. The enemy passed the night in the parian and at Dilao, making carts, mantelets, scaling-ladders, artificial fire, and other contrivances, for approaching and assaulting the wall, and for burning the gates, and setting fire to everything. At dawn of the next day, Monday, the Sangleys came together with these arms and tools, and having reached the wall with their bravest and best-armed men, attacked it with great fury and resolution. The artillery destroyed their machines, and caused them so great injury and resistance with it and the arquebuses, that the Sangleys were forced to retire again to the parian and to Dilao, with heavy loss. Joan Xuarez Gallinato, accompanied by some soldiers and a Japanese troop, made a sally from the Dilao gate upon the Sangleys. They reached the church, when the Sangleys turned upon them and threw the Japanese into disorder. The latter were the cause of all retreating again to seek the protection of the walls, whither the Sangleys pursued them. At this juncture Captain Don Luys de Velasco entered Manila. He came from the Pintados in a stout caracoa, manned by some good arquebusiers, while others manned some bancas that sailed in the shelter of the caracoa. They approached the parian and Dilao by the river, and harassed the enemy quartered there on that and the two following days, so that they were compelled to abandon those positions. These vessels set fire to the parian, and burned everything, and pursued the enemy wherever they could penetrate. The Sangleys, upon beholding their cause waning, and their inability to attain the end desired, resolved to retire from the city, after having lost more than four thousand men; to advise China, so that that country would reenforce them;

and for their support to divide their men into three divisions in different districts—one among the Tingues of Passic, the second among those of Ayonbon, and the third at La Laguna de Bay, San Pablo, and Batangas. On Wednesday they abandoned the city completely, and, divided as above stated, marched inland. Don Luys de Velasco, with some soldiers and armed Indians who came from all sides to the relief of Manila, accompanied by some Spaniards who guided them, and the religious from their missions, went by way of the river in pursuit of them, and pressed them, so that they killed and annihilated the bands bound for the Tingues of Passic and for Ayombon. The majority and main body of the Sangleys went to La Laguna de Bay, the mountains of San Pablo, and Batangas, where they considered themselves more secure. Burning towns and churches, and everything in their path, they fortified themselves in the above-mentioned sites. Don Luys de Velasco, with seventy soldiers, continued to pursue them, killing each day a great number of them. On one occasion Don Luys was so closely engaged with the enemy, that the latter killed him and ten soldiers of his company, and fortified themselves again in San Pablo and Batangas, where they hoped to be able to sustain themselves until the arrival of reenforcements from China. [185]

The governor, fearful of this danger, and desirous of finishing the enemy, and giving entire peace to the country, sent Captain and Sargento-mayor Cristoval de Axqueta Menchaca with soldiers to pursue and finish the enemy. This man left with two hundred Spaniards—soldiers and volunteers—three hundred Japanese, and one thousand five hundred Pampanga and Tagal Indians, [186] on the twentieth of October. He was so expeditious, that with little or no loss of men, he found the Sangleys fortified in San Pablo and Batangas, and, after fighting with them, killed and destroyed them all. None escaped, except two hundred, who were taken alive to Manila for the galleys. The captain was occupied in this for twenty days, and with it the war was ended. Very few merchants were left in Manila, and they had taken the good counsel to betake themselves, with their possessions, among the Spaniards in the city. At the beginning of the war there were not seven hundred Spaniards in the city capable of bearing arms. [187]

After the end of the war, the need of the city began, for, because of not having Sangleys who worked at the trades, and brought in all the provisions, there was no food, nor any shoes to wear, not even at excessive prices. The native Indians are very far from exercising those trades, and have even forgotten much of farming, and the raising of fowls, cattle, and cotton, and the weaving of cloth, which they used to do in the days of their paganism and for a long time after the conquest of the country. [188] In addition to this, people thought that Chinese vessels would not come to the islands with food and merchandise, on account of the late revolution. Above all, they lived not without fear and suspicion that, instead of the merchant vessels, an armed fleet would attack Manila, in order to avenge the death of their Sangleys. All conspired to sadden the minds of the Spaniards. After having sent Fray Diego de Guevara, prior of the monastery of St. Augustine in Manila, to the court of Espana by way of India, with news of this event—but who was unable to reach Madrid for three years, because of his various fortunes in India, Persia, and Italia, through which countries he went—they immediately sent Captain Marco de la Cueva, together with Fray Luys Gandullo of the Order of St. Dominic, to the city of Macao in China, where the Portuguese were living, with letters for the chief captain and the council of that city. These letters advised the latter of the revolt of the Sangleys, and of the result of the war, so that, if they should hear any rumors of a Chinese fleet, they could send word. At the same time letters were taken from the governor to the Tutons, Aytaos, and visitors of the provinces of Canton and Chincheo, recounting the outbreak of the Chinese, which obliged the Spaniards to kill them. Upon their arrival at Macao, Marcos de la Cueva and Fray Luys Gandullo found no news of a fleet, but that everything was quiet—although the Chinese had already heard of the insurrection and much of the result, from some Sangleys who had fled from Manila in champans, upon that occasion. It was immediately learned in Chincheo that these Spaniards were in Macao, whereupon Captains Guansan Sinu and Guachan, wealthy men and usually engaged in trade with Manila, went to look for them. Having learned the truth of the event, they took the letters for the mandarins and promised to deliver them. They urged other merchants and vessels of Chincheo, who were afraid, to go to Manila that year. This was very useful, for through them much of the necessity that the city [of Manila] was suffering was supplied. With this result and with some powder, saltpeter, and lead which Marcos de la Cueva had provided for the magazines, the latter left Macao, and sailed to Manila, which he reached in May, to the universal joy of the city over the news that he brought—which began to be verified immediately by the coming of the fleet of thirteen Chinese vessels bearing food and merchandise.

In the month of June of this year six hundred and three, [189] two vessels were despatched from Manila to Nueva Espana, under command of Don Diego de Mendoca who had been sent that year by the viceroy, Marques de Montesclaros, with the usual reenforcements for the islands. The flagship was "Nuestra Senora de los Remedios" and the almiranta "Sant Antonio."

Many rich men of Manila, warned by the past troubles, took passage in these vessels with their households and property, for Nueva Espana—especially in the almiranta—with the greatest wealth that has ever left the Filipinas. Both vessels experienced so severe storms during the voyage, in the altitude of thirty-four degrees, and before having passed Japon, that the flagship, without masts and greatly lightened and damaged, put back in distress to Manila. The almiranta was swallowed up in the sea, and no one was saved. This was one of the greatest shipwrecks and calamities that the Filipinas have suffered since the past ones.

During the rest of that year and that of six hundred and five, until the sailing of the vessels which were to go to Castilla, [190] the governor occupied himself in repairing the city, and supplying it with provisions and ammunition, with the special object and care that the decision which he was awaiting from the court for making an expedition to Maluco—of which he had been advised and warned—should not find him so unprepared as to cause him to delay the expedition. In this he was very successful, for at that same time, the master-of-camp, Joan de Esquivel, had arrived in Mexico with six hundred soldiers from Espana. In Mexico more men were being enrolled, and a great preparation was made of ammunition, food, money, and arms, which the viceroy sent to the governor from Nueva Espana in March of that year, by order of his Majesty, in order that he might go to Maluco. All this arrived safely and in due season at Manila.

Shortly after the ships had left Manila for Nueva Espana, and those despatched thence by the viceroy had entered, Archbishop Don Fray Miguel de Benavides died of a long illness. His body was buried amid the universal devotion and grief of the city. [191] At this same time, Don Pedro de Acuna received three letters, by the ships that continued to come from China that year, with the merchandise and with their principal captains. They were all of the same tenor—when translated into Castilian—from the Tuton and Haytao, and from the inspector-general of the province of Chincheo, and were on the matter of the insurrection of the Sangleys and their punishment. They were as follows:[*]

The letter of the inspector-general was written on the twelfth of the second month—which according to our reckoning is March of the twenty-third year of the reign of Vandel [i.e., Wanleh]. The eunuch's [192]

---

[*] This letter occupies folios 113b-115a of the original edition of Morga. We have already presented that document in our VOL. XIII, p. 287, which is translated from a copy of the original manuscript. The answer of Acuna to this letter will be found in VOL. XIV, in the second document of that volume.

letter was written on the sixteenth of the said month and year; and that of the viceroy, on the twenty-second of the month.

The governor answered these letters through the same messengers, civilly and authoritatively. He gave an explanation of the deed and justified the Spaniards, and offered friendship and trade anew with the Chinese. He said that their property, which had remained in Manila, would be restored to the owners, and that those imprisoned in the galleys would be freed in due season. First, however, he intended to use them for the Maluco expedition, which he was undertaking.

The entrances into various provinces of Japon by the discalced religious of St. Francis and those of St. Dominic and St. Augustine, continued to be made, both in the Castilian vessel itself which was despatched that year to the kingdoms of Quanto, [193] and in other Japanese vessels which came to Manila with the silver and flour of the Japanese, in order to trade. This was permitted and allowed by Daifu, now called Cubosama, who that year sent the governor, through one of his servants, certain weapons and presents, in return for others which the governor had sent him. He answered the latter's letter as follows:

> Letter from Daifusama, lord of Japon, to governor Don Pedro de Acuna, in the year one thousand six hundred and five.
>
> I received two letters from your Lordship, and all the gifts and presents mentioned in the memorandum. Among them, when I received them, the wine made from grapes pleased me greatly. During former years, your Lordship requested permission for six vessels, and last year for four, and I always granted your request. But, what angers me greatly is that among the four vessels that your Lordship requested was that one called "Antonio," which made the voyage without my orders. This was a very lawless act, and in contempt of me. Can it be, perhaps, that your Lordship would send to Japon without my permission any vessel that you wished? Besides this, your Lordship and others have often negotiated about the sects of Japon, and requested many things in regard to them. This likewise I cannot concede; for this region is called Xincoco [Shinkoku], or "dedicated to the idols." These have been honored with the highest adoration from the time of our ancestors until now, and their acts I alone cannot undo or destroy. Consequently, it is not at all advisable that your religion be promulgated or preached in Japon; and if your

Lordship wish to preserve friendship with these kingdoms of Japon and with me, do what I wish, and never do what is displeasing to me. Lastly, many have told me that many wicked and perverse Japanese, who go to that kingdom and live there for many years, afterward return to Japon. This makes me very angry. Consequently, your Lordship will, in the future, allow no one of the Japanese to come here in the vessels that come from your country. In other matters, your Lordship shall act advisedly and prudently, and shall so conduct affairs, that henceforth I may not be angered on account of them.

The governor, carrying out his dearest wish, was to make the expedition to Terrenate in the Malucos, which should be done quickly, before the enemy could gather more strength than he had then; for he had been informed that the Dutch, who had seized the island and fortress of Amboino, had done the same with that of Tidore, whence they had driven the Portuguese who had settled therein, and had entered Terrenate, where they had established a trading-post for the clove-trade. Accordingly, as soon as the despatches in regard to this undertaking arrived from Espana, in June of six hundred and five, and the men and supplies from Nueva Espana, which were brought at the same time by the master-of-camp, Joan de Esquivel, the governor spent the balance of this year in preparing the ships, men, and provisions that he deemed necessary for the undertaking. Leaving behind in Manila sufficient force for its defense, he went to the provinces of Pintados, where the fleet was collected, in the beginning of the year six hundred and six.

By the fifteenth day of the month of March, the governor had thoroughly prepared the fleet—which consisted of five ships, four galleys with poop-lanterns [galeras de fanal], three galliots, four champans, three funeas, two English lanchas, two brigantines, one barca chata [194] for the artillery, and thirteen fragatas with high freeboard. There were one thousand three hundred Spaniards, counting regulars, captains and officers, substitutes [entretenidos], and volunteers. Among them were some Portuguese captains and soldiers, under charge of the chief captain of Tidore, [195] who was at that island when the Dutch seized it. These Portuguese came from Malaca to serve in the expedition. There were also four hundred Indian pioneers—Tagals and Pampangos of Manila—who went to serve at their own cost, under their own officers, and with their own weapons. There was a quantity of artillery of all kinds, ammunition, tools, and provisions for nine months. [196] Don Pedro de Acuna left the point of Hilohilo, which is near the town of Arevalo in the island of Panai, [on the above day] with all this equipment, and coasting the island of Mindanao, made port at La Caldera, in order to replenish his water, wood, and other necessaries.

The governor embarked in the galley "Santiago" and took under his charge the other galleys and oared vessels. The ship "Jesus Maria" acted as flagship of the other vessels, and was commanded by the master-of-camp, Joan de Esquivel. Captain and Sargento-mayor Cristoval de Azcueta Menchaca acted as admiral of the fleet, which, after attending to its necessities at La Caldera, left that port. On setting sail, the flagship, which was a heavy vessel, was unable to leave port, and the currents drove it shoreward so that, without the others being able to help it, it grounded. It was wrecked there, but the crew, artillery, and a portion of its ammunition and clothing, were saved. After setting fire to the ship, and taking what nails and bolts they could, so that the Mindanaos could not make use of them, the fleet continued its voyage. The galleys coasted along the island of Mindanao, and the ships and other deep-draught vessels sailed in the open sea, all making for the port of Talangame, in the island of Terrenate. The vessels, although experiencing some changes of weather, first sighted the islands of Maluco, after they had been reconnoitered by a large Dutch ship, well equipped with artillery, which was anchored at Terrenate. This vessel fired some heavy artillery at our vessels, and then immediately entered the port, where it fortified itself under shelter of the land, and with its artillery and crew and the people of Terrenate. The master-of-camp went with his vessels to the island of Tidore, where he was well received by the Moro chiefs and cachils; for the king was away, as he had gone to the island of Bachan to be married. The master-of-camp found four Dutch factors there, who were trading for cloves. He learned from them that the ship at Terrenate was from Holland, and was one of those which had sailed from Amboino and seized Tidore, whence it had driven the Portuguese, and that it was being laden with cloves. It was awaiting other vessels of its convoy, for they had made friendship and treaties with Tidore and Terrenate, in order to be protected against the Castilians and Portuguese. The master-of-camp had the king of Tidore summoned immediately, and, while awaiting Don Pedro de Acuna, rested his men and cleaned the ships, and made gabions and other things necessary for the war. Don Pedro de Acuna, through his pilots' fault, had gone thirty leguas to leeward of the island of Terrenate toward the island of Celebes, otherwise called Mateo. Recognizing that island, he returned to Terrenate, and passing in sight of Talangame, discovered the Dutch vessel. He tried to reconnoiter it, but after seeing that it was harming his galleys with its artillery, and that the master-of-camp was not there, he proceeded to Tidore, where he found the latter, to the great joy of all. There they spent the remainder of the month of March. At this juncture the king of Tidore arrived, with twelve well-armed caracoas. He expressed joy at the governor's coming, to whom he complained at length of the tyranny and subjection in which he was kept by Sultan Zayde, [197] king of Terrenate, who was aided by the Dutch. He offered to go in person to serve his Majesty in the fleet, with six hundred men of Tidore. Don Pedro received him and feasted him. Then, without any further delay at Tidore, or any more concern about the ship at Talangame, he set about the chief purpose for which they had come. On the last of March he started to return to Terrenate. On that day he anchored in a harbor between the settlement and the port, as did also the king of Tidore with his caracoas. That same night the Dutch ship weighed anchor and went to Amboino. At dawn of next day, April first, soldiers were landed with some difficulty, with the intention of marching along the shore (which was a very close and narrow stretch) to the fort, in order to plant the artillery, with which to bombard it. As the governor thought that mischief would ensue because of the narrowness and closeness of the pass, he landed a number of pioneers on the high ground, to open another road, so that the remainder of the army might pass, and the enemy be diverted in several directions. By these efforts, he placed his camp under the walls, although a great number of Terenatans came from various directions to prevent him. The vanguard of the camp was in charge of Joan Xuarez Gallinato and Captains Joan de Cuevas, Don Rodrigo de Mendoca, Pasqual de Alarcon, Joan de Cervantes, Captain Vergara, and Cristoval de Villagra, with their companies. The other captains were in the body of the squadron. The rearguard was under command of Captain Delgado, while the master-of-camp aided in all parts. The army came up within range of the enemy's artillery, which suddenly began to play. The governor came to see how the troops were formed, and, leaving them at their post, returned to the fleet to have the pieces brought out for bombarding, and to obtain refreshment for the soldiers. Some high trees intervened between the troops and the wall, in which the enemy had posted some scouts to reconnoiter the field. They were driven down, and our own scouts posted there, who gave advice from above of what was being done in the fort. Captain Vergara, and after him, Don Rodrigo de Mendoca and Alarcon, went to reconnoiter the walls, the bastion of Nuestra Senora, and the pieces mounted on the ground there, and a low wall of rough stone which extended to the mountain, where there was a bastion in which the wall ended. It was called Cachiltulo, and was defended with pieces of artillery and a number of culverins, muskets, arquebuses, and pikes; while many other weapons peculiar to the Terenatans were placed along the wall for its defense.

Having seen and reconnoitered all this, although not with impunity, because the enemy had killed six soldiers with the artillery and wounded Alferez Joan de la Rambla in the knee with a musket-ball, the Spaniards returned to the army. A trifle past noon, a lofty site was reconnoitered, in the direction of the bastion of Cachiltulo, whence the enemy could be attacked and driven from the wall; and Captain Cuevas was ordered to occupy it with twenty-five musketeers. Having done this, the enemy sent out a crowd of men to prevent him from occupying it. A skirmish ensued, and the Moros turned and retreated to their wall. Cuevas followed them so closely and persisted so long, that he needed reenforcement. The scouts in the trees gave information of what was being done, whereupon Captains Don Rodrigo de Mendoca, Alarcon, Cervantes, and Vergara reenforced him with their light-armed pikemen and halberdiers. They pursued the enemy with so great rapidity and resolution that they entered the walls behind them. However, some of the Spaniards were wounded, and Captain Cervantes was pushed down from the wall and his legs broken, which caused his death. Captain Don Rodrigo de Mendoca, pursuing the enemy, who were retiring, ran inside the wall as far as the cavalier of Nuestra Senora, while Vergara ran in the opposite direction along the curtain of the wall to the bastion of Cachiltulo, and went on as far as the mountain. By this time the main body of the army had already assaulted the wall. Mutually aiding one another, they mounted the wall and entered the place on all sides, although with the loss of some dead and wounded soldiers. The soldiers were stopped by a trench beyond the fort of Nuestra Senora, for the enemy had retreated to a shed, which was fortified with a considerable number of musketeers and arquebusiers, and four light pieces. They discharged their arquebuses and muskets at the Spaniards, and threw cane spears hardened in fire, and bacacaes, [198] after their fashion. The Spaniards assaulted the shed, whereupon a Dutch artilleryman trying to fire a large swivel-gun, with which he would have done great damage, being confused did not succeed, and threw down the linstock, turned, and fled. The enemy did the same after him, and abandoned the shed, fleeing in all directions. Those who would do so embarked with the king and some of his wives and the Dutch in one caracoa and four juangas [199] which they had armed near the king's fort. Captain Vergara entered the fort immediately, but found it deserted. Don Rodrigo de Mendoca and Villagra pursued the enemy toward the mountain for a long distance, and killed many Moros. With this, at two o'clock in the afternoon, the settlement and fort of Terrenate was completely gained. The Spanish banners and standards were flung from it, without it having been necessary for them to bombard the walls, as they had expected; and the fort was taken at so slight cost to the Spaniards. Their dead numbered fifteen men, and the wounded twenty more. The whole town was reconnoitered, even its extremity—a small fort, called Limataen—which contained two pieces of artillery, and two other pieces near the mosque on the seashore. The loot of the place was of small importance, for already the things of most value, and the women and children, had been removed to the island of Moro, whither the king fled and took refuge in a fort that he had there. Some products of that land were found, and a great quantity of cloves. In the factory of the Dutch were found two thousand ducados, some cloth goods and linens, and many weapons, while in many places were excellent Portuguese and Dutch artillery, a number of culverins and a quantity of ammunition, of which possession was taken for his Majesty. [200] A guard was placed over what was gained, and the place was put in a condition for defense with some pieces taken from the fleet, while the governor ordered and provided whatever else was advisable.

Cachil Amuxa, the king's nephew and the greatest chief of Terrenate, came with other cachils to make peace with the governor. He said that he and all the Terenatans wished to be vassals of his Majesty, and that they would have rendered homage long before, but the king prevented them. The latter as a proud man, and, confident in his own opinion, although he had been advised to surrender the fort to his Majesty and render him homage, had steadily refused to do so, having been encouraged and emboldened by the success that he had gained upon other occasions. That was the reason that he found himself in his present wretched condition. He offered to induce the king to leave the fort of Moro if given assurance of life. Don Pedro de Acuna received this Moro well, and as a Portuguese, Pablo de Lima—one of those whom the Dutch had driven from Tidore, a man of high standing, and well acquainted with the king—offered to accompany him, the governor despatched them with a written passport as follows:

> Passport from Don Pedro de Acuna to the king of Terrenate
> I, Don Pedro de Acuna, governor, captain-general, and president of the Filipinas Islands, and general of this army and fleet, declare that, over my signature, I hereby give security of life to the king of Terrenate, in order that he may come to talk with me—both to him and those whom he may bring with him—reserving to myself the disposal of all the others as I may see fit. I certify this in his Majesty's name. And I order that no person of this fleet molest him or any of his possessions, and that all observe what is

herein contained. Given in Terrenate, April six, one thousand six hundred and six.

DON PEDRO DE ACUÑA

Within nine days Cachilamuja and Pablo de Lima returned to Terrenate with the king, the prince, his son, [201] and others of his relatives, cachils and sangajes, [202] under the said passport. They placed themselves under the governor's power, and he received them with great affection and respect. He lodged the king and his son in a good house in the settlement, under guard of a company. The king restored the villages of Christians that his Majesty had possessed in the island of Moro, when the fort of Terrenate was lost by the Portuguese. He placed his person and kingdom in his Majesty's power, and surrendered a quantity of muskets and heavy artillery that he had in some forts of the said island. The governor did not despoil him of his kingdom, but on the contrary allowed him to appoint two of his men to govern, whose choice was to be ratified by himself. The king, his son the prince, and their cachils and sangajes swore homage to his Majesty. The kings of Tidore and Bachan, and the sangaje of La Bua did the same, and covenanted and promised not to admit either the Dutch or other nations into Maluco for the clove-trade. They promised, as his Majesty's vassals, to go on all occasions to serve him with their persons, men, and ships, whenever summoned by whomever commanded the fort of Terrenate; that they would oppose no obstacles to the Moros who wished to become Christians; that if any wicked Christian went to their lands to turn renegade, they would surrender him; and other suitable things. Therewith great and small were content and pleased, since they were freed from the tyranny of the king of Terrenate. The governor remitted to them the third part of the tributes which they were wont to pay their king, and gave the Moros other advantages. Then he planned a new and modern fort, in a very conspicuous and suitable location, and began to build it. In order that the old fort might be better defended while the new one was being completed, he reduced it to a less size, by making new cavaliers and bastions, which he finished and furnished with ramparts and stout gates. He commenced another fort in the island of Tidore, on a good location near the settlement. After placing in order whatever he judged necessary in Terrenate and Tidore, and in the other towns and fortresses of Maluco, he returned with his fleet to the Filipinas. He left the master-of-camp, Joan de Esquivel, with a garrison of six hundred soldier—five hundred, in five companies, for Terrenate—in the fort of Terrenate to act as his assistant and as governor of Maluco; he also left there one large forge and a number of smiths, sixty-five pioneers, thirty-five stonecutters, two galliots, two well-armed brigantines, and crews of rowers. The other company of soldiers [was to be stationed] in Tidore under command of Captain Alarcon; while ammunition and provisions for one year were left in both forts. In order to be more assured of the [peaceful] condition of the country, he took the king of Terrenate from it and carried him to Manila, as well as his son the prince, and twenty-four cachils and sangajes, most of them the king's relatives, to whom he showed every honor and good treatment. He explained to them why he took them, and that their return to Maluco depended upon the security and tranquillity with which the Moros should conduct themselves in their obedience and service to his Majesty. [203] The three Portuguese galliots returned to Malaca, taking with them the Dutch who were in Maluco and the Portuguese captains and soldiers who had come to take part in this expedition. The governor entered Manila in triumph with the remainder of the fleet, on the last day of May, six hundred and six. He was received there with acclamations of joy and praise from the city, who gave thanks to God for so happy and prompt result in an undertaking of so great weight and importance.

During the governor's absence in Maluco, the royal Audiencia of the islands governed the Filipinas. The Audiencia wished to drive a number of Japanese from the city, for they were a turbulent people and promised little security for the country. When this was attempted and force employed, the Japanese resisted, and the matter came to such a pass that they took arms to oppose it, and it was necessary for the Spaniards to take their arms also. The affair assumed definite proportions, and some on either side wished to give battle. However, it was postponed by various means until, through the efforts of certain religious, the Japanese were quieted; and afterward as many as possible were embarked in vessels, although they resented it greatly. This was one of the greatest dangers that has threatened Manila, for the Spaniards were few in number, and the Japanese more than one thousand five hundred, and they are a spirited and very mettlesome race. Had they come to blows on this occasion, the Spaniards would have fared ill. [204]

The governor, upon entering Manila, took over immediately the affairs of his government, especially the despatching of two vessels about to sail to Nueva Espana. He was present in person in the port of Cabit at the equipment and lading of the ships, and the embarcation of the passengers. He was seized by some indisposition of the stomach which compelled him to return to Manila and take to his bed. His pain and vomiting increased so rapidly that, without its being possible to relieve him, he died in great anguish on St. John's day, to the great sorrow and grief of the country. Especially did the king of Terrenate show and express his grief, for he had always received great honor and kind treatment from the governor. It was suspected that his death had been violent, because of the severity and the symptoms of his illness. The suspicion increased, because the physicians and surgeons, having opened his body, declared, from the signs that they found, that he had been poisoned, which made his death more regrettable. [205] The Audiencia buried the governor in the monastery of St. Augustine at Manila, with the pomp and ostentation due to his person and offices. Then, again taking charge of the government, the Audiencia despatched the vessels to Nueva Espana, whence advice was sent to his Majesty of the taking of Maluco and the death of the governor.

The flagship, in which Don Rodrigo de Mendoca was sailing as general and captain, reached Nueva Espana quickly with this news. The almiranta, notwithstanding that it left the islands at the same time, delayed more than six months. Eighty persons who perished from disease were buried in the sea, while many others stricken by the disease died of it upon landing at the port of Acapulco. Among these was the licentiate Don Antonio de Ribera, auditor of Manila, who had been appointed auditor of Mexico.

At the arrival of these vessels, it was learned that since the death of Don Pedro de Acuna, and the taking over of the government by the Audiencia, no change had occurred in the affairs of the islands; but that their commerce was restricted because of the prohibition which forbade sending to the islands more than five hundred thousand pesos each year of the proceeds from the sale of the merchandise in Nueva Espana. On account of this the people were in need, as this amount appeared little for the many Spaniards and for the extent of the trade—by which all classes are sustained, as they have no other resources or capital. Also, although the gaining of Maluco had been so important for affairs in those islands themselves, and their punishment for the reduction of the other rebels—especially those of Mindanao and Jolo, from whom the Filipinas had received so great injury—the desirable quiet and stability had not been secured. For the Mindanaos and the Joloans were not yet discontinuing their descents upon the provinces of the Pintados in their war-vessels, to seize booty according to their custom—and this will continue until a suitable expedition be sent against them—and Maluco affairs were not failing to give Joan de Esquivel, the master-of-camp, sufficient to do. He was acting as governor there and had but little security from the natives, who, being a Mahometan people, and by nature easily persuaded and fickle, are restless, and ready for disturbances and wars. Daily and in different parts the natives were being incited and aroused to rebellion; and although the master-of-camp and his captains were endeavoring to punish and pacify them, they could not do what was necessary to quiet so many disturbances as arose. The soldiers were dying, and the food giving out; and the aid sent from Manila could not arrive at the time or in so great quantity as was requested, because of the perils of the voyage and the straits of the royal treasury. [206] The coming of vessels to Maluco at this time from Holanda and Zelanda was not less prejudicial to all our interests; for the Dutch, having so great interests in the islands, and having established their interests there so firmly, were coming in squadrons by the India route, to recover what they had lost in Amboino, Terrenate, and other islands. With their countenance, the Moros were revolting against the Spaniards, who had their hands full with them, and more so with the Dutch, for the latter were numerous, and more dangerous enemies than the natives.

The Dutch interest in these regions is so vast—both in the clove-trade and that of other drugs and spices, and because they think that they will have a gateway there for the subjugation of the whole Orient—that, overcoming all the toil and dangers of the voyage, they are continually coming to these islands in greater numbers and with larger fleets. If a very fundamental and timely remedy be not administered in this matter, it will increase to such an extent in a short time that afterward no remedy can be applied.

The English and Flemish usually make this voyage by way of the strait of Magallanes. Francisco Draque [Drake] was the first to make it, and some years later Tomas Liscander [Candish or Cavendish], who passed by Maluco.

Lately Oliver del Nort, a Fleming, made the voyage. The Spanish fleet fought with his fleet amid the Filipinas Islands, at the end of the year one thousand six hundred. In this fight, after the capture of his almiranta (which was commanded by Lamberto Biezman) the flagship, having lost nearly all its crew, and being much disabled, took to flight. And as it afterward left the Filipinas, and was seen in Sunda and the Java channels, so disabled, it seemed impossible for it to navigate, and that it would surely be lost, as was recounted above when treating of this.

This pirate, although so crippled, had the good fortune to escape from the Spaniards, and, after great troubles and hardships, he returned to Amstradam with his ship "Mauricio," with only nine men alive, reaching it on the twenty-sixth of August in the year six hundred and one. He wrote the relation and the events of his voyage, and gave plates of the battle and of the ships. This was afterward translated into Latin and printed by Teodoro de Bri, a German, at Francfort, in the year six hundred and two. Both relations are going the rounds, and the voyage is

211

regarded as a most prodigious feat and one of so great hardships and perils. [207]

Bartolome Perez, a pilot, gave the same news from the island of La Palma. He, having come from England by way of Holanda, conversed with Oliver del Nort, and the latter narrated to him his voyage and sufferings, as mentioned by Licentiate Fernando de la Cueva in a letter from the island of La Palma, [208] on the last of July, of the year six hundred and four, to Marcos de la Cueva, his brother, who was a resident of Manila, and one of the volunteers who embarked on the Spanish flagship which fought with the pirate. This letter is as follows.

> I answer two of your Grace's letters in this: one dated July, six hundred and one, and the other July, six hundred and two. In both of them your Grace relates to me the shipwreck that befell you and how you saved yourself by swimming. Long before I saw your Grace's letters, I had learned of your mishap, whereat I was very anxious and even quite grieved; because of what was reported here, I imagined that your Grace had a part in it. Consequently, I was singularly overjoyed at the assurance that your Grace still possessed life and health. Having them, one can conquer other things; and without them human treasure has no value. By way of Flandes (whence ships come daily to this island), I learned much, nay, all the event, although not so minutely. For Oliver de Nort, who was the Dutch general, with whom the engagement occurred, arrived safely in Holanda, with eight men—and he made nine—and without money. His purpose when he left the rebellious states of Holanda and Zelanda, with five armed vessels laden with merchandise—which were worth, principal and merchandise, one hundred and fifty or two hundred thousand ducados—was to trade and carry on commerce through the strait (and such were his orders), in whatever parts he should be, with friends or enemies. He was not to attack anyone, but only to defend himself and to incline the Indians to trade and exchange with him. All the vessels having reached the strait together, three of them became separated there because of storms, and must have been wrecked; for up to the present nothing has been heard of them. Having seen himself so abandoned, and that he could not restore his loss by trade, or else because he did not receive a hospitable reception from the inhabitants of

Piru, he determined to exceed his orders, and make that voyage one of plundering. Accordingly he stationed himself at the mouth of the river to await ships. The rest that befell, your Grace knows. Oliver de Nort is a native of the city of Roterdam, and he reached it with an anchor of wood. [209] He had no other with which to anchor, nor indeed had he any other left. It is said that this is a very heavy wood of the Indias, and he has placed it at the door of his house, as a mark of distinction. He arrived, as I say, with nine men, all told, very much worn out, and as by a miracle. He has printed a book of his voyage, with engravings of his vessels, and many other details of what happened to him, and the hardships that they endured in the fight and throughout the voyage, both to show his own glory and to incite others to similar deeds.

A pilot of this island, one Bartolome Perez, was seized and taken to Inglaterra before the peace or truce. He came through Holanda, where he conversed at great length with Oliver. The latter told him all that had happened to him, which is known to all, and was discussed in this island before that voyage. Bartolome Perez says that Oliver de Nort praised the Spaniards greatly, and said they were the bravest men he had seen in his life. They had gained the deck of his ship, and all the upper works, when he cried out from below deck to set fire to the powder, whereupon he believes that the Spaniards left for fear of being blown up. The Dutch then had an opportunity to escape, but so crippled were they that their reaching port seems a miracle. The pilot says that he saw the anchor and the book, and what pertains to the book is stated here. I have recounted this to your Grace, because of the statements in your letter, namely, that people considered them as lost, and so that so singular a case may be known there.

Now the Dutch make the voyage more quickly and more safely, going and coming, by way of India, but not touching at its ports or coasts, until they reach the islands of the Javas [210]—Java major and Java minor—and Samatra, Amboino, and the Malucas. Since they know the district so well, and have experienced the immense profits ensuing to them therefrom, it will be difficult to drive them from the Orient, where they have inflicted so many losses in both spiritual and temporal affairs.

Chapter 8

¶ Relation of the Filipinas Islands and of their natives, antiquity, customs, and government, both during the period of their paganism and after their conquest by the Spaniards, and other details.

The islands of the eastern Ocean Sea, adjacent to farther Asia, belonging to the crown of Espana, are generally called, by those who navigate thither by way of the demarcation of Castilla and Castilla's seas and lands of America, "the Western Islands;" for from the time that one leaves Espana, he sails in the course of the sun from east to west, until he reaches them. For the same reason they are called "Eastern Islands" by those who sail from west to east by way of Portuguese India, each of them circumscribing the world by voyaging in opposite directions, until they meet at these islands, which are numerous and of varying size; they are properly called Filipinas, and are subject to the crown of Castilla. They lie within the tropic of Cancer, and extend from twenty-four degrees north latitude to the equinoctial line, which cuts the islands of Maluco. There are many others on the other side of the line, in the tropic of Capricorn, which extend for twelve degrees in south latitude. [211] The ancients affirmed that each and all of them were desert and uninhabitable, [212] but now experience has demonstrated that they deceived themselves; for good climates, many people, and food and other things necessary for human life are found there, besides many mines of rich metals, with precious gems and pearls, and animals and plants, which nature has not stinted.

It is impossible to number all the islands—counting larger and smaller—of this vast archipelago. Those comprised in the name and government of Filipinas, number about forty large islands, besides other smaller ones, all consecutive. The chiefest and best known are Luzon, Mindoro, Tendaya, [213] Capul, Burias, Mazbate, Marinduque, Leite, Camar, Ybabao, Sebu, Panay, Bohol, Catenduanes, Calamianes, Mindanao, and others of less renown.

The first island conquered and colonized by the Spaniards was Sebu. [214] From there the conquest was started and continued in all the neighboring islands. Those islands are inhabited by people, natives of the same islands, called Vicayas; or by another name, Pintados—for the more prominent of the men, from their youth, tattoo their whole bodies, by pricking them wherever they are marked and then throwing certain black powders over the bleeding surface, the figures becoming indelible. But, as the chief seat of the government, and the principal Spanish settlement, was moved to the island of Luzon—the largest island, and that one nearest and opposite to Great China and Japon—I shall treat of it first; for much that will be said of it is similar in the others, to each of whose particulars and distinctive details I shall pass in due time.

This island of Luzon extends lengthwise, from the point and head where one enters the Filipinas Islands (by the channel of Capul, which lies in thirteen and one-half degrees north latitude) to the other point in the province of Cagayan, called Cape Bojeador (and located opposite China, in twenty degrees), more than two hundred leguas. In some parts its width is more constricted than in others, especially in the middle of the island, where it is so narrow that it is less than thirty leguas from sea to sea, or from one coast to the other. The whole island is more than four hundred leguas in circumference.

The climates of this island are not harmonious; on the contrary, they present a great diversity in its different districts and provinces. The head and beginning of the island, in the region of the channel, is more temperate in the interior, although the coasts are hot. The site of the city of Manila is hot, for it is on the coast and is low; but in its vicinity, quite near the city, there are districts and settlements much cooler, where the heat is not oppressive. The same is true of the other head of the island, opposite China, named Cagayan. The seasons of the year—winter and summer—are contrary to those in Europe; for the rains generally last in all these islands from the month of June until the month of September, and are accompanied by heavy showers, whirlwinds, and storms on sea and land. The summer lasts from October to the end of May, with clear skies and fair winds at sea. However, the winter and rainy season begins earlier in some provinces than in others. [215] In Cagayan winter and summer almost coincide with those of Espana, and come at the same seasons.

The people inhabiting the province of Camarines and almost as far as the provinces of Manila, in this great island of Luzon, both along the coast and in the interior, are natives of this island. They are of medium height, with a complexion like stewed quinces; and both men and women are well-featured. They have very black hair, and thin beards; and are very

215

clever at anything that they undertake, keen and passionate, and of great resolution. All live from their labor and gains in the field, their fishing, and trade, going from island to island by sea, and from province to province by land.

The natives of the other provinces of this island as far as Cagayan are of the same nature and disposition, except that it has been learned by tradition that those of Manila and its vicinity were not natives of this island, but came thither in the past and colonized it; and that they are Malay natives, and come from other islands and remote provinces. [216]

In various parts of this island of Luzon are found a number of natives black in color. Both men and women have woolly hair, and their stature is not very great, although they are strong and robust. These people are barbarians, and have but little capacity. They possess no fixed houses or settlements, but wander in bands and hordes through the mountains and rough country, changing from one site to another according to the season. They support themselves in certain clearings, and by planting rice, which they do temporarily, and by means of the game that they bring down with their bows, in the use of which they are very skilful and certain. [217] They live also on honey from the mountains, and roots produced by the ground. They are a barbarous people, in whom one cannot place confidence. They are much given to killing and to attacking the settlements of the other natives, in which they commit many depredations; and there is nothing that can be done to stop them, or to subdue or pacify them, although this is always attempted by fair or foul means, as opportunity and necessity demand.

The province of Cagayan is inhabited by natives of the same complexion as the others of the island, although they are better built, and more valiant and warlike than the others. They wear their hair long and hanging down the back. They have been in revolt and rebellion twice since the first time when they were pacified; and there has been plenty to do, on different occasions, in subduing them and repacifying them.

The apparel and clothing of these natives of Luzon before the entrance of the Spaniards into the country were generally, for the men, certain short collarless garments of cangan, sewed together in the front, and with short sleeves, and reaching slightly below the waist; some were blue and others black, while the chiefs had some red ones, called chinanas. [218] They also wore a strip of colored cloth wrapped about the waist, and passed between the legs, so that it covered the privy parts, reaching half-way down the thigh; these are called bahaques. [219] They go with legs bare, feet unshod, and the head uncovered, wrapping a narrow cloth, called potong [220] just below it, with which they bind the forehead and temples. About their necks they wear gold necklaces, wrought like spun wax, [221] and with links in our fashion, some larger than others. On their arms they wear armlets of wrought gold, which they call calombigas, and which are very large and made in different patterns. Some wear strings of precious stones—cornelians and agates; and other blue and white stones, which they esteem highly. [222] They wear around the legs some strings of these stones, and certain cords, covered with black pitch in many foldings, as garters. [223]

In a province called Zambales, they wear the head shaved from the middle forward. On the skull they have a huge lock of loose hair. [224] The women throughout this island wear small jackets [sayuelos] with sleeves of the same kinds of cloth and of all colors, called varos. [225] They wear no shifts, but certain white cotton garments which are wrapped about the waist and fall to the feet, while other dyed cloths are wrapped about the body, like kirtles, and are very graceful. The principal women have crimson ones, and some of silk, while others are woven with gold, and adorned with fringe and other ornaments. They wear many gold necklaces about the neck, calumbigas on the wrists, large earrings of wrought gold in the ears, and rings of gold and precious stones. Their black hair is done up in a very graceful knot on the head. Since the Spaniards came to the country many Indians do not wear bahaques, but wide drawers of the same cloths and materials, and hats on their heads. The chiefs wear braids of wrought gold containing many designs, while many of them wear shoes. The chief women also wear beautiful shoes, many of them having shoes of velvet adorned with gold, and white garments like petticoats.

Men and women, and especially the chief people, are very clean and neat in their persons and clothing, and of pleasing address and grace. They dress their hair carefully, and regard it as being more ornamental when it is very black. They wash it with water in which has been boiled the bark of a tree called gogo. [226] They anoint it with aljonjoli oil, prepared with musk, and other perfumes. All are very careful of their teeth, which from a very early age they file and render even, with stones and iron. [227] They dye them a black color, which is lasting, and which preserves their teeth until they are very old, although it is ugly to look at. [228]

They quite generally bathe the entire body in the rivers and creeks, both young and old, without reflecting that it could at any time be injurious to them; [229] for in their baths do they find their best medicines. When an infant is born, they immediately bathe it, and the mother likewise. The women have needlework as their employment and occupation, and they are very clever at it, and at all kinds of sewing. They weave cloth and spin cotton, and serve in the houses of their husbands and fathers. They pound the rice for eating, [230] and prepare the other food. They raise fowls and swine, and keep the houses, while the men are engaged in the labors of the field, and in their fishing, navigation, and trading. They are not very chaste, either single or married women; while their husbands, fathers, or brothers are not very jealous or anxious about it. Both men and women are so selfish and greedy that, if they are paid, they are easily won over. When the husband finds his wife in adultery, he is smoothed and pacified without any trouble—although, since they have known Spaniards, some of those who assume to be more enlightened among them have sometimes killed the adulterers. Both men and women, especially the chiefs, walk slowly and sedately when upon their visits, and when going through the streets and to the temples; and are accompanied by many slaves, both male and female, with parasols of silk which they carry to protect them from the sun and rain. The women walk ahead and their female servants and slaves follow them; behind these walk their husbands, fathers, or brothers, with their man-servants and slaves. [231]

Their ordinary food is rice pounded in wooden mortars, and cooked—this is called morisqueta, [232] and is the ordinary bread of the whole country—boiled fish (which is very abundant), the flesh of swine, deer, and wild buffaloes (which they call carabaos). Meat and fish they relish better when it has begun to spoil and when it stinks. [233] They also eat boiled camotes (which are sweet potatoes), beans, quilites [234] and other vegetables; all kinds of bananas, guavas, pineapples, custard apples, many varieties of oranges, and other varieties of fruits and herbs, with which the country teems. Their drink is a wine made from the tops of cocoa and nipa palm, of which there is a great abundance. They are grown and tended like vineyards, although without so much toil and labor. Drawing off the tuba, [235] they distil it, using for alembics their own little furnaces and utensils, to a greater or less strength, and it becomes brandy. This is drunk throughout the islands. It is a wine of the clarity of water, but strong and dry. If it be used with moderation, it acts as a medicine for the stomach, and is a protection against humors and all sorts of rheums. Mixed with Spanish wine, it makes a mild liquor, and one very palatable and healthful.

In the assemblies, marriages, and feasts of the natives of these islands, the chief thing consists in drinking this wine, day and night, without ceasing, when the turn of each comes, some singing and others drinking. As a consequence, they generally become intoxicated without this vice being regarded as a dishonor or disgrace. [236]

The weapons of this people are, in some provinces, bow and arrows. But those generally used throughout the islands are moderate-sized spears with well-made points; and certain shields of light wood, with their armholes fastened on the inside. These cover them from top to toe, and are called carasas [kalasag]. At the waist they carry a dagger four fingers in breadth, the blade pointed, and a third of a vara in length; the hilt is of gold or ivory. The pommel is open and has two cross bars or projections, without any other guard. They are called bararaos. They have two cutting edges, and are kept in wooden scabbards, or those of buffalo-horn, admirably wrought. [237] With these they strike with the point, but more generally with the edge. When they go in pursuit of their opponent, they show great dexterity in seizing his hair with one hand, while with the other they cut off his head with one stroke of the bararao, and carry it away. They afterward keep the heads suspended in their houses, where they may be seen; and of these they make a display, in order to be considered as valiant, and avengers of their enemies and of the injuries committed by them. [238]

Since they have seen the Spaniards use their weapons, many of the natives handle the arquebuses and muskets quite skilfully. Before the arrival of the Spaniards they had bronze culverins and other pieces of cast iron, with which they defended their forts and settlements, although their powder is not so well refined as that of the Spaniards.

Their ships and boats are of many kinds; for on the rivers and creeks inland they use certain very large canoes, each made from one log, and others fitted with benches and made from planks, and built up on keels. They have vireys and barangays, which are certain quick and light vessels that lie low in the water, put together with little wooden nails. These are as slender at the stern as at the bow, and they can hold a number of rowers on both sides, who propel their vessels with bucceyes or paddles, and with gaones [239] on the outside of the vessel; and they time their rowing to the accompaniment of some who sing in their language refrains by which they understand whether to hasten or retard their rowing. [240] Above the rowers is a platform or gangway, built of bamboo, upon which the fighting-men stand, in order not to interfere with the rowing of the oarsmen. In accordance with the capacity of the vessels is the number of men on these gangways. From that place they manage the sail, which is square and made of linen, and hoisted on a support or yard made of two thick bamboos, which serves as a mast. When the vessel is large, it also has a foresail of the same form. Both yards, with their tackle, can be lowered upon the gangway when the weather is rough. The helmsmen are stationed in the stern to steer. It carries another bamboo framework on the gangway itself, and upon this, when the sun shines hot, or it rains, they stretch an awning made from some mats, woven from palm-leaves. These are very bulky and close, and are called cayanes [241] Thus all the ship and its crew are covered and protected. There are also other bamboo frameworks for each side of the vessel, which are so long as the vessel, and securely fastened on. They skim the water, without hindering the rowing, and serve as a counterpoise, so that the ship cannot overturn nor upset, however heavy the sea, or strong the wind against the sail. It may happen that the entire hull of these vessels, which have no decks, may fill with water and remain between wind and water, even until it is destroyed and broken up, without sinking, because of these counterpoises. These vessels have been used commonly throughout the islands since olden times. They have other larger vessels called caracoas, lapis, and tapaques, which are used to carry their merchandise, and which are very suitable, as they are roomy and draw but little water. They generally drag them ashore every night, at the mouths of rivers and creeks, among which they always navigate without going into the open sea or leaving the shore. All the natives can row and manage these boats. Some are so long that they can carry one hundred rowers on a side and thirty soldiers above to fight. The boats commonly used are barangays and vireys, which carry a less crew and fighting force. Now they put many of them together with iron nails instead of the wooden pegs and the joints in the planks, while the helms and bows have beaks like Castilian boats. [242]

The land is well shaded in all parts by trees of different kinds, and fruit-trees which beautify it throughout the year, both along the shore and inland among the plains and mountains. It is very full of large and small rivers, of good fresh water, which flow into the sea. All of them are navigable, and abound in all kinds of fish, which are very pleasant to the taste. For the above reason there is a large supply of lumber, which is cut and sawed, dragged to the rivers, and brought down, by the natives. This lumber is very useful for houses and buildings, and for the construction of small and large vessels. Many very straight thick trees, light and pliable, are found, which are used as masts for ships and galleons. Consequently, vessels of any size may be fitted with masts from these trees, made of one piece of timber, without its being necessary to splice them or make them of different pieces. For the hulls of the ships, the keels, futtock-timbers, top-timbers, and any other kinds of supports and braces, compass-timbers, transoms, knees small and large, and rudders, all sorts of good timber are easily found; as well as good planking for the sides, decks, and upper-works, from very suitable woods. [243]

There are many native fruit-trees, such as the sanctors, mabolos, tamarinds, nancas, custard-apples, papaws, guavas, and everywhere many oranges, of all kinds—large and small, sweet and sour; citrons, lemons, and ten or twelve varieties of very healthful and palatable bananas. [244] There are many cocoa-palms bearing fruit of pleasant taste—from which is made wine and common oil, which is a very healing remedy for wounds; and other wild palms of the forests—that do not yield cocoa-nuts, but serve as wood, and from whose bark is made bonote, a tow for rigging and cables, and also for calking ships. Efforts have been made to plant olives and quinces, and other fruit-trees of Espana, but as yet they have had no success, except with pomegranates and grapevines, which bear fruit the second year. These bear abundance of exceedingly good grapes three times a year; and some fig-trees have succeeded. Vegetables of every kind grow well and very abundantly, but do not seed, and it is always necessary to bring the seeds from Castilla, China, or Japon.

In the Cagayan provinces are found chestnut-trees, which produce fruit. In other districts are found pines and other trees which yield certain very large pine-nuts, with a hard shell and a pleasant taste, which are called piles. [245] There is abundance of cedar which is called calanta, a beautiful red wood called asana, [246] ebony of various qualities, and many other precious woods for all uses. The meat generally eaten is that of swine, of which there is a great abundance, and it is very palatable and wholesome.

Beef is eaten, cattle being raised abundantly in stock-farms in many different parts of the islands. The cattle are bred from those of China and Nueva Espana. [247] The Chinese cattle are small, and excellent breeders. Their horns are very small and twisted, and some cattle can move them. They have a large hump upon the shoulders, and are very manageable beasts. There are plenty of fowls like those of Castilla, and others very large, which are bred from fowls brought from China. They are very pal-atable, and make fine capons. Some of these fowls are black in feather, skin, flesh, and bones, and are pleasant to the taste. [248] Many geese are raised, as well as swans, ducks, and tame pigeons brought from China. There is abundance of flesh of wild game, such as venison, and wild boars, and in some parts porcupines. There are many buffaloes, which are called carabaos, which are raised in the fields and are very spirited; others are brought tame from China; these are very numerous, and very handsome. These last are used only for milking, and their milk is thicker and more palatable than that of cows.

Goats and kids are raised, although their flesh is not savory, because of the humidity of the country. These animals sicken and die for that reason, and because they eat certain poisonous herbs. Ewes and rams, although often brought from Nueva Espana, never multiply. Conse-quently there are none of these animals, for the climate and pasturage has not as yet seemed suitable for them. [249] There were no horses, mares, or asses in the islands, until the Spaniards had them brought from China and brought them from Nueva Espana. Asses and mules are very rare, but there are many horses and mares. Some farms are being stocked with them, and those born there (mixed breeds for the most part) turn out well, and have good colors, are good tempered and willing to work, and are of medium size. Those brought from China are small, very strong, good goers, treacherous, quarrelsome, and bad-tempered. Some horses of good colors are brought from Japon. They have well-shaped bodies, thick hair, large fetlocks, large legs and front hoofs, which makes them look like draft-horses. Their heads are rather large, and their mouths hard. They run but slowly, but walk well, and are spirited, and of much mettle. The daily feed of the horses consists throughout the year of green provender, [250] besides rice in the husk, which keeps them very fat. [251]

There are many fowls and field birds, and wild birds of wonderful colors and very beautiful. There are no singing birds suitable for keeping in cages, although some calendar larks [Calandrias] called fimbaros, [252] smaller than those of Espana, are brought from Japon, whose song is most sweet. There are many turtle-doves, ring-doves; other doves with an extremely green plumage, and red feet and beaks; and others that are white with a red spot on the breast, like a pelican. Instead of quail, there are certain birds resembling them, but smaller, which are called povos [253] and other smaller birds called mayuelas. [254] There are many wild chickens and cocks, which are very small, and taste like partridge. There are royal, white, and grey herons, flycatchers, and other shore birds, ducks, lavancos, [255] crested cranes, sea-crows, eagles, eagle-owls, and other birds of prey, although none are used for hawking. There are jays and thrushes as in Espana, and white storks and cranes. [256] They do not rear peacocks, rabbits, or hares, although they have tried to do so. It is believed that the wild animals in the forests and fields eat and destroy them, namely, the cats, foxes, badgers, and large and small rats, which are very numerous, and other land animals. [257]

Throughout these islands are found a great number of monkeys, of various sizes, with which at times the trees are covered. There are green and white parrots, but they are stupid in talking; and very small parroquets, of beautiful green and red colors, which talk as little. The forests and settlements have many serpents, of various colors, which are generally larger than those of Castilla. Some have been seen in the forests of unusual size, and wonderful to behold. [258] The most harmful are certain slender snakes, of less than one vara in length, which dart down upon passersby from the trees (where they generally hang), and sting them; their venom is so powerful that within twenty-four hours the person dies raving.

There are many very large scorpions in the rivers and creeks, and a great number of crocodiles, which are very bloodthirsty and cruel. They quite commonly pull from their bancas the natives who go in those boats, and cause many injuries among the horned cattle and the horses of the stock-farms, when they go to drink. And although the people fish for them often and kill them, they are never diminished in number. For that reason, the natives set closely-grated divisions and enclosures in the rivers and creeks of their settlements, where they bathe. There they enter the water to bathe, secure from those monsters, which they fear so greatly that they venerate and adore them, as if they were beings superior to themselves. All their oaths and execrations, and those which are of any weight with them (even among the Christians) are, thus expressed: "So may the crocodile kill him!" They call the crocodile buhaya in their language. It has happened when some one has sworn falsely, or when he has broken his word, that then some accident has occurred to him with the crocodile, which God, whom he offends, has so permitted for the sake of the authority and purity of the truth, and the promise of it. [259]

The fisheries of sea and rivers are most abundant, and include all kinds of fish; both of fresh and salt water. These are generally used as food throughout the entire country. There are many good sardines, sea-eels, sea-breams (which they call bacocos), daces, skates, bicudas, tanguingues, soles, plantanos, [260] taraquitos, needle-fish, gilt-heads, and eels; large oysters, mussels, [261] porcebes, crawfish, shrimp, sea-spiders, center-fish, and all kinds of cockles, shad, white fish, and in the Tajo River of Cagayan, [262] during their season, a great number of bobos, which come down to spawn at the bar. In the lake of Bonbon, a quantity of tunny-fish, not so large as those of Espana, but of the same shape, flesh, and taste, are caught. Many sea-fish are found in the sea, such as whales, sharks, caellas, marajos, bufeos, and other unknown species of extraordinary forms and size. In the year of five hundred and ninety-six, during a furious storm in the islands, a fish was flung into shallow water on one of the Luzon coasts near the province of Camarines. It was so huge and misshapen, that although it lay in more than three and one-half bracas of water, it could not again get afloat, and died there. The natives said that they had never seen anything like it, nor another shaped like it. Its head was of wonderful size and fierce aspect. On its frontal it bore two horns, which pointed toward its back. One of them was taken to Manila. It was covered with its skin or hide, but had no hair or scales. It was white, and twenty feet long. Where it joined the head it was as thick as the thigh, and gradually tapered proportionally to the tip. It was somewhat curved and not very round; and to all appearances, quite solid. It caused great wonder in all beholders. [263]

There is a fresh-water lake in the island of Luzon, five leguas from Manila, which contains a quantity of fish. Many rivers flow into this lake, and it empties into the sea through the river flowing from it to Manila. It is called La Laguna de Bay ["Bay Lake"]. It is thirty leguas in circumference, and has an uninhabited island in its middle, where game abounds. [264] Its shores are lined with many native villages. The natives navigate the lake, and commonly cross it in their skiffs. At times it is quite stormy and dangerous to navigate, when the north winds blow, for these winds make it very boisterous, although it is very deep.

Twenty leguas from Manila, in the province of Bonbon, is another lake of the same name [Bonbon], not so extensive as the former, but with a great abundance of fish. The natives' method of catching them is by making corrals [265] of bejucos, which are certain slender canes or rushes, solid and very pliant and strong; these are employed for making cables for the natives' boats, as well as other kinds of ropes. They catch the fish inside these corrals, having made the enclosures fast by means of stakes. They also catch the fish in wicker baskets made from the bejucos, but most generally with atarrayas, [266] esparaveles, other small barrederas, [267] and with hand lines and hooks. [268] The most usual food of the natives is a fish as small as pejerreyes. [269] They dry and cure these fish in the sun and air, and cook them in many styles. They like them better than large fish. It is called laulau among them. [270]

Instead of olives and other pickled fruit, they have a green fruit, like walnuts, which they call paos. [271] Some are small, and others larger in size, and when prepared they have a pleasant taste. They also prepare charas [272] in pickle brine, and all sorts of vegetables and greens, which are very appetizing. There is much ginger, and it is eaten green, pickled, and preserved. There are also quantities of cachumba [273] instead of saffron and other condiments. The ordinary dainty throughout these islands, and in many kingdoms of the mainland of those regions, is buyo [betel]. This is made from a tree, [274] whose leaf is shaped like that of the mulberry. The fruit resembles an oak acorn, and is white inside. [275] This fruit, which is called bonga, is cut lengthwise in strips, and each strip is put into an envelope or covering made from the leaf. With the bonga is thrown in a powder of quick lime. [276] This compound is placed in the mouth and chewed. It is so strong a mixture, and burns so much, that it induces sleep and intoxication. It burns the mouths of those not used to it, and causes them to smart. The saliva and all the mouth are made as red as blood. It does not taste bad. After having been chewed [277] for a considerable time it is spit out, when it no longer has any juice, which is called capa [sapa]. They consider very beneficial that quantity of the juice which has gone into the stomach, for strengthening it, and for various diseases. It strengthens and preserves the teeth and gums from all inflammations, decay, and aches. They tell other wonderful effects of it. What has been seen is that the natives and Spaniards—laymen and religious, men and women—use it so commonly and generally that mornings and afternoons, at parties and visits, and even alone in their houses, all their refreshments and luxuries consist of buyos served on heavily-gilded and handsomely adorned plates and trays like chocolate in Nueva Espana. In these poison has been often administered from which the persons eating them have died, and that quite commonly.

The natives (especially the chiefs) take whenever they leave their houses, for show and entertainment, their boxes of buyos—which they call buccetas [278]—ready to use, and the leaf, bonga, and quick lime, separately. With these handsome boxes, which are made of metal and of other materials, they carry the scissors and other tools for making the buyo with cleanliness and neatness. Wherever they may stop, they make and use their buyo. In the parians, or bazars, buyos are sold ready made, and the outfit for making them. [279]

The natives of these islands quite commonly use as venoms and poisons the herbs of that class found throughout the islands. They are so efficacious and deadly that they produce wonderful effects. There is a lizard, commonly found in the houses, somewhat dark-green in color, one palmo long, and as thick as three fingers, which is called chacon. [280] They put this in a joint of bamboo, and cover it up. The slaver of this animal during its imprisonment is gathered. It is an exceedingly strong poison, when introduced as above stated, in the food or drink, in however minute quantities. There are various herbs known and gathered by the natives for the same use. Some of them are used dry, and others green; some are to be mixed in food, and others inhaled. Some kill by simply touching them with the hands or feet, or by sleeping upon them. The natives are so skilful in making compounds from these substances, that they mix and apply them in such a manner that they take effect at once, or at a set time—long or short, as they wish, even after a year. Many persons usually die wretchedly by these means—especially Spaniards, who lack foresight, and who are tactless and hated because of the ill-treatment that they inflict upon the natives with whom they deal, either in the collection of their tributes, or in other matters in which they employ them, without there being any remedy for it. There are certain poisonous herbs, with which, when the natives gather them, they carry, all ready, other herbs which act as antidotes. In the island of Bohol is one herb of such nature that the natives approach it from windward when they cut it from the shrub on which it grows; for the very air alone that blows over the herb is deadly. Nature did not leave this danger without a remedy, for other herbs and roots are found in the same islands, of so great efficacy and virtue that they destroy and correct the poison and mischief of the others, and are used when needed. Accordingly, when

225

one knows what poison has been given him, it is not difficult, if recourse be had in time, to cure it, by giving the herb that is antidotal to such poison. At times it has happened that pressure has been put upon the person suspected of having committed the evil to make him bring the antidote, by which it has been remedied. There are also other general antidotes, both for preservation against poison and for mitigating the effects of poison that has been administered. But the most certain and efficacious antidotes are certain small flies or insects, of a violet color, found on certain bushes in the islands of Pintados. These are shut up in a clean bamboo joint, and covered over. There they breed and multiply. Ground rice is put in with them, and they exist thereon. Every week they are visited [281] and the old rice removed and new rice put in, and they are kept alive by this means. If six of these insects are taken in a spoonful of wine or water—for they emit no bad odor, and taste like cress—they produce a wonderful effect. Even when people go to banquets or dinners where there is any suspicion, they are wont to take with them these insects, in order to preserve and assure themselves from any danger of poison and venom.

All these islands are, in many districts, rich in placers and mines of gold, a metal which the natives dig and work. However, since the advent of the Spaniards in the land, the natives proceed more slowly in this, and content themselves with what they already possess in jewels and gold ingots, handed down from antiquity and inherited from their ancestors. [282] This is considerable, for he must be poor and wretched who has no gold chains, calombigas [bracelets], and earrings.

Some placers and mines were worked at Paracali in the province of Camarines, where there is good gold mixed with copper. This commodity is also traded in the Ylocos, for at the rear of this province, which borders the seacoast, are certain lofty and rugged mountains which extend as far as Cagayan. On the slopes of these mountains, in the interior, live many natives, as yet unsubdued, and among whom no incursion has been made, who are called Ygolotes. These natives possess rich mines, many of gold and silver mixed. They are wont to dig from them only the amount necessary for their wants. They descend to certain places to trade this gold (without completing its refining or preparation), with the Ylocos; there they exchange it for rice, swine, carabaos, cloth, and other things that they need. [283] The Ylocos complete its refining and preparation, and by their medium it is distributed throughout the country. Although an effort has been made with these Ygolotes to discover their mines, and how they work them, and their method of working the metal, nothing definite has been learned, for the Ygolotes fear that the Spaniards will go to seek them for their gold, and say that they keep the gold better in the earth than in their houses. [284]

There are also many gold mines and placers in the other islands, especially among the Pintados, on the Botuan River in Mindanao, and in Sebu, where a mine of good gold is worked, called Taribon. If the industry and efforts of the Spaniards were to be converted into the working of the gold, as much would be obtained from any one of these islands as from those provinces which produce the most in the world. But since they attend to other means of gain rather than to this, as will be told in due time, they do not pay the proper attention to this matter.

In some of these islands pearl oysters are found, especially in the Calamianes, where some have been obtained that are large and exceedingly clear and lustrous. [285] Neither is this means of profit utilized. In all parts, seed pearls are found in the ordinary oysters, and there are oysters as large as a buckler. From the [shells of the] latter the natives manufacture beautiful articles. There are also very large sea turtles in all the islands. Their shells are utilized by the natives, and sold as an article of commerce to the Chinese and Portuguese, and other nations who go after them and esteem them highly, because of the beautiful things made from them.

On the coasts of any of these islands are found many small white snail shells, called siguei. The natives gather them and sell them by measure to the Siamese, Cambodians, Pantanes, and other peoples of the mainland. It serves there as money, and those nations trade with it, as they do with cacao-beans in Nueva Espana. [286]

Carabao horns are used as merchandise in trading with China; and deerskins and dye-wood with Japon. The natives make use of everything in trading with those nations and derive much profit therefrom.

In this island of Luzon, especially in the provinces of Manila, Panpanga, Pangasinan, and Ylocos, certain earthenware jars [tibores] are found among the natives. They are very old, of a brownish color, and not handsome. Some are of medium size, and others are smaller, and they have certain marks and stamps. The natives are unable to give any explanation of where or when they got them, for now they are not brought to the islands or made there. The Japanese seek them and esteem them, for they have found that the root of a plant called cha [tea]—which is drunk hot, as a great refreshment and medicine, among the kings and lords of Japon—is preserved and keeps only in these tibors. These are so highly valued throughout Japon, that they are regarded as the most precious jewels of their closets and household furniture. A tibor is worth a great sum, and the Japanese adorn them outside with fine gold beautifully chased, and keep them in brocade cases. Some tibors are valued and sold for two thousand taes of eleven reals to the tae, or for less, according to the quality of the tibor. It makes no difference if they are cracked or chipped, for that does not hinder them from holding the tea. The natives of these islands sell them to the Japanese for the best price possible, and seek them carefully for this profit. However, few are found now, because of the assiduity with which the natives have applied themselves to that search. [287]

At times the natives have found large pieces of ambergris on the coasts. When they discovered that the Spaniards value it, they gathered it, and have made profit from it. The past year of six hundred and two, some natives found in the island of Sebu a good-sized piece of ambergris, and when their encomendero heard of it, he took it, and traded with them secretly for it, on the account of their tribute. It is said that it weighed a good number of libras. Afterward he brought it out and sold it by the ounce at a higher rate. [288]

In the province and river of Butuan—which is pacified and assigned to Spaniards, and is located in the island of Mindanao—the natives practice another industry, which is very useful. As they possess many civet cats, although smaller than those of Guinea, they make use of the civet and trade it. This they do easily, for, when the moon is in the crescent, they hunt the cats with nets, and capture many of them. Then when they have obtained the civet, they loose the cats. They also capture and cage some of them, which are sold in the islands at very low prices. [289]

Cotton is raised abundantly throughout the islands. It is spun and sold in the skein to the Chinese and other nations, who come to get it. Cloth of different patterns is also woven from it, and the natives also trade that. Other cloths, called medrinaques, are woven from the banana leaf. [290]

The islands of Babuytanes [291] consist of many small islands lying off the upper coast of the province of Cagayan. They are inhabited by natives, whose chief industry consists in going to Cagayan, in their tapaques, with swine, fowls, and other food, and ebony spears, for exchange. The islands are not assigned as encomiendas, nor is any tribute collected from them. There are no Spaniards among them, as those natives are of less understanding and less civilized [than the others]. Accordingly no Christians have been made among them, and they have no justices.

Other islands, called the Catenduanes, lie off the other head of the island of Luzon, opposite the province of Camarines, in fourteen degrees of north latitude, near the strait of Espiritu Santo. They are islands densely populated with natives of good disposition, who are all assigned to Spaniards. They possess instruction and churches, and have an alcalde-mayor who administers justice to them. Most of them cultivate the soil, but some are engaged in gold-washing, and in trading between various islands, and with the mainland of Luzon, very near those islands. [292]

The island of Luzon has a bay thirty leguas in circumference on its southern coast, situated about one hundred leguas from the cape of Espiritu Santo, which is the entrance to the Capul channel. Its entrance is narrow, and midway contains an island called Miraveles [i.e., Corregidor] lying obliquely across it, which makes the entrance narrow. This island is about two leguas long and one-half legua wide. It is high land and well shaded by its many trees. It contains a native settlement of fifty persons, and there the watchman of the bay has his fixed abode and residence. There are channels at both ends of the island, where one may enter the bay. The one at the south is one-half legua wide, and has a rock in its middle called El Fraile ["the friar"]. The one on the north is much narrower, but any ships of any draft whatever can enter and go out by both channels. The entire bay is of good depth, and clean, and has good anchorages in all parts. It is eight leguas from these entrances to the colony of Manila and the bar of the river. A large harbor is formed two leguas south of Manila, with a point of land that shelters it. That point has a native settlement called Cabit, [293] and it gives name to the harbor, which is used as a port for the vessels. It is very capacious and well sheltered from the vendavals—whether the southeast, and southwest, the west, and west-southwest, or the north-northeast and north winds. It has a good anchorage, with a clean and good bottom. There is a good entrance quite near the land, more than one and one-half leguas wide, for the ingress and egress of vessels. All the shores of this bay are well provided with abundant fisheries, of all kinds. They are densely inhabited by natives. Above Manila there is a province of more than twenty leguas in extent called La Pampanga. This province possesses many rivers and creeks that irrigate it. They all flow and empty into the bay. This province contains many settlements of natives, and considerable quantities of rice, fruits, fish, meat, and other foods. [294]

The bar of the river of Manila, which is in the same bay, near the colony of Manila on one side and Tondo on the other, is not very deep because of certain sand shoals on it, which change their position at the time of the freshets and obstruct it. Consequently, although the water is deep enough for any vessel past the bar, still, unless they are fragatas, vireys, or other small vessels, they cannot pass the bar to enter the river. In respect to galleys, galliots, and the vessels from China, which draw but little water, they must enter empty, and at high tide, and by towing. Such vessels anchor in the bay outside the bar, and, for greater security enter the port of Cabit.

There is another good port called Ybalon, [295] twenty leguas from the channel of the same island of Luzon, which is sheltered from the vendavals, and has a good entrance and anchorage. There the vessels that enter to escape the vendaval find shelter, and wait until the brisa returns, by which to go to Manila, eighty leguas away.

On the coasts of Pangasinan, Ylocos, and Cagayan, there are some ports and bars, where ships can enter and remain, such as the harbor of Marihuma, [296] the port El Frayle ["the friar"], [297] that of Bolinao, the bar of Pangasinan, that of Bigan, the bar of Camalayuga, at the mouth of the Tajo River (which goes up two leguas to the chief settlement of Cagayan)—besides other rivers, bars, harbors, and shelters of less account for smaller vessels throughout the coasts of this island.

Quite near this large island of Luzon, many other islands, large and small, are located; they are inhabited by the same natives as Luzon, who have gold placers, sowed fields, and their trading. Such are Marinduque, Tablas Island, Mazbate, Burias, Banton, Bantonillo, and others of less importance. The nearest of them to Manila is the island of Mindoro. It is more than eighty leguas long and about two hundred in circumference. It has many settlements of the same natives, and the side lying next the provinces of Balayan and Calilaya is so near and close to the island of Luzon, that it forms a strait which contains powerful currents and races, through which the ships going to and from Manila enter and leave. The winds and currents there are very strong. It is about one-half a legua wide. In that part is the chief town of this island of Mindoro. It has a port that is called El Varadero ["the place for laying up ships"] for large vessels. There are also other anchorages and bars throughout this island for smaller vessels; and many settlements and natives on all the coasts of this island. All of the settlements abound in rice, food, and gold-placers, and all kinds of game and timber. [298]

The cape of Espiritu Santo, which is sighted by ships entering the Filipinas Islands on the way from Nueva Espana, is in an island called Tendaya, [299] in about thirteen degrees. Twenty leguas south after turning this cape of Espiritu Santo lie the island of Viri, and many others which are sighted. Through them an entrance opens to the island of Sebu by a strait called San Juanillo, which is formed by these islands. It is not very good or safe for the larger ships. But toward the north after leaving this course, one reaches the island of Capul, which forms a strait and channel of many currents and rough waves, through which the ships enter. Before reaching the strait there is a rock, or barren islet, called San Bernardino; this strait is formed by the coast of the island of Luzon and that of the island of Capul. Its channel is about one legua long and less wide.

On leaving this strait, after having entered by it, three small islets form a triangle. They are called the islands of Naranjos ["Oranges"], and are lofty and inaccessible with steep rocks. Upon them ships are wont to be driven by the powerful currents, even though they try to escape them. These are not inhabited, but the others [Capul, Viri, etc.] are large islands containing many settlements of natives and all kinds of provisions and food.

South of this district lie the islands of Bicayas, or, as they are also called, Pintados. They are many in number, thickly populated with natives. Those of most renown are Leite, Ybabao, [300] Camar [Samar], Bohol, island of Negros, Sebu, Panay, Cuyo, and the Calamianes. All the natives of these islands, both men and women, are well-featured, of a good disposition, and of better nature, and more noble in their actions than the inhabitants of the islands of Luzon and its vicinity.

They differ from them in their hair, which the men wear cut in a cue, like the ancient style in Espana. Their bodies are tattooed with many designs, but the face is not touched. [301] They wear large earrings of gold and ivory in their ears, and bracelets of the same; certain scarfs wrapped round the head, very showy, which resemble turbans, and knotted very gracefully and edged with gold. They wear also a loose collarless jacket with tight sleeves, whose skirts reach half way down the leg. These garments are fastened in front and are made of medrinaque and colored silks. They wear no shirts or drawers, but bahaques [i.e., breech-clouts] of many wrappings, which cover their privy parts, when they remove their skirts and jackets. The women are good-looking and graceful. They are very neat, and walk slowly. Their hair is black, long, and drawn into a knot on the head. Their robes are wrapped about the waist and fall downward. These are made of all colors, and they wear collarless jackets of the same material. Both men and women go naked and without any coverings, [302] and barefoot, and with many gold chains, earrings, and wrought bracelets.

Their weapons consist of large knives curved like cutlasses, spears, and caracas [i.e., shields]. They employ the same kinds of boats as the inhabitants of Luzon. They have the same occupations, products, and means of gain as the inhabitants of all the other islands. These Visayans are a race less inclined to agriculture, and are skilful in navigation, and eager for war and raids for pillage and booty, which they call mangubas. [303] This means "to go out for plunder."

Near the principal settlement of the island of Sebu, there is a fine port for all manner of vessels. It has a good entrance and furnishes shelter at all times. It has a good bottom and is an excellent anchorage. There are also other ports and bars of less importance and consideration, as in all these islands, for smaller vessels.

This island of Sebu is an island of more than one hundred leguas in circumference. It has abundance of provisions, and gold mines and placers, and is inhabited by natives.

Beyond it lie other islands, very pleasant and well populated, especially the island of Panay. Panay is a large island, more than one hundred leguas in circumference, containing many native settlements. [304] It produces considerable quantities of rice, palm-wine, and all manner of provisions. It has flourishing and wealthy settlements, on what is called the river of Panay. The chief one is Oton, which has a bar and port for galleys and ships, shipyards for building large ships, and a great amount of timber for their construction. There are many natives, who are masters of all kinds of shipbuilding. Near this island lies an islet eight leguas in circumference, which is densely populated by natives who are all carpenters. They are excellent workmen, and practice no other trade or occupation; and, without a single tree of any size on this whole islet, they practice this art with great ability. From there all the islands are furnished with workmen for carpentry. The island is called that of the Cagayanes.

After the island of Sebu follow immediately the island of Mindanao, an island of more than three hundred leguas in circumference, and Jolo, which is small. Lower down is the island of Borneo, a very large island, more than five hundred leguas in circumference. All of these islands are densely populated, although that of Borneo is not subdued. Neither is that of Mindanao in entirety, but only the river of Botuan, Dapitan, and the province and coast of Caragan.

Below this island [Mindanao], before reaching that of Borneo, lie the islands of the Calamianes. They are very numerous, and consist of islands of various sizes, which are densely inhabited with natives; they have some supply of provisions and engage in certain kinds of husbandry. However the most usual occupation is that of their navigations from island to island in pursuit of their trading and exchange, and their fisheries; while those who live nearest the island of Borneo are wont to go on piratical raids and pillage the natives in other islands.

The flow- and ebb-tides, and the high and low tides among these islands are so diverse in them that they have no fixed rule, either because of the powerful currents among these islands, or by some other natural secret of the flux and reflux which the moon causes. No definite knowledge has been arrived at in this regard, for although the tides are highest during the opposition of the moon, and are higher in the month of March than throughout the rest of the year, there is so great variation in the daily tides that it causes surprise. Some days there are two equal tides between day and night, while other days there is but one. At other times the flow during the day is low, and that of the night greater. They usually have no fixed hour, for it may happen to be high-tide one day at noon, while next day high-tide may be anticipated or postponed many hours. Or the tide of one day may be low, and when a smaller one is expected for next day, it may be much greater.

The language of all the Pintados and Bicayas is one and the same, by which they understand one another when talking, or when writing with the letters and characters of their own which they possess. These resemble those of the Arabs. The common manner of writing among the natives is on leaves of trees, and on bamboo bark. Throughout the islands the bamboo is abundant; it has huge and misshapen joints, and lower part is a very thick and solid tree. [305]

The language of Luzon and those islands in its vicinity differs widely from that of the Bicayas. [306] The language of the island of Luzon is not uniform, for the Cagayans have one language and the Ylocos another. The Zambales have their own particular language, while the Pampangos also have one different from the others. The inhabitants of the province of Manila, the Tagals, have their own language, which is very rich and copious. By means of it one can express elegantly whatever he wishes, and in many modes and manners. It is not difficult, either to learn or to pronounce.

The natives throughout the islands can write excellently with certain characters, almost like the Greek or Arabic. These characters are fifteen in all. Three are vowels, which are used as are our five. The consonants number twelve, and each and all of them combine with certain dots or commas, and so signify whatever one wishes to write, as fluently and easily as is done with our Spanish alphabet. The method of writing was on bamboo, but is now on paper, commencing the lines at the right and running to the left, in the Arabic fashion. Almost all the natives, both men and women, write in this language. There are very few who do not write it excellently and correctly.

This language of the province of Manila [i.e., the Tagal] extends throughout the province of Camarines, and other islands not contiguous to Luzon. There is but little difference in that spoken in the various districts, except that it is spoken more elegantly in some provinces than in others. [307]

The edifices and houses of the natives of all these Filipinas Islands are built in a uniform manner, as are their settlements; for they always build them on the shores of the sea, between rivers and creeks. The natives generally gather in districts or settlements where they sow their rice, and possess their palm trees, nipa and banana groves, and other trees, and implements for their fishing and sailing. A small number inhabit the interior, and are called tinguianes; they also seek sites on rivers and creeks, on which they settle for the same reasons.

The houses and dwellings of all these natives are universally set upon stakes and arigues [i.e., columns] high above the ground. Their rooms are small and the roofs low. They are built and tiled with wood and bamboos, [308] and covered and roofed with nipa-palm leaves. Each house is separate, and is not built adjoining another. In the lower part are enclosures made by stakes and bamboos, where their fowls and cattle are reared, and the rice pounded and cleaned. One ascends into the houses by means of ladders that can be drawn up, which are made from two bamboos. Above are their open batalanes [galleries] used for household duties; the parents and [grown] children live together. There is little adornment and finery in the houses, which are called bahandin. [309]

Besides these houses, which are those of the common people and those of less importance, there are the chiefs' houses. They are built upon trees and thick arigues, with many rooms and comforts. They are well constructed of timber and planks, and are strong and large. They are furnished and supplied with all that is necessary, and are much finer and more substantial than the others. They are roofed, however, as are the others, with the palm-leaves called nipa. These keep out the water and the sun more than do shingles or tiles, although the danger from fires is greater.

The natives do not inhabit the lower part of their houses, because they raise their fowls and cattle there, and because of the damp and heat of the earth, and the many rats, which are enormous and destructive both in the houses and sowed fields; and because, as their houses are generally built on the sea shore, or on the banks of rivers and creeks, the waters bathe the lower parts, and the latter are consequently left open.

There were no kings or lords throughout these islands who ruled over them as in the manner of our kingdoms and provinces; but in every island, and in each province of it, many chiefs were recognized by the natives themselves. Some were more powerful than others, and each one had his followers and subjects, by districts and families; and these obeyed and respected the chief. Some chiefs had friendship and communication with others, and at times wars and quarrels. [310]

These principalities and lordships were inherited in the male line and by succession of father and son and their descendants. If these were lacking, then their brothers and collateral relatives succeeded. Their duty was to rule and govern their subjects and followers, and to assist them in their interests and necessities. What the chiefs received from their followers was to be held by them in great veneration and respect; and they were served in their wars and voyages, and in their tilling, sowing, fishing, and the building of their houses. To these duties the natives attended very promptly, whenever summoned by their chief. They also paid the chiefs tribute (which they called buiz), in varying quantities, in the crops that they gathered. The descendants of such chiefs, and their relatives, even though they did not inherit the lordship, were held in the same respect and consideration. Such were all regarded as nobles, and as persons exempt from the services rendered by the others, or the plebeians, who were called timaguas. [311] The same right of nobility and chieftainship was preserved for the women, just as for the men. When any of these chiefs was more courageous than others in war and upon other occasions, such a one enjoyed more followers and men; and the others were under his leadership, even if they were chiefs. These latter retained to themselves the lordship and particular government of their own following, which is called barangai among them. They had datos and other special leaders [mandadores] who attended to the interests of the barangay.

The superiority of these chiefs over those of their barangai was so great that they held the latter as subjects; they treated these well or ill, and disposed of their persons, their children, and their possessions, at will, without any resistance, or rendering account to anyone. For very slight annoyances and for slight occasions, they were wont to kill and wound them, and to enslave them. It has happened that the chiefs have made perpetual slaves of persons who have gone by them, while bathing in the river, or who have raised their eyes to look at them less respectfully and for other similar causes. [312]

When some natives had suits or disputes with others over matters of property and interest, or over personal injuries and wrongs received, they appointed old men of the same district, to try them, the parties being present. If they had to present proofs, they brought their witnesses there, and the case was immediately judged according to what was found, according to the usages of their ancestors on like occasions; and that sentence was observed and executed without any further objection or delay. [313]

The natives' laws throughout the islands were made in the same manner, and they followed the traditions and customs of their ancestors, without anything being written. Some provinces had different customs than others in some respects. However, they agreed in most, and in all the islands generally the same usages were followed [314]

There are three conditions of persons among the natives of these islands, and into which their government is divided: the chiefs, of whom we have already treated; the timaguas, who are equivalent to plebeians; and slaves, those of both chiefs and timaguas.

The slaves were of several classes. Some were for all kinds of work and slavery, like those which we ourselves hold. Such are called saguiguilires; [315] they served inside the house, as did likewise the children born of them. There are others who live in their own houses with their families, outside the house of their lord; and come, at the season, to aid him in his sowings and harvests, among his rowers when he embarks, in the construction of his house when it is being built, and to serve in his house when there are guests of distinction. These are bound to come to their lord's house whenever he summons them, and to serve in these offices without any pay or stipend. These slaves are called namamahays, [316] and their children and descendants are slaves of the same class. From these slaves—saguiguilirs and namamahays—are issue, some of whom are whole slaves, some of whom are half slaves, and still others one-fourth slaves. It happens thus: if either the father or the mother was free, and they had an only child, he was half free and half slave. If they had more than one child, they were divided as follows: the first follows the condition of the father, free or slave; the second that of the mother. If there were an odd number of children, the last was half free and half slave. Those who descended from these, if children of a free mother or father, were only one-fourth slaves, because of being children of a free father or mother and of a half-slave. These half slaves or one-fourth slaves, whether saguiguilirs or namamahays, served their masters during every other moon; and in this respect so is such condition slavery.

In the same way, it may happen in divisions between heirs that a slave will fall to several, and serves each one for the time that is due him. When the slave is not wholly slave, but half or fourth, he has the right, because of that part that is free, to compel his master to emancipate him for a just price. This price is appraised and regulated for persons according to the quality of their slavery, whether it be saguiguilir or namamahay, half slave or quarter slave. But, if he is wholly slave, the master cannot be compelled to ransom or emancipate him for any price.

The usual price of a sanguiguilir slave among the natives is, at most, generally ten taes of good gold, or eighty pesos; if he is namamahay, half of that sum. The others are in the same proportion, taking into consideration the person and his age.

No fixed beginning can be assigned as the origin of these kinds of slavery among these natives, because all the slaves are natives of the islands, and not strangers. It is thought that they were made in their wars and quarrels. The most certain knowledge is that the most powerful made the others slaves, and seized them for slight cause or occasion, and many times for loans and usurious contracts which were current among them. The interest, capital, and debt, increased so much with delay that the borrowers became slaves. Consequently all these slaveries have violent and unjust beginnings; and most of the suits among the natives are over these, and they occupy the judges in the exterior court with them, and their confessors in that of conscience. [317]

These slaves comprise the greatest wealth and capital of the natives of these islands, for they are very useful to them and necessary for the cultivation of their property. They are sold, traded, and exchanged among them, just as any other mercantile article, from one village to another, from one province to another, and likewise from one island to another. Therefore, and to avoid so many suits as would occur if these slaveries were examined, and their origin and source ascertained, they are preserved and held as they were formerly.

The marriages of these natives, commonly and generally were, and are: Chiefs with women chiefs; timaguas with those of that rank; and slaves with those of their own class. But sometimes these classes intermarry with one another. They considered one woman, whom they married, as the legitimate wife and the mistress of the house; and she was styled ynasaba. [318] Those whom they kept besides her they considered as friends. The children of the first were regarded as legitimate and whole heirs of their parents; the children of the others were not so regarded, and were left something by assignment, but they did not inherit.

The dowry was furnished by the man, being given by his parents. The wife furnished nothing for the marriage, until she had inherited it from her parents. The solemnity of the marriage consisted in nothing more than the agreement between the parents and relatives of the contracting parties, the payment of the dowry agreed upon to the father of the bride, [319] and the assembling at the wife's parents' house of all the relatives to eat and drink until they would fall down. At night the man took the woman to his house and into his power, and there she remained. These marriages were annulled and dissolved for slight cause, with the examination and judgment of the relatives of both parties, and of the old men, who acted as mediators in the affairs. At such a time the man took the dowry (which they call vigadicaya), [320] unless it happened that they separated through the husband's fault; for then it was not returned to him, and the wife's parents kept it. The property that they had acquired together was divided into halves, and each one disposed of his own. If one made any profits in which the other did not have a share or participate, he acquired it for himself alone.

The Indians were adopted one by another, in presence of the relatives. The adopted person gave and delivered all his actual possessions to the one who adopted him. Thereupon he remained in his house and care, and had a right to inherit with the other children. [321]

Adulteries were not punishable corporally. If the adulterer paid the aggrieved party the amount adjudged by the old men and agreed upon by them, then the injury was pardoned, and the husband was appeased and retained his honor. He would still live with his wife and there would be no further talk about the matter.

In inheritances all the legitimate children inherited equally from their parents whatever property they had acquired. If there were any movable or landed property which they had received from their parents, such went to the nearest relatives and the collateral side of that stock, if there were no legitimate children by an ynasaba. This was the case either with or without a will. In the act of drawing a will, there was no further ceremony than to have written it or to have stated it orally before acquaintances.

If any chief was lord of a barangai, then in that case, the eldest son of an ynasaba succeeded him. If he died, the second son succeeded. If there were no sons, then the daughters succeeded in the same order. If there were no legitimate successors, the succession went to the nearest relative belonging to the lineage and relationship of the chief who had been the last possessor of it.

If any native who had slave women made concubines of any of them, and such slave woman had children, those children were free, as was the slave. But if she had no children, she remained a slave. [322]

These children by a slave woman, and those borne by a married woman, were regarded as illegitimate, and did not succeed to the inheritance with the other children, neither were the parents obliged to leave them anything. Even if they were the sons of chiefs, they did not succeed to the nobility or chieftainship of the parents, nor to their privileges, but they remained and were reckoned as plebeians and in the number and rank of the other timaguas.

The contracts and negotiations of these natives were generally illegal, each one paying attention to how he might better his own business and interest.

Loans with interest were very common and much practiced, and the interest incurred was excessive. The debt doubled and increased all the time while payment was delayed, until it stripped the debtor of all his possessions, and he and his children, when all their property was gone, became slaves. [323]

Their customary method of trading was by bartering one thing for another, such as food, cloth, cattle, fowls, lands, houses, fields, slaves, fishing-grounds, and palm-trees (both nipa and wild). Sometimes a price intervened, which was paid in gold, as agreed upon, or in metal bells brought from China. These bells they regard as precious jewels; they resemble large pans and are very sonorous. [324] They play upon these at their feasts, and carry them to the war in their boats instead of drums and other instruments. There are often delays and terms for certain payments, and bondsmen who intervene and bind themselves, but always with very usurious and excessive profits and interests.

Crimes were punished by request of the aggrieved parties. Especially were thefts punished with greater severity, the robbers being enslaved or sometimes put to death. [325] The same was true of insulting words, especially when spoken to chiefs. They had among themselves many expressions and words which they regarded as the highest insult, when said to men and women. These were pardoned less willingly and with greater difficulty than was personal violence, such as wounding and assaulting. [326]

Concubinage, rape, and incest, were not regarded at all, unless committed by a timagua on the person of a woman chief. It was a quite ordinary practice for a married man to have lived a long time in concubinage with the sister of his wife. Even before having communication with his wife he could have had access for a long time to his mother-in-law, especially if the bride were very young, and until she were of sufficient age. This was done in sight of all the relatives.

Single men are called bagontaos, [327] and girls of marriageable age, dalagas. Both classes are people of little restraint, and from early childhood they have communication with one another, and mingle with facility and little secrecy, and without this being regarded among the natives as a cause for anger. Neither do the parents, brothers, or relatives, show any anger, especially if there is any material interest in it, and but little is sufficient with each and all.

As long as these natives lived in their paganism, it was not known that they had fallen into the abominable sin against nature. But after the Spaniards had entered their country, through communication with them—and still more, through that with the Sangleys, who have come from China, and are much given to that vice—it has been communicated to them somewhat, both to men and to women. In this matter it has been necessary to take action.

The natives of the islands of Pintados, especially the women, are very vicious and sensual. Their perverseness has discovered lascivious methods of communication between men and women; and there is one to which they are accustomed from their youth. The men skilfully make a hole in their virile member near its head, and insert therein a serpent's head, either of metal or ivory, and fasten it with a peg of the same material passed through the hole, so that it cannot become unfastened. With this device, they have communication with their wives, and are unable to withdraw until a long time after copulation. They are very fond of this and receive much pleasure from it, so that, although they shed a quantity of blood, and receive other harm, it is current among them. These devices are called sagras, and there are very few of them, because since they have become Christians, strenuous efforts are being made to do away with these, and not consent to their use; and consequently the practice has been checked in great part. [328]

Herbalists and witches are common among these natives, but are not punished or prohibited among them, so long as they do not cause any special harm. But seldom could that be ascertained or known.

There were also men whose business was to ravish and take away virginity from young girls. These girls were taken to such men, and the latter were paid for ravishing them, for the natives considered it a hindrance and impediment if the girls were virgins when they married.

In matters of religion, the natives proceeded more barbarously and with greater blindness than in all the rest. For besides being pagans, without any knowledge of the true God, they neither strove to discover Him by way of reason, nor had any fixed belief. The devil usually deceived them with a thousand errors and blindnesses. He appeared to them in various horrible and frightful forms, and as fierce animals, so that they feared him and trembled before him. They generally worshiped him, and made images of him in the said forms. These they kept in caves and private houses, where they offered them perfumes and odors, and food and fruit, calling them anitos. [329]

Others worshiped the sun and the moon, and made feasts and drunken revels at the conjunction of those bodies. Some worshiped a yellow-colored bird that dwells in their woods, called batala. They generally worship and adore the crocodiles when they see them, by kneeling down and clasping their hands, because of the harm that they receive from those reptiles; they believe that by so doing the crocodiles will become appeased and leave them. Their oaths, execrations, and promises are all as above mentioned, namely, "May buhayan eat thee, if thou dost not speak truth, or fulfil what thou hast promised," and similar things.

There were no temples throughout those islands, nor houses generally used for the worship of idols; but each person possessed and made in his house his own anitos, [330] without any fixed rite or ceremony. They had no priests or religious to attend to religious affairs, except certain old men and women called catalonas. These were experienced witches and sorcerers, who kept the other people deceived. The latter communicated to these sorcerers their desires and needs, and the catalonas told them innumerable extravagancies and lies. The catalonas uttered prayers and performed other ceremonies to the idols for the sick; and they believed in omens and superstitions, with which the devil inspired them, whereby they declared whether the patient would recover or die. Such were their cures and methods, and they used various kinds of divinations for all things. All this was with so little aid, apparatus, or foundation—which God permitted, so that the preaching of the holy gospel should find those of that region better prepared for it, and so that those natives would confess the truth more easily, and it would be less difficult to withdraw them from their darkness, and the errors in which the devil kept them for so many years. They never sacrificed human beings as is done in other kingdoms. They believed that there was a future life where those who had been brave and performed valiant feats would be rewarded; while those who had done evil would be punished. But they did not know how or where this would be. [331]

They buried their dead in their own houses, and kept their bodies and bones for a long time in chests. They venerated the skulls of the dead as if they were living and present. Their funeral rites did not consist of pomp or assemblages, beyond those of their own house—where, after bewailing the dead, all was changed into feasting and drunken revelry among all the relatives and friends. [332]

A few years before the Spaniards subdued the island of Luzon, certain natives of the island of Borneo began to go thither to trade, especially to the settlement of Manila and Tondo; and the inhabitants of the one island intermarried with those of the other. These Borneans are Mahometans, and were already introducing their religion among the natives of Luzon, and were giving them instructions, ceremonies, and the form of observing their religion, by means of certain gazizes [333] whom they brought with them. Already a considerable number, and those the chiefest men, were commencing, although by piecemeal, to become Moros, and were being circumcised [334] and taking the names of Moros. Had the Spaniards' coming been delayed longer, that religion would have spread throughout the island, and even through the others, and it would have been difficult to extirpate it. The mercy of God checked it in time; for, because of being in so early stages, it was uprooted from the islands, and they were freed from it, that is, in all that the Spaniards have pacified, and that are under the government of the Filipinas. That religion has spread and extended very widely in the other islands outside of this government, so that now almost all of their natives are Mahometan Moros, and are ruled and instructed by their gazizes and other morabitos; [335] these often come to preach to and teach them by way of the strait of Ma[la]ca and the Red Sea, through which they navigate to reach these islands.

241

The arrival of the Spaniards in these Filipinas Islands, since the year one thousand five hundred and sixty-four, the pacification and conversion that has been made therein, their mode of governing, and the provisions of his Majesty during these years for their welfare, have caused innovations in many things, such as are usual to kingdoms and provinces that change their religion and sovereign. The foremost has been that, besides the name of Filipinas which all the islands took and received from the beginning of their conquest, they belong to a new kingdom and seigniory to which his Majesty, Filipo Second, our sovereign, gave the name of Nuevo Reyno de Castilla ["New Kingdom of Castilla"]. By his royal concession, he made the city of Manila capital of it, and gave to it as a special favor, among other things, a crowned coat-of-arms which was chosen and assigned by his royal person. This is an escutcheon divided across. In the upper part is a castle on a red field, and in the lower a lion of gold, crowned and rampant, holding a naked sword in its right paw. One-half of the body is in the form of a dolphin upon the waters of the sea, to signify that the Spaniards crossed the sea with their arms to conquer this kingdom for the crown of Castilla. [336]

The city of Manila was founded by the adelantado Miguel Lopez de Legazpi, first governor of the Filipinas, in the island of Luzon. It occupies the same site where Rajamora had his settlement and fort—as has been related more at length—at the mouth of the river which empties into the bay, on a point between the river and the sea. The whole site was occupied by this new settlement, and Legazpi apportioned it to the Spaniards in equal building-lots. It was laid out with well-arranged streets and squares, straight and level. A sufficiently large main square [Plaza mayor] was left, fronting which were erected the cathedral church and municipal buildings. He left another square, that of arms [Plaza de armas], fronting which was built the fort, as well as the royal buildings. He gave sites for the monasteries, [337] hospital, and chapels which were to be built, as being a city which was to grow and increase continually—as already it has done; for, in the course of the time that has passed, that city has flourished as much as the best of all the cities in those regions.

The city is completely surrounded with a stone wall, which is more than two and one-half varas wide, and in places more than three. It has small towers and traverses at intervals. [338] It has a fortress of hewn stone at the point that guards the bar and the river, with a ravelin close to the water, upon which are mounted some large pieces of artillery. This artillery commands the sea and river, while other pieces are mounted farther up to defend the bar, besides some other moderate-sized field-pieces and swivel-guns. These fortifications have their vaults for storing supplies and munitions, and a magazine for the powder, which is well guarded and situated in the inner part; and a copious well of fresh water. There are also quarters for the soldiers and artillerymen, and the house of the commandant [alcayde]. The city has been lately fortified on the land side at the Plaza de armas, where it is entered by a strong wall and two salient towers, defended with artillery, which command the wall and gate. This fortress is called Santiago, and has a company of thirty soldiers with their officers, and eight artillerymen who guard the gate and entrance by watches—all in charge of a commandant who lives inside, and has the guard and custody of the fort.

There is another fortress, also of stone, in the same wall, within culverin range, located at the end [339] of the curtain, which extends along the shore of the bay. It is called Nuestra Senora de Guia, and is a very large round tower. It has its own court, well, and quarters inside, as well as the magazine, and other rooms for work. It has a traverse extending to the beach, on which are mounted a dozen large and moderate-sized pieces, which command the bay and sweep the wall, which extends along the shore to the gate and to the fort of Santiago. On the other side the fortress has a large salient tower, mounted with four large pieces, which command the shore ahead in the direction of the chapel of Nuestra Senora de Guia. The gate and entrance is within the city and is guarded by a company of twenty soldiers and their officers, six artillerymen, and one commandant and his lieutenant, who live inside.

On the land side, where the wall extends, there is a rampart called Sant Andres, which mounts six pieces of artillery that command in all directions, and some swivel-guns. Farther on is another traverse called San Gabriel, opposite the parian of the Sangleys, with a like amount of artillery. Both have some soldiers and an ordinary guard.

The wall has a sufficient height, and is furnished with battlements and turrets, built in the modern style, for its defense. It has a circuit of about one legua, which can be made entirely on top. It has many broad steps of the same hewn stone, at intervals inside. There are three principal city gates on the land side, and many other posterns opening at convenient places on the river and beach, for the service of the city. Each and all of them are locked before nightfall by the ordinary patrols. These carry the keys to the guard-room of the royal buildings. In the morning when day comes, the patrols return with the keys and open the city. [340]

The royal arsenals front on the Plaza de armas. In them are kept and guarded all the supplies of ammunition, food, rigging, iron, copper, lead, artillery, arquebuses, and other things belonging to the royal estate. They have their own officers and workmen, and are placed in charge of the royal officials.

Near these arsenals is located the powder-house, with its master, workmen, and convicts, where powder is generally ground in thirty mortars, and that which is spoiled is refined. [341]

The building for the founding of artillery is located on a suitable site in another part of the city. It has its molds, ovens, and tools, founders, and workmen who work it. [342]

The royal buildings are very beautiful and sightly, and contain many rooms. They have many windows opening toward the sea and the Plaza de armas. They are all built of stone and have two courts, with upper and lower galleries raised on stout pillars. The governor and president lives inside with his family. There is a hall for the royal Audiencia, which is very large and stately; also a separate chapel, a room for the royal seal, [343] and offices for the scriveners of the Audiencia, and the government. There are also other apartments for the royal treasury and the administration of the royal officials, while a large porch opens on the street with two principal doors, where the guardroom is located. There is one company of regular arquebusiers, who come in daily with their banners to stand guard. Opposite, on the other side of the street, is another edifice for the royal treasury and those in charge of it. [344]

The houses of the cabildo, located on the square, are built of stone. They are very sightly and have handsome halls. On the ground floor is the prison, and the court of the alcaldes-in-ordinary. [345]

On the same square is situated the cathedral church. It is built of hewn stone, and has three naves, and its main chapel, and choir, with high and low seats. The choir is shut in by railings, and has its organ, missal-stands, and other necessary things. The cathedral has also its sacristan [346] and his apartments and offices.

Within the city is the monastery of St. Augustine. It is very large and has many dormitories, a refectory and kitchens. They are now completing a church, which is one of the most sumptuous in those districts. This convent has generally fifty religious. [347]

The monastery of St. Dominic is inside the walls. It contains about forty religious. It was built of stone, and was very well constructed. It has a church, house, and all offices. It has lately been rebuilt, and much better; for it was completely destroyed in the burning of the city in the year six hundred and three.

The monastery of St. Francis is farther on. It is well constructed of stone, and its church is being rebuilt. It contains about forty discalced religious.

The residence [colegio] of the Society of Jesus is established near the fortress of Nuestra Senora de Guia. It contains twenty religious of their order, and is an excellent stone house and church. There they study

Latin, the arts, and cases of conscience. Connected with them is a seminary and convictorio [348] for Spanish scholars, with their rector. These students wear gowns of tawny-colored frieze with red facings. [349]

In another part of the city stands a handsome house, walled in, with its stone church, called San Andres and Santa Potenciana. It is a royal foundation, and a rectoress lives there. It has a revolving entrance and a parlor, and the rectoress has other confidential assistants; and there shelter is given to needy women and girls of the city, in the form of religious retirement. Some of the girls leave the house to be married, while others remain there permanently. It has its own house for work, and its choir. His Majesty assists them with a portion of their maintenance; the rest is provided by their own industry and property. They have their own steward and their priest, who administers the sacraments to them. [350]

In another part is the royal hospital for Spaniards, with its physician, apothecary, surgeons, managers, and servants. It and its church are built of stone; and it has its sick rooms and the bed service. In it all the Spaniards are treated. It is usually quite full; it is under the royal patronage. His Majesty provides the most necessary things for it. Three discalced religious of St. Francis act there as superintendents, and they prove very advantageous for the corporal and spiritual relief of the sick. It was burned in the conflagration of the former year six hundred and three, and is now being rebuilt.

There is another charitable hospital in charge of the Confraternity of that name. It was founded in the city of Manila by the Confraternity of La Misericordia of Lisboa, and by the other confraternities of India. [351] It has apostolic bulls for works of charity, such as burying the dead, supporting the modest poor, marrying orphans, and relieving many necessities. There the slaves of the city are treated, and lodgings are likewise provided for poor women.

Next to the monastery of St. Francis is located the hospital for natives, [352] which is under royal patronage. It was founded with alms, by a holy lay-brother of St. Francis, one Fray Joan Clemente. A great many natives, suffering from all diseases, are treated there with great care and attention. It has a good edifice and workrooms built of stone. The discalced religious of St. Francis manage it; and three priests and four lay-brothers, of exemplary life, live there. These are the physicians, surgeons, and apothecaries of the hospital, and are so skilful and useful, that they cause many marvelous cures, both in medicine and in surgery.

The streets of the city are compactly built up with houses, mostly of stone, although some are of wood. Many are roofed with clay tiling, and others with nipa. They are excellent edifices, lofty and spacious, and have large rooms and many windows, and balconies, with iron gratings, that embellish them. More are daily being built and finished. There are about six hundred houses within the walls, and a greater number, built of wood, in the suburbs; and all are the habitations and homes of Spaniards.

The streets, squares, and churches are generally filled with people of all classes, especially Spaniards—all, both men and women, clad and gorgeously adorned in silks. They wear many ornaments and all kinds of fine clothes, because of the ease with which these are obtained. Consequently this is one of the settlements most highly praised, by the foreigners who resort to it, of all in the world, both for the above reason, and for the great provision and abundance of food and other necessaries for human life found there, and sold at moderate prices.

Manila has two drives for recreation. One is by land, along the point called Nuestra Senora de Guia. It extends for about a legua along the shore, and is very clean and level. Thence it passes through a native street and settlement, called Bagunbayan, to a chapel, much frequented by the devout, called Nuestra Senora de Guia, and continues for a goodly distance further to a monastery and mission-house of the Augustinians, called Mahalat. [353]

The other drive extends through one of the city gates to a native settlement, called Laguio, by which one may go to a chapel of San Anton, and to a monastery and mission-house of discalced Franciscans, a place of great devotion, near the city, called La Candelaria. [354]

This city is the capital of the kingdom and the head of the government of all the islands. It is the metropolis of the other cities and settlements of the islands. In it reside the Audiencia and Chancilleria of his Majesty, and the governor and captain-general of the islands. [355]

Manila has a city cabildo with two alcaldes-in-ordinary, twelve perpetual regidors, an alguacil-mayor [i.e., chief constable], a royal standard-bearer, the scrivener of the cabildo, and other officials.

The archbishop of the Filipinas Islands resides in this city. He has his metropolitan church, and all the cathedral dignitaries—canons, racioneros, medias racioneros, [356] chaplains, and sacristans—and a music-choir, who chant to the accompaniment of the organ and of flutes [ministriles]. The cathedral is quite ornate and well decorated, and the Divine offices are celebrated there with the utmost gravity and ceremony. As suffragans the cathedral has three bishops—namely, in the island of Sebu, and in Cagayan and Camarines. [357]

There is a royal treasury with three royal officials—factor, accountant, and treasurer—by whom the royal revenue of all the islands is managed. [358]

The vessels sailing annually to Nueva Espana with the merchandise and investments of all the islands are despatched from the city of Manila;

and they return thither from Nueva Espana with the proceeds of this merchandise, and the usual reenforcements.

In the city is established the camp of the regular soldiers whom his Majesty has had stationed in the islands.

Several galleys are also stationed at Manila with their general and captains, as well as other war-vessels, of deep draft, and smaller ones built like those used by the natives, to attend to the needs of all the islands.

The majority of the vessels from China, Japon, Maluco, Borney, Sian, Malaca, and India, that come to the Filipinas with their merchandise and articles of trade, gather in the bay and river of Manila. In that city they sell and trade for all the islands and their settlements.

In the province [of Cagayan] of this same island of Luzon was founded the city of Segovia, [359] during the term of Don Goncalo Ronquillo, the third governor. It has two hundred Spanish inhabitants who live in wooden houses on the shore of the Tajo River, two leguas from the sea and port of Camalayuga. There is a stone fort near the city for the defense of it and of the river. This fort mounts some artillery, and has its own commandant. Besides the inhabitants, there are generally one hundred regular soldiers, arquebusiers, and their officers. They are all in charge and under command of the alcalde-mayor of the province, who is its military commander.

In that city is established a bishop and his church, although at present the latter has no dignitaries or prebendaries. [360] There is a city cabildo consisting of two alcaldes, six regidors, and an alguacil-mayor. The city abounds in all kinds of food and refreshment at very cheap prices.

The city of Caceres was founded in the province of Camarines of the same island of Luzon, during the term of Doctor Sande, governor of the Filipinas. It has about one hundred Spanish inhabitants; and has its cabildo, consisting of alcaldes, regidors, and officials. A bishop of that province is established there and has his church, although without dignitaries or prebendaries. A monastery of discalced Franciscans is located there. The government and military affairs of that province are under one alcalde-mayor and war-captain, who resides in Caceres. The latter is a place abounding in and furnished with all kinds of provisions, at very low rates. It is founded on the bank of a river, four leguas inland from the sea, and its houses are of wood.

The fourth city is that called Santisimo Nombre de Jesus; it is located in the island of Sebu, in the province of Bicayas or Pintados. It was the first Spanish settlement and was founded by the adelantado Miguel Lopez de Legazpi, the first governor. It is a fine seaport, whose water is very clear and deep, and capable of holding many vessels. The city has an excellent stone fort, which mounts a considerable quantity of artillery, and which has its commandant and officers for the guard and defense of the port and of the city. It is sufficiently garrisoned with regulars, and is under command of the alcalde-mayor, the military commander of the province, who lives in the city. The settlement contains about two hundred Spanish inhabitants who live in houses of wood. It has a cabildo, consisting of two alcaldes-in-ordinary, eight regidors, and an alguacil-mayor and his officers. It has a bishop and his church, like those of other cities of these islands, without prebendaries. [361]

The city is provided with food by, and is a station for, the ships going from Maluco to Manila. Through his Majesty's concession they keep there a deep-draft merchant vessel, which generally leaves its port for Nueva Espana, laden with the merchandise of the products gathered in those provinces. It has a monastery of Augustinian religious and a seminary of the Society of Jesus.

The town of Arevalo was founded on the island of Oton [Panay], during the term of Don Goncalo Ronquillo. [362] It contains about eighty Spanish inhabitants, and is located close to the sea. It has a wooden fort, which mounts some artillery, and a monastery of the Order of St. Augustine; also a parish church, with its own vicar and secular priest. This church belongs to the diocese of the Sebu bishopric.

It has a cabildo, consisting of alcaldes, regidors, and other officials. There is one alcalde-mayor and military leader in those provinces. The town is well supplied with all kinds of provisions, sold at very low rates.

The settlement of Villa Fernandina, [363] which was founded in the province of the Ilocos on the island of Luzon, is settled by Spaniards, but very few of them remain there. It has a church, with its own vicar and secular priest. Now no mention will be made of it, on account of what has been said. The alcalde-mayor of the province resides there, and the town is situated in the diocese of the Cagayan bishopric.

From the earliest beginning of the conquest and pacification of the Filipinas Islands, the preaching of the holy gospel therein and the conversion of the natives to our holy Catholic faith were undertaken. The first to set hand to this task were the religious of the Order of St. Augustine, who went there with the adelantado Legazpi in the fleet of discovery, and those of the same order who went afterward to labor in this work, and toiled therein with great fervor and zeal. Thus, finding the harvest in good season, they gathered the first fruits of it, and converted and baptized many infidels throughout the said islands. [364]

Next to them in the fame of this conversion, the discalced religious of the Order of St. Francis went to the islands by way of Nueva Espana;

then those of the Order of St. Dominic, and of the Society of Jesus. [365] Lastly, the discalced Augustinian Recollects went. One and all, after being established in the islands, worked in the conversion and instruction of the natives. Consequently they have made—and there are now in all the islands—a great number of baptized natives, besides many others in many parts, who, for want of laborers, have been put off, and are awaiting this blessing and priests to minister to them. Hitherto there have been but few missions in charge of secular priests, as not many of these have gone to the islands; and as very few have been ordained there, for lack of students.

The Order of St. Augustine has many missions in the islands of Pintados and has established and occupied monasteries and various visitas. [366] In the island of Luzon, they have those of the province of Ylocos, some in Pangasinan, and all those of La Pampanga—a large number of monasteries; while in the province of Manila and its vicinity they have others, which are flourishing.

The Order of St. Dominic has the missions of the province of Cagayan, and others in the province of Pangasinan, where are many monasteries and visitas. They also administer others about the city.

The Order of St. Francis has some missions and monasteries about Manila, all the province of Camarines and the coast opposite, and La Laguna de Bay. These include many missions.

The Society of Jesus has three large missions in the neighborhood of Manila, which have many visitas. In the Pintados it has many others on the islands of Sebu, Leite, Ybabao, Camar [Samar], Bohol, and others near by. They have good men, who are solicitous for the conversion of the natives.

These four orders have produced many good results in the conversion of these islands, as above stated; and in good sooth the people have taken firm hold of the faith, as they are a people of so good understanding. They have recognized the errors of their paganism and the truths of the Christian religion; and they possess good and well-built churches and monasteries of wood with their reredoses and beautiful ornaments, and all the utensils, crosses, candlesticks, and chalices of silver and gold. Many devotions are offered, and there are many confraternities. There is assiduity in taking the sacraments and in attendance on the Divine services; and the people are careful to entertain and support their religious (to whom they show great obedience and respect) by the many alms that they give them, as well as by those that they give for the suffrages and the burial of their dead, which they provide with all punctuality and liberality.

At the same time that the religious undertook to teach the natives the precepts of religion, they labored to instruct them in matters of their own improvement, and established schools for the reading and writing of Spanish among the boys. They taught them to serve in the church, to sing the plain-song, and to the accompaniment of the organ; to play the flute, to dance, and to sing; and to play the harp, guitar, and other instruments. In this they show very great adaptability, especially about Manila; where there are many fine choirs of chanters and musicians composed of natives, who are skilful and have good voices. There are many dancers, and musicians on the other instruments which solemnize and adorn the feasts of the most holy sacrament, and many other feasts during the year. The native boys present dramas and comedies, both in Spanish and in their own language, very charmingly. This is due to the care and interest of the religious, who work tirelessly for the natives' advancement. [367]

In these islands there is no native province or settlement which resists conversion or does not desire it. But, as above stated, baptism has been postponed in some districts, for lack of workers to remain with the people, in order that they may not retrograde and return to their idolatries. In this work, the best that is possible is done, for the mission-fields are very large and extensive. In many districts the religious make use, in their visitas, of certain of the natives who are clever and well instructed, so that these may teach the others to pray daily, instruct them in other matters touching religion, and see that they come to mass at the central missions; and in this way they succeed in preserving and maintaining their converts.

Hitherto, the orders who control these missions in virtue of the omnimodo and other apostolic concessions [368] have attended to the conversion of the natives, administered the sacraments, looked after the spiritual and temporal and ecclesiastical affairs of the natives, and absolved them in cases of difficulty. But now that there are an archbishop and bishops, this is being curtailed, and the management of these affairs is being given to the bishops, as the archbishop's vicars—although not to such an extent, nor has the administration of these natives been placed in their charge, in matters of justice, and under the inspection and superintendence of the bishops, as they have endeavored to obtain. [369]

The governor and royal Audiencia of Manila attend to what it is advisable to provide and direct for the greatest accomplishment and advancement of this conversion, and the administration of the natives and their missions—both by causing the encomenderos to assist the religious and churches, in the encomiendas that they enjoy, with the stipends and necessary expenses of the missions; and by furnishing from the royal revenues what pertains to it, which is no less a sum. [370] They also ordain whatever else is required to be provided and remedied for the said missions and for the advancement of the natives. This also is attended to by the archbishop and the bishops in what pertains to them in their duty and charge as pastors.

The Holy Office of the Inquisition, residing in Mexico of Nueva Espana, has its commissaries, servants, and helpers in Manila and in the bishoprics of the islands, who attend to matters touching the Holy Office. They never fail to have plenty to do there because of the entrance of so many strangers into those districts. However, this holy tribunal does not have jurisdiction of the causes pertaining to the natives, as the latter are so recently converted.

All these islands are subdued, and are governed from Manila by means of alcaldes-mayor, corregidors, and lieutenants, each of whom rules and administers justice in his own district and province. Appeals from their acts and sentences go to the royal Audiencia. The governor and captain-general provides what pertains to government and war.

The chiefs, who formerly held the other natives in subjection, now have no power over them in the tyrannical manner of former days. This was not the least benefit received by these natives in having been freed from such servitude. However, it is true that matters touching the slavery of former days have remained on the same footing as before. The king our sovereign has ordered by his decrees that the honors of the chiefs be preserved to them as such; and that the other natives recognize them and assist them with certain of the labors that they used to give when pagans. This is done with the lords and possessors of barangays, and those belonging to such and such a barangay are under that chief's control. When he harvests his rice, they go one day to help him; and the same if he builds a house, or rebuilds one. This chief lord of a barangay collects tribute from his adherents, and takes charge of these collections, to pay them to the encomendero. [371]

Besides the above, each village has a governor [372] who is elected. He and his constables who are called vilangos [373] comprise the usual magistracy among the natives. The governor hears civil suits where a moderate sum is involved; in appeal, the case goes to the corregidor or alcalde-mayor of the province. These governors are elected annually by the votes of all the married natives of such and such a village. The governor of Manila confirms the election, and gives the title of governor to the one elected, and orders him to take the residencia of the outgoing governor. [374] This governor, in addition to the vilangos and scrivener (before whom he makes his acts in writing, in the language of the natives of that province), [375] holds also the chiefs—lords of barangays, and those who are not so—under his rule and government, and, for any special service, such as collections of tributes, and assignments of personal services, as his datos and mandones. [376] They do not allow the chiefs to oppress the timaguas or slaves under their control.

The same customs observed by these natives in their paganism, are observed by them since they have become Christians, in so far as they are not contrary to natural law, especially as to their slavery, successions, inheritances, adoptions, wills, and lawful trading. In their suits, they always allege and prove the custom, and are judged by it, according to royal decrees to that effect. In other causes which do not involve their customs, and in criminal cases, the matter is determined by law as among Spaniards.

All of these islands and their natives, so far as they were pacified, were apportioned into encomiendas from the beginning. To the royal crown were allotted those which were chief towns and ports, and the dwellers of the cities and towns; and also other special encomiendas and villages in all the provinces, for the necessities and expenses of the royal estate. All the rest was assigned to the conquerors and settlers who have served and labored for the conquest and pacification, and in the war. This matter is in charge of the governor, who takes into consideration the merits and services of the claimants. [377] In like manner the villages that become vacant are assigned. There are many very excellent encomiendas throughout the islands, and they offer many profits, both by the amount of their tributes and by the nature and value of what is paid as tribute. [378] The encomienda lasts, according to the royal laws and decrees, and by the regular order and manner of succession to them, for two lives; but it may be extended to a third life, by permission. After it becomes vacant, it is again assigned and granted anew.

The tributes paid to their encomenderos by the natives were assigned by the first governor, Miguel Lopez de Legazpi, in the provinces of Vicayas and Pintados, and in the islands of Luzon and its vicinity; they were equal to the sum of eight reals annually for an entire tribute from each tributario. The natives were to pay it in their products—in gold, cloth, cotton, rice, bells, fowls, and whatever else they possessed or harvested. The fixed price and value of each article was assigned so that, when the tribute was paid in any one of them, or in all of them, it should not exceed the value of the eight reals. So it has continued until now, and the governors have increased the appraisements and values of the products at different times, as they have deemed advisable.

The encomenderos have made great profits in collecting in kind, for, after they acquired possession of the products, they sold them at higher prices. By this they increased their incomes and the proceeds of their encomiendas considerably; until a few years ago his Majesty, by petition of the religious and the pressure that they brought to bear on him in this matter, ordered for this region that the natives should pay their tribute in whatever they wished—in kind or in money—without being compelled to do otherwise. Consequently, when they should have paid their eight reals, they would have fulfilled their obligation. Accordingly this rule was initiated; but experience demonstrates that, although it seemed a merciful measure, and one favorable to the natives, it is doing them great injury. For, since they naturally dislike to work, they do not sow, spin, dig gold, rear fowls, or raise other food supplies, as they did before, when they had to pay the tribute in those articles. They easily obtain, without so much work, the peso of money which is the amount of their tribute. Consequently it follows that the natives have less capital and wealth, because they do not work; and the country, which was formerly very well provided and well-supplied with all products, is now suffering want and deprivation of them. The owners of the encomiendas, both those of his Majesty and those of private persons who possess them, have sustained considerable loss and reduction in the value of the encomiendas.

When Gomez Perez Dasmarinas was appointed governor of the Filipinas, he brought royal decrees ordering the formation of the camp in Manila, with an enrollment of four hundred paid soldiers, with their officers, galleys, and other military supplies, for the defense and security of the country. Before that time all the Spanish inhabitants had attended to that without any pay. Then an increase of two reals to each tributario over the eight reals was ordered. This was to be collected by the encomenderos at the same time when they collected the eight reals of the tribute, and was to be delivered and placed in the royal treasury. There this amount was to be entered on an account separate from that of the other revenue of his Majesty, and was to be applied in the following manner: one and one-half reals for the expenses of the said camp and war stores; and the remaining half real for the pay of the prebendaries of the Manila church, which his Majesty pays from his treasury, until such time as their tithes and incomes suffice for their sustenance. [379]

These tributes are collected from all the natives, Christians and infidels, in their entirety—except that in those encomiendas without instruction the encomendero does not take the fourth part of the eight reals (which equals two reals) for himself, since that encomienda has no instruction or expenses for it; but he takes them and deposits them in Manila, in a fund called "the fourths." [380] The money obtained from this source is applied to and spent in hospitals for the natives, and in other works beneficial to them, at the option of the governor. As fast as the encomiendas are supplied with instruction and religious, the collection of these fourths and their expenditure in these special works cease.

Some provinces have taken the census of their natives; and according to these the tributes and the assignment of the two reals are collected.

In most of the provinces no census has been taken, and the tributes are collected when due by the encomenderos and their collectors, through the chiefs of their encomiendas, by means of the lists and memoranda of former years. From them the names of the deceased and of those who have changed their residence are erased, and the names of those who have grown up, and of those who have recently moved into the encomienda, are added. When any shortage is perceived in the accounts, a new count is requested and made.

The natives are free to move from one island to another, and from one province to another, and pay their tribute for that year in which they move and change their residence in the place to which they move; and to move from a Christian village that has instruction to another village possessing it. But, on the other hand, they may not move from a place having instruction to one without it, nor in the same village from one barangay to another, nor from one faction to another. In this respect, the necessary precautions are made by the government, and the necessary provisions by the Audiencia, so that this system may be kept, and so that all annoyances resulting from the moving of the settled natives of one place to another place may be avoided.

Neither are the natives allowed to go out of their villages for trade, except by permission of the governor, or of his alcaldes-mayor and justices, or even of the religious, who most often have been embarrassed by this, because of the instruction. This is done so that the natives may not wander about aimlessly when there is no need of it, away from their homes and settlements.

Those natives who possess slaves pay their tributes for them if the slaves are saguiguilirs. If the slaves are namamahays living outside their owners' houses, they pay their own tributes, inasmuch as they possess their own houses and means of gain.

The Spaniards used to have slaves from these natives, whom they had bought from them, and others whom they obtained in certain expeditions during the conquest and pacification of the islands. This was stopped by a brief of his Holiness [381] and by royal decrees. Consequently, all of these slaves who were then in the possession of the Spanish, and who were natives of these islands, in whatever manner they had been acquired, were freed; and the Spaniards were forever prohibited from holding them as slaves, or from capturing them for any reason, or under pretext of war, or in any other manner. The service rendered by these natives is in return for pay and daily wages. The other slaves and captives that the Spaniards possess are Cafres and blacks brought by the Portuguese by way of India, and are held in slavery justifiably, in accordance with the provincial councils and the permissions of the prelates and justices of those districts.

The natives of these islands have also their personal services, which they are obliged to render—in some parts more than in others—to the Spaniards. These are done in different ways, and are commonly called the polo. [382] For, where there are alcaldes-mayor and justices, they assign and distribute certain natives by the week for the service of their houses. They pay these servants a moderate wage, which generally amounts to one-fourth real per day, and rice for their food. The same is done by the religious for the mission, and for their monasteries and churches, and for their works, and for public works. [383]

The Indians also furnish rice, and food of all kinds, at the prices at which they are valued and sold among the natives. These prices are always very moderate. The datos, vilangos, and fiscals make the division, collect, and take these supplies from the natives; and in the same manner they supply their encomenderos when these go to make the collections.

The greatest service rendered by these natives is on occasions of war, when they act as rowers and crews for the vireys and vessels that go on the expeditions, and as pioneers for any service that arises in the course of the war, although their pay and wages are given them.

In the same way natives are assigned and apportioned for the king's works, such as the building of ships, the cutting of wood, the trade of making the rigging, [384] the work in the artillery foundry, and the service in the royal [385] magazines; and they are paid their stipend and daily wage.

In other things pertaining to the service of the Spaniards and their expeditions, works, and any other service, performed by the natives, the service is voluntary, and paid by mutual agreement; [386] for, as hitherto, the Spaniards have worked no mines, nor have they given themselves to the gains to be derived from field labors, there is no occasion for employing the natives in anything of that sort.

Most of the Spaniards of the Filipinas Islands reside in the city of Manila, the capital of the kingdom, and where the chief trade and commerce is carried on. Some encomenderos live in provinces or districts adjacent to Manila, while other Spaniards live in the cities of Segovia, Caceres, Santisimo Nombre de Jesus (in Sebu), and in the town of Arevalo, where they are settled, and where most of them have their encomiendas.

Spaniards may not go to the Indian villages, [387] except for the collection of the tributes when they are due; and then only the alcaldes-mayor, corregidors, and justices. It is not permitted these to remain continually in one settlement of their district, but they must visit as much of it as possible. They must change their residence and place of abode every four months to another chief village and settlement, where all the natives may obtain the benefit of their presence; and so that the natives may receive as slight annoyance as possible in supporting them and in the ordinary service that they render them. [388]

The governor makes appointments to all offices. When the term of office expires, the royal Aurdiencia orders the residencia of each official to be taken, and his case is decided in accordance therewith; and until the residencia is completed, the incumbent cannot be appointed to any other duty or office. The governor also appoints commandants of forts, companies, and other military officials, in all the cities, towns, and hamlets of the islands. [389]

Certain offices of regidors and notaries have been sold by royal decree for one life. But the sale of these offices has been superseded, as it is now considered that the price paid for them is of little consideration, while the disadvantage of perpetuating the purchasers in office by this method is greater.

Elections of alcaldes-in-ordinary for all the Spanish towns are held on New Year's day by the cabildo and magistracy. The residencias of these alcaldes-in-ordinary and their cabildos are ordered by his Majesty to be taken at the same time as that of the governor and captain-general of the islands is taken; and they give account of the administration of the revenues and the estates under their care. However, the governor may take it before this, every year, or whenever he thinks it expedient and cause the balances of their accounts to be collected. With the governor's advice and permission the expenses desired by the towns are made.

The city of Manila has sufficient public funds for certain years, through the fines imposed by its judges; in its own particular possessions, inside and outside the city; in the reweighing of the merchandise and the rents of all the shops and sites of the Sangleys in the parian; and in the monopoly on playing cards. All this was conceded to the city by his Majesty, especially for the expenses of its fortification. [390] These revenues are spent for that purpose; for the salaries of its officials, and those of the agents sent to Espana; and for the feasts of the city, chief of which are St. Potenciana's day, May nineteen, when the Spaniards entered and seized the city, and the day of St. Andrew, November 30, the date on which the pirate Limahon was conquered and driven from the city. On that day the city officials take out the municipal standard, and to the sound of music go to vespers and mass at the church of San Andres, where the entire city, with the magistracy and cabildo and the royal Audiencia, assemble with all solemnity. The above revenues are also used in receiving the governors at their first arrival in the country, in the kings' marriage feasts, and the births of princes, and in the honors and funeral celebrations for the kings and princes who die. In all the above the greatest possible display is made.

The other cities and settlements do not possess as yet so many sources of wealth or revenue, or the occasions on which to spend them—although, as far as possible, they take part in them, in all celebrations of the same kind.

The Spaniards living in the islands are divided into five classes of people: namely, prelates, religious, and ecclesiastical ministers, both secular and regular; encomenderos, settlers, and conquerors; soldiers, officers, and officials of war (both on land and sea), and those for navigation; merchants, business men, and traders; and his Majesty's agents for government, justice, and administration of his royal revenue.

The ecclesiastical prelates have already been stated, and are as follows: The archbishop of Manila, who resides in the city, as metropolitan, in charge of his cathedral church; he has a salary of four thousand pesos, [391] which is paid from the royal treasury annually. Likewise the salaries paid to the holders of the dignidades, [392] canonries, and other prebends, and those performing other services, are paid in the same manner. They are all under royal patronage, and are provided in accordance with the king's orders. The archbishop's office and jurisdiction consists of and extends to all, both the spiritual and temporal, that is ecclesiastic, and to its management. [393]

The bishop of the city of Santisimo Nombre de Jesus in Sibu, that of Segovia in Cagayan, and that of Caceres in Camarines, have the same rights of jurisdiction and enjoy the same privileges in their dioceses, since they are suffragans of the archbishop of Manila; appeal from their judgments is made to the latter, and he summons and convokes them to his provincial councils whenever necessary. They receive each an annual salary of five hundred thousand maravedis for their support, which is paid from the royal treasury of Manila, besides their offerings and pontifical dues. All together it is quite sufficient for their support, according to the convenience of things and the cheapness of the country. At present the bishops do not possess churches with prebendaries nor is any money set aside for that. [394]

The regular prelates are the provincials of the four mendicant orders, namely, St. Dominic, St. Augustine, St. Francis, the Society of Jesus, and the discalced Augustinians [395] Each prelate governs his own order and visits the houses. The orders have nearly all the missions to the natives under their charge, in whatever pertains to the administration of the sacraments and conversion—by favor of, and in accordance with, their privileges and the apostolic bulls, in which until now they have main-

257

tained themselves—and in what pertains to judicial matters, as vicars of the bishops, and through appointment and authorization of the latter. The discalced Augustinians as yet have no missions, as they have but recently entered the islands.

The monasteries are supported by certain special incomes that they possess and have acquired—especially those of the Augustinians and those of the Society—and by help and concessions granted by his Majesty. The Dominicans and Franciscans do not possess or allow incomes or properties; [396] and for them, as for the other orders, the principal source of revenue is in the alms, offerings, and aid given by the districts where they are established and where they have charge. This help is given by both Spaniards and natives, very piously and generously. They are aided also by the stipend given them from the encomiendas for the instruction that they give there. Consequently the religious of the orders live well and with the comfort necessary.

The first encomenderos, conquerors, and settlers of the islands, and their issue, are honorably supported by the products of their encomiendas, and by certain means of gain and trading interests that they possess, as do the rest of the people. There are a great number of them, each one of whom lives and possesses his house in the city and settlement of Spaniards in whose province he has his encomienda. This they do in order not to abandon their encomiendas, and thus they are nearer the latter for their needs and for collections.

Now but few of the first conquerors who gained the country and went there for its conquest with the adelantado Miguel Lopez de Legaspi remain alive.

The soldiers and officers of war and of naval expeditions formerly consisted of all the dwellers and inhabitants of the islands, who rendered military service without any pay or salary. They went on all the expeditions and pacifications that arose, and guarded the forts and presidios, and cities and settlements. This was their principal exercise and occupation. They were rewarded by the governor, who provided them with encomiendas, offices, and profits of the country according to their merits and services. [397]

At that time the soldiers of the islands were the best in the Indias. They were very skilful and well-disciplined by both land and sea, and were esteemed and respected by all those nations. They gloried in their arms, and in acquitting themselves valiantly.

Afterward, when Gomez Perez Das Marinas entered upon the government of the Filipinas, he founded the regular camp of four hundred soldiers: the arquebusiers, with pay of six pesos per month; the musketeers, with eight pesos; six captains, with annual pay of four hundred and twenty pesos apiece; their alfereces, sergeants, corporals, standard-bearers, and drummers, with pay in proportion to their duties; one master-of-camp, with annual pay of one thousand four hundred pesos; one sargento-mayor with captain's pay; one adjutant of the sargento-mayor and field-captain, with monthly pay of ten pesos; two castellans; commandants of the two fortresses of Manila, with four hundred pesos apiece annually; their lieutenants; squads of soldiers and artillerymen; one general of galleys, with annual pay of eight hundred pesos; each galley one captain, with annual pay of three hundred pesos; their boatswains, boatswains' mates, coxswains, alguacils of the galleys, soldiers, artillerymen, master-carpenters, riggers, sailors, conscripts, [398] galley-crews of Spanish, Sangley, and native convicts, condemned for crimes; and, when there is lack of convicts, good rowers are obtained from the natives for pay, for the period of the expedition and the occasion of the voyage. [399]

In the vessels and fleets of large vessels for the Nueva Espana line, the ships that are sent carry a general, admiral, masters, boatswains, commissaries, stewards, alguacils, sergeants of marine artillery [condestables], artillerymen, sailors, pilots and their assistants, common seamen, carpenters, calkers, and coopers, all in his Majesty's pay, on the account of Nueva Espana, from whose royal treasury they are paid. All that is necessary for this navigation is supplied there. Their provisions and appointments are made by the viceroy; and this has hitherto pertained to him, even though the ships may have been constructed in the Filipinas. They sail thence with their cargo of merchandise for Nueva Espana, and return thence to the Filipinas with the reenforcements of soldiers and supplies, and whatever else is necessary for the camp, besides passengers and religious, and the money proceeding from the investments and merchandise. [400]

After the establishment of a regular camp for guard and expeditions, the other inhabitants, dwellers, and residents were enrolled without pay under the banners of six captains of the Filipinas, for special occasions requiring the defense of the city. But they were relieved of all other duties pertaining to the troops, unless they should offer of their own accord to go upon any expedition, or volunteer for any special occasion, in order to acquire merits and benefits, so that they may be given encomiendas that become vacant, and offices, and the means of profit of the country. They are not compelled or obliged to do this, unless they are encomenderos. Consequently all have given themselves to trading, as there is no other occupation, but they are not unmindful of military service.

His Majesty prohibits all who are in his pay in the military forces of the islands from engaging in commerce; and orders the governor not to allow this, or permit them to export goods to Nueva Espana. If the governors would observe that order, it would not be amiss. [401]

The merchants and business men form the bulk of the residents of the islands, because of the great amount of merchandise brought there—outside of native products—from China, Japon, Maluco, Malaca, Sian, Camboja, Borneo, and other districts. They invest in this merchandise and export it annually in the vessels that sail to Nueva Espana, and at times to Japon, where great profits are made from raw silk. Thence on the return to Manila are brought the proceeds, which hitherto have resulted in large and splendid profits.

Through the very great increase of this trade—which was harmful and prejudicial to the Spanish merchants who shipped goods to Peru and Nueva Espana, and to the royal duties collected on the shipments from Espana—and through the business men of Mexico and Peru having become greedy of trade and commerce with the Filipinas, by means of their agents and factors, so that the trade with Espana was ceasing in great measure, and the merchants were sending to the Filipinas for their investments great consignments of silver, which by that means flowed yearly from his Majesty's kingdoms, to fall into the possession of infidels: all persons of Nueva Espana and Peru were prohibited from trading and engaging in commerce in the Filipinas, and from taking the Chinese merchandise to those regions. [402] Permission was given to the inhabitants and residents of the Filipinas that they alone might trade in the said merchandise, and export it. They are to take these goods themselves, or send them with persons who belong to the islands, so that they may sell them. From the proceeds of the said merchandise, they may not carry to the Filipinas more than five hundred thousand pesos each year. [403]

A considerable number of somas and junks (which are large vessels) generally come from Great China to Manila, laden with merchandise. Every year thirty or even forty ships are wont to come, and although they do not come together, in the form of a trading and war fleet, still they do come in groups with the monsoon and settled weather, which is generally at the new moon in March. They belong to the provinces of Canton, Chincheo, and Ucheo [Fo-Kien], and sail from those provinces. They make their voyage to the city of Manila in fifteen or twenty days, sell their merchandise, and return in good season, before the vendavals set in—the end of May and a few days of June—in order not to endanger their voyage.

These vessels come laden with merchandise, and bring wealthy merchants who own the ships, and servants and factors of other merchants who remain in China. They leave China with the permission and license of the Chinese viceroys and mandarins. The merchandise that they generally bring and sell to the Spaniards consists of raw silk in bundles, of the fineness of two strands [dos cabecas], and other silk of poorer quality; fine untwisted silk, white and of all colors, wound in small skeins; quantities of velvets, some plain, and some embroidered in all sorts of figures, colors, and fashions—others with body of gold, and embroidered with gold; woven stuffs and brocades, of gold and silver upon silk of various colors and patterns; quantities of gold and silver thread in skeins over thread and silk—but the glitter of all the gold and silver is false, and only on paper; damasks, satins, taffetans, gorvaranes, picotes, [404] and other cloths of all colors, some finer and better than others; a quantity of linen made from grass, called lencesuelo [handkerchief]; [405] and white cotton cloth of different kinds and qualities, for all uses. They also bring musk, benzoin, and ivory; many bed ornaments, hangings, coverlets, and tapestries of embroidered velvet; damask and gorvaran of different shades; tablecloths, cushions, and carpets; horse-trappings of the same stuff, and embroidered with glass beads and seed-pearls; also some pearls and rubies, sapphires and crystal-stones; metal basins, copper kettles, and other copper and cast-iron pots; quantities of all sorts of nails, sheet-iron, tin and lead; saltpetre and gunpowder. They supply the Spaniards with wheat flour; preserves made of orange, peach, scorzonera, [406] pear, nutmeg, and ginger, and other fruits of China; salt pork and other salt meats; live fowls of good breed, and very fine capons; quantities of green fruit, oranges of all kinds; excellent chestnuts, walnuts, pears, and chicueyes [407] (both green and dried, a delicious fruit); quantities of fine thread of all kinds, needles, and knick-knacks; little boxes and writing-cases; beds, tables, chairs, and gilded benches, painted in many figures and patterns. They bring domestic buffaloes; geese that resemble swans; horses, some mules and asses; even caged birds, some of which talk, while others sing, and they make them play innumerable tricks. The Chinese furnish numberless other gewgaws and ornaments of little value and worth, which are esteemed among the Spaniards; besides a quantity of fine crockery of all kinds; cangantes, [408] sines, and black and blue robes; tacley, which are beads of all kinds; strings of cornelians, and other beads and precious stones of all colors; pepper and other spices; and rarities which, did I refer to them all, I would never finish, nor have sufficient paper for it.

As soon as the ship reaches the mouth of the bay of Manila, the watchman stationed at the island of Miraveles goes out to it in a light vessel. Having examined the ship, he puts a guard of two or three soldiers on it, so that it may anchor upon the bar, near the city, and to see that no one shall disembark from the vessel, or anyone enter it from outside, until the vessel has been inspected. By the signal made with fire by the watchman from the said island, and the advice that he sends in all haste to the city—of what ship it is, whence it has come, what merchandise and people it brings—before the vessel has finished anchoring, the governor and the city generally know all about it. [409]

When the vessel has arrived and anchored, the royal officials go to inspect it and the register of the merchandise aboard it. At the same time the valuation of the cargo is made according to law, of what it is worth in Manila; for the vessel immediately pays three per cent on everything to his Majesty. [410] After the register has been inspected and the valuation made, then the merchandise is immediately unloaded by another official into champans, and taken to the Parian, or to other houses and magazines, outside of the city. There the goods are freely sold.

No Spaniard, Sangley, or other person is allowed to go to the ship to buy or trade merchandise, food, or anything else. Neither is it allowed, when the merchandise is ashore, to take it from them or buy it with force and violence; but the trade must be free, and the Sangleys can do what they like with their property.

The ordinary price of the silks (both raw and woven) and the cloths—which form the bulk of the cargo—is settled leisurely, and by persons who understand it, both on the part of the Spaniards and that of the Sangleys. The purchase price is paid in silver and reals, for the Sangleys do not want gold, or any other articles, and will not take other things to China. All the trading must be completed by the end of the month of May, or thereabout, in order that the Sangleys may return and the Spaniards have the goods ready to lade upon the vessels that go to Nueva Espana by the end of June. However, the larger dealers and those who have most money usually do their trading after that time, at lower rates, and keep the merchandise until the following year. Certain Sangleys remain in Manila with a portion of their merchandise for the same purpose, when they have not had a good sale for it, in order to go on selling it more leisurely. The Sangleys are very skilful and intelligent traders, and of great coolness and moderation, in order to carry on their business better. They are ready to trust and accommodate freely whoever they know treats them fairly, and does not fail in his payments to them when these are due. On the other hand, as they are a people without religion or conscience, and so greedy, they commit innumerable frauds and deceits in their merchandise. The purchaser must watch them very closely, and know them, in order not to be cheated by them. The purchasers, however, acquit themselves by their poor payments and the debts that they incur; and both sides generally keep the judges and Audiencia quite busy.

Some Japanese and Portuguese merchantmen also come every year from the port of Nangasaque in Japon, at the end of October with the north winds, and at the end of March. They enter and anchor at Manila in the same way. The bulk of their cargo is excellent wheat-flour for the provisioning of Manila, and highly prized salt meats. They also bring some fine woven silk goods of mixed colors; beautiful and finely-decorated screens done in oil and gilt; all kinds of cutlery; many suits of armor, spears, catans, and other weapons, all finely wrought; writing-cases, boxes and small cases of wood, japanned and curiously marked; other pretty gewgaws; excellent fresh pears; barrels and casks of good salt tunny; cages of sweet-voiced larks, called fimbaros; and other trifles. In this trading, some purchases are also made, without royal duties being collected from those vessels. The bulk of the merchandise is used in the country, but some goods are exported to Nueva Espana. The price is generally paid in reals, although they are not so greedy for them as the Chinese, for there is silver in Japon. They generally bring a quantity of it as merchandise in plates, and it is sold at moderate rates.

These vessels return to Japon at the season of the vendavals, during the months of June and July. They carry from Manila their purchases, which are composed of raw Chinese silk, gold, deerskin, and brazil-wood for their dyes. They take honey, manufactured wax, palm and Castilian wine, civet-cats, large tibors in which to store their tea, glass, cloth, and other curiosities from Espana.

Some Portuguese vessels sail to Manila annually during the monsoon of the vendavals, from Maluco, Malaca, and India. They take merchandise consisting of spices—cloves, cinnamon, and pepper; slaves, both blacks and Cafres; cotton cloth of all sorts, fine muslins [caniquies], linens, gauzes, rambuties, and other delicate and precious cloths; amber, and ivory; cloths edged with pita, [411] for use as bed-covers; hangings, and rich counterpanes from Vengala [Bengal], Cochin, and other countries; many gilt articles and curiosities; jewels of diamonds, rubies, sapphires, topazes, balas-rubies, and other precious stones, both set and loose; many trinkets and ornaments from India; wine, raisins, and almonds; delicious preserves, and other fruits brought from Portugal and prepared in Goa; carpets and tapestries from Persia and Turquia, made of fine silks and wools; beds, writing-cases, parlor-chairs, and other finely-gilded furniture, made in Macao; needle-work in colors and in white, of chain-lace and royal point lace, and other fancy-work of great beauty and perfection. Purchases of all the above are made in Manila, and paid in reals and gold. The vessels return in January with the brisas, which is their favorable monsoon. They carry to Maluco provisions of rice and wine, crockery-ware, and other wares needed there; while to Malaca they take only the gold or money, besides a few special trinkets and curiosities from Espana, and emeralds. The royal duties are not collected from these vessels.

A few smaller vessels also sail from Borneo, during the vendavals. They belong to the natives of that island, and return during the first part of the brisas. They enter the river of Manila and sell their cargoes in their vessels. These consist of fine and well-made palm-mats, a few slaves for the natives, sago—a certain food of theirs prepared from the pith of palms—and tibors; large and small jars, glazed black and very fine, which are of great service and use; and excellent camphor, which is produced on that island. Although beautiful diamonds are found on the opposite coast, they are not taken to Manila by those vessels, for the Portuguese of Malaca trade for them on that coast. These articles from Borneo are bought more largely by the natives than by the Spaniards. The articles taken back by the Borneans are provisions of wine and rice, cotton cloth, and other wares of the islands, which are wanting in Borneo.

Very seldom a few vessels sail to Manila from Sian and Camboja. They carry some benzoin, pepper, ivory, and cotton cloth; rubies and sapphires, badly cut and set; a few slaves; rhinoceros horns, and the hides, hoofs, and teeth of this animal; and other goods. In return they take the wares found in Manila. Their coming and return is between the brisas and the vendavals, during the months of April, May, and June.

In these classes of merchandise, and in the products of the islands—namely, gold, cotton cloth, mendrinaque, and cakes of white and yellow wax—do the Spaniards effect their purchases, investments, and exports for Nueva Espana. They make these as is most suitable for each person, and lade them on the vessels that are to make the voyage. They value and register these goods, for they pay into the royal treasury of Manila, before the voyage, the two per cent royal duties on exports, besides the freight charges of the vessel, which amount to forty Castilian ducados [412] per tonelada. This latter is paid at the port of Acapulco in Nueva Espana, into the royal treasury of the said port, in addition to the ten per cent duties for entrance and first sale in Nueva Espana. [413]

Inasmuch as the ships which are despatched with the said merchandise are at his Majesty's account, and other ships cannot be sent, there is generally too small a place in the cargo for all the purchases. For that reason the governor divides the cargo-room among all the shippers, according to their wealth and merits, after they have been examined by intelligent men, appointed for that purpose. Consequently every man knows from his share how much he can export, and only that amount is received in the vessel; and careful and exact account is taken of it. Trustworthy persons are appointed who are present at the lading; and space is left for the provisions and passengers that are to go in the vessels. When the ships are laden and ready to sail, they are delivered to the general and the officials who have them in charge. Then they start on their voyage at the end of the month of June, with the first vendavals.

This trade and commerce is so great and profitable, and easy to control—for it only lasts three months in the year, from the time of the arrival of the ships with their merchandise, until those vessels that go to Nueva Espana take that merchandise—that the Spaniards do not apply themselves to, or engage in, any other industry. Consequently, there is no husbandry or field-labor worthy of consideration. Neither do the Spaniards work the gold mines or placers, which are numerous. They do not engage in many other industries that they could turn to with great profit, if the Chinese trade should fail them. That trade has been very hurtful and prejudicial in this respect, as well as for the occupations and farm industries in which the natives used to engage. Now the latter are abandoning and forgetting those labors. Besides, there is the great harm and loss resulting from the immense amount of silver that passes annually by this way [of the trade], into the possession of infidels, which can never, by any way, return into the possession of the Spaniards.

His Majesty's agents for the government and justice, and the royal officials for the management of his Majesty's revenue, are as follows: First, the governor and captain-general of all the islands, who is at the same time president of the royal Audiencia of Manila. He has a salary of eight thousand pesos de minas per year for all his offices. [414] He possesses his own body-guard of twelve halberdiers, whose captain receives three hundred pesos per year. The governor alone provides and regulates all that pertains to war and government, with the advice of the auditors of the Audiencia in difficult matters. He tries in the first instance the criminal cases of the regular soldiers, and any appeals from his decisions go to the Audiencia. [415] The governor appoints many alcaldes-mayor, corregidors, deputies, and other magistrates, throughout the islands and their provinces, for carrying on the government and justice, and for military matters. These appointments are made before a government chief scrivener appointed by his Majesty, who helps the governor.

The governor likewise takes part with the royal Audiencia, as its president, in whatever pertains to its duties. The Audiencia consists of four auditors and one fiscal—each of whom receives an annual salary of two thousand pesos de minas [416]—one reporter, one court scrivener, one alguacil-mayor, with his assistants, one governor of the prison of the court, one chancellor, one registrar, two bailiffs, one chaplain and sacristan, one executioner, attorneys, and receivers. The Audiencia tries all causes, civil and criminal, taken to it from all the provinces of its district. [417] These include the Filipinas Islands and the mainland of China, already discovered or to be discovered. The Audiencia has the same authority as the chancillerias of Valladolid and Granada in Espana. At the same time, the Audiencia provides whatever is advisable for the proper and systematic management of the royal exchequer.

His Majesty's revenues in the Filipinas Islands are in charge of and their tribunal consists of three royal officials. They are appointed by his Majesty, and consist of a factor, an accountant, and a treasurer. They each receive an annual salary of five hundred and ten thousand maravedis. They have their clerk of mines, and registrars of the royal revenues, and their executive and other officials, all of whom reside in Manila. From that city they manage and attend to everything pertaining to the royal revenues throughout the islands.

His Majesty has a number of encomiendas apportioned to his royal crown throughout the provinces of the Filipinas Islands. The tributes of those encomiendas are collected for his royal treasury by his royal officials and the collectors engaged for that purpose by the royal officials. From year to year these amount to thirty thousand pesos, after deducting costs and expenses. They collect, from one year to another, eight thousand pesos in tributes from the Sangleys—both Christians and infidels. 418

They also collect the fifth of all gold dug in the islands. By special concession for a limited period, the tenth is collected instead of the fifth. There is a declaration concerning it, to the effect that the natives shall pay no fifths or other duties on the jewels and gold inherited by them from their ancestors before his Majesty owned the country. Sufficient measures have been taken for the clear understanding of this concession and its investigation, for that on which the tenth has once been paid, and the steps to be taken in the matter. From one year to another they collect ten thousand pesos from these fifths, for much is concealed. 419

The assignment of two reals from each tributario inures to the royal treasury and is paid into it, for the pay of the soldiers and the stipend of the prebendaries. These are collected from the encomenderos, in proportion to, and on the account of, their tributes, and amount annually to thirty-four thousand pesos.

The fines and expenses of justice are committed to the care of the treasurer of the royal revenues, and are kept in the treasury. They amount annually to three thousand pesos.

The three per cent duties on the Chinese merchandise of the Sangley vessels average forty thousand pesos annually. 420

The two per cent duties paid by the Spaniards for exporting merchandise to Nueva Espana amount annually to twenty thousand pesos. On the merchandise and money sent from Nueva Espana to the Filipinas, result eight thousand pesos more. Consequently, in these things and in other dues of less importance that belong to the royal treasury, his Majesty receives about one hundred and fifty thousand pesos, or thereabout, annually in the Filipinas. [421]

Inasmuch as this amount does not suffice for the expenses that are incurred, the royal treasury of Nueva Espana sends annually to that of the Filipinas, in addition to the above revenues, some assistance in money—a greater or less sum, as necessity requires. For his Majesty has thus provided for it from the proceeds of the ten per cent duties on the Chinese merchandise that are collected at the port of Acapulco in Nueva Espana. This assistance is given into the keeping of the royal officials in Manila, and they take charge of it, with the rest of the revenues that they manage and collect.

From all this gross sum of his Majesty's revenue, the salaries of the governor and royal Audiencia are paid, as well as the stipends of prelates and ecclesiastical prebendaries, the salaries of the magistrates, and of the royal officials and their assistants; the pay of all the military officers and regular soldiers; his Majesty's share of the stipends for instruction, and the building of churches and their ornaments; the concessions and gratifications that he has allowed to certain monasteries, and private persons; the building of large vessels for the navigation to Nueva Espana, and of galleys and other vessels for the defense of the islands; expenses for gunpowder and ammunition; the casting of artillery, and its care; the expense arising for expeditions and individual undertakings in the islands, and in their defense; that of navigations to, and negotiations with, the kingdoms in their vicinity, which are quite common and necessary. Consequently, since his Majesty's revenues in these islands are so limited, and his expenses so great, the royal treasury falls short, and suffers poverty and need. [422]

The proceeds from the ten per cent duties and the freight charges of the ships, which are collected at Acapulco in Nueva Espana, on the merchandise sent there from the Filipinas, although considerable, are also not always sufficient for the expenses incurred in Nueva Espana with the ships, soldiers, ammunition, and other supplies sent annually to the Filipinas. These expenses are generally greatly in excess of those duties, and the amount is made up from the royal treasury of Mexico. Consequently, the king our sovereign derives as yet no profit from any revenues of the Filipinas, but rather an expenditure, by no means small, from his revenues in Nueva Espana. He sustains the Filipinas only for the christianization and conversion of the natives, and for the hopes of greater fruits in other kingdoms and provinces of Asia, which are expected through this gateway, at God's good pleasure.

Every year the Audiencia audits the accounts of the royal officials of his Majesty's revenues, strikes the balances, and sends the accounts to the tribunal of accounts in Mexico. [423]

In the city of Manila, and in all those Spanish settlements of the islands, reside Sangleys, who have come from Great China, besides the merchants. They have appointed settlements and are engaged in various trades, and go to the islands for their livelihood. Some possess their parians and shops. Some engage in fishing and farming among the natives, throughout the country; and go from one island to another to trade, in large or small champans. [424]

The annual vessels from Great China bring these Sangleys in great numbers, especially to the city of Manila, for the sake of the profits that are gained from their fares. As there is a superabundance of population in China, and the wages and profits there are little, they regard as of importance whatever they get in the Filipinas.

Very great annoyances result from this; for, not only can there be little security to the country with so many infidels, but the Sangleys are a wicked and vicious race. Through intercourse and communication with them, the natives improve little in Christianity and morals. And since they come in such numbers and are so great eaters, they raise the price of provisions, and consume them.

It is true that the city could not be maintained or preserved without these Sangleys; for they are the mechanics in all trades, and are excellent workmen and work for suitable prices. But a less number of them would suffice for this, and would avoid the inconvenience of so many people as are usually in Manila when the ships arrive—to say nothing of the many Chinese who go about among the islands, under pretext of trading with the natives, and there commit innumerable crimes and offenses. At the least, they explore all the country, the rivers, creeks, and ports, and know them better than the Spaniards do; and they will be of great harm and injury in case of any revolt or hostile invasion of the islands.

In order to remedy all the above, it was ordered that the vessels should not bring so many people of this kind, under penalties that are executed; that, when the vessels return to China, they take these Sangleys back with them; that only a convenient number of merchants remain in Manila, in the Parian, and the mechanics of all necessary trades; and that these must have written license, under severe penalties. In the execution of this, an auditor of the Audiencia is engaged by special commission every year, together with some assistants. On petition of the city cabildo, he usually allows as many Sangleys to remain as are necessary for the service of all trades and occupations. The rest are embarked and compelled to return in the vessels going to China, and a great deal of force and violence [425] is necessary to accomplish it.

Those merchants and artisans who remained in Manila before the revolt of the year six hundred and three had settled the Parian and its shops. The Parian is a large enclosed alcaiceria of many streets, at some distance from the city walls. It is near the river, and its location is called San Graviel. There they have their own governor, who has his tribunal and prison, and his assistants; these administer justice to them, and watch them day and night, so that they may live in security, and not commit disorders.

Those who cannot find room in this Parian live opposite, on the other side of the river, where Tondo is, in two settlements called Baybay and Minondoc. They are in charge of the alcalde-mayor of Tondo, and under the ministry of the religious of St. Dominic, who labor for their conversion, and for that purpose have learned the Chinese language.

The Dominicans have two monasteries with the requisite assistants, and a good hospital for the treatment of Sangleys. In a district kept separate from the infidels, they have a settlement of baptized Sangleys, with their wives, households, and families, numbering five hundred inhabitants; and the religious are continually baptizing others and settling them in that village. But few of them turn out well, for they are a vile and restless race, with many vices and bad customs. Their having become Christians is not through the desire or wish for salvation, but for the temporal conveniences that they have there, and because some are unable to return to China because of debts incurred and crimes committed there.

Each and all, both Christians and infidels, go unarmed and in their national garb. This consists of long garments with wide sleeves, made of blue cangan (but white for mourning, while the chief men wear them of black and colored silks); wide drawers of the same material; half hose of felt; very broad shoes, according to their fashion, made of blue silk embroidered with braid—with several soles, well-sewed—and of other stuffs. Their hair is long and very black, and they take good care of it. They do it up on the head in a high knot, [426] under a very close-fitting hood or coif of horsehair, which reaches to the middle of the forehead. They wear above all a high round cap made of the same horsehair, in different fashions, by which their different occupations, and each man's rank, are distinguished. The Christians differ only in that they cut their hair short, and wear hats, as do the Spaniards.

They are a light-complexioned people and tall of body. They have scant beards, are very stout-limbed, and of great strength. They are excellent workmen, and skilful in all arts and trades. They are phlegmatic, of little courage, treacherous and cruel when opportunity offers, and very covetous. They are heavy eaters of all kinds of meat, fish, and fruits; but they drink sparingly, and then of hot beverages.

They have a governor of their own race, a Christian, who has his officials and assistants. He hears their cases in affairs of justice, in their domestic and business affairs. Appeals from him go to the alcalde-mayor of Tondo or of the Parian, and from all these to the Audiencia, which also gives especial attention to this nation and whatever pertains to it.

No Sangley can live or own a house outside these settlements of the Parian, and of Baybay and Minondoc. Native settlements are not allowed in Sangley settlements, or even near them. No Sangley can go among the islands, or as much as two leguas from the city, without special permission. Much less can he remain in the city at night, after the gates are shut, under penalty of death.

There are generally some Japanese, both Christian and infidel, in Manila. These are left by the vessels from Japon, although they are not so numerous as the Chinese. They have their special settlement and location outside the city, between the Sangley Parian and the suburb of Laguio, near the monastery of La Candelaria. There they are directed by discalced religious of St. Francis, by means of interpreters whom the fathers keep for that purpose. They are a spirited race, of good disposition, and brave. They wear their own costume, namely, kimonos of colored silks and cotton, reaching half way down the leg, and open in front; wide, short drawers; close-fitting half-boots of leather, [427] and shoes like sandals, with the soles of well-woven straw. They go bare-headed, and shave the top of the head as far back as the crown. Their back hair is long, and fastened upon the skull in a graceful knot. They carry their catans, large and small, in the belt. They have scant beards, and are a race of noble bearing and behavior. They employ many ceremonies and courtesies, and attach much importance to honor and social standing. They are resolute in any necessity or danger.

Those who become Christians prove very good, and are very devout and observant in their religion; for only the desire for salvation incites them to adopt our religion, so that there are many Christians in Japon. Accordingly they return freely, and without opposition, to their own country. At most there are about five hundred Japanese of this nation in Manila, for they do not go to other parts of the islands, and such is their disposition that they return to Japon, and do not tarry in the islands; consequently very few of them usually remain in the islands. They are treated very cordially, as they are a race that demand good treatment, and it is advisable to do so for the friendly relations between the islands and Japon. [428]

Few people come from the other nations—Sian, Camboja, Borneo, Patan, and other islands—outside our government; and they immediately return in their vessels. Consequently, there is nothing special to be said of them, except that care is exercised in receiving and despatching them well, and seeing that they return quickly to their own countries.

Since I have told, in the short time at my disposal, the characteristics of the Filipinas Islands, and their customs and practices, it will not be inappropriate to discuss the navigation to them since it is made thither from Nueva Espana; the return voyage, which is not short, or without great dangers and hardships; and that made in the eastern direction.

When the islands were conquered in the year of one thousand five hundred and seventy-four [sic; sc. 1564], the Spanish fleet sailed under command of the adelantado Miguel Lopez de Legaspi, from Puerto de la Navidad [429] situated in the South Sea, on the coast of Nueva Espana, in the province and district of Xalisco and Galicia, where resides the royal Audiencia of Guadalajara. A few later voyages were made also from the same port, until the point for the sending of these vessels was removed, for better and greater convenience, to the port of Acapulco, located farther south on the same coast, in sixteen and one-half degrees of latitude; it is eighty leguas from Mexico, and in its district. It is an excellent port, sheltered from all weather; and has a good entrance and good anchorages. Its vicinity is advantageous, being better provisioned and more populous than that of La Navidad. There a large Spanish colony has been established, with its alcalde-mayor, and royal officials who have charge of his Majesty's treasury; and these attend to the despatch of the vessels.

The vessels that sail to the Filipinas, as they are despatched annually on his Majesty's account, must necessarily leave in the certain season of the brisas, which begin in the month of November and last until the end of March. This navigation should not be made at any other season, for from June the vendavals blow, and they are contrary to the voyage.

As a rule, these ships sail and are despatched at the end of February, or at the latest by the twentieth of March. They sail west toward the islands of Las Velas, [430] otherwise called the Ladrones. The island of Guan, one of them, lies in thirteen degrees of latitude. Inasmuch as the vessels on leaving Acapulco are wont sometimes to encounter calms, they sail south from sixteen and one-half degrees, in which the port is situated, until they strike the brisas, which is generally at ten or eleven degrees. By this route they sail continually before the wind, and without changing the sails, with fresh and fair brisas, and in other moderate weather, for one thousand eight hundred leguas, without sighting any mainland or island. Then leaving to the south the Barbudos and other islands, and advancing gradually to a latitude of thirteen degrees, they sail until they sight the island of Guan; and above it, in fourteen degrees, that of La Carpana [Seypan]. This voyage to those Ladrones Islands lasts generally seventy days.

The natives of those islands, who go naked, and are a very robust and barbarous race, go out to sea to meet the ships as soon as they discover them, at a distance of four to six leguas, with many vessels; these are one-masted, and are very slender and light. These vessels have a counterpoise of bamboo to leeward, and their sails are made of palm-leaves and are lateen-sails. Two or three men go in each one with oars and paddles. They carry loads of flying-fish, dorados, [431] cocoa-nuts, ba-nanas, sweet potatoes, bamboos full of water, and certain mats; and when they reach the ships, they trade these for iron from the hoops of casks, and bundles of nails, which they use in their industries, and in the building of their ships. Since some Spaniards and religious have lived among them, because of Spanish ships being wrecked or obliged to take refuge there, they come more freely to our ships and enter them.

Our ships sail between the two islands of Guan and Carpana toward the Filipinas and the cape of Espiritu Santo, a distance of three hundred leguas farther on, in the latitude of about thirteen degrees. This distance is made in ten or twelve days with the brisas; but it may happen, if the ships sail somewhat late, that they encounter vendavals, which endanger their navigation, and they enter the islands after great trouble and stormy weather.

From the cape of Espiritu Santo, the ships enter the strait of Capul at the islands of Mazbate and Burias; thence they sail to Marinduque and the coast of Calilaya, the strait of Mindoro, the shoals of Tuley, and the mouth of Manila Bay. Thence, they go to the port of Cabit. This is a voy-age of one hundred leguas from the entrance to the islands and is made in one week. This is the end of the voyage, which is good and generally without storms, if made in the proper time.

These vessels now make the return voyage from the Filipinas to Nueva Espana with great difficulty and danger, for the course is a long one and there are many storms and various temperatures. The ships de-part, on this account, very well supplied with provisions, and suitably equipped. Each one sails alone, hoisting as much sail as possible, and one does not wait for the other, nor do they sight one another during the voyage.

They leave the bay and port of Cabit at the first setting-in of the vendavals, between the same islands and by the same straits, by the twen-tieth of June and later. As they set out amid showers, and are among islands, they sail with difficulty until they leave the channel at Capul. Once in the open sea, they catch the vendaval, and voyage east, making more progress when they reach the latitude of fourteen or fifteen degrees.

Then the brisa starts. This wind is the ordinary one in the South Sea, especially in low latitudes. Since it is a head wind, the course is changed, and the bow is pointed betwen the north and east, as much as the wind will allow. With this they reach a higher latitude, and the ship is kept in this course until the vendaval returns. Then, by means of it, the ship again takes an eastern course in that latitude where it happens to be, and keeps that direction as long as that wind lasts. When the vendaval dies, the ship takes the best course that the winds allow, by the winds then blowing between north and east. If the wind is so contrary that it is north or northwest, so that the ship cannot take that course, the other course is taken so that they may continue to maintain their voyage without losing time. At four hundred leguas from the islands they sight certain volcanoes and ridges of the islands of Ladrones, which run north as far as twenty-four degrees. [432] Among these they generally encounter severe storms and whirl-winds. At thirty-four degrees is the cape of Sestos, [433] at the northern head of Japon, six hundred leguas from the Filipinas. They sail among other islands, which are rarely seen, in thirty-eight degrees, encountering the same dangers and storms, and in a cold climate, in the neighborhood of the islands Rica de Oro ["rich in gold"] and Rica de Plata ["rich in silver"], which are but seldom seen. [434] After passing them the sea and open expanse of water is immense, and the ship can run free in any weather. This gulf is traversed for many leguas with such winds as are encountered, until a latitude of forty-two degrees is reached, toward the coast of Nueva Espana. They seek the winds that generally prevail at so high a latitude, which are usually northwest. After a long voyage the coast of Nueva Espana is sighted, and from Cape Mendocino (which lies in forty-two and one-half degrees) the coast extends nine hundred leguas to the port of Acapulco, which lies in sixteen and one-half degrees.

When the ships near the coast, which they generally sight betwen forty and thirty six degrees, the cold is very severe, and the people suffer and die. Three hundred leguas before reaching land, signs of it are seen, by certain aguas malas, [435] as large as the hand, round and violet colored, with a crest in the middle like a lateen sail, which are called caravelas ["caravels"] This sign lasts until the ship is one hundred leguas from land; and then are discovered certain fish, with half the body in the form of a dog; [436] these frolic with one another near the ship. After these perrillos ["little dogs"] are seen the porras ["knobsticks"], which are certain very long, hollow shoots of a yellow herb with a ball at the top, and which float on the water. At thirty leguas from the coast are seen many

273

great bunches of grass which are carried down to the sea by the great rivers of the country. These grasses are called balsas ["rafts or floats"]. Also many perrillos are seen, and, in turn, all the various signs. Then the coast is discovered, and it is very high and clear land. Without losing sight of land, the ship coasts along it with the northwest, north-northwest, and north winds, which generally prevail on that coast, blowing by day toward the land, and by night toward the sea again. With the decrease of the latitude and the entrance into a warm climate the island of Cenizas [ashes] is seen, and afterward that of Cedros [cedars]. Thence one sails until the cape of San Lucas is sighted, which is the entrance of [the gulf of] California. From that one traverses the eighty leguas intervening to the islands of Las Marias and the cape of Corrientes ["currents"], which is on the other side of California in Val de Vanderas ["valley of banners"], and the provinces of Chametla. Thence one passes the coast of Colima, Sacatul, Los Motines ["the mutinies"], and Ciguatanejo, and enters the port of Acapulco—without having made a way-station or touched land from the channel of Capul in the Filipinas throughout the voyage. The voyage usually lasts five months or thereabout, but often six and even more. [437]

By way of India, one may sail from the Filipinas to Espana, by making the voyage to Malaca, and thence to Cochin and Goa, a distance of one thousand two hundred leguas. This voyage must be made with the brisas. From Goa one sails by way of India to the cape of Buena Esperanca [Good Hope], and to the Terceras [i.e., Azores] Islands, and thence to Portugal and the port of Lisboa. This is a very long and dangerous voyage, as is experienced by the Portuguese who make it every year. From India they usually send letters and despatches to Espana by way of the Bermejo ["Red"] Sea, by means of Indians. These send them through Arabia to Alexandria, and thence by sea to Venecia [Venice] and thence to Espana.

A galleon bound for Portugal sails and is despatched from the fort of Malaca, in certain years, by the open sea, without touching at India or on its coasts. It reaches Lisboa much more quickly than do the Goa vessels. It generally sails on the fifth of January, and does not leave later than that; nor does it usually anticipate that date. However, not any of these voyages are practiced by the Castilians—who are prohibited from making them—except the one made by way of Nueva Espana, both going and coming, as above described. And although the effort has been made, no better or shorter course has been found by way of the South Sea. [438]
Laus Deo

Notes

¹ Cea is a small town situated in the old kingdom of Leon, on a river of the same name. It was a seat of a chateau and a duchy. The name of the first duke of Lerma was Francisco Gomez de Sandoval y Rojas. Hume's Spain (Cambridge, 1898), mentions one of his sons as duke of Cea, who is probably the Cristoval Gomez de Sandoval y Rojas of Morga's dedication.

² The facts of Doctor Antonio de Morga's life are meager. He must have been born in Sevilla, as his birth register is said to exist in the cathedral of that city. He sailed from Acapulco for the Philippines in 1595 in charge of the vessels sent with reenforcements that year. He remained there eight years, during which time he was continually in office. In 1598, upon the reestablishment of the Manila Audiencia he was appointed senior auditor. In 1600 he took charge of the operations against the Dutch and commanded in the naval battle with them. He left the islands July 10, 1603, in charge of the ships sailing that year to Mexico. After that period he served in the Mexico Audiencia; and as late as 1616 was president of the Quito Audiencia, as appears from a manuscript in the British Museum. His book circulated, at least, in part, in manuscript before being published. Torrubia mentions a manuscript called Descubrimiento, conquista, pacificacion y poblacion de ias Islas Philipinas, which was dated 1607, and dedicated to "his Catholic Majesty, King Don Phelipe III, our sovereign." Morga combined the three functions of historian, politician, and soldier, and his character is many sided and complex. He is spoken of in high terms as an historian, and Rizal, as well as Blumentritt, exalts him above all other historians of the Philippines.

³ Throughout this work, all notes taken entire or condensed from Jose Rizal's edition of Sucesos de las Islas Filipinas por el Doctor Antonio de Morga (Paris, 1890), will be signed Rizal, unless Rizal is given as authority for the note or a portion of it in the body of the note. Similarly those notes taken or condensed from Lord Henry E. J. Stanley's translation of Morga, The Philippine Islands…. by Antonio de Morga (Hakluyt

Soc. ed., London, 1868), will be signed Stanley, unless Stanley is else-where given as authority as above.

Dr. Jose Rizal, the Filipino patriot, was born in 1861 at Calamba in Luzon, of pure Tagal stock, although some say that it was mixed with Chinese blood. Through the advice of Father Leontio, a Tagal priest, he was sent to Manila to the Jesuit institution Ateneo Municipal—where he was the pupil of Rev. Pablo Pastells, now of Barcelona. His family name was Mercado, but at the advice of his brother, who had become involved in the liberal movement, he took that of Rizal. After taking his degree at Manila, he studied in Spain, France, and Germany. He founded the Liga Filipina, whose principal tenet was "Expulsion of the friars and the con-fiscation of their property," and which was the basis of the revolutionary society of the Sons of the Nation. On Rizal's return to Manila, after sev-eral years of travel, in 1892, he was arrested and exiled to Dapitan. In 1895, he was allowed to volunteer for hospital service in Cuba, but was arrested in Barcelona, because of the breaking out of the Filipino insur-rection, and sent back to Manila, where he was shot on December 30, 1896, by native soldiers. Besides being a skilled physician, Dr. Rizal was a poet, novelist, and sculptor, and had exhibited in the salon. His first novel Noli me tangere appeared in Berlin in 1887, and was, as Dr. T. H. Pardo de Tavera remarks, the first book to treat of Filipino manners and customs in a true and friendly spirit. It was put under the ban by the Church. Its sequel El Filibusterismo appeared in 1891.

Sir Henry Edward John Stanley, third Baron of Alderley, and sec-ond Baron Eddisbury of Sinnington, a member of the peerage of the United Kingdom, and a baronet, died on December 10, 1903, at the age of seventy-six. He was married in 1862 to Fabia, daughter of Senor Don Santiago Federico San Roman of Sevilla, but had no issue. He spent many years in the East, having been first attache at Constantinople and Secretary of Legation at Athens. He embraced the Mahometan religion and was buried by its rites privately by Ridjag Effendi, Imaum of the Turkish embassy.

[4] Charles chose as his motto Plus ultra, being led thereto by the re-cent world discoveries and the extension of Spanish dominions. This motto is seen on his coins, medals, and other works.

[5] Perhaps Morga alludes to Argensola, who published his Historia de la conquista de las Molucas this same year of 1609.—Rizal.

[6] This was the second establishment of the Audiencia, in 1598.

[7] The term "proprietary governor" refers to the regularly appointed (hence governor in his own right) royal representative who governed the islands; all others were governors ad interim, and were appointed in dif-ferent manners at different periods. The choice of governors showed a

gradual political evolution. In the earliest period, the successor in case of death or removal was fixed by the king or the Audiencia of Mexico (e.g., in the case of Legazpi). Some governors (e.g., Gomez Perez Dasmarinas) were allowed to name their own successor. After the establishment of the Audiencia, the choice fell upon the senior auditor. The latest development was the appointment of a segundo cabo, or second head (about the equivalent of lieutenant-governor), who took the office ad interim in case of the governor's death or removal, or a vacancy arising from any other cause.

[8] Morga may refer to accounts of the battle with Oliver van Noordt, or the manuscripts of Juan de Plasencia, Martin de Rada, and others.—Rizal.

[9] Magalhaes and Serrano died on the same day. Argensola commenting on this fact says: "At this time his friend Serrano was going to India; and although in different parts, the two navigators died on the same day, almost under like circumstances."

[10] This is too strong a statement, and Morga's knowledge is inexact, as Magalhaes had sailed the eastern seas while in the service of the Portuguese monarch.

[11] Argensola (Conquistas de las Islas Malucas, Madrid, 1609) mentions the expedition sent out by the bishop of Plasencia, Don Gutierre de Vargas.

[12] An error for 1542.

[13] Urdaneta received Felipe II's order to accompany the expedition while in Mexico.—Rizal.

See VOL. II of this series for Urdaneta's connection with this expedition.

[14] See abstract of these instructions, VOL. II, pp. 89-100.

[15] Called Villa de San Miguel at first, according to San Agustin.—Rizal.

[16] Ruy Lopez de Villalobos, not Legazpi, first gave the name Filipinas to the archipelago.

[17] Rizal identifies Rajamora with Soliman, and says that he was called Rajamora or Rahang mura in opposition to Rajamatanda or Rahang matanda, signifying, as Isabelo de los Reyes y Florentino partially points out in an article entitled "Los Regulos de Manila," pp. 87-111 of Artículos varios (Manila, 1887), the young raja and the old raja. In the above article, the latter seeks to identify Rajamora or Soliman with the Raxobago of San Agustin, and declares that Rajamatanda and Lacandola are identical. The confusion existing in later writers regarding these names is lacking in Morga, and Rizal's conjecture appears correct.

[18] Arigues comes from the Tagal word haligi, which are stout wooden posts, used to support the frames of buildings. The word is in quite common use in the Philippines among the Spanish speaking people. It is sometimes used to denote simply a column.—Rizal (in part).

[19] This was the date of Legazpi's arrival at Manila and not of the assault, which occurred in 1570.—Rizal.

Goiti took possession of Manila for the king, June 6, 1570. See various documents in VOL. III of this series.

[20] The inhabitants of Sebu aided the Spaniards on this expedition, and consequently were exempted from tribute for a considerable period.—Rizal.

[21] Rizal conjectures that this is a typographical error and should read de Bisayas o de los Pintados, i.e., Bisayas or Los Pintados.

[22] The Tagals called it Maynila.—Rizal.

For the meaning of this name, see VOL. III, p. 148, note 41.

[23] Rather it was his grandson Salcedo. This hero, called the Hernan Cortes of the Filipinas, was truly the intelligent arm of Legazpi. By his prudence, his fine qualities, his talent, and personal worth, the sympathies of the Filipinos were captured, and they submitted to their enemies. He inclined them to peace and friendship with the Spaniards. He likewise saved Manila from Limahon. He died at the age of twenty-seven, and is the only one to our knowledge who named the Indians as his heirs to a large portion of his possessions, namely his encomienda of Bigan. (San Agustin).—Rizal.

See also VOL. III, p. 73, note 21.

[24] "He assigned the tribute that the natives were to pay to their encomenderos," says San Agustin. "This was one piece of cotton cloth, in the provinces where cloth was woven, of the value of four reals; two fanegas of rice; and one fowl. This was to be given once each year. Those who did not possess cloth were to give its value in kind of another product of their own harvest in that town; and where there was no rice harvested, they were to give two reals, and one-half real for the fowl, estimated in money."—Rizal.

[25] Legazpi dies August 20, 1572.

[26] "One thousand five hundred friendly Indians from the islands of Zebu, Bohol, Leyte, and Panay, besides the many other Indians of service, for use as pioneers and boat-crews, accompanied the Spaniards..." Lacandola and his sons and relatives, besides two hundred Bissayans and many other Indians who were enrolled in Pangasinan, aided them. (San Agustin).—Rizal.

[27] According to San Agustin, more than one thousand five hundred Indian bowmen from the provinces of Pangasinan, Cagayan, and Pinta-

dos accompanied this expedition. Its apparent motive was to place on the throne Sirela, or Malaela, as Colin calls him, who had been dethroned by his brother.—Rizal.

See the relation of this expedition in VOL. IV, pp. 148-303.

[28] This expedition did not succeed because of the development of the disease beriberi among the Spanish forces, from which more than four-fifths of the soldiers died. More than one thousand five hundred of the most warlike natives, mostly from Cagayan and Pampanga, accompanied the expedition.—Rizal.

[29] By making use of the strife among the natives themselves, because of the rivalry of two brothers, as is recounted by San Agustin.—Rizal.

[30] His name was Zaizufa.—Rizal.

La Concepcion, vol. ii, p. 33, gives the founding of the city of Nueva Segovia as the resultant effect of this Japanese pirate. He says: "He [i.e., Joan Pablos de Carrion] found a brave and intrepid Japanese pirate in possession of the port, who was intending to conquer it and subdue the country. He attacked the pirate boldly, conquered him, and frustrated his lofty designs. For greater security he founded the city of Nueva Segovia, and fortified it with a presidio."

[31] Captain Ribera was the first envoy from the Philippines to confer with the king on the needs of the country.—Rizal.

See VOL. V of this series, pp. 207-209, for his complaints against the governor.

[32] The fire caught from the candles placed about the catafalque of Governor Gonzalo Ronquillo.—Rizal.

[33] This Pedro Sarmiento was probably the one who accompanied Fathers Rada and Marin, and Miguel Loarca to China in 1575; see this series, VOL. IV, p. 46, and VOL. VI, p. 116. The celebrated mathematician and navigator, Pedro Sarmiento de Gamboa doubtless belonged to a different branch of the same family. The latter was born in Alcahl de Henares, in 1532, and died toward the end of the century. Entering the Spanish army he went to America, perhaps in 1555. As early as 1557 he sailed in the south seas, and being led to the belief of undiscovered islands there, several times proposed expeditions for their discovery to the viceroy of Peru. He was captain of Mendana's ship in the expedition that discovered the Solomon Islands. Shortly after, at the instance of the viceroy, Francisco de Toledo, he visited Cuzco, and wrote a full description of that country. He was the first to study the ancient history and institutions of the Incas in detail. When Drake made his memorable expedition into the South Sea, Sarmiento was sent in his pursuit, and he wrote a detailed account of the Strait of Magellan and his voyage through it. He

later founded a Spanish colony in the strait, but it was a failure, and was known afterward as Famine Port. He was a prisoner, both in England and France, being ransomed by Felipe II from the latter country. In navigation he was ahead of his times, as his writings attest. He was persecuted for many years by the Holy Inquisition on various charges. See Lord Amherst's Discovery of the Solomon Islands (Hakluyt Soc. ed., London, 1901), vol. i, pp. 83-94; and Clements R. Markham's Narratives of the voyages of Pedro Sarmiento de Gamboa (Hakluyt Soc. ed., 1895). Argensola gives (Conquistas de las islas Malucas), some account of Sarmiento's expedition to the strait in pursuit of Drake. He seems (pp. 167-168) when speaking of the incident in our text to confuse these two men. An excellent atlas containing fourteen illuminated and colored maps is also attributed to Sarmiento the navigator, number five being a map of India, including the Moluccas and the Philippines.

[34] See letter by Juan de Moron, VOL. VI, of this series, pp. 275-278.

[35] It was divulged by a Filipino woman, the wife of a soldier (Sinibaldo de Mas).—Rizal.

[36] Thomas Cavendish or Candish. He is named by various authors as Escandesch, Cande, Eschadesch, Embleg, and Vimble.—Rizal. See also appendix A.

[37] This memorable expedition of Sir Francis Drake left Plymouth November 15, 1577, but an accident caused their return to the same port, whence they again sailed on the thirteenth of December. After various fortunes the Strait of Magellan was reached on August 17, 1578. They coasted along the western part of South America, where a valuable prize was taken. At the island of Canno "wee espyed a shippe, and set sayle after her, and tooke her, and found in her two Pilots and a Spanish Gouernour, going for the Ilands of the Philippinas: Wee searched the shippe, and tooke some of her Merchandizes, and so let her goe." Thence they voyaged to the Moluccas, which were reached November 14. Next day they anchored at Yerrenate, where they were welcomed. The voyage was continued through the islands, around the Cape of Good Hope, and thence to England, where they arrived November 3, 1580. See Purchas: His Pilgrims (London, 1625), i, book ii, ch. iii, pp. 46-57. For accounts of the life and voyages of Drake, see also, Purchas: ut supra, v, book vii, ch. v, pp. 1391-1398; Bry: Collectiones peregrinationum (Francofurti, 1625), ser. i, vol. iii, pars viii, pp. 3-34; Francis Fletcher; The World encompassed by Sir Francis Drake (London, 1635); Knox: New Collection of voyages and travels (London, 1767), iii, pp. 1-27; John Barrow: Life, voyages, and exploits of Admiral Sir Francis Drake (John Murray, Albemarle St., 1843); Thomas Maynarde: Sir Francis Drake, his voyage 1595 (Hakluyt Soc. ed., London, 1849); W. S. W. Vaux: The

world encompassed by Sir Francis Drake (Hakluyt Soc. ed., London, 1854).

³⁸ See VOL. VI of this series for various documents concerning Father Alonso Sanchez's mission to Spain and Rome.

³⁹ San Agustin says that these walls were twelve thousand eight hundred and forty-three geometrical feet in extent, and that they were built without expense to the royal treasury.—Rizal.

⁴⁰ See references to this expedition, VOL. VIII, pp. 242, 250, 251; and VOL. XIV.

⁴¹ This emperor, also called Hideyosi, had been a stable boy, called Hasiba.—Rizal.

See VOL. X, p. 25, note I, and p. 171, note 19; also Trans. Asiatic Soc. (Yokohama), vols. vi, viii, ix, and xi.

⁴² See VOL. VIII of this series, pp. 260-267.

⁴³ San Agustin [as does Argensola] says there were two hundred and fifty Chinese.—Rizal.

⁴⁴ Marikaban.—Rizal.

⁴⁵ The original is ballesteras, defined in the old dictionaries as that part of the galley where the soldiers fought.

⁴⁶ A sort of knife or saber used in the Orient.

⁴⁷ This lack and defect are felt even now ¹⁸⁹⁰ after three centuries.—Rizal.

⁴⁸ Cho-da-mukha, in Siamese the place of meeting of the chief mandarins, i.e., the capital.—Stanley.

⁴⁹ Phra-Unkar. Phra or Pra is the title given to the kings of Siam and Camboja.—Rizal.

⁵⁰ Si-yuthia, or the seat of the kings.—Stanley.

⁵¹ Id est, the supercargo, in Chinese.—Stanley.

⁵² Father Alonso Ximenez or Jimenez took the Dominican habit in the Salamanca convent. His best years were passed in the missions of Guatemala. He was one of the first Dominicans to respond to the call for missionaries for the Dominican province in the Philippines, leaving for that purpose the Salamanca convent, whither he had retired. His first mission was on the river of Bataan. A severe illness compelled him to go to the Manila convent, where he was later elected prior, and then provincial of the entire Dominican field of the islands, being the second to hold that office. He later engaged in the two disastrous expeditions as mentioned in our text, and died December 31, 1598. See Resena biografica.

⁵³ Lantchang or Lanxang is the name of an ancient city in the north of Cambodia. (Pallegoix's Dictionary).—Stanley.

⁵⁴ Rizal says: "There exists at this point a certain confusion in the order, easy, however, to note and correct. We believe that the author

must have said 'Vencidas algunas dificultades, para la falida, por auer ydo a efte tiempo, de Camboja a Lanchan, en los Laos vn madarin llamado Ocuna de Chu, con diez paroes, etc.;'" whereas the book reads the same as the above to "Camboja," and then proceeds "a los Laos, vn madarin llamado Ocuna de Chu, Alanchan con diez paroes." We have accordingly translated in accordance with this correction. Stanley translates the passage as follows: "Some difficulties as to setting out from Alanchan having been overcome, by the arrival at this time in Laos from Cambodia of a mandarin named Ocunia de Chu, with ten prahus, etc." In the above we follow the orthography of the original.

55 The river Me-Kong.—Rizal.

56 Laksamana, a general or admiral in Malay.—Stanley.

57 Chow Phya is a title in Siam and Cambodia.—Rizal.

58 That is, his son or other heir was to inherit the title.

59 Rizal conjectures that this word is a transformation of the Tagal word, lampitaw, a small boat still used in the Philippines.

60 We follow Stanley's translation. He derives the word cacatal [zacatal] from zacate, or sacate, signifying "reed," "hay," or other similar growths, zacatal thus being a "place of reeds" or a "thicket."

61 From kalasag, a shield.—Rizal.

62 Argensola says that this native, named Ubal, had made a feast two days before, at which he had promised to kill the Spanish commander.—Rizal.

63 Perhaps the arquebuses of the soldiers who had been killed in the combat with Figueroa, for although culverins and other styles of artillery were used in these islands, arquebuses were doubtless unknown.—Rizal.

64 These considerations might apply to the present 1890 campaigns in Mindanao.—Rizal.

65 Argensola says that Cachil is probably derived from the Arabic Katil, which signifies "valiant soldier." "In the Malucas they honor their nobles with this title as with Mosiur in Francia, which means a trifle more than Don in Espana." See also VOL. X, p. 61, note 6.

66 The Solomon Islands (Islas de Salomon) were first discovered in 1568 by Alvaro de Mendana de Neyra while on an expedition to discover the supposed southern continent between Asia and America. Various reasons are alleged for the name of this group: one that Mendana called them thus because of their natural richness; another that King Solomon obtained wood and other materials there for his temple; and the third and most probable that they were called after one of the men of the fleet. As narrated in our text, the expedition of 1595 failed to rediscover the islands. They remained completely lost, and were even expunged from the maps until their rediscovery by Carteret in 1767. The discoverers and

explorers Bougainville, Surville, Shortland, Manning, d'Entrecasteaux, Butler, and Williamson, made discoveries and explorations in the same century. In 1845, they were visited by d'Urville. H.B. Guppy made extensive geological studies there in 1882. The French Marist fathers went there first in 1845, but were forced, in 1848, to abandon that field until 1861. They were the least known of all the Pacific and South Sea islands. They extend a distance of over 600 miles, and lie approximately between 4° 30'-12° south latitude and 154° 40'-162° 30' east longitude. They lie southeast of New Britain and northwest of New Hebrides. The larger islands are: Bougainville, Choiseul, Santa Isabel, Guadalconar, Malaita, and San Cristobal, and are generally mountainous, and volcanic in origin, containing indeed several active volcanoes. The smaller islands are generally volcanic and show traces of coral limestone. The climate is unhealthful, and one of the rainiest in the world. They are extremely fertile and contain excellent water. The inhabitants are of the Malay race and were formerly cannibals. They form parts of the British and German possessions. See Lord Amherst: Discovery of the Solomon Islands (London, Hakluyt Soc. ed., 1901); H. B. Guppy: The Solomon Islands (London, 1887); Justo Zaragoza: Historia del descubrimiento australes (Madrid, 1876).

[67] These places are all to be found on the old maps. Paita or Payta is shown just above or below five degrees south latitude. Callao was properly the port of Lima.

[68] Called by the natives Fatuhiwa, situated in 10° 40' south latitude, and west longitude 138° 15', one of the Marquesas group belonging to France.—Rizal.

[69] According to Captain Cook, cited by Wallace, these islanders surpassed all other nations in the harmony of their proportions and the regularity of their features. The stature of the men is from 175 to 183 cm.—Rizal.

[70] The three islands are identified as Motane (probably), Hiwaoa, Tahuata or Tanata; the channel as the strait of Bordelais; and the "good port" as Vaitahu (Madre de Dios) (?).—Rizal.

[71] The breadfruit, which grows on the tree artocarpus incisa. It is called rima in Spanish, the name by which it was perhaps known throughout Polynesia.—Rizal.

In the Bissayan Islands this tree was called colo. It reaches a height of about sixty feet. Its bark exudes a gummy sap, that is used for snaring birds. For want of areca, the bark is also used by the Indians as a substitute. The wood is yellow, and is used for making canoes, and in the construction of houses. See Delgado's Historia General, and Blanco's Flora de Filipinas.

[72] Probably the Pukapuka group or Union Islands.—Rizal.

[73] Perhaps Sophia Island, which is about this distance from Lima.—Rizal.

[74] Nitendi.—Rizal.

[75] The small islets may have been the Taumako Islands; the shoals, Matema, and the "island of no great size," Vanikoro.—Rizal.

[76] Called kilitis in the Philippines, but we are not aware that indigo is made of it.—Rizal.

Delgado (Historia, Manila, 1892) describes the wild amaranths which he calls quiletes (an American word, according to Blanco) doubtless the plant indicated in the text. The native generic name is haroma. There are numerous varieties, all edible.

[77] This word is untranslated by Stanley. Rizal conjectures that it may come from the Tagal word saga or jequiriti. But it may be a misprint for the Spanish sagu or sagui, "sago."

[78] Pingre's translation of the Descubrimiento de las Islas de Salomon says, p. 41: "On the 17th October there was a total eclipse of the moon: this luminary, on rising above the horizon, was already totally eclipsed. Mendana, by his will, which he signed with difficulty, named as lady governor of the fleet his wife Dona Isabella de Barreto." And in a note, he [i.e., Pingre] says that he calculated this eclipse by the tables of Halley: the immersion must have happened at Paris at 19 hours 6 minutes, and the moon had already been risen since 5 or 6 minutes; so that the isle of Sta. Cruz would be at least 13h. 2m. west of Paris, which would make it 184 degrees 30 minutes longitude, or at most 190 degrees, allowing for the Spaniards not having perceived the eclipse before sunset.—Stanley.

[79] Probably Ponape.—Rizal.

[80] The Descubrimiento de las Islas de Salomon says: "The frigate was found cast away on the coast with all the crew dead. The galliot touched at Mindanao, in 10 degrees, where the crew landed on the islet of Camaniguin; and while wandering on the shore, and dying of hunger, met with some Indians, who conducted them to a hospital of the Jesuits. The corregidor of the place sent five men of this ship prisoners to Manila, upon the complaint of their captain, whom they had wished to hang. He wrote to Don Antonio de Morga the following letter: 'A Spanish galliot has arrived here, commanded by a captain, who is as strange a man as the things which he relates. He pretends to have belonged to the expedition of General Don Alvaro de Mendana, who left Peru for the Solomon isles, and that the fleet consisted of four ships. You will perhaps have the means of knowing what the fact is.' The soldiers who were prisoners de-

clared that the galliot had separated from the general only because the captain had chosen to follow another route."—Stanley.

⁸¹ Dr. T. H. Pardo de Tavera in his Historia del descubrimiento de las regiones australes (Madrid, 1876), identifies this bay with the present Harbor of Laguan.—Rizal.

⁸² Lord Stanley translates the above passage, which reads in the original "que por quede della razon (si acaso Dios dispusiese de mi persona, o aya otra qualquiera ocasion; que yo, o la que lleuo faltemos), aya luz della," etc., as "that an account may remain (if perchance God should dispose of my life, or anything else should arise, or I or she that I take with me should be missing), and that it may give light," etc. Rizal points out that the words "o la que lleuo faltemos" do not refer to Dona Isabel de Barreto, but to a similar relation of the voyage that Quiros carried with him. We have accordingly adopted the latter's rendering, which is by far more probable.

⁸³ On the island of Shikoku.—Rizal.

⁸⁴ From the Japanese fune, boat. This may be etymologically equivalent to the English word funny, a kind of small boat.

⁸⁵ Lord Stanley connects this word, which he translates "monks," with the Nembuds Koo. These, according to Engelbert Kaempfer, historian and physician at the Dutch embassy in Japan, and who lived from 1651 to 1716, are devout fraternities who chant the Namanda, the abbreviation of "Nama Amida Budsu" ("Great Amida help us"). The Dai-Nembudzsui are persons especially devoted to Amida's worship. Rizal however refutes this, and derives Nambaji from the Japanese word Nambanjin, signifying "dweller of the barbaric south," as the missionaries came from the south.

⁸⁶ See note 85, ante, p. 119.

⁸⁷ The Spanish word is dojicos, which is etymologically the same as the French dogiques. This latter term is defined in The Jesuit Relations (Cleveland, 1896-1901), xxvii, p. 311, note 1, as a name given, in foreign missions, to those natives who instruct their countrymen. They officiated in the absence of the priests.

⁸⁸ Fushimi, Osaka, and Sakai.—Rizal.

⁸⁹ See VOL. X, p. 171, note 19.

⁹⁰ Santa Ines publishes a translation of the same sentence that varies somewhat in phraseology from the above, but which has the same sense. It is dated however: "the first year of Queicho, on the twentieth day of the eleventh moon." J.J. Rein (Japan, London, 1884) publishes a version different from either, which is as follows: "Taiko—sama. I have condemned these people to death, because they have come from the Philippine Islands, have given themselves out as ambassadors, which they

are not, and because they have dwelt in my country without my permission, and proclaimed the law of the Christians against my command. My will is that they be crucified at Nagasaki." For the persecutions in this and succeeding administrations, see Rein, ut supra.

[91] Santa Ines gives the names and order of the crucifixion of religious and converts, twenty-six in all. They were crucified in a row stretching east and west as follows: ten Japanese converts, the six Franciscans, three Jesuits, and seven Japanese converts, with about four paces between each two. The Japanese served the Franciscans in various religious and secular capacities. The six Franciscans were: Francisco Blanco, of Monte Rey, Galicia; Francisco de San Miguel, lay-brother, of Parrilla, in the Valladolid bishopric; Gonzalo Garcia, lay-brother, of Bazain, East India, son of a Portuguese father and a native woman; Felipe de Jesus, or de las Casas, of Mexico; Martin de la Ascension, theological lecturer, of Beasain, in the province of Guipuzcoa; and Pedro Bautista, of San Esteban, in the Avila bishopric. The Jesuits were, at least two of them, Japanese, and were not above the rank of brother or teacher. Five Franciscans of the eleven in Japan escaped crucifixion, namely, Agustin Rodriguez, Bartolome Ruiz, Marcelo de Rivadeneira, Jeronimo de Jesus, and Juan Pobre. The first three were forced to leave Japan in a Portuguese vessel sailing to India.

[92] The Lequios Islands are identified by Rizal as the Riukiu or Lu-Tschu Islands. J. J. Rein (Japan, London, 1884) says that they form the second division of the modern Japanese empire, and lie between the thirtieth and twenty-fourth parallels, or between Japan proper and Formosa. They are called also the Loochoo Islands.

[93] See Stanley, appendix v, pp. 398-402, and Rizal, note 4, p. 82, for extracts and abstracts of a document written by Father Alexander Valignano, visitor of the Society of Jesus in Japan, dated October 9, 1598. This document states that three Jesuits were crucified by mistake with the others. The document is polemical in tone, and explains on natural grounds what the Franciscans considered and published as miraculous. The above letter to Morga is published by Santa Ines, ii, p. 364.

[94] Santa Ines publishes a letter from this religious to another religious of the same order. From this letter it appears that he later went to Macan, whence he returned to Manila.

[95] Called Alderete in Argensola, doubtless an error of the copyist.—Rizal.

[96] The same king wrote a letter of almost the same purport to Father Alonso Ximenez, which is reproduced by Aduarte.—Rizal.

[97] Diego Aduarte, whose book Historia de la Provincia del Santo Rosario (Manila, 1640), will appear later in this series.

⁹⁸ Morga's own account of this, ante, says distinctly that there were two vessels and that Bias Ruiz had entered the river ahead of Diego Belloso. Hernando de los Rios Coronel, however, explains this in his Relacion of 1621, by stating that one of the two vessels had been wrecked on the Cambodian coast.

⁹⁹ The original is en la puente, which translated is "on the bridge." We have regarded it as a misprint for en el puerto, "in the port."

¹⁰⁰ This kingdom has disappeared. The ancient Ciampa, Tsiampa, or Zampa, was, according to certain Jesuit historians, the most powerful kingdom of Indochina. Its dominions extended from the banks of the Menam to the gulf of Ton-King. In some maps of the sixteenth century we have seen it reduced to the region now called Mois, and in others in the north of the present Cochinchina, while in later maps it disappears entirely. Probably the present Sieng-pang is the only city remaining of all its past antiquity.—Rizal.

¹⁰¹ That is, his mother and grandmother.

¹⁰² From which to conquer the country and the king gradually, for the latter was too credulous and confiding.—Rizal.

¹⁰³ Rizal misprints Malaca.

¹⁰⁴ Stanley thinks that this should read "since the war was not considered a just one;" but Rizal thinks this Blas Ruiz's own declaration, in order that he might claim his share of the booty taken, which he could not do if the war were unjust and the booty considered as a robbery.

¹⁰⁵ Aduarte says: "The matter was opposed by many difficulties and the great resistance of influential persons in the community, but as it was to be done without expense to the royal treasury, all were overcome."— Rizal.

La Concepcion says, vol. iii, p. 234, that the royal officials did not exercise the requisite care in the fitting of Luis Dasmarinas's vessels, as the expedition was not to their taste.

¹⁰⁶ A Chinese vessel, lighter and swifter than the junk, using oars and sails.

¹⁰⁷ Aduarte says that the fleet left the bay on September 17.—Rizal.

La Concepcion gives the same date, and adds that Dasmarinas took in his vessel, the flagship, Father Ximinez, while Aduarte sailed in the almiranta. The complement of men, sailors and soldiers was only one hundred and fifty. Aduarte left the expedition by command of the Dominican superior after the almiranta had put in to refit at Nueva Segovia, "as he [i.e., the superior] did not appear very favorable to such extraordinary undertakings." He returned with aid to Dasmarinas, sailing from Manila September 6, almost a year after the original expedition had sailed.

[108] The island of Corregidor, also called Mirabilis.—Rizal.

[109] The almiranta was wrecked because of striking some shoals, while pursuing a Chinese craft with piratical intent. The Spanish ship opened in two places and the crew were thrown into the sea. Some were rescued and arrested by the Chinese authorities.—Rizal.

La Concepcion says that the majority of the Spaniards determined to pursue and capture the Chinese vessel contrary to the advice of the pilot and a few others, and were consequently led into the shoals.

[110] This man became a religious later. We present his famous relation of 1621 in a later volume of this series. Hernando de los Rios was accompanied by Aduarte on his mission.

[111] It has been impossible to verify this citation. Of the four generally known histories of the Indias written at the time of Los Rios Coronel's letter, that of Las Casas only contains chapters of the magnitude cited, and those chapters do not treat of the demarcation question. Gonzalez Fernandez de Oviedo y Valdes: Historia general y natural de las Indias (Madrid, Imprenta de la Real Academia de la Historia, 1851), edited by Amador de los Rios, discusses the demarcation in book ii, ch. viii, pp. 32, 33, and book xxi, ch. ii, pp. 117, 118; Bartolome de las Casas: Historia de las Indias (Madrid, 1875), edited by Marquis de la Fuensanta del Valle (vols. 62-66 of Documentos ineditos para la historia de Espana), in book i, ch. lxxix, pp. 485, 486; Antonio de Herrera: Historia general de los Indios occidentalis (Madrid, 1601), in vol. i, ch. iiii, pp. 50-53, and ch. x, pp. 62-64; Joseph de Acosta: Historia de las Indias (first published in Spanish in Sevilla in 1590) does not discuss the matter. Neither is the reference to Giovanni Pietro Maffei's Historiarum Indicarum (Coloniae Agrippinae, 1590), where the demarcation is slightly mentioned.

[112] Costa in the original, misprinted cosa in Rizal.

[113] From the context, one would suppose that Los Rios Coronel wrote Jesuita instead of Theatino.

[114] Undoubtedly the famous Father Mateo Ricci, called Li-Ma-Teou and Si-Thai by the Chinese. He was born in Macerata in 1552, and died in Pekin in 1610. He was one of the greatest Chinese scholars of Europe, and wrote a number of works in Chinese, which were highly esteemed and appreciated by the Chinese themselves. He extended Christianity in the celestial empire more than anyone else, by his tolerance and keen diplomacy, by composing with great skill what he could not combat openly. This excited the wrath of the Dominicans, and gave rise to many controversies....Father Ricci was the associate of the famous Father Alessandro Valignani.—Rizal.

[115] The latitude of Toledo is 39° 52'; Nankin [Lanquien] 32°; and Pekin [Paquien] 39° 58'.

[116] The pico is a measure of weight. Gregorio Sancianco y Goson (El Progreso de Filipinas, Madrid, 1881) gives its table thus: 1 pico = 10 chinantes = 100 cates = 1 tael, 6 decimas = 137 libras, 5 decimas = 62 kilogramos, 262 gramos, 1 tael = 22 adarmes = 39 gramos, 60 centimos. The pico is not a fixed weight. In Manila its equivalent has been fixed at 137 libras, 6 decimas. In the ports of China and Singapore the English have adopted the following equivalents: 1 pico = 133 1/3 English pounds; 1 pico in Manila is equal to 140 English pounds; and 1 English pico equals 131.4 Castilian pounds.

[117] Certain shells found in the Philippines, and used as money in Siam, where they are called sigay.

[118] Father Juan Maldonado de San Pedro Martir was born in Alcala de Guadaira in the province of Sevilla. After a course in the humanities and philosophy, he went to Salamanca University to study canonical law. He made his profession at the Dominican convent in Valladolid, where he lived in great austerity. He was one of the first to respond to the call of Father Juan Crisostomo for workers in the Philippines. He was associated with Father Benavides in the Chinese mission, but was unable to learn the language because of other duties. He was later sent to Pangasinan, where, in 1588, he was appointed vicar of Gabon (now Calasiao). He was definitor in the Manila chapter in 1592, by which he was appointed vicar of Abucay, in the Bataan district. Shortly after he was again appointed to the Chinese work, and learned the language thoroughly. In 1596, while on the unfortunate voyage to Camboja, Father Alonso Jimenez appointed him vicar-general, but he resigned from this, as well as from the office of commissary-general of the Holy Office, which he was the first to hold in the islands. In 1598 he was appointed lecturer on theology, and in November of the same year went to Camboja. His death occurred within sight of Cochinchina, December 22, 1598, and he was buried in Pulocatouan. He was confessor to Luis Dasmarinas. (Resena Biografica, Manila, 1891.)

[119] Rizal misprints guardia de sus personas que podian, as guardia de sus personas que pedian.

[120] This happened afterward and was a constant menace to the Spaniards, as many letters, reports, and books attest.

[121] This was the first piratical expedition made against the Spaniards by the inhabitants of the southern islands.—Rizal.

Barrantes (Guerras Piraticas) wrongly dates the abandonment of La Caldera and the incursion of the Moros 1590. Continuing he says: "The following year they repeated the expedition so that the Indians retired to the densest parts of the forests, where it cost considerable trouble to induce them to become quiet. For a woman, who proclaimed herself a sibyl

289

or prophetess, preached to them that they should not obey the Spaniards any longer, for the latter had allied themselves with the Moros to exterminate all the Pintados."

[122] From the Malay tingi, a mountain.—Rizal.

[123] The island of Guimaras, southeast of Panay, and separated from it by the strait of Iloilo.

[124] Neither Stanley nor Rizal throws any light on this word. The Spanish dictionaries likewise fail to explain it, as does also a limited examination of Malay and Tagal dictionaries. Three conjectures are open: 1. A derivative of tifatas, a species of mollusk—hence a conch; 2. A Malay or Tagal word for either a wind or other instrument—the Malay words for "to blow," "to sound a musical instrument," being tiyup and tiyupkan; 3. A misprint for the Spanish pifas—a possible shorthand form of pifanos—signifying fifes.

[125] J. J. Rein (Japan, London, 1884) say that the son of Taicosama or Hideyoshi was called Hideyosi, and was born in 1592. He was recognized by Taicosama as his son, but Taicosama was generally believed not to have been his father. The Yeyasudono of Morga was Tokugawa Iyeyasu, lord of the Kuwanto, who was called Gieiaso by the Jesuits. He was already united by marriage to Taicosama. The men appointed with Iyeyasu to act as governors were Asano Nagamasa, Ishida, Mitsunari, Masuda Nagamori, Nagatsuka Masaiye, and Masuda Geni. Iyeyasu, the Daifusama of our text, tried to exterminate Christianity throughout the empire. He established the feudal system that ruled Japan for three centuries, dividing society into five classes, he himself being the most powerful vassal of the mikado. He framed a set of laws, known by his name, that were in force for three centuries. Their basis was certain doctrines of Confucius that recognized the family as the basis of the state. Iyeyasu was a true statesman, an attractive personage, and a peace-loving man. He was revered after death under the name of Gongensama. See also Trans. Asiatic Soc. (Yokohama), vol. iii, part ii, p. 118, "The Legacy of Iyeyasu."

[126] A manuscript in the British Museum, Dutch Memorable Embassies, says that he died September 16, 1598, at the age of sixty-four, after reigning fifteen years. The regent is there called Ongoschio.—Stanley.

[127] Recueil des voyages (Amsterdam, 1725) ii, pp. 94-95 divides Japanese society into five classes: those having power and authority over others, called tones, though their power may be dissimilar; priests or bonzes; petty nobility and bourgeoisie; mechanics and sailors; and laborers.

[128] This battle was fought at Sekigahara, a little village on the Nakasendo, in October, 1600. Some firearms and cannon were used but the

old-fashioned spears and swords predominated in this battle, which was fought fiercely all day. (Murray: Story of Japan, New York, 1894).

[129] John Calleway, of London, a musician, as stated in van Noordt's account.—Stanley.

[130] See appendix B, end of this volume, for resume of Dutch expeditions to the East Indies.

[131] Cuckara, the ladle formerly used to charge cannon which used no cartridge, but the loose powder from the barrel.

[132] The count of Essex, who in command of an English squadron captured the city of Cadiz in 1596. He sacked the city and killed many of the inhabitants, leaving the city in ruins. Drake in 1587 had burned several vessels in the same harbor.

[133] Called "San Antonio" above.

[134] Portuguese, above.

[135] The present port of Mariveles, as is seen from Colin's map.—Rizal.

[136] Juan Francisco Valdes was preacher in the convent of Santo Nino de Cebu in 1599, and was a missionary in Caruyan from 1600 until 1606. He died in 1617. Juan Gutierrez was assistant in the council [discreto] of the general chapter of his order of 1591. He returned to Manila after three years and was definitor and minister of Tondo in 1596, and of Paranaque 1602-1603. After that he returned to Rome a second time as definitor-general, whence he went to Mexico, where he exercised the duties of procurator in 1608. See Perez's Catalogo.

[137] Perhaps "in the direction of the island Del Fraile" is meant here, since no port of that name is known.—Rizal.

The expression occurs, however, in at least one other contemporaneous document.

[138] Now Punta de Fuego [i.e., Fire Promontory].—Rizal.

[139] The Dutch account of this combat says that their flagship carried fifty-three men before the fight, of whom only five were killed and twenty-six wounded.—Rizal.

[140] This is perhaps the brother of Fernando de los Rios Coronel, mentioned in his letter to Morga, ante, p. 180.

[141] This is the present Nasugbu, which is located in the present province of Batangas, a short distance below Punta de Fuego or Fire Promontory, on the west coast of Luzon.

[142] The governor appears to have ordered this execution of his own authority, without trial or the intervention of the Audiencia. Since the independence of Holland was not recognized by Spain until 1609, it is likely that these men were executed as rebels. If the ground was that they were pirates, the Dutchmen's own account of their burning villages, etc.,

where there were no Spaniards, is more damaging to themselves than the statements of Morga, and enough to make them out to have been hostes humani generis.—Stanley.

[143] Van Noordt was not wrecked, as will be seen later in this work. He returned to Holland after many misfortunes and adventures.—Rizal.

The Sunda is the strait between the islands of Sumatra and Java.

[144] Hernando de los Rios Coronel in his Memorial y Relacion attributes both the loss of these two vessels and also that of the "San Felipe" to Don Francisco Tello's indolence. "For this same reason other vessels were lost afterward—one called 'Santa Margarita,' which was wrecked in the Ladrones, another, called 'San Geronimo,' wrecked in the Catanduanes, near the channel of those islands, and a third which sailed from Cibu, called 'Jesus Maria.'" But the last-named, which sailed during Pedro de Acuna's administration, was not wrecked, as claimed by the above author.—Rizal.

[145] Port of Baras (?).—Rizal.

[146] Kachil Kota. Kachil is the title of the nobles. Kota or Kuta signifies fortress.—Rizal.

[147] Leonardo y Argensola (Conquesta de las Molucas, Madrid, 1609, pp. 262, 263), reproduces this letter translated into Spanish.

[148] These considerations were very narrow, and contrary to the international obligations of mutual assistance incurred by the Spanish by their trading with Japan; such treatment of Japan furnished that country with an additional motive for secluding itself and declining relations, the benefits of which were so one-sided: however, the Spaniards themselves may have felt this only nine years later, for, according to the Dutch Memorable Embassies, part i, p. 163, a large Spanish ship, commanded by Don Rodrigo de Riduera, came from Mexico to Wormgouw, near Yeddo, in August of 1611; these Spaniards were requesting permission from the Japanese emperor to sound the Japanese ports, because the Manila ships were frequently lost on the voyage to New Spain, for want of knowledge of those ports. "Moreover, these same Spaniards requested permission to build ships in Japan, because, both in New Spain and in the Philippines, there was a scarcity of timber fit for ships, and also of good workmen." In the Philippines there was no scarcity of timber, so that the statement to that effect was either an error of the Dutch author, or a pretext on the part of the Spaniards.—Stanley.

[149] The Dominican Francisco Morales was born at Madrid, October 14, 1567. He professed at the Valladolid convent, where he became lecturer on philosophy. In the same convent he fulfilled various duties until 1602, in which year it was determined to send him to Japan as vicar-general. With other missionaries he was driven from the kingdom of

Satzuma in 1609. Father Morales worked, however, in the capital until the persecution of 1614, when he remained hidden in the country. He was arrested March 15, 1619. A week after he was conducted, with other priests, to the island of Juquinoxima, distant three leagues from Nagasaki. In August they were removed to the prison of Ormura. On September 21, 1622, they were taken again to Nagasaki, where they were executed next day. He was beautified by order of the pope. He wrote La relacion del glorioso martirio de los BB. Alonso Navarrete y Hernando Ayala de San Jose, a quarto of thirty pages. (Resena Biografica, Manila, 1891.)

[150] The Augustinian Diego de Guevara was born in the town of Baeza, in the province of Jaen, of a noble family. He took the habit in Salamanca. He arrived at Manila in 1593 with twenty-four other religious of his order. In May, 1595, he was chosen sub-prior and procurator of Manila, and in June definitor and discreto [i.e., assistant in the council] to the general chapter. He was wrecked at Japan while on his way to attend the chapter at Rome, however, and returned to Manila with Father Juan Tamayo, his companion. After the Chinese insurrection in Manila in 1603, he was sent to Spain, which he reached by way of Rome. He remained for three years in San Felipe el Real, but was again sent (1610) to the islands, as visitor of the Augustinian province. From 1616-1621 he was bishop of Nueva Caceres, dying in the latter year. He was the author of various Actas, which have been used extensively by the province. (Catalogo de los Agustinos, Manila, 1901.)

[151] Santa Ines mentions this religious as one of those sent back to Manila by way of a Portuguese vessel about to sail to Portuguese India, at the time of the persecution.

[152] Probably the Sibukaw.—Rizal. This tree—also spelled sibucao—grows to a height of twelve or fifteen feet. Its flowers grow in clusters, their calyx having five sepals. The pod is woody and ensiform and contains three or four seeds, separated by spongy partition-walls. The wood is so hard that nails are made of it, while it is used as a medicine. It is a great article of commerce as a dye, because of the beautiful red color that it yields.

[153] The Philippines then exported silk to Japan, whence today comes the best silk.—Rizal.

[154] These must be the precious ancient china jars that are even yet found in the Philippines. They are dark gray in color, and are esteemed most highly by the Chinese and Japanese.—Rizal.

[155] From this point the Rizal edition lacks to the word and in the second sentence following. The original reads: "que hizieron su camino por tierra. Entre tanto, se padecian en la nao muchas molestias, de los Iapones que auia en el puerto."

293

[156] The word in the original is cabria, which signifies literally the sheers or machine for raising a temporary mast. It is evidently used here for the mast itself.

[157] Perhaps to perform the hara-kiri, which was an ancient custom among the Japanese, and consisted in the criminal's making an incision in his abdomen, and then afterward sinking the knife in his bosom, or above the clavicle, in order to run it through the heart. Then the victim's head was cut off with a stroke of the sword.—Rizal.

[158] Andrea Furtado de Mendoza began his military career at the age of sixteen, when he accompanied King Sebastian on his ill-fated expedition to Morocco. A year or two later he went to India and became famous by his relief of Barcelor. He had charge of many arduous posts and achieved many military and naval successes. He opposed the Dutch attempts of Matelief at Malacca. In 1609, he was elected as thirty-seventh Portuguese governor of India, and filled the office with great credit to himself and country. (Voyage of Pyrard de Laval, Hakluyt Society ed., London, 1888, part i, vol. ii, p. 267, note 3.)

[159] The accounts of voyages made for the Dutch East India Company (Recueil des voyages, Amsterdam, 1725) mention a town Jaffanapatan in Ceylon, evidently the Jabanapatan of our text.

[160] Hernando de los Rios attributed to these wars of the Moluccas the reason why the Philippines were at first more costly than profitable to the king, in spite of the immense sacrifices of the inhabitants in the almost gratuitous construction of galleons, in their equipment, etc.; and in spite of the tribute, duty, and other imposts and taxes. These Molucca expeditions, so costly to the Philippines, depopulated the islands and depleted the treasury, without profiting the country at all, for they lost forever and shortly what had been won there so arduously. It is also true that the preservation of the Philippines for Spain must be attributed to the Moluccas, and one of the powerful arguments presented to Felipe II as to the advisability of sustaining those islands was for the possession of the rich spice islands.—Rizal.

[161] Argensola says that the following things were also sent for this expedition: "300 blankets from Ilocos, 700 varas of wool from Castilla, 100 sail-needles, and 30 jars of oil; while the whole cost of the fleet amounted to 22,260 pesos per month." The expedition, which was profitless, lasted six months.—Rizal.

[162] See VOLS. XII and XII for documents concerning the coming of these mandarins, and the subsequent Chinese insurrection.

[163] Ignacio or Inigo de Santa Maria, of the Dominican convent of Salamanca, on arriving at the Philippines, was sent to Cagayan. He was later elected prior of the Manila convent, and then definitor. In 1603 he

went to Camboja as superior of that mission. Returning thence for more workers that same year, he died at sea. (Resena Biografica, Manila, 1891.)

[164] Diego de Soria was born in Yebenes, in the province and diocese of Toledo, and took the Dominican habit in Ocana. Showing signs of a great preacher he was sent to the College of Santo Tomas in Alcala de Henares. Thence he went to Manila in 1587 and was one of the founders of the Dominican convent in Manila, of which he was vicar-president until June 10, 1588, when he was chosen its prior in the first provincial chapter of the Philippine province. In 1591 he was sent to Pangasinan, where he remained until 1595, whence he was sent to Cagayan at the instance of Luis Perez Dasmarinas. In 1596, after many successes in Cagayan, he was recalled to Manila as prior of the convent for the second time. Shortly after he was sent to Spain and Rome as procurator. He refused the nomination to the bishopric of Nueva Caceres, but was compelled to accept that of Nueva Segovia, and reached the islands somewhat later. In 1608 he was in Vigan, his residence. He died in 1613 and was buried in the parish church of Vigan. In 1627 his remains were removed to the Dominican convent at Lallo-c, in accordance with his wishes. (Resena Biografica, Manila, 1891.)

[165] Buzeta and Bravo say that Baltasar Covarrubias was appointed to the bishopric in 1604, at which time he entered upon his duties; but that he died in 1607 without having been consecrated.

[166] Copied and condensed from Purchas: His Pilgrimes (London, 1625), book ii, chap. iiii, pp. 55-71, "the third circumnavigation of the globe." For other accounts of Candish, see Purchas: ut supra, iv, book vi, chap. vi, pp. 1192-1201, and chap. vii, pp. 1210-1242; Bry: Collectiones peregrinationum (Francofurti, 1625), ser. i, vol. iii, pars viii, pp. 35-59; Pieter van der Aa: Zee en landreysen (Leyden, 1706) xx deel, pp. 1-64; and Hakluyt's Voyages (Goldsmid ed., Edinburgh, 1890), xvi, pp. 1-84.

[167] The area of England and Wales is 58,186 sq. mi., that of Scotland, with its 787 islands, 30,417 (mainland 26,000) sq. mi., and that of Luzon, about 41,000 sq. mi.

[168] See also VOL. XI of this series.

[169] Oliver van Noordt was the first Dutch circumnavigator. For an account of the fight with the Spanish from the side of the Dutch, see Stanley's translation of Morga, pp. 173-187.

[170] "L'Amsterdam ... avoit ete amene a Manille avec 51 morts a son bord ... que le yacht le Faucon en avoit 34   que le Faucon avoit ete aussi emmene avec 22 morts."

[171] Spanish accounts, some of which will be published later in this series, relate Spielberg's bombardment of Iloilo, and his defeat, after dis-

embarking by Diego Quinones in 1616; while he was later completely defeated by Juan Ronquillo at Playa Honda, in 1617.

[172] Following in a translation of the title-page of the other edition of Morga's work, which shows that a second edition of the Sucesos was published in the same year as was the first. A reduced facsimile of this title-page—from the facsimile reproduction in the Zaragoza edition (Madrid, 1887)—forms the frontispiece to the present volume. It reads thus: "Events in the Philipinas Islands: addressed to Don Christoval Gomez de Sandoval y Rojas, duke de Cea, by Doctor Antonio de Morga, alcalde of criminal causes in the royal Audiencia of Nueva Espana, and consultor for the Holy Office of the Inquisition. At Mexico in the Indias, in the year 1609." In the lower left-hand corner of the engraved title appears the engraver's name: "Samuel Estradanus, of Antwerp, made this."

[173] The month is omitted in the text.—Stanley.

[174] Fray Diego Bermeo, a native of Toledo, became a Franciscan friar; and in 1580 went to Mexico, and three years later to the Philippines. After spending many years as a missionary in Luzon and Mindoro, he was elected provincial of his order in the islands (in 1599, and again in 1608). Going to Japan as commissary provincial—in 1603, according to Morga, but 1604 as given by Huerta (Estado, p. 446)—he was obliged by severe illness to return to Manila; he died there on December 12, 1609.

[175] Luis Sotelo, belonging to an illustrious family of Sevilla, made his profession as a Franciscan in 1594. Joining the Philippine mission, he reached the islands in 1600; and he spent the next two years in ministering to the Japanese near Manila, and in the study of their language. In 1600 he went to Japan, where he zealously engaged in missionary labors. Ten years later, he was sentenced to death for preaching the Christian religion; but was freed from this danger by Mazamune, king of Boxu, who sent the Franciscan as his ambassador to Rome and Madrid. Returning from this mission, Sotelo arrived in the Philippines in 1618, and four years later resumed his missionary labors in Japan. In 1622 he was again imprisoned for preaching, and was confined at Omura for two years, during which time he wrote several works, in both the Spanish and Japanese languages. Sotelo was finally burned at the stake in Omura, August 25, 1624. See Huerta's Estado, pp. 392-394.

[176] The present towns of San Nicolas, San Fernando, etc., lying between Binondo and the sea.—Rizal.

[177] This remark of Morga can be applied to many other insurrections that occurred later—not only of Chinese, but also of natives—and probably even to many others which, in the course of time, will be contrived.—Rizal.

¹⁷⁸ These devices, of which certain persons always avail themselves to cause a country to rebel, are the most efficacious to bring such movements to a head. "If thou wishest thy neighbor's dog to become mad, publish that it is mad," says an old refrain.—Rizal.

¹⁷⁹ This is the famous Eng-Kang of the histories of Filipinas.—Rizal.

¹⁸⁰ The Rizal edition of Morga omits the last part of this sentence, the original of which is "entre vnos esteros y cienagas, lugar escondido."

¹⁸¹ "The Chinese killed father Fray Bernardo de Santo Catalina, agent of the holy office, of the order of St. Dominic … They attacked Quiapo, and after killing about twenty people, set fire to it. Among these they burned alive a woman of rank, and a boy."—Rizal. This citation is made from Leonardo de Argensola's Conquistas de las Molucas (Madrid, 1609), a synopsis of which will follow Morga's work.

¹⁸² We are unaware of the exact location of this settlement of Laguio. It is probably the present village of Kiapo, which agrees with the text and is mentioned by Argensola. Nevertheless, from the description of this settlement given by Morga (post, chapter viii) and Chirino, it can be inferred that Laguio was located on the present site of the suburb of La Concepcion. In fact, there is even a street called Laguio between Malate and La Ermita.—Rizal.

¹⁸³ "Fine helmets were found broken in with clubs… About thirty also escaped (among whom was Father Farfan), who were enabled to do so because of being in the rear, and lightly armed" (Argensola).—Rizal.

¹⁸⁴ Argensola says that the Chinese killed many peaceful merchants in the parian, while others hanged themselves of their own accord. Among these Argensola mentions General Hontay and the rich Chican—according to the relation of Fray Juan Pobre, because the latter had refused to place the famous Eng-Kang at the head of the movement.—Rizal.

¹⁸⁵ "And they tried to persuade the natives to unite with them; but the latter refused, and on the contrary killed as many of the Sangleys as they caught" (Argensola).—Rizal.

¹⁸⁶ Argensola says that "four thousand Pampangos, armed in the custom of their country, with bows and arrows, half-pikes, shields, and long broad daggers," were sent by the alcalde of Pampanga to the relief of Manila, which now needed soldiers.—Rizal.

¹⁸⁷ In this struggle many cruelties were committed and many quiet and friendly Chinese killed. Don Pedro de Acuna, who could not prevent or stifle this terrible insurrection in its beginnings, also contributed to the horrible butcheries that ensued. "Accordingly many Spaniards and natives went to hunt the disbanded Sangleys, at Don Pedro's order."

297

Hernando de Avalos, alcalde of La Pampanga, seized more than 400 pacific Sangleys, "and leading them to an estuary, manacled two and two, delivered them to certain Japanese, who killed them. Father Fray Diego de Guevara of the order of St. Augustine, prior of Manila, who made this relation, preached to the Sangleys first, but only five abandoned their idolatry." … Would he not have done better to preach to Alcalde Avalos, and to remind him that he was a man? The Spanish historians say that the Japanese and Filipinos showed themselves cruel in the killing of the Chinese. It is quite probable, considering the rancor and hate with which they were regarded. But their commanders contributed to it also by their example. It is said that more than 23,000 Chinese were killed. "Some assert that the number of Sangleys killed was greater, but in order that the illegality committed in allowing so many to enter the country contrary to the royal prohibitions might not be known, the officials covered up or diminished the number of those who perished" (Argensola).—Rizal.

[188] The coming of the Spaniards to the Filipinas, and their government, together with the immigration of the Chinese, killed the industry and agriculture of the country. The terrible competition of the Chinese with any individual of another race is well known, for which reason the United States and Australia refuse to admit them. The indolence, then, of the inhabitants of the Filipinas, is derived from the lack of foresight of the government. Argensola says the same thing, and could not have copied Morga, since their works were published in the same year, in countries very distant from one another, and the two contain wide differences.—Rizal.

The Chinese question has always been of great importance in the Philippines. The dislike of the Filipino for the Chinese seemed instinctive and was deep-rooted. The subject of the Chinese immigration to the islands has served for special legislation on many occasions in Spain, but they have nevertheless persisted in their trading and occupations therein. See Stanley's edition of Morga, appendix II, pp. 363-368; and Los Chinos en Filipinos (Manila, 1886).

[189] This should be six hundred and four.—Rizal.

[190] Nueva Espana.—Rizal.

[191] This archbishop seems to have been a principal cause of the disturbance and massacre of the Chinese, by taking a leading part in exciting suspicion against them.—Stanley.

[192] The Arab travelers of the ninth century mention that eunuchs were employed in China, especially for the collection of the revenue, and that they were called thoucam.—Stanley.

[193] "In earlier times a barrier, which ran from Osaka to the border of Yamato and Omi, separated the thirty-three western from the thirty-three

eastern provinces. The former were collectively entitled Kuwansei (pronounce Kanse), i.e., westward of the Gate; the latter Kuwanto (pronounce Kanto), i.e., eastward of the Gate. Later, however, when under the Tokugawa regime the passes leading to the plain in which Yedo, the new capital of Shogune, grew up were carefully guarded; by the Gate (Kuwan) was understood the great guard on the Hakone Pass, and Kuwanto or Kuwanto-Hashiu, the eight provinces east of it: Sagami, Musashi, Kotsuke, Shimotsuke, Hitachi, Shimosa, Katsusa, and Awa." Thus defined by Rein, in his Japan, p. II, Cf. Griffis, Mikado's Empire, p. 68, note.

[194] A flat-bottomed boat, capable of carrying heavy loads.

[195] Pedro Alvares de Abreu.—Rizal.

[196] According to Argensola, who gives a succinct relation of this expedition, the number engaged in it were as follows: Spaniards and their officers, 1,423; Pampangos and Tagals (without their chiefs), 344; idem, for maritime and military service, 620; rowers, 649; Indian chiefs, 5; total 3,041. But he adds that all those of the fleet, exclusive of the general's household and followers, numbered 3,095. Probably the 54 lacking in the above number were the Portuguese under command of Abreu and Camelo, although Argensola does not mention Portuguese soldiers.... The names of the Indian chiefs attending the expedition at their own cost were: Don Guillermo (Palaot), master-of-camp; and Captains Don Francisco Palaot, Don Juan Lit, Don Luis Lont, and Don Agustin Lont. These must have behaved exceedingly well, for after the assault on Ternate, Argensola says: "Not a person of consideration among the Spaniards or the Indians remained unwounded."—Rizal.

[197] Said Dini Baraka ja.—Rizal.

[198] Combes (Mindanao, Retana's ed., cols. 73, 74) describes the bagacay as a small, slender reed, hardened in fire and sharp-pointed; it is hurled by a Moro at an enemy with unerring skill, and sometimes five are discharged in one volley. He narrates surprising instances of the efficacy of this weapon, and says that "there is none more cruel, at close range."

[199] Stanley translates this "flat-boats." Retana and Pastells (Combes's Mindanao, col. 787) derive this word from Chinese chun, "a boat," and regard the joanga (juanga) as a small junk.

[200] "The soldiers, having entered the city, gave themselves universally to violence and pillage. Don Pedro had issued a proclamation conceding that all of the enemy captured within those four days, should be slaves" (Argensola). During the sack, which Don Pedro was unable to restrain, neither children nor young girls were spared. One girl was killed because two soldiers disputed for her.—Rizal.

[201] "The prince's name was Sulamp Gariolano. This step was contrary to the advice of Queen Celicaya" (Argensola).—Rizal.

[202] Sangajy, a Malay title (Marsden).—Stanley.

[203] The Jesuit Father Luis Fernandez, Gallinato, and Esquivel made negotiations with the king for this exile, and Father Colin attributes its good outcome to the cleverness of the former. What was then believed to be prudent resulted afterward as an impolitic measure, and bore very fatal consequences; for it aroused the hostility of all the Molucas, even that of their allies, and made the Spanish name as odious as was the Portuguese. The priest Hernando de los Rios, Bokemeyer, and other historians, moreover, accuse Don Pedro de Acuna of bad faith in this; but, strictly judged, we believe that they do so without foundation. Don Pedro in his passport assured the lives of the king and prince, but not their liberty. Doubtless a trifle more generosity would have made the conqueror greater, and the odium of the Spanish name less, while it would have assured Spanish domination of that archipelago. The unfortunate king never returned to his own country. Hernando de los Rios says that during Don Pedro de Acuna's life he was well treated, but that during the administration of Don Juan de Silva "I have seen him in a poor lodging where all the rain fell on him, and they were starving him to death." He is described by Argensola as of "robust proportions, and his limbs are well formed. His neck and much of his breast are bare. His flesh is of a cloudy color, rather black than gray. The features of his face are like those of an European. His eyes are large and full, and he seems to dart sparks from them. His large eyelashes, his thick bristling beard, and his mustaches add to his fierceness. He always wears his campilan, dagger, and kris, both with hilts in the form of gilded serpents' heads." This description was taken from a picture sent to Spain.—Rizal.

[204] Other disturbances occurred also, because of Don Pedro's enemies having spread the news that the expedition had been destroyed, and most of those making it killed. "This report, having come to the ears of the Indians, was so harmful that they began to mutiny, especially in the provinces of Camarines and Pintados. The friars who instructed them could already do, nothing with them, for they asked why, since the inhabitants of the Malucos were victorious, should they be subject to the Spaniards, who did not defend them from the Moros. They said that the Moros would plunder them daily with the help of Ternate, and that it would be worse henceforth" (Argensola).—Rizal.

La Concepcion states (Hist. de Philipinas, iv, p. 103) that these Japanese were settled in Dilao; and that the immediate cause of their mutiny was the killing of a Japanese by a Spaniard, in a quarrel.

[205] The authors of this poisoning were then known in Manila, and according to Argensola were those envious of the governor. "But although they were known as such, so that the suspicion of the crowd makes them the authors of the poisoning we shall repress their names ... for all are now dead" (Argensola).—Rizal.

Cf. La Concepcion (Hist. de Philipinas, iv, pp. 105, 106); he ascribes the report of Acuna's poisoning to the physicians, who sought thus to shield their own ignorance of his disease.

[206] These were the results of having taken the king and his chiefs, who had entrusted themselves to Don Pedro de Acuna, prisoners to Manila, the king of Tidore, the ally of Espana, had already found means to break the alliance. The governors appointed by the captive king refused to have anything to do with the Spaniards. Fear was rampant in all parts, and the spirit of vengeance was aroused. "When his vassals saw the ill-treatment that the Spaniards inflicted on their king, they hated us so much that they acquired an equal liking for our enemies. (Her. de los Rios)." Don Pedro lacked the chief characteristic of Legazpi.—Rizal.

[207] This relation forms an appendix to Theodore de Bry's Ninth part of America (Frankfort, 1601), and was printed by Matthew Becker (Frankfort, 1602). The copper plates are different from those of the Dutch edition of the relation.—Stanley.

The plates representing Oliver van Noordt's fleet, presented in the preceding volume, are taken from tome xvi of Theodore de Bry's Peregrinationes (first ed.), by courtesy of the Boston Public Library. The title-page of the relation reads in part: "Description dv penible voyage faict entovr de l'univers ou globe terrestre, par Sr. Olivier dv Nort d'Avtrecht, ... Le tout translate du Flamand en Franchois, . . . Imprime a Amsterdame. Ches Cornille Claessz fur l'Eau au Livre a Escrire, l'An 1602." This relation was reprinted in 1610, and numerous editions have appeared since.

[208] One of the Canary Islands.

[209] This anchor was given him by a Japanese captain, in Manila Bay, on December 3, 1600.—Stanley.

[210] What we now call Java used to be called Java major, and the island of Bali was Java minor.—Stanley.[*]

---

[*] Inasmuch as Morga enters somewhat largely into the ancient customs of the Tagals and other Filipino peoples in the present chapter, and as some of Rizal's notes indicative of the ancient culture of those peoples are incorporated in notes that follow, we deem it advisable to invite attention to Lord Stanley's remarks in the preface to his translation of Morga (p. vii), and Pardo de Tavera's comment in his Biblioteca Filipina (Washington, 1903), p. 276. Stanley says: "The inhabi-

[211] More exactly from 25° 40' north latitude to 12° south latitude, if we are to include Formosa in the group, which is inhabited likewise by the same race.—Rizal.

[212] We confess our ignorance with respect to the origin of this belief of Morga, which, as one can observe, was not his belief in the beginning of the first chapter. Already from the time of Diodorus Siculus (first century B. C.), Europe received information of these islands by one Iamboule, a Greek, who went to them (to Sumatra at least), and who wrote afterward the relation of his voyage. He gave therein detailed information of the number of the islands, of their inhabitants, of their writing, navigation, etc. Ptolemy mentions three islands in his geography, which are called Sindae in the Latin text. They are inhabited by the Aginnatai. Mercator interprets those islands as Celebes, Gilolo, and Amboina. Ptolemy also mentions the island Agathou Daimonos (Borneo), five Baroussai (Mindanao, Leite, Sebu, etc.), three Sabadeibai (the Java group—Iabadiou) and ten Masniolai where a large loadstone was found. Colin surmises that these are the Manilas.—Rizal.

Colin (Labor Evangelica, Madrid, 1663) discusses the discovery and naming of the Philippines. He quotes Ptolemy's passage that speaks of islands called the Maniolas, whence many suppose came the name Manilas, sometimes given to the islands. But as pointed out in a letter dated March 14, 1904, by James A. LeRoy, Spanish writers have wasted more time on the question than it merits. Mr. LeRoy probably conjectures rightly that many old Chinese and Japanese documents will be found to contain matter relating to the Philippines prior to the Spanish conquest.

---

tants of the Philippines previous to the Spanish settlement were not like the inhabitants of the great Indian Peninsula, people with a civilization as that of their conquerors. Excepting that they possessed the art of writing, and an alphabet of their own, they do not appear to have differed in any way from the Dayaks of Borneo as described by Mr. Boyle in his recent book of adventures amongst that people. Indeed there is almost a coincidence of verbal expressions in the descriptions he and De Morga give of the social customs, habits, and superstitions of the two peoples they are describing; though many of these coincidences are such as are incidental to life in similar circumstances, there are enough to lead one to suppose a community of origin of the inhabitants of Borneo and Luzon." Pardo de Tavera says after quoting the first part of the above: "Lord Stanley's opinion is dispassionate and not at all at variance with historical truth." The same author says also that Blumentritt's prologue and Rizal's notes in the latter's edition of Morga have so aroused the indignation of the Spaniards that several have even attacked Morga.

213 It is very difficult now to determine exactly which is this island of Tendaya, called Isla Filipina for some years. According to Father Urdaneta's relations, this island was far to the east of the group, past the meridian of Maluco. Mercator locates it in Panay, and Colin in Leyte, between Abuyog and Cabalian—contrary to the opinion of others, who locate it in Ibabao, or south of Samar. But according to other documents of that period, there is no island by that name, but a chief called Tendaya, lord of a village situated in that district; and, as the Spaniards did not understand the Indians well at that time, many contradictions thus arose in the relations of that period. We see that, in Legazpi's expedition, while the Spaniards talked of islands, the Indians talked of a man, etc. After looking for Tandaya for ten days they had to continue without finding it "and we passed on without seeing Tandaya or Abuyo." It appears, nevertheless, that the Spaniards continued to give this name to the southwestern part of Samar, calling the southeastern part Ibabao or Zibabao and the northern part of the same island Samar.—Rizal.

214 Sugbu, in the dialect of the country.—Rizal.

215 Morga considers the rainy season as winter, and the rest of the year as summer. However this is not very exact, for at Manila, in December, January, and February, the thermometer is lower than in the months of August and September. Consequently, in its seasons it is like those of Espana and those of all the rest of the northern hemisphere.—Rizal.

216 The ancient traditions made Sumatra the original home of the Filipino Indians. These traditions, as well as the mythology and genealogies mentioned by the ancient historians, were entirely lost, thanks to the zeal of the religious in rooting out every national pagan or idolatrous record. With respect to the ethnology of the Filipinas, see Professor Blumentritt's very interesting work, Versuch einer Etnographie der Philippinen (Gotha, Justus Perthes, 1882).—Rizal.

217 This passage contradicts the opinion referred to in Boyle's Adventures among the Dyaks of Borneo, respecting the ignorance of the Dyaks in the use of the bow, which seems to imply that other South Sea islanders are supposed to share this ignorance. These aboriginal savages of Manila resemble the Pakatans of Borneo in their mode of life. - Stanley.

218 We do not know the origin of this word, which does not seem to be derived from China. If we may make a conjecture, we will say that perhaps a poor phonetic transcription has made chinina from the word tinina (from tina) which in Tagal signifies tenido ["dyed stuff"], the name of this article of clothing, generally of but one color throughout. The chiefs wore these garments of a red color, which made, according to Colin, "of fine gauze from India."—Rizal.

[219] Bahag "a richly dyed cloth, generally edged with gold" among the chiefs.—Rizal.

[220] "They wrapped it in different ways, now in the Moro style, like a turban without the top part, now twisted and turned in the manner of the crown of a hat. Those who esteemed themselves valiant let the ends of the cloth, elaborately embroidered, fall down the back to the buttocks. In the color of the cloth, they showed their chieftaincy, and the device of their undertakings and prowess. No one was allowed to use the red potong until he had killed at least one man. And in order to wear them edged with certain edgings, which were regarded as a crown, they must have killed seven men" (Colin). Even now any Indian is seen to wear the balindang in the manner of the putong. Putong signifies in Tagal, "to crown" or "to wrap anything around the head."—Rizal.

[221] This is the reading of the original (cera hilada). It seems more probable that this should read "spun silk," and that Morga's amanuensis misunderstood seda ("silk") as cera ("wax"), or else it is a misprint.

[222] "They also have strings of bits of ivory" (Colin).—Rizal.

[223] "The last complement of the gala dress was, in the manner of our sashes, a richly dyed shawl crossed at the shoulder and fastened under the arm" (even today the men wear the lambong or mourning garment in this manner) "which was very usual with them. The Bisayans, in place of this, wore robes or loose garments, well made and collarless, reaching to the instep, and embroidered in colors. All their costume, in fact, was in the Moorish manner, and was truly elegant and rich; and even today they consider it so" (Colin).—Rizal.

[224] This manner of headdress, and the long robe of the Visayans, have an analogy with the Japanese coiffure and kimono.—Rizal.

[225] Baro.—Rizal.

[226] A tree (Entada purseta) which grows in most of the provinces of the Philippines. It contains a sort of filament, from which is extracted a soapy foam, which is much used for washing clothes. This foam is also used to precipitate the gold in the sand of rivers. Rizal says the most common use is that described above.

[227] This custon still exists.—Rizal.

[228] This custom exists also among the married women of Japan, as a sign of their chastity. It is now falling into disuse.—Rizal.

[229] The Filipinos were careful not to bathe at the hour of the siesta, after eating, during the first two days of a cold, when they have the herpes, and some women during the period of menstruation.—Rizal.

[230] This work, although not laborious, is generally performed now by the men, while the women do only the actual cleaning of the rice.—Rizal.

²³¹ This custom is still to be seen in some parts.—Rizal.

²³² A name given it by the Spaniards. Its Tagal name is kanin.—Rizal.

²³³ The fish mentioned by Morga is not tainted, but is the bagoong.—Rizal.

²³⁴ A term applied to certain plants (Atmaranthus, Celosia, etc.) of which the leaves are boiled and eaten.

²³⁵ From the Tagal tuba, meaning sap or juice.—Rizal.

²³⁶ The Filipinos have reformed in this respect, due perhaps to the wine-monopoly. Colin says that those intoxicated by this wine were seldom disagreeable or dangerous, but rather more witty and sprightly; nor did they show any ill effects from drinking it.—Rizal.

²³⁷ This weapon has been lost, and even its name is gone. A proof of the decline into which the present Filipinos have fallen is the comparison of the weapons that they manufacture now, with those described to us by the historians. The hilts of the talibones now are not of gold or ivory, nor are their scabbards of horn, nor are they admirably wrought.—Rizal.

Balarao, dagger, is a Vissayan word.—Stanley.

²³⁸ The only other people who now practice head-hunting are the Mentenegrins.—Stanley.

²³⁹ A Tagal word meaning oar.—Stanley.

²⁴⁰ A common device among barbarous or semi-civilized peoples, and even among boatmen in general. These songs often contain many interesting and important bits of history, as well as of legendary lore.

²⁴¹ Karang, signifying awnings.—Rizal and Stanley.

²⁴² The Filipinos, like the inhabitants of the Marianas—who are no less skilful and dexterous in navigation—far from progressing, have retrograded; since, although boats are now built in the islands, we might assert that they are all after European models. The boats that held one hundred rowers to a side and thirty soldiers have disappeared. The country that once, with primitive methods, built ships of about 2,000 toneladas, today ¹⁸⁹⁰ has to go to foreign ports, as Hong-Kong, to give the gold wrenched from the poor, in exchange for unserviceable cruisers. The rivers are blocked up, and navigation in the interior of the islands is perishing, thanks to the obstacles created by a timid and mistrusting system of government; and there scarcely remains in the memory anything but the name of all that naval architecture. It has vanished, without modern improvements having come to replace it in such proportion as, during the past centuries, has occurred in adjacent countries....—Rizal.

[243] It seems that some species of trees disappeared or became very scarce because of the excessive ship-building that took place later. One of them is the betis.—Rizal.

Blanco states (Flora, ed. 1845, p. 281) that the betis (Azaola betis) was common in Pampanga and other regions.

Delgado describes the various species of trees in the Philippines in the first six treatises of the first part of the fourth book of Historia general de Filipinas (Manila, 1892). He mentions by name more than seventy trees grown on the level plains and near the shores; more than forty fruit-trees; more than twenty-five species grown in the mountains; sixteen that actually grow in the water; and many kinds of palms. See also Gazetteer of the Philippine Islands (Washington, 1902), pp. 85-95, and Buzeta and Bravo's Diccionario (Madrid, 1850), i, pp. 29-36.

[244] Sanctor is called santol (Sandoricum indicum—Cavanilles), in Delgado (ut supra, note 71). The tree resembles a walnut-tree. Its leaves are rounded and as large as the palm of the hand, and are dark green in color. Excellent preserves are made from the fruit, which was also eaten raw by the Indians. The leaves of the tree have medicinal properties and were used as poultices. Mabolo (Diospyros discolor—Willd.) signifies in Tagal a thing or fruit enclosed in a soft covering. The tree is not very high. The leaves are large, and incline to a red color when old. The fruit is red and as large as a medium-sized quince, and has several large stones. The inside of the fruit is white, and is sweet and firm, and fragrant, but not very digestible. The wood resembles ebony, is very lustrous, and is esteemed for its solidity and hardness. The nanca [nangka, nangca; translated by Stanley, jack-fruit] (Artocarpus integrifolia—Willd.), was taken to the Philippines from India, where it was called yaca. The tree is large and wide-spreading, and has long narrow leaves. It bears fruit not only on the branches, but on the trunk and roots. The fruit is gathered when ripe, at which time it exhales an aromatic odor. On opening it a yellowish or whitish meat is found, which is not edible. But in this are found certain yellow stones, with a little kernel inside resembling a large bean; this is sweet, like the date, but has a much stronger odor. It is indigestible, and when eaten should be well masticated. The shells are used in cooking and resemble chestnuts. The wood is yellow, solid, and especially useful in making certain musical instruments. Buzeta and Bravo (Diccionario, i, p. 35) say that there are more than fifty-seven species of bananas in the Philippines.

[245] Pile (Canarium commune—Linn.). Delgado (ut supra) says that this was one of the most notable and useful fruits of the islands. It was generally confined to mountainous regions and grew wild. The natives used the fruit and extracted a white pitch from the tree. The fruit has a

strong, hard shell. The fruit itself resembles an almond, both in shape and taste, although it is larger. The tree is very high, straight, and wide-spreading. Its leaves are larger than those of the almond-tree.

246 Delgado (ut supra) describes the tree (Cedrela toona—Roxb.) called calanta in Tagal, and lanipga in Visayan. The tree is fragrant and has wood of a reddish color. It was used for making the hulls of vessels, because of its strength and lightness. The same author describes also the asana (Pterocarpus indicus—Willd.) or as it is called in the Visayas, naga or narra—as an aromatic tree, of which there are two varieties, male and female. The wood of the male tree is pinkish, while that of the female tree is inclined to white. They both grow to a great size and are used for work requiring large timber. The wood has good durable qualities and is very impervious to water, for which reason it was largely used as supports for the houses. Water in which pieces of the wood were placed, or the water that stood in vessels made of this wood, had a medicinal value in dropsy and other diseases. In the provinces of Albay and Camarines the natives made curiously-shaped drinking vessels from this wood.

247 So many cattle were raised that Father Gaspar de San Agustin, when speaking of Dumangas, says: "In this convent we have a large ranch for the larger cattle, of so many cows that they have at times numbered more than thirty, thousand ... and likewise this ranch contains many fine horses."—Rizal.

248 To the flesh of this fowl, called in Tagal ulikba, are attributed medicinal virtues.—Rizal.

249 These animals now 1890 exist in the islands, but are held in small esteem.—Rizal.

250 See chapter on the mammals of the islands, in Report of U. S. Philippine Commission, 1900, iii, pp. 307-312. At its end is the statement that but one species of monkey is known, and one other is reported, to exist in the Philippines; and that "the various other species of monkey which have been assigned to the Philippines by different authors are myths pure and simple."

251 Camalote, for gamalote, a plant like maize, with a leaf a yard long and an inch wide. This plant grows to a height of two yards and a half, and when green serves for food for horses (Caballero's Dictionary, Madrid, 1856).—Stanley.

At that time the name for zacate (hay).—Rizal.

252 In Japanese fimbari, larks (Medhurst's Japanese Vocabulary).—Stanley.

253 Pogos, from the Tagal pugo.—Rizal.

Delgado (ut supra) describes the pogos as certain small gray birds, very similar to the sparrows in Spain. They are very greedy, and if undisturbed would totally destroy the rice-fields. Their scientific name is Ex-calfactoria chinensis (Linn.).

[254] Stanley conjectures that this word is a misprint for maynelas, a diminutive of maina, a talking bird. Delgado (ut supra) describes a bird called maya (Munia jagori—Cab.; Ploceus baya—Blyth.; and Ploceus hy-poxantha—Tand.), which resembles the pogo, being smaller and of a cinnamon color, which pipes and has an agreeable song.

[255] Stanley translates this as "wild ducks." Delgado (ut supra) de-scribes a bird called lapay (Dendrocygna vagans—Eyton.), as similar to the duck in body, but with larger feet, which always lives in the water, and whose flesh is edible.

[256] For descriptions of the birds in the Philippines, see Delgado (ut supra) book v, part i, 1st treatise, pp. 813-853; Report of U.S. Philippine Commission, 1900, iii, pp. 312-316; and Gazetteer of the Philippine Is-lands (Washington, 1902), pp. 170, 171. There are more than five hundred and ninety species of birds in the islands, of which three hun-dred and twenty-five are peculiar to the archipelago, and largely land birds. There are thirty-five varieties of doves and pigeons, all edible.

[257] There are now domestic rabbits, and plenty of peacocks.—Rizal.

[258] Doubtless the python, which is often domesticated in the Philip-pines. See VOL. XII, p. 259, note 73.

[259] La Gironiere (Twenty Years in the Philippines—trans. from French, London, 1853) describes an interesting fight with a huge croco-dile near his settlement of Jala-Jala. The natives begged for the flesh in order to dry it and use it as a specific against asthma, as they believed that any asthmatic person who lived on the flesh for a certain time would be infallibly cured. Another native wished the fat as an antidote for rheu-matic pain. The head of this huge reptile was presented to an American, who in turn presented it to the Boston Museum. Unfortunately La Giro-niere's picturesque descriptions must often be taken with a grain of salt. For some information regarding the reptiles of the islands see Report of U.S. Philippine Commission,, 1900, iii, pp. 317-319.

[260] Unless we are mistaken, there is a fish in the Filipinas called Pampano.—Rizal.

[261] For catalogue and scientific description of the mollusks of the Philippines, see the work of Joaquin Gonzalez Hidalgo—now (1904) in course of publication by the Real Academia de Ciencias of Madrid—Estudios preliminares sobre la fauna malacologica de las Islas Filipinas.

[262] The Rio Grande.—Rizal.

[263] No fish is known answering to this description.—Stanley.

[264] The island of Talim.—Rizal.

265 Retana thinks (Zuniga, ii, p. 545*) that this device was introduced among the Filipinos by the Borneans.

266 A species of fishing-net. Stanley's conjecture is wrong.

267 Esparavel is a round fishing-net, which is jerked along by the fisher through rivers and shallow places. Barredera is a net of which the meshes are closer and tighter than those of common nets, so that the smallest fish may not escape it.

268 Cf. methods of fishing of North American Indians, Jesuit Relations, vi, pp. 309-311, liv, pp. 131, 306-307.

269 A species of fish in the Mediterranean, about three pulgadas [inches] long. Its color is silver, lightly specked with black.

270 The fish now called lawlaw is the dry, salted sardine. The author evidently alludes to the tawilis of Batangas, or to the dilis, which is still smaller, and is used as a staple by the natives.—Rizal.

For information regarding the fishes of the Philippines, see Delgado (ut supra), book v, part iv, pp. 909-943; Gazetteer of the Philippine Islands (ut supra), pp. 171-172; and (with description of methods of fishing) Report of U. S. Philippine Commission, 1900, iii, pp. 319-324.

271 Paho. A species of very small mango from one and one-half to five centimeters in its longer diameter. It has a soft pit, and exhales a strong pitchy odor.—Rizal.

272 A Spanish word signifying a cryptogamous plant; perhaps referring to some species of mushroom.

273 In Tagal this is kasubha. It comes from the Sanskrit kasumbha, or Malay kasumba (Pardo de Tavera's El Sanscrito en la lengua tagalog).—Rizal.

This plant is the safflower or bastard saffron (Certhamus tinctorius); its flowers are used in making a red dye.

274 Not a tree, but a climber. The plants are cultivated by training them about some canes planted in the middle of certain little channels which serve to convey irrigation to the plant twice each day. A plantation of betel—or ikmo, as the Tagals call it—much resembles a German hop-garden.—Rizal.

275 This fruit is not that of the betel or buyo, but of the bonga (Tagal bunga), or areca palm.—Rizal.

276 Not quicklime, but well slaked lime.—Rizal.

Rizal misprints un poco de cal viva for vn poluc de cal viua.

277 The original word is marcada. Rizal is probably correct in regarding it as a misprint for mascada, chewed.

278 It is not clear who call these caskets by that name. I imagine it to be the Spanish name, properly spelt buxeta. The king of Calicut's betel box is called buxen in the Barcelona MS. of the Malabar coasts.—Stanley.

[279] See VOL. IV, p. 222, note 31; also Delgado (ut supra), pp. 667-669. Delgado says that bonga signifies fruit.

[280] Tagal, tuko.—Rizal.

[281] This word in the original is visitandolas; Rizal makes it irritando-las (shaking or irritating them), but there are not sufficient grounds for the change.

[282] The Indians, upon seeing that wealth excited the rapacity of the encomenderos and soldiers, abandoned the working of the mines, and the religious historians assert that they counseled them to a similar action in order to free them from annoyances. Nevertheless, according to Colin (who was "informed by well-disposed natives") more than 100,000 pesos of gold annually, conservatively stated, was taken from the mines during his time, after eighty years of abandonment. According to "a manuscript of a grave person who had lived long in these islands" the first tribute of the two provinces of Ilocos and Pangasinan alone amounted to 109,500 pesos. A single encomendero, in 1587, sent 3,000 taheles of gold in the "Santa Ana," which was captured by Cavendish.—Rizal.

[283] This was prohibited later.—Rizal.

[284] See VOL. XIV, pp. 301-304.

According to Hernando de los Rios the province of Pangasinan was said to contain a quantity of gold, and that Guido de Labazaris sent some soldiers to search for it; but they returned in a sickly state and suppressed all knowledge of the mines in order not to be sent back there. The Dominican monks also suppressed all knowledge of the mines on account of the tyranny of which gold had been the cause in the West Indies.—Stanley.

[285] Pearl-fishing is still carried on along the coasts of Mindanao and Palawan, and in the Sulu archipelago. In the latter region pearls are very abundant and often valuable; the fisheries there are under the control of the sultan of Sulu, who rents them, appropriating for himself the largest pearls.

[286] Probably the cowry (Cypraea moneta). Crawfurd states (Dict. Ind. Islands, p. 117) that in the Asiatic archipelago this shell is found only on the shores of the Sulu group, and that it "seems never to have been used for money among the Indian Islanders as it has immemorially been by the Hindus."

[287] Jagor, Travels in the Philippines (Eng. trans., London, 1875), devotes a portion of his chapter xv to these jars. He mentions the great prices paid by the Japanese for these vessels. On p. 164, occurs a translation of the above paragraph, but it has been mistranslated in two places. Stanley cites the similar jars found among the Dyaks of Borneo—the best called gusih—which were valued at from $1,500 to $3,000, while the

second grade were sold for $400. That they are very ancient is proved by one found among other remains of probably the copper age. From the fact that they have been found in Cambodia, Siam, Cochinchina, and the Philippines, Rizal conjectures that the peoples of these countries may have had a common center of civilization at one time.

[288] "Not many years ago," says Colin (1663), "a large piece [of ambergris] was found in the island of Jolo, that weighed more than eight arrobas, of the best kind, namely, the gray."—Rizal.

[289] This industry must now be forgotten, for it is never heard of.—Rizal.

[290] Perhaps Morga alludes to the sinamay, which was woven from abaka, or filament of the plant Musa textilis. The abaka is taken from the trunk and not the leaf.—Rizal.

[291] This name seems to be Malay, Babu-utan, wild swine.—Stanley.

[292] The men of these islands were excellent carpenters and ship-builders. "They make many very light vessels, which they take through the vicinity for sale in a very curious manner. They build a large vessel, undecked, without iron nail or any fastening. Then, according to the measure of its hull, they make another vessel that fits into it. Within that they put a second and a third. Thus a large biroco contains ten or twelve vessels, called biroco, virey, barangay, and binitan." These natives were "tattooed, and were excellent rowers and sailors; and although they are upset often, they never drown." The women are very masculine. "They do not drink from the rivers, although the water is very clear, because it gives them nausea.... The women's costumes are chaste and pretty, for they wear petticoats in the Bisayan manner, of fine medrinaque, and lamboncillos, which resemble close-fitting sayuelos [i.e., woolen shifts worn by certain classes of religious]. They wear long robes of the same fine medrinaque. They gather the hair, which is neatly combed, into a knot, on top of the head, and place a rose in it. On their forehead they wear a band of very fine wrought gold, two fingers wide. It is very neatly worked and on the side encircling the head it is covered with colored taffeta. In each ear they wear three gold earrings, one in the place where Spanish women wear them, and two higher up. On their feet they wear certain coverings of thin brass, which sound when they walk." (The citations herein are from Colin.) These islands have also retrograded.—Rizal.

[293] Cavite derives its name from the Tagal word cavit, a creek, or bend, or hook, for such is its form.—Stanley.

[294] This province had decreased so greatly in population and agriculture, a half century later, that Gaspar de San Agustin said: "Now it no longer has the population of the past, because of the insurrection of that province, when Don Sabiniano Manrique de Lara was governor of these

islands, and because of the incessant cutting of the timber for the building of his Majesty's ships, which prevents them from cultivating their extremely fertile plain." Later, when speaking of Guagua or Wawa, he says: "This town was formerly very wealthy because of its many chiefs, and because of the abundant harvests gathered in its spacious plains, which are now submerged by the water of the sea."—Rizal.

[295] Now the port of Sorsogon.—Rizal.

[296] Now the port of Mariveles (?).—Rizal.

[297] Subik (?).—Rizal.

[298] Mindoro is at present [1890] so depopulated that the minister of the Colonies, in order to remedy this result of Spanish colonization, wishes to send there the worst desperadoes of the peninsula, to see if great criminals will make good colonists and farmers. All things considered, given the condition of those who go, it is indubitable that the race that succeeds must know how to defend itself and live, so that the island may not be depopulated again.—Rizal.

[299] Samar. This proves contrary to the opinion of Colin, who places Tendaya in Leite.—Rizal.

[300] Southeastern part of Samar.—Rizal.

[301] Colin says, however, that they did tattoo the chins and about the eyes [barbas y cejas]. The same author states also that the tattooing was done little by little and not all at once. "The children were not tattooed, but the women tattooed one hand and part of the other. In this island of Manila the Ilocos also tattooed themselves, although not so much as did the Visayans." The Negritos, Igorrotes, and other independent tribes of the Filipinas still tattoo themselves. The Christians have forgotten the practice. The Filipinas used only the black color, thus differing from the Japanese, who employ different colors, as red and blue, and carry the art to a rare perfection. In other islands of the Pacific, the women tattoo themselves almost as much as the men. Dr. Wilhelm Joest's Taetowiren Narbenzeichnen und Koerperbemahlen (Berlin, 1887) treats the matter very succinctly.—Rizal.

[302] This is a confused statement, after what just precedes it and according to the evidence of Father Chirino (see VOL. XII, chapter vii). Morga must mean that they wore no cloak or covering when they went outside the house, as did the Tagals (both men and women), who used a kind of cape.—Rizal.*

[303] Gubat, grove, field, in Tagal. Mangubat [so printed in the text of Rizal's edition] signifies in Tagal "to go hunting, or to the wood," or even "to fight."—Rizal.

---

* This is the sense in which Stanley understood and translated this passage.

³⁰⁴ "At the arrival of the Spaniards at this island (Panay)" says San Agustin, "it was said to have more than 50,000 families. But they decreased greatly ... and at present it has about 14,000 tributarios—6,000 apportioned to the crown, and 8,000 to individual encomenderos." They had many gold-mines, and obtained gold by washing the sand in the Panay River; "but instigated by the outrages received from the alcaldes-mayor," says the same historian, "they have ceased to dig it, preferring to live in poverty than to endure such troubles."—Rizal.

³⁰⁵ This entire paragraph is omitted in the Rizal edition. In the original it is as follows:

La Lengua de todos, los Pintados y Bicayas, es vna mesma, por do se entienden, hablando y escriuiendo, en letras y caratores que tienen particulares, que semejan a los Arabigos, y su comun escribir entre los naturales, es en hojas de arboles, y en canas, sobre la corteza; que en todas las islas ay muchas, de disforme grueso los canutos, y el pie es vn arbol muy grueso y macico.

³⁰⁶ This difference is no greater than that between the Spanish, Portuguese, and Italian.—Rizal.

³⁰⁷ See Chirino (Relacion de las islas Filipinas) VOL. XII, chapters xv-xvii. His remarks, those of Morga, and those of other historians argue a considerable amount of culture among the Filipino peoples prior to the Spanish conquest. A variety of opinions have been expressed as to the direction of the writing. Chirino, San Antonio, Zuniga, and Le Gentil, say that it was vertical, beginning at the top. Colin, Ezguerra, and Marche assert that it was vertical but in the opposite direction. Colin says that the horizontal form was adopted after the arrival of the Spaniards. Mas declares that it was horizontal and from left to right, basing his arguments upon certain documents in the Augustinian archives in Manila. The eminent Filipino scholar, Dr. T. H. Pardo de Tavera has treated the subject in a work entitled "Contribucion para el estudio de los antiguos alfabetos filipinos" (Losana, 1884). See Rizal's notes on p. 291 of his edition of Morga.

³⁰⁸ This portion of this sentence is omitted in Stanley.

³⁰⁹ Bahay is "house" in Tagal; pamamahay is that which is in the interior and the house. Bahandin may be a misprint for bahayin, an obsolete derivative.—Rizal.

³¹⁰ Cf. this and following sections with Loarca's relation, VOL. V, of this series; and with Plasencia's account, VOL. VII, pp. 173-196.

³¹¹ Timawa.—Rizal.

³¹² The condition of these slaves was not always a melancholy one. Argensola says that they ate at the same table with their masters, and married into their families. The histories fail to record the assassination

for motives of vengeance of any master or chief by the natives, as they do of encomenderos. After the conquest the evil deepened. The Spaniards made slaves without these pretexts, and without those enslaved being Indians of their jurisdiction—going moreover, to take them away from their own villages and islands. Fernando de los Rios Coronel, in his memorial to the king (Madrid, 1621) pp. 24-25, speaks in scathing terms of the cruelties inflicted on the natives in the construction of ships during the governorship of Juan de Silva. A letter from Felipe II to Bishop Domingo de Salazar shows the awful tyranny exercised by the encomenderos upon the natives, whose condition was worse than that of slaves.—Rizal.

[313] For remarks on the customs formerly observed by the natives of Pampanga in their suits, see appendix to this volume.

[314] This fundamental agreement of laws, and this general uniformity, prove that the mutual relations of the islands were widespread, and the bonds of friendship more frequent than were wars and quarrels. There may have existed a confederation, since we know from the first Spaniards that the chief of Manila was commander-in-chief of the sultan of Borneo. In addition, documents of the twelfth century that exist testify the same thing.—Rizal.

[315] This word must be sagigilid in its Tagal form. The root gilid signifies in Tagal, "margin," "strand," or "shore." The reduplication of the first syllable, if tonic, signifies active future action. If not tonic and the suffix an be added, it denotes the place where the action of the verb is frequently executed. The preposition sa indicates place, time, reference. The atonic reduplication may also signify plurality, in which case the singular noun would be sagilid, i.e., "at the margin," or "the last"—that is, the slave. Timawa signifies now in Tagal, "in peace, in quietness, tranquil, free," etc. Maginoo, from the root ginoo, "dignity," is now the title of the chiefs; and the chief's reunion is styled kaginoohan. Colin says, nevertheless, that the Chiefs used the title gat or lakan, and the women dayang. The title of mama applied now to men, corresponds to "uncle," "Senor," "Monsieur," "Mr.," etc.; and the title al of women to the feminine titles corresponding to these.—Rizal.

[316] Namamahay (from bahay, "house"), "he who lives in his own house." This class of slaves, if they may be so called, exists even yet. They are called kasama (because of being now the laborers of a capitalist or farmer), bataan ("servant," or "domestic"), kampon, tao, etc.

[317] This class of slavery still exists [1890] in many districts, especially in the province of Batangas; but it must be admitted that their condition is quite different from that of the slave in Greece or Rome, or that of the negro, and even of those made slaves formerly by the Spaniards. Thanks

to their social condition and to their number in that time, the Spanish domination met very little resistance, while the Filipino chiefs easily lost their independence and liberty. The people, accustomed to the yoke, did not defend the chiefs from the invader, nor attempt to struggle for liberties that they never enjoyed. For the people, it was only a change of masters. The nobles, accustomed to tyrannize by force, had to accept the foreign tyranny, when it showed itself stronger than their own. Not encountering love or elevated feelings in the enslaved mass, they found themselves without force or power.—Rizal.

[318] Inasawa, or more correctly asawa (consort).—Rizal.

[319] This dowry, if one may call it so, represented to the parents an indemnity for the care and vigilance that they had exercised in their daughter's education. The Filipina woman, never being a burden to any one (either to her parents or to her husband), but quite the contrary, represents a value, whose loss to the possessor must be substituted.... The Tagal wife is free, and treated with consideration; she trades and contracts, almost always with the approbation of her husband, who consults her in all his acts. She takes care of the money, and educates the children, half of whom belong to her...—Rizal.

[320] Bigay-kaya, "to give what one can," "a voluntary offering, a present of good will" ... This bigay-kaya devolved entire to the married couple, according to Colin, if the son-in-law was obedient to his parents-in-law; if not, it was divided among all the heirs. "Besides the dowry, the chiefs used to give certain gifts to the parents and relatives, and even to the slaves, which were great or less according to the rank of the one married." (Colin).—Rizal.

[321] This good custom still exists, ... although it is gradually passing away.—Rizal.

[322] Such is the law throughout most parts of Asia; in Siam the woman becomes free without having children. It is only in America that fathers could and did sell their own children into slavery.—Stanley.

[323] This condition of affairs and the collection of usury is true still [1890]. Morga's words prove true not only of the Indian, but also of the mestizos, the Spaniards, and even of various religious. So far has it gone that the government itself not only permits it, but also exacts the capital and even the person to pay the debts of others, as happens with the cabeza de barangay [head of a barangay].—Rizal.

[324] The tam-tam and the pum-piang are still used.—Rizal.

[325] The early Filipinos had a great horror of theft, and even the most anti-Filipino historian could not accuse them of being a thievish race. Today, however, they have lost their horror of that crime. One of the old Filipino methods of investigating theft was as follows: "If the crime was

proved, but not the criminal, if more than one was suspected ... each suspect was first obliged to place a bundle of cloth, leaves, or whatever he wished on a pile, in which the thing stolen might be hidden. Upon the completion of this investigation if the stolen property was found in the pile, the suit ceased." The Filipinos also practiced customs very similar to the "judgments of God" of the middle ages, such as putting suspected persons, by pairs, under the water and adjudging guilty him who first emerged.—Rizal.

326 The Filipino today prefers a beating to scoldings or insults.—Rizal.

327 From bago, new, and tao, man: he who has become a man.—Rizal.

328 In speaking of a similar custom in Australia, Eyre (Central Australia, i, p. 213), says: "This extraordinary and inexplicable custom must have a great tendency to prevent the rapid increase of the population."—Stanley.*

329 It appears that the natives called anito a tutelary genius, either of the family, or extraneous to it. Now, with their new religious ideas, the Tagals apply the term anito to any superstition, false worship, idol, etc.—Rizal.

330 Others besides Morga mention oratories in caves, where the idols were kept, and where aromatics were burned in small brasiers. Chirino found small temples in Taitay adjoining the principal houses. [See VOL. XII. of this series, chapter xxi.] It appears that temples were never dedicated to bathala maykapal, nor was sacrifice ever offered him. The temples dedicated to the anito were called ulango.—Rizal.

331 San Agustin says that hell was called solad, and paradise, kalualhatian (a name still in existence), and in poetical language, ulugan. The blest abodes of the inhabitants of Panay were in the mountain of Madias.—Rizal.

332 Cf. the "wake" of the Celtic and Gaelic peasants. Cf. also the North-American Indian burial ceremonies, and reverence paid to the dead, in Jesuit Relations, i, p. 215; ii, pp. 21, 149; viii, p. 21; x, pp. 169, 247, 283-285, 293; xiii, 259; xxi, 199; xxiii, 31; lxv, 141; etc.

In the Filipino burials, there were mourners who composed panegyrics in honor of the dead, like those made today. "To the sound of this sad music the corpse was washed, and perfumed with storax, gum-resin, or other perfumes made from tree gums, which are found in all these woods. Then the corpse was shrouded, being wrapped in more or less cloth according to the rank of the deceased. The bodies of the more

---

* Stanley does not translate this paragraph of the text.

wealthy were anointed and embalmed in the manner of the Hebrews, with aromatic liquors, which preserved them from decay.... The burial-place of the poor was in pits dug in the ground under their own houses. After the bodies of the rich and powerful were kept and bewailed for three days, they were placed in a chest or coffin of incorruptible wood, adorned with rich jewels, and with small sheets of gold in the mouth and over the eyes. The coffin was all in one piece, and the lid was so adjusted that no air could enter. Because of these precautions the bodies have been found after many years, still uncorrupted. These coffins were deposited in one of three places, according to the inclination and arrangement of the deceased, either on top of the house among the treasures ... or underneath it, but raised from the ground; or in the ground itself, in an open hole surrounded with a small railing ... nearby they were wont to place another box filled with the best clothes of the deceased; and at meal-time they set various articles of food there in dishes. Beside the men were laid their weapons, and beside the women their looms or other implements of work" (Colin).—Rizal.

[333] Kasis. This is another instance of the misapplication of this Arabic term, which means exclusively a Christian priest.—Stanley.

[334] This custom has not fallen into disuse among the Filipinos, even among the Catholics.—Rizal.

Lieutenant Charles Norton Barney, of the medical department of the U. S. Army, has an article in Journal of the Association of Military Surgeons for September, 1903, on "Circumcision and Flagellation among the Filipinos." In regard to circumcision he states that it "is a very ancient custom among the Philippine indios, and so generalized that at least seventy or eighty per cent of males in the Tagal country have undergone the operation." Those uncircumcised at the age of puberty are taunted by their fellows, and such are called "suput," a word formerly meaning "constricted" or "tight," but now being extended to mean "one who cannot easily gain entrance in sexual intercourse." The "operation has no religious significance," nor is it done for cleanliness, "but from custom and disinclination to be ridiculed," probably [as Morga proves] having been learned from the Moros. The friars were unable to check the custom. Among the Tagals the operation is called "tuli," and the method of circumcising is described at length. The author derives his information from a mestizo and a full-blooded native. The custom is mentioned by Foreman.

[335] Appellation given to their ecclesiastical sages by Mahometans.

[336] See the king's decree granting this coat-of-arms, in VOL. IX, pp. 211-215, with two representations of the coat-of-arms.

[337] Convents occupy almost one-third part of the walled city.—Rizal.

[338] The walls did not even have any moats then; these were dug after the English invasion of 1762. The walls were also rearranged at that time, and perfected with the lapse of time and the needs that arose in the city.—Rizal.

[339] Rizal misprints al cabo del lienco as al campo del lienzo.

[340] Now [1890] the gates of the city are open all night, and in certain periods, passage along the streets and through the walls is allowed at all hours.—Rizal.

[341] This powder-mill has several times changed its site. It was afterward near Maalat on the seashore, and then was moved to Nagtaha, on the bank of the Pasig.—Rizal.

[342] Probably on the same site where the great Tagal cannon-foundry had formerly stood, which was burned and destroyed by the Spaniards at their first arrival in Manila. San Agustin declares the Tagal foundry to have been as large as that at Malaga.—Rizal.

[343] The Rizal edition omits the words, muy grande y autorizada, capilla aparte, camara del sello real.

[344] The treasury building. The governor's palace was destroyed in 1863.—Rizal.

[345] The Audiencia and cabildo buildings were also destroyed, but the latter has been rebuilt.—Rizal.

[346] The Rizal edition misprints sacristan as sacristias.

[347] This is the largest convent in Manila.—Rizal.

[348] Among the Jesuits, that part of a college where the pensioners or boarders live and receive their instruction.

[349] This college of San Jose was founded in 1601, although the royal decree for it had been conceded in 1585. The number of collegiates to enter was thirteen, among whom was a nephew of Francisco Tello and a son of Dr. Morga. From its inception Latin was taught there. In a suit with the College of Santo Tomas, the Jesuits obtained a favorable decision; and it was recognized as the older institution, and given the preference in public acts. The historians say that at its inauguration the students wore bonnets covered with diamonds and pearls. At present [1890] this college, after having moved from house to house, has become a school of pharmacy attached to Santo Tomas, and directed by the Dominican rector.—Rizal.

[350] After many varying fortunes, this institution has wholly disappeared.—Rizal.

[351] The Confraternity of Mercy [Hermandad de la Misericordia] was founded in 1594, by an ecclesiastic named Juan Fernandez de Leon.—Rizal.

[352] San Juan de Dios [St. John of God].—Rizal.

[353] Better, Maalat. The Spaniards pronounced this later Malate. There lived the chief Tagals after they were deprived of their houses in Manila, among whom were the families of Raja Matanda and Raja Soliman. San Augustin says that even in his day many of the ancient nobility dwelt there, and that they where very urbane and cultured. "The Men hold various positions in Manila, and certain occupations in some of the local public functions. The women make excellent lace, in which they are so skilfull that the Dutch women cannot surpass them." This is still true of the women.—Rizal.

[354] Now the town of Paco.—Rizal.

[355] Recopilacion de leyes, lib. ii, tit. xv, ley xi, defines the district of the Audiencia and states certain perogatives of the governor and auditors as follows: "In the city of Manila, in the island of Luzon, capital of the Felipinas, shall reside our royal Audiencia and Chancilleria, with a president who shall be governor and captain-general, four auditors, who shall also be alcaldes of criminal cases, one fiscal, one alguacil-mayor, one lieutenant of the grand chancillor, and the other ministers and officials necessary. It shall have as its district the said island of Luzon, and all the rest of the Filipinas, the archipelago of China and its mainland as yet discovered and to be discovered. We order the governor and captain-general of the said islands and provinces and president of the royal Audiencia in them, to hold personal charge in peace and war of the superior government of all the district of the said Audiencia, and to make the provisions and concessions in our royal name, which in accordance with the laws of this Recopilacion and of these kingdoms of Castilla, and with the instructions and powers that he shall get from us, he should and can make. In things and matters of importance that arise in the government, the said president governor shall discuss them with the auditors of the said Audiencia, so that they, after consulting, may give him their opinion. He, after hearing them, shall take what course is most advisable to the service of God and to ours, and the peace and quiet of that province and community." Felipe II, Aranjuez, May 5, 1583; Toledo, May 25, 1596, in ordinance of the Audiencia; Felipe IV in this Recopilacion.

[356] The original is canongias, raciones, y medias raciones, which literally refers to the office or prebend instead of the individual. We retain the above terms as expressing the persons who held these prebends.

[357] Literaly, the original translates "in the islands of Sebu, Cagayan, and Camerines."

[358] This is so changed now [1890] and the employees so increased in number, that the annual expenses amount to more than 2,000,000 pesos, while the intendant's salary is 12,000 pesos.—Rizal.

[359] This city has disapeared from the map and from the earth. An inconsiderable town named Lal-lo occupies its site. It is still [1890], however, named as the appointment of the bishopric of Bigan, the actual residence of the bishop.—Rizal.

[360] An attempt was made to supply the lack of prebends in the cathedral cities of the Philippines by the following law: "Inasmuch as the bishops of the churches of Nueva Caceres, Nueva Segovia, and of the Name of Jesus of the Filipinas Islands should have men to assist them in the pontifical acts, and the bishops should have all the propriety possible in their churches, and divine worship more reverence; and inasmuch as there are no tithes with which a few prebendaries can be sustained in the churches: therefore our governor of those islands shall appoint to each of the said churches two ecclesiastics of good life and example, who shall aid and assist the bishop in the pontifical acts, and in all else relating to divine worship. He shall assign them a certain modest sum for their support from our royal treasury, so that with that they may for the present serve the churches, until there be more opportunity for endowing them with prebendaries and providing other necessary things." Felipe III, San Lorenzo, October 5, 1606. Recopilacion de leyes, lib. i, tit. vi, ley xviii.

[361] The Rizal edition omits a considerable portion of this paragraph. The omission is as follows: para guarda del puerto, y defensa de la ciudad, con bastante guarnicion de soldados de paga, a orden del alcalde mayor, capitan a guerra de la prouincia que reside en la ciudad. Sera la poblazon, de dozientos vezinos Espanoles, con casas de madera, tiene Cabildo, de dos alcaldes ordinarios, ocho rejidores, alguazil mayor y sus oficiales.

[362] Now [1890] of slight importance. Of its former grandeur there remain only 1,000 inhabitants, with a parochial house, a justice's house, a prison, and a primary school.—Rizal.

[363] Vigan or Bigan.—Rizal.

[364] Legazpi also had two secular priests, Juan de Vivero and Juan de Villanueva, who had part in the first conversions.—Rizal.

[365] The Jesuits preceded the Dominicans seven years as missionaries to the Filipinas. The first Jesuits came over with Domingo de Salazar, the first bishop, and his Dominican associate.—Rizal.

[366] Visita: here meaning a district which has no resident missionary, but is visited by religious from some mission station, on which the visita is therefore dependent.

367 Cf. with the musical ability of the Filipinos that displayed by the North American Indians, as described in The Jesuit Relations, vols. vi, p. 183; xviii, p. 161; xxiii, p. 213; xxvii, p. 117; xxxi, p. 219; xxxviii, pp. 259, 263; etc.

368 Chirino (chapter vii) mentions the apportionment, by the king, of distinct districts to the different orders. The Augustinian authorities in Mexico granted permission to those of their order going to the Philippines to establish themselves wherever they wished in the islands (see VOL. II, pp. 161-168), and the latter exercised the omnimodo [i.e., entire] ecclesiastical authority, as conceded by the popes, until the arrival of the Franciscans in 1577. Papal concessions probably marked out the districts as apportioned by the king.

369 Morga refers, with his characteristic prudence, to the great question of diocesan visits, which commenced with Fray Domingo de Salazar, and which could not be ended until 1775, in the time of Anda—thanks to the energy of the latter and the courage of Archbishop Don Basilio Sancho de Santa Justa y Rufina, when after great disturbances they succeeded in subjecting the regular curas to the inspection of the bishops. Morga, however, shows that he did not approve the claims of the religious to independence, but does not dare to state so distinctly.—Rizal.

370 The Augustinians received also one-fourth part of the tribute from the villages while they were building churches; and 200 pesos fuertes [i.e., ten-real pieces] and 200 cavans [the cavan equals 25 gantas, or 137 Spanish libras] of cleaned rice for four religious who heard confessions during Lent. Fifty cavans of cleaned rice per person seems to us too much. It results that each friar consumes 12 1/2 libras of rice or 27 chupas [the chupa is 1/8 ganta or 3 litros] daily, thirteen times as much as any Indian.—Rizal.

371 Recopilacion de leyes, lib. vi, tit. vii, ley xvi, contains the following in regard to the native chiefs: "It is not right that the Indian chiefs of Filipinas be in a worse condition after conversion; rather should they have such treatment that would gain their affection and keep them loyal, so that with the spiritual blessings that God has communicated to them by calling them to His true knowledge, the temporal blessings may be joined, and they may live contentedly and comfortably. Therefore, we order the governors of those islands to show them good treatment and entrust them, in our name, with the government of the Indians, of whom they were formerly the lords. In all else the governors shall see that the chiefs are benefited justly, and the Indians shall pay them something as a recognition, as they did during the period of their paganism, provided it be without prejudice to the tributes that are to be paid us, or prejudicial

to that which pertains to their encomenderos." Felipe II, Madrid, June 11, 1594.

[372] The gobernadorcillo ["little or petty governor"].

[373] Bilango signifies today in Tagal "the act of imprisoning," and bilanguan "the prison."—Rizal.

[374] For good expositions of local government in modern times, see Bowring, Visit to the Philippine Isles (London, 1859), pp. 87-93; and Montero y Vidal, Archipielago Filipino (Madrid, 1886), pp. 162-168.

[375] These are now [1890] made in Spanish.—Rizal.

[376] Names of petty officers: the former the name of an officer in oriental countries; the second signifying one who commands. Dr. T. H. Pardo de Tavera (Costumbres de los Tagalos, Madrid, 1892, p. 10, note 1) says the word dato is now unused by the Tagals. Datu or datuls primitively signified "grandfather," or "head of the family," which was equivalent to the head of the barangay. This name is used in Mindanao and Jolo to designate certain chiefs.

[377] A later law in Recopilacion de leyes (lib. vi, tit. viii, ley xi) regulates the encomienda—giving power as follows: "The governor and captain-general of Filipinas shall apportion the encomiendas, in accordance with the regulations to worthy persons, without having other respect than to the service of God our Lord, and our service, the welfare of the public cause, and the remuneration of the most deserving. Within sixty days, reckoned from the time that he shall have heard of the vacancy, he shall be obliged to apportion them. If he does not do so, the right to apportion them shall devolve upon and pertain to our royal Audiencia of those islands, and we order the Audiencia to apportion them, paying heed to the laws, within six days, and to avail itself of the edicts and diligences issued by the governor without other new ones. In case the governor shall not have issued edicts and diligences, the Audiencia shall issue them and make the provision within twenty days." Felipe III, Madrid, June 4, 1620.

[378] The rapidity with which many of these encomenderos amassed great wealth in a few years is known, and that they left colossal fortunes at their death. Some were not satisfied with the tributes and with what they demanded, but made false measures, and balances that weighed twice as much as was indicated. They often exacted the tributes in certain products only, and appraised the same at what value they wished.—Rizal.

[379] A law in Recopilacion de leyes (lib. vi, tit. v, ley lxv) cites the above provision and confirms it anew: "In order to provide instruction for certain villages of the Filipinas Islands, which did not enjoy it, or if they had it, it was not sufficient, it was resolved to increase the tribute, which was formerly eight reals, or its value, per peso, to the proportion

of ten Castilian reals apiece. It was ordered that the increased amount be placed in our royal treasury, and one-half real of it be applied to paying the obligations which had to be met in regard to the tithes, while the one and one-half reals would remain to pay those soldiers there and for other purposes; in consideration of the fact that the funds necessary to send out religious, who are employed in the preaching of the holy gospel, are supplied from our royal treasury, and that the encomenderos were obliged to pay for the ordinary instruction from the eight reals, and the part of the building of churches that fell to their share, while the Indians had the choice of paying all the tribute in money or in products, or in both. Thus was it enacted and voted. We order no innovation to be made in this regard, in consideration of the welfare and conservation of those provinces and their natives, and so that the choice of paying in money shall not occasion any lack of products and cause sterility." Felipe II, San Lorenzo, August 1589; Felipe III, Zamora, February 16, 1602.

380 The following law regulates supervision of the accounts of this fund: "Inasmuch as, when any encomienda of the Filipinas Islands happens to be without instruction, the fourth part of the tribute collected by the encomendero is deposited in a box with three keys, in order that it may be converted into benefices for the Indians; and as it is advisable that that ordinance be executed sensibly and properly, and that we should know the amount of it and how it is apportioned: therefore, we order our presidents, the governors of the Filipinas Islands, that whenever they deem it advisable to examine the account, they shall appoint for that purpose one of the officials of our royal treasury of those islands—the one most suitable for it—who shall examine them. The fiscal of our royal Audiencia shall investigate them before they are finished; and shall ask and see that they are executed with the care that the matter requires in regard to their items, charges, articles, and balances, and whatever else is advisable. He shall advise our president and governor of it all, so that he may assist him in what may be necessary, and advise us of the result." Felipe III, Madrid, June 4, 1620, in Recopilacion de leyes, lib. i, tit. xiii, ley xiv.

381 The bull here referred to was issued by Gregory XIV, and dated April 18, 1591. The seventh section reads as follows: "Finally, since, as we have learned, our very dear son in Christ, Philip, Catholic King of the Spains, on account of the many deceits wont to be practised therein, has forbidden any Spaniard in the aforesaid Philippine Islands to dare to take, or have, or hold any slaves, or servants, even by right of just and unjust war, or of purchase, or by whatsoever other title, or pretext; although some, despite the edict, or mandate, of King Philip himself, still keep the same slaves in their power: therefore in order that, as is befitting to rea-

son and equity, the Indians themselves may freely and safely without any fear of bondage come and go to their Christian doctrinas, and to their own homes and possessions, we order and command all and singular the persons living in the same islands, of whatsoever state, degree, condition, order, and rank they may be, in virtue of holy obedience and under pain of excommunication, on the publication of these presents, in accordance with the edict, or mandate of the said King Philip, to release wholly free, without deceit and guile, whatsoever Indian slaves and servants they may have, or hold; nor ever for the future in any manner to take or keep captives, or servants."[*]

[382] This [1890] has disappeared from legislation, although the personal services for Espana are still continued, and are fifteen days.—Rizal.

[383] Recopilacion de leyes, lib. vi, tit. xii, ley xii, treating of personal services, reads as follows: "The religious and the ministers of the instruction, and the alcaldes-mayor of the Filipinas Islands have a weekly repartimiento of Indians which they call tanores, so that the Indians may serve them without pay; and besides the villages contribute to them the fish necessary to them on Fridays, which is against reason and justice. We order the governor and captain-general, the Audiencia, and any other of our justices, to stop and not allow this personal service and contribution, so that the villages shall in no manner perform it, and we declare the villages free from any obligation that they have or may have." This law is dated Madrid, March 17, 1608.

[384] Taal was one of the villages where the most rigging was made for the royal ships.—Rizal.

[385] This word reales is omitted in the Rizal edition.

[386] A comparatively early law (Recopilacion de leyes, lib. vi, tit. i, ley xv), prohibits the forcible removal of the natives for expeditions of conquest from one island to another. It is as follows: "We order that the Indians in the Filipinas Islands be not taken from one island to another forcibly in order to make incursions, and against their will, unless it be under very necessary circumstances, and paying them for their work and trouble. They shall be well treated and receive no injury." Felipe II, Madrid, November 7, 1574.

[387] In Java also the Dutch restrict Europeans from roaming about the country; this is a good regulation for the protection of the inhabitants.—Stanley.

[388] Stanley praises these regulations; Rizal deplores them, as keeping the men in authority out of touch with the people.

---

[*] Translated from the original by REV. T. C. MIDDLETON, O.S.A.

389 Recopilacion de leyes, lib. iv, tit. x, ley vii, has the following law, dated Madrid, March 17, 1608: "The governor and captain-general of Filipinas shall for the present appoint the magistracy [regimiento] of the city of Manila, choosing persons who shall prove to be suitable for the office and zealous for the service of God our Lord, and for ours; and he shall not remove them without our special order."

390 Many royal decrees related to playing cards. The monopoly ceased to exist perhaps before the government monopoly on betel was initiated.—Rizal (in part).

391 In 1890 he received 12,000 pesos.—Rizal.

392 The prebend, in Spanish cathedrals, superior to a canonry.

The following laws (xvi and xvii, respectively) as to the appointments of vacant prebends, are found in Recopilacion de leyes, lib. i, tit. vi.

"Because of the great distance from these kingdoms to the Filipinas Islands and the inconvenience that might result from the prebends falling vacant without any provision being made until we present those who shall take them, we order the governor and captain-general of the said islands that, when dignidades, canonries, and other prebends in the metropolitan church become vacant, he shall present other persons of the sufficiency and characteristics required, so that they may serve in place of their predecessors, until we provide persons for them. They shall receive the stipend that their predecessors shall have received. The governor shall observe the rules made by the laws of this titulo in his presentations." Felipe II, Guadalupe, March 26, 1580.

"We order our governors of the Filipinas Islands, and charge the archbishops of Manila, that when any prebends of that church become vacant, they send us three nominations for each one, instead of one only, with very minute advice of their sufficiency, learning, degrees, and all other qualities that are found in those proposed, so that after examination, we may appoint the one most suitable." Felipe III, Lerma, June 28, 1608.

393 In 1890 the Filipinas were paying 36,670 pesos annually for one dean, four dignitarios, five canons, four racioneros, four medio-racioneros, and other inferior helpers, including the choir, a total of twenty-six individuals; 3,330 pesos annually is to be added for sacristans, singers, and orchestra.—Rizal.

394 Their salary amounted to from 750 to 1,000 pesos. Now 1890 the salary of each bishop is 6,000 pesos, with two father assistants at 100 to 150 pesos per month.—Rizal.

395 Thus in original, but it is carelessly worded; for the Society of Jesus is not one of the mendicant orders.

[396] All of the orders held property and had regular means of revenue, later; while the Dominicans held enormous property in both the islands and at Hong Kong.—Rizal.

[397] The following law is from Recopilacion de leyes (lib. iii, tit. x, ley xiv): "The governor and captain-general of the Filipinas Islands shall be careful to reward the soldiers who shall have served us there, and their sons, with the posts and emoluments at his disposal, in accordance with the ordinances, and [he shall do it] with all fairness, so that they may have some remuneration. He shall keep in toto the laws relating to this." Felipe III, Lerma, July 23, 1605; Madrid, December 19, 1618.

[398] Consejeles: men sent to service by order of a municipal council.

[399] The pay of various of the above officers and men in 1890 was as follows: Filipino infantrymen, 4 pesos per month; Spanish artillerymen, 13-15 pesos, plus some centimos, per month; Filipino artillerymen, 4 pesos, plus some centimos, per month; captains, 1,500-1,800 pesos per year; alfereces, 975-1,050 pesos per year; first sergeants, European, 318-360 pesos per year—native, 180 pesos per year; second sergeants, European, 248.06-307.50 pesos per year—native, 156 pesos per year; first corporals, European, 189.56-202 pesos per year—native, 84 pesos per year; second corporals, European, 174-192 pesos per year—native corporals, 72 pesos per year; the segundo cabo [lieutenant-commander], 12,000 pesos per year; sargento-mayor de plaza (now lieutenant-colonel), 225 pesos per month; vice-admiral [contra-almirante, general de galeras], 16,392 pesos per year; frigate and ship captains, 2,700-5,760 pesos per year, according to their duties and grades.—Rizal.

The following laws from Recopilacion de leyes regulate the pay of the soldiers and some of the officers, and impose certain restrictions on the soldiers, and provide for certain appointments: "Each soldier established in the Filipinas Islands shall be paid eight pesos per month, each captain, fifty, each alferez, twenty, and each sergeant, ten. The governor and captain-general of the said islands shall give all the men of the companies thirty ducados to each company of additional pay, as is done in other districts, providing the additional pay of each one does not exceed ten pesos per year. We order that all be well paid. When the governor shall provide any of the captains, officers, or soldiers with an encomienda, or other post, he shall not allow him to draw pay. While they draw pay they shall not be allowed to trade or traffic, so that that occupation may not divert or distract them from their proper exercise and employment of war. For the same reason, no pay shall be granted to any soldier who serves any other person, whomsoever he be." Felipe II, Anover, August 9, 1589, clause 34 of his instructions; Felipe III, Ventosilla, November 4, 1606; lib. iii, tit. x, ley xiii.

"We order that when the post of general of artillery of the Filipinas Islands becomes vacant, either by the death or promotion of its occupant, or for any other cause, the governor and captain-general shall not fill it without first notifying us and without our special order for it. We permit him to appoint a captain of artillery and a sargento-mayor, and he may assign each of them thirty pesos' pay. We approve the increase of two pesos in the pay of the musketeers. It is our will that the pay of the governor's captain of the guard be increased five pesos, in addition to his fifteen pesos, and that a like sum be granted to the commandants of forts when they have a captain of infantry." Felipe II, clause of letter, Madrid, June 11, 1594; Felipe IV, Madrid, January 30, 1631; lib. iii, tit. v, ley iii.

[400] A definite law, as is shown in Recopilacion de leyes, lib. iii. tit. iv, ley xiii, charged the viceroys of Nueva Espana to send help to the Philippines. The law is as follows: "We charge and order the viceroys of Nueva Espana to aid the governor and captain-general of Filipinas on all occasions that arise, with very special care, promptness, and diligence, with whatever the latter shall request; and with the men, arms, ammunition, and money, that he deems necessary for the conservation of those islands, salaries [the original is sueldos, perhaps a misprint for suelos, signifying 'provinces' or 'districts'], presidios, and whatever else is under his charge." Felipe III, Aranjuez, May 25, 1607.

The two following laws impose certain restrictions on the reenforcements sent to the Philippines from Nueva Espana:

"One of the captains who shall raise men in Nueva Espana as reenforcements for the Filipinas Islands, shall act as their agent to the port of Acapulco. There he shall deliver them to the general, or commander of the ships about to sail; but no captain shall take passage or go to the islands with the men of his company." Felipe III, Zamora, February 16, 1602; lib. iii, tit. iv, ley xvi.

"Among the men sent by the viceroy, who shall go as a reenforcement from Nueva Espana to Filipinas, he shall not allow, under any circumstances, or admit, any mestizos or mulattoes, because of the annoyances that have been experienced from them." Felipe III, Valladolid, August 30, 1608; lib. iii, tit. iv, ley xv.

[401] See ante, note 227, the citation of the law from Recopilacion de leyes, lib. iii, tit. x, ley xiii.

[402] See VOL. XII ("Various documents relating to commerce"), pp. 51-75.

Banuelos y Carrillo, in his relation to the king, says: "That the inhabitants of the Manilas should be allowed to export as many boat-loads as possible of the country's produce—such as wax, gold, perfumes, ivory, and cotton cloth [lampotes]—which they must buy from the natives of the country, who would thus be hindered from selling them to the Dutch. In this way we would make those peoples friendly, and supply Nueva Espana with their merchandise; and the money taken to Manila would not leave that city. ... Your Majesty should consider that one and one-half millions in gold go to China annually." This commerce was advantageous to the Celestial empire alone and to certain individuals of Manila. It was fatal to Espana, and harmful to the islands, whose industry was gradually perishing like that of the metropolis.—Rizal.

[403] See in VOL. VIII, pp. 316-318, a royal decree enforcing these prohibitions under severe penalties.

[404] Coarse stuff made of goat's hair, or a glossy silk stuff; probably the latter is intended in the text. Gorvoran or gorgoran is a sort of silk grogram.

[405] This fabric is now called Pina. It is made from threads stripped from fibers of the leaf of that plant or fruit, and which are never longer than half a yard. It cannot be woven at all times, as extreme heat or humidity affects the fiber. The machinery employed is of wood, unmixed with any metal, and of rude construction. This fabric is stronger than any other of equal fineness, and its color is unaffected by time or washing. The pieces are generally only 1 1/2 feet wide: the price varies from 1.s. 4d. to 2s. 6d. per yard. Pina of a yard wide is from six reals to a dollar (of eight reals) a yard. All the joinings of the threads are of knots made by the fingers. It is fabricated solely by native Indians in many parts of the Philippines, but especially in Ilo-Ilo. The use of this stuff is extensive, and the value is estimated at 500,000 dollars or L120,000; the value of the annual export of it to Europe for dresses, handkerchiefs, collars, scarfs, and wristbands, which are beautifully embroidered at Manila, is estimated at 20,000 dollars annually. (Mr. Consul Farren, January 21, 1851).—Stanley.

In order to obtain the fiber of this plant, the fruit is first cut, so that the leaf may become as long and broad as possible. When the leaves are well developed they are torn off, and scraped with a sharp instrument to separate the fleshy part and leave the fiber; this is washed, dried in the sun, combed out, and classed in four grades according to its fineness. The cloth has a peculiar softness and delicacy; and it is said that that made formerly (one or two centuries ago) was much finer than that made now.

[406] Scorzonera is a genus of composite plants, of numerous species; the leaves or roots of many are used as vegetables or salads. S. tuberosa and other Eastern species have edible roots.

[407] Delgado (ut supra) says that this fruit (Diospyros kaki, Linn.) was brought by the Chinese traders, and called Xi-cu in their language,

whence is derived the word chiquey. It is a beautiful scarlet fruit, although there is another species of a yellow color. Both are sweet and pleasant to the taste. Some of the yellow variety were grown in the Visayas, but Delgado says the tree is not indigenous to the islands. The fruit is shaped like an acorn but is about as large as a lemon. The peel is soft and the interior like honey, and it contains several seeds. The tree is wide-spreading but not very tall. The leaves are small and almost round. D. kaki is the Chinese or Japanese persimmon; D. virginiana is the American persimmon. From other species is obtained the valuable wood called ebony.

[408] This must be the cloth and not the porcelain of Kaga, which even today is so highly esteemed.—Rizal.

[409] With very slight differences, this custom and ceremony is continued to the present [1890].—Rizal.

[410] "A three per cent duty was imposed in the Filipinas on merchandise, for the payment of the troops. We order that part of the law to be observed, but that pertaining to the other things paid from those duties to be repealed." Anover, August 9, 1589. (Ley xxii.)

"We ordain that the Chinese, Japanese, Siamese, Borneans, and all other foreigners, who go to the ports of the Filipinas Islands, pay no duty on food, supplies, and materials that they take to those islands, and that this law be kept in the form in w, hich it may have been introduced, and not otherwise." Anover, August 9, 1589. (Ley xxiv.)

"On the Chinese merchandise and that from other countries, shipped to Nueva Espana by way of Filipinas, an impost ad valorem tax of ten per cent shall be collected, based on their value in the ports and regions where the goods shall be discharged. This tax shall be imposed mildly according to the rule, and shall be a tax additional to that usually paid on departure both from the said Filipinas Islands and from the provinces of Nueva Espana, to any other places where they may and shall be taken." El Pardo, November 1, 1591. (Ley xxi.)

"We order that the duty of three per cent collected in the Filipinas Islands on the merchandise taken thither by the Chinese be increased by another three per cent." El Pardo, November 20, 1606. (Ley xxiii.) The above laws are from Recopilacion de leyes, lib. viii, tit. xv.

[411] The agave (Agave americana; the maguey of Mexico) is found in the Philippines, and is called pita, but Delgado and Blanco think that it was not indigenous there. Its fibers were used in former times for making the native textile called nipis, manufactured in the Visayas. As used in the text, pita means, apparently, some braid or other ornament of agave fibers.

412 The ducado of Castilla was worth slightly more than two pesos.—Rizal.

413 These imposts and fetters, which the products of the country did not escape, are still 1890 in force, so that foreign markets must be sought, since the markets of the mother-country offer no greater advantages. According to a document of 1640, this commerce netted the government 350,000 pesos annually.—Rizal.

414 The salary is now 1890 40,000 pesos.—Rizal.

415 Recopilacion de leyes (lib. iv, tit. i, ley v) outlines the governor's and Audiencia's power in regard to conquests by private individuals, as follows: "We grant permission to the governor and president of the Filipinas Islands and its Audiencia to make contracts for new explorations and conquests [pacificaciones] with persons, who are willing to covenant to do it at their own expense and not at that of our royal treasury; and to give them the titles of captains and masters-of-camp, but not those of adelantados [i.e., governors] and marshals. Those contracts and agreements such men may execute, with the concurrence of the Audiencia, until we approve them, provided that they observe the laws enacted for war, conquest, and exploration, so straitly, that for any negligence, the terms of their contract will be observed, and those who exceed the contract shall incur the penalties imposed; also provided the parties shall receive our confirmation within a brief period assigned by the governor." Felipe II, Guadalupe, April 1, 1580; Toledo, May 25, 1596, a clause of instructions.

416 There are eight auditors now 1890, and their salary has increased to 4,700 pesos, while that of the fiscal is 5,500 pesos.—Rizal.

417 Recopilacion de leyes, lib. v, tit. xv, ley xxviii, contains the following on suits arising from residencias, dated Lerma, June 23, 1608: "Suits brought during the residencia against governors, captains-general, presidents, auditors, and fiscals of our Audiencia of Manila, and against any other officials, both civil and criminal, shall pass in appeal and be concluded in that Audiencia, if they do not exceed one thousand pesos of the current money."

418 The tributes of the Indians in the Filipinas amount to more than 4,000,000 pesos now 1890; and from the Chinese are derived 225,000 pesos.—Rizal.

419 Now since there is no exploitation of gold mines, and since the Indians have no jewels that would justify this tenth or fifth, the Spaniards substitute for this the imposts upon property, which amount to 105,400 pesos, and that upon industry, which amounts to 1,433,200 pesos. In 1640, the revenue from the above source [fifths or tenths] had decreased so greatly, that only 750 pesos were collected annually.—Rizal.

330

[420] Import duties now [1890] amount to 1,700,000 pesos.—Rizal.

[421] Export duties now [1890] amount to 285,000 pesos.—Rizal.

[422] According to Hernando de los Rios, the Filipinas Islands could have been self-sustaining from the beginning from their own products, had it not been for the expeditions and adventurous conquests in the Moluccas, Camboja, etc. ... In the governorship of Don Juan de Silva, the treasury owed, for the war in the Moluccas, more than 2,000,000 pesos to the Indians, besides what it must have owed to the inhabitants of Manila.—Rizal.

[423] This excellent custom has entirely perished.—Rizal.

"The president of our royal Audiencia of Filipinas and one auditor of that body, shall, at the beginning of each year, examine the accounts of our royal officials, and shall finish their examination within the two months of January and February. On finishing their examination they shall send a copy of them to our council for the reason contained in the following law. Should the examination not be finished in the said time, our officials shall receive no salary. The auditor who shall assist in examining the accounts shall receive as a compensation the twenty-five thousand maravedis that are ordained; but he shall receive that amount only in that year that he shall send the said accounts concluded to our council." Ordinance 97, Toledo, May 15, 1596. (Ley ix.)

"For the accounts of our royal treasury, which must be furnished in the usual form by our officials of the Filipinas Islands annually, during the administration of their duties, the officials shall deliver for inventory all the books and orders pertaining to those accounts, and all that shall be requested from them and that shall be necessary. They shall continue the course of their administration [of their duties] with new and similar books. These accounts shall be concluded before the governor of those islands, and the auditor whom the Audiencia and the fiscal of that body may appoint. In case of the finding of any doubts and remarks it is our will that the auditor and governor resolve and determine them, so that they may be concluded and finished. And inasmuch as the factor and overseer must give account of certain things in kind and products of great weight and tediousness, we order that that account be examined every three years, and that the concluding and settling of the doubts and remarks shall be made in the form declared. And we order that when the said accounts of the said islands are completed and the net balances struck, they shall be sent to our Council of the Indies, so that the accountants of its accounts may revise and make additions to them according to the manner of the accountancy." Valladolid, January 25, 1605. (Ley x.)

The above two laws are taken from Recopilacion de leyes, lib. viii, tit. xxix.

424 The Chinese engaged in agriculture and fishing now 1890 are very few.—Rizal.

425 The Rizal edition misprints fuerca e premio as fuerza a premio.

426 The custom of shaving the head, now prevalent among the Chinese, was imposed upon them by their Tartar conquerors.

427 A kind of stocking called tabi.—Rizal.

428 The following law was issued at Segovia July 4, 1609, and appears in Recopilacion de leyes, lib. iii, tit. iv, ley xviii: "The governor and captain-general of the Filipinas Islands shall ever strive to maintain friendly relations, peace, and quiet, with the emperor of Japon. He shall avail himself, for that purpose, of the most prudent and advisable means, as long as conditions permit; and he shall not risk the reputation of our arms and state in those seas and among oriental nations."

429 This port (established before 1540) was in Colima, Mexico, near the present Manzanillo. It was plundered and burned by the English adventurer Thomas Candish, on August 24-25, 1587.

430 Thus named because seamen and voyagers noticed especially the lateen sails of the light vessels used by the natives of the Marianas.—Rizal.

431 A marine fish (Sparus auratus), thus named because it has spots of golden-yellow color.

432 A chart of the Indian Ocean, by L. S. de la Rochette (pub. London, 1803, by W. Faden, geographer to the king) shows three volcanoes in about 25° north latitude, and but a few degrees north of the Ladrones. One of them is called "La Desconocida, or Third Volcano," and the following is added: "The Manilla ships always try to make this Volcano."

433 A group of islands called Shidsi To, lying in 34° 20'.—Rizal.

434 "Thirty-eight degrees" is probably an error for "twenty-eight degrees," and these islands [the first ones mentioned in the above sentence] would be the Mounin-Sima Islands, lying between 26° 35' and 27° 45'; and Lot's Wife in 29° 51', and Crespo, in 32° 46', which [latter] are supposed by the Univers Pittoresque to be the Roca de Oro [rock of gold] and the Roca de Plata of the ancient maps.—Stanley.

For these latter islands, see VOL. XIV, p. 272, note 45.

435 A fungous substance that grows in the sea, and contains signs of life.

436 Probably the dogfish, a species of shark.

437 Most of these places can be identified on the old maps of the seventeenth and eighteenth centuries, and most of the names are retained today. The island of Cedros is shown on a map of 1556 (Ramusio: Vni-

versale della parte del mondo nvovamente ritrovata). The island of Cenizas is shown, on the old maps, in about 32°, and Cedros in about 29°.
The Marias or Tres Marias Islands are Maria Madre, Maria Magdalena,
and Maria Cleofas. Cape Corrientes is south of La Valle de Banderas and
Chametla. Socatul is called Socatula and Zocatula. An English map of
1626, engraved by Abraham Goos, shows the town of Ciguatlan, north
of Aquapulco, which may be the same as Morga's Ciguatanejo. Los
Motines cannot be identified.

[438] Acosta in his History of the Indies (Hakluyt Soc. edition, London, 1880) says of the courses between the Philippines and New Spain:
"The like discourse is of the Navigation made into the South sea, going
from New Spaine or Peru to the Philippines or China, and returning
from the Philippines or China to New Spaine, the which is easie, for that
they saile alwaies from East to West neere the line, where they finde the
Easterly windes to blow in their poope. In the yeere 1584, there went a
shippe from Callao in Lima to the Philippines, which sailed 2000 and 700
leagues without sight of land, and the first it discovered was the Iland of
Lusson, where they tooke port, having performed their voiage in two
moneths, without want of winde or any torment, and their course was
almost continually vnder the line; . . . The returne is like vnto the voiage
from the Indies vnto Spaine, for those which returne from the Philippines or China to Mexico, to the end they may recover the Westerne
windes, they mount a great height, vntill they come right against the
Ilands of Iappon, and, discovering the Caliphornes, they returne by the
coast of New Spaine to the port of Acapulco."

Also from Benediction Books ...
Wandering Between Two Worlds: Essays on Faith and Art
Anita Mathias
Benediction Books, 2007
152 pages
ISBN: 0955373700

Available from www.amazon.com, www.amazon.co.uk

In these wide-ranging lyrical essays, Anita Mathias writes, in lush, lovely prose, of her naughty Catholic childhood in Jamshedpur, India; her large, eccentric family in Mangalore, a sea-coast town converted by the Portuguese in the sixteenth century; her rebellion and atheism as a teenager in her Himalayan boarding school, run by German missionary nuns, St. Mary's Convent, Nainital; and her abrupt religious conversion after which she entered Mother Teresa's convent in Calcutta as a novice. Later rich, elegant essays explore the dualities of her life as a writer, mother, and Christian in the United States-- Domesticity and Art, Writing and Prayer, and the experience of being "an alien and stranger" as an immigrant in America, sensing the need for roots.

About the Author

Anita Mathias is the author of *Wandering Between Two Worlds: Essays on Faith and Art.* She has a B.A. and M.A. in English from Somerville College, Oxford University, and an M.A. in Creative Writing from the Ohio State University, USA. Anita won a National Endowment of the Arts fellowship in Creative Nonfiction in 1997. She lives in Oxford, England with her husband, Roy, and her daughters, Zoe and Irene.

Visit Anita's website
   http://www.anitamathias.com,
and Anita's blog
   http://dreamingbeneaththespires.blogspot.com, (Dreaming Beneath the Spires).

The Church That Had Too Much
Anita Mathias
Benediction Books, 2010
52 pages
ISBN: 9781849026567

Available from www.amazon.com, www.amazon.co.uk

The Church That Had Too Much was very well-intentioned. She
wanted to love God, she wanted to love people, but she was both
hampered by her muchness and the abundance of her possessions, and beset by ambition, power struggles and snobbery.
Read about the surprising way The Church That Had Too Much
began to resolve her problems in this deceptively simple and en-
chanting fable.

About the Author

Anita Mathias is the author of *Wandering Between Two Worlds:
Essays on Faith and Art.* She has a B.A. and M.A. in English
from Somerville College, Oxford University, and an M.A. in
Creative Writing from the Ohio State University, USA. Anita
won a National Endowment of the Arts fellowship in Creative
Nonfiction in 1997. She lives in Oxford, England with her husband, Roy, and her daughters, Zoe and Irene.

Visit Anita's website
    http://www.anitamathias.com,
and Anita's blog
    http://dreamingbeneaththespires.blogspot.com (Dreaming Beneath the Spires).

www.ingramcontent.com/pod-product-compliance
Lightning Source LLC
LaVergne TN
LVHW011910080426
835508LV00007BA/313

9 781781 390160